AN EMPIRE UNDONE

AN EMPIRE UNDONE

THE WILD RISE AND HARD FALL OF CHRIS WHITTLE

BY VANCE H. TRIMBLE

A Birch Lane Press Book
Published by Carol Publishing Group

A Birch Lane Press Book
Published by Carol Publishing Group
Birch Lane Press is a registered trademark of Carol Communications, Inc.
Editorial Offices: 600 Madison Avenue, New York, NY 10022
Sales and Distribution Offices: 120 Enterprise Avenue, Secaucus, NJ 07094
In Canada: Canadian Manda Group, One Atlantic Avenue, Suite 105, Toronto, Ontario M6K 3E7

Queries regarding rights and permissions should be addressed to
Carol Publishing Group, 600 Madison Avenue, New York, NY 10022

Carol Publishing Group books are available at special discounts for bulk purchases, sales promotion, fund-raising, or educational purposes. Special editions can be created to specifications. For details, contact: Special Sales Department, Carol Publishing Group, 120 Enterprise Avenue, Secaucus, NJ 07094

Manufactured in the United States of America
10 9 8 7 6 5 4 3 2 1

Library of Congress Cataloging-in-Publication Data
Trimble, Vance H.
    An empire undone : the wild rise and hard fall of Chris Whittle /
    Vance H. Trimble.
      p. cm.
    "A Birch Lane Press book."
    ISBN 1-55972-309-2 (hc)
    1. Whittle, Chris. 2. Businessmen—United States—Biography.
3. Advertising—United States. 4. Business failure—United States.
I. Title.
HC102.5.W514T75   1995
338.7'610701'092—dc20   95-19236
                                           CIP

For our lifelong friends in Harrison, Arkansas; Wewoka, Oklahoma; Houston, Texas; Washington, D.C.; Cincinnati, Ohio; and Covington, Kentucky.

Adminiculum in amicissimo quoque dulcissimum est.

—Cicero

═══CONTENTS═══

CHRONOLOGY

1947

Born in Knoxville, Tennessee, August 23, 1947, and grows up in Etowah, Tennessee.

1965

Enters the University of Tennessee at Knoxville, becoming student leader and political activist.

1968

Joins three collegians, David White, Brient Mayfield, and Phillip Moffitt, in publishing freshman guide called *Knoxville in a Nutshell*.

1969

Starts Columbia University law school and drops out in two months.

Works as oilfield laborer in Morgan City, Louisiana.

Helps run Wally Barnes's campaign for governor of Connecticut.

Begins year and a half of world travels.

1970

Continues world travels.

1971

Returns to Knoxville mid-year and rejoins expanding *Nutshell* operation, called 13–30 Corporation, as national sales manager. Helps start new publications.

1972

Floundering 13–30 Corporation falls $1 million in debt.

1973

13–30 loses another half million dollars.

1974–75

13–30 turns profitable and repays start-up loans to family and friends.

1977

Bonnier Magazine Group, Sweden's largest publisher, buys half interest in 13–30 for $3.2 million.

1979

With Phillip Moffitt, acquires struggling *Esquire* magazine from London's Associated Newspapers, which replaces Bonnier as 13–30 partner.

1981–84

Launches dozens of new 13–30 magazines to support *Esquire,* which turns a profit for the first time in thirteen years.

1986

13–30 maintains 32 percent growth rate for ten years.

Breaks with Moffitt, who buys control of *Esquire* while Chris takes over 13–30, which is renamed Whittle Communications L.P.

1987

Considers political career, expands magazine empire, begins hiring top-flight executives.

1988

Decides to build $55 million Ivy League–style headquarters in downtown Knoxville.

Starts *Tennessee Illustrated* magazine to further his political ambitions.

Sells half-interest in Whittle Communications to Time Inc. (later Time Warner) for $185 million, of which Chris personally receives $40 million.

1989

Channel One debuts in schools, causes uproar over advertising content.

Begins construction of Knoxville headquarters.

Begins publishing books by noted authors containing advertising, distributed free to opinion makers.

1990

Marries Priscilla Rattazzi.

Special Report magazines in doctors' waiting rooms hit by advertising slump, changes to television program.

Tennessee Illustrated folds.

1991

Desperate for new financing, Chris induces Forstmann Little to invest $350 million, but deal falls through.

Moves into "Historic Whittlesburg" headquarters.

1992

Chris reveals two mammoth projects, $2.5 billion for-profit Edison Schools and $300 million Medical News Network, with $147 million pledged by pharmaceutical advertisers for launch.

Whittle revenue hits all-time high of $207 million.

Philips Electronics buys 25 percent of Whittle Communications for $175 million, later increasing stake to 33.4 percent.

1993

Handwriting on the wall foretells collapse of Whittle empire as twenty-year growth streak ends and banks and investors threaten to foreclose.

Chris fails to raise $750 million to finance start-up of Edison Schools and buyout of Time Warner's stake.

1994

Frustrated partners oust Chris as chief executive and bring in Philips's Don Johnstone to liquidate Whittle Communications, closing down every operation except Channel One, which is sold to K-III. Headquarters building is sold to federal government to be converted into courthouse. Debts are basically liquidated.

Chris salvages interest in Edison Schools and manages to obtain 11th hour financing to stave off bankruptcy.

1995

Chris sells most of his homes to raise $15 million to acquire half-interest in Edison Schools, his last remaining venture, but steps aside as chairman to appease Benno Schmidt who remains CEO.

Edison contracts to operate four elementary schools starting in the fall of 1995 and plans second wave of expansion to seven additional cities in 1996.

AN
EMPIRE
UNDONE

1

WOOING
THE PRESIDENT OF
YALE

Benno Schmidt Jr., the president of Yale University, kept lifting his eyebrows and shooting wry looks at Peter Jennings, the ABC television network anchor who sat across the candlelit black marble table set for twelve. In considerable amazement, he listened at a Long Island beach house dinner party in the summer of 1990 to a bizarre scheme being vigorously espoused by one guest he had only met this night.

Calmly and persuasively, Chris Whittle was suggesting that America's bankrupt public school system should be turned upside down—"reinvented"—and that he was ready to tackle the job himself while making a profit doing so.

Not surprisingly, the powerful and sophisticated president of Yale and Jennings, a knowledgeable education buff, fired challenging questions. Between bites of grilled tuna the other guests, sophisticates all, leaped in and fueled a stimulating debate that rattled on for three or four hours. At times it was heated.

The hosts were Ed Victor, an international literary agent in London, and his lawyer wife Carol Ryan. Both Americans, they regularly came home to spend summers at Two Barns on Long Island's Little Noyac Pass in Bridgehampton. Their beach house, romantic, historic, and aptly named, was constructed from two seventeenth-century English barns they had dismantled and numbered board by board in 1981 and then shipped across the Atlantic to be reassembled and joined as their vacation home.

This dinner highlighted the weekend Benno Schmidt and his wife, Helen Cutting Whitney, a documentary filmmaker, were spending as the Victors' guests at Two Barns, as they did every year,

Mort Janklow, a New York literary agent, was another one of Victor and Ryan's dinner guests that evening. He recalls thinking that Chris Whittle—"a really smart guy"—was sending up trial balloons and "noodling" an idea he hadn't yet thought out.

"I don't think there is anything that Chris Whittle has not thought out," rejoins Victor. "In a sense it was a trial balloon. I think it was one of the first public outings of the Edison Project, but I remember the dinner table was, to make a terrible pun of the Edison Project, 'lit up' by this conversation.

"It really did dominate the evening. I know that very heated words were exchanged between Chris and Peter [Jennings]. They really went at it. Peter is an expert on education. It's a regular part of his American Agenda on the nightly news. They crossed swords a lot, as did Harry Evans and Chris."

Ed Victor was referring to another guest, Harold Evans, former editor of the London *Times,* who had become head of Random House's trade book division. He was present with his wife, Tina Brown, then editor of *Vanity Fair* and soon to be named editor of the *New Yorker.* The other three at the table were Peter Jennings's wife, the author Kati Ilona Marton; Mort Janklow's wife, Linda, who headed New York City's ghetto school cultural program; and Chris Whittle's fiancée, Priscilla Rattazzi. Daughter of an Italian count and niece of billionaire Gianni Agnelli, Italy's richest man and chairman of the Fiat automobile empire, she occupied her family's summer house nearby in East Hampton. She knew the Victors because her five-year-old son Maximilian played in the Long Island "brat pack" with the Victors' small boy, Gary. Priscilla Rattazzi currently was awaiting a divorce from Maxi's father, her second husband, Claus Moehlmann, a German investment banker.

Despite Machiavellian overtones that could be suspected later, the dinner party was not a deliberate ploy for letting Chris Whittle try out wacky ideas on Benno Schmidt or, for that matter, on any guest. "Benno and Chris are both pals of mine," says Ed Victor, "and I thought they should get to know each other."

Schmidt later said of the dinner party, "I've often wondered whether my old friend Ed had any thought that an oak tree might grow out of that acorn."

Throughout the evening, Chris Whittle was definitely on the defensive, countering sharp blows from every side. Ed Victor watched and marveled at his poise and argumentive skills. Though Whittle had bought and was remodeling his own house in East Hampton across a pond from Priscilla Rattazzi's, Victor had first met him in 1989 in London. A mutual friend in Hollywood had asked the agent to introduce Chris to the London *literati*, which included going to Ken Follett's Christmas party and a photo exhibit by Koo Stark, the actress who dated Prince Andrew in the mid-eighties. However, no one at the table knew more about him than Tina Brown, who had just published in her March 1990 issue of *Vanity Fair* (whose cover displayed near-nude actress Kathleen Turner) a thorny profile: "Is Chris Whittle the Devil?" The introductory deck read:

> Chris Whittle, the marketing whiz from Tennessee, has seen the future and it is "enlightened commercialism"—ads everywhere, even in doctors' waiting rooms and between the pages of books. With the launch this month of Channel One, a news program for classrooms with commercials and expected revenues of $100 million, Whittle has raised an uproar. Is he a visionary? Or is he asking us "to sell access to our kids' minds"?

At this dinner party, no one rehashed Chris Whittle's image as a maverick of controversy in American media for the past two decades. The talk centered on his private-public school brainstorm and his impending challenge of America's elementary education with a multi-billion-dollar scheme that had not yet been publicly announced.

"We were talking about education," says Janklow, "lamenting the failure of the American public school system. Linda is chairman of Arts Connection, which is the largest inner-city school cultural program in the United States. They give 2,600 cultural performances in the ghetto schools every year. She was talking about the schools she visits in the ghetto where the educational system is failing. I recalled the time in the forties when I was in public school and we still had the first-generation children of immigrant parents for whom teaching was a big deal. And how we had such wonderful public education in New York and how that was now failing.

"Chris began to talk, asking, wouldn't it be wonderful if there could be a way to really take the kinds of things that are possible in private schools and do them in a broad-based educational structure. It seems this was something he was noodling with. But it was clear to me that he was convinced then there was a way to improve the education system that might not be possible in the public context which has been traditional in this country.

"Some of us argued we weren't getting the right kind of teaching and the ghettos had become uncivilized. That it became dangerous and impossible to teach in those environments. And the illegitimacy of children . . . That kind of thing. Really far-ranging discussions. . . . And Chris was the only one who had obviously focused on trying to find a solution to this problem."

Peter Jennings objected to the "reinventing" idea. He feared 200 to 250 alternative Edison schools scattered across the United States would "take away" from the state educational system. Ed Victor recalls Jennings arguing that the country's energy and resources should go to improve the existing system, not create an untried alternative. Chris Whittle countered that millions spent by Edison on research and development would inspire states to emulate its anticipated revolutionary methods.

Benno Schmidt has a vivid recollection of the dinner-table debate.

"Chris Whittle said he had in mind creating a new nationwide system of schools that would be rethought from the ground up. He thought we needed a revolution in education, that the existing schools were so fragmented, so constrained by politics and by the sort of inherited model and approaches they had. Hence they were not capable of the kind of revolutionary change he thought education needed. That the way to do it was to create a new nationwide system of schools, get investors to finance it, because it couldn't be financed any other way. And that was about it.

"Jennings jumped in. Said he had been around to a lot of schools. Thought there was a lot of innovation going on, and a lot of new thinking. And that the problem really wasn't so much with the schools but with the problems of family and kids that they bring to the schools. So there was a lot of discussion about what current schools are doing. And some skepticism, I guess, about whether it would be possible to create a whole new system."

When the last guest had departed and the Schmidts relaxed for a nightcap with the Victors, the president of Yale was of the opinion that he had experienced a stimulating dinner-table joust over the future of American education with an intense, articulate, and serious young man with notable powers of persuasion. And that was all.

But he did not know Chris Whittle. It was not to be their last encounter on that subject.

When Chris phoned him at Yale weeks later it took Schmidt a moment to remember who he was. "I didn't think anything more about him or the idea after that dinner, just an interesting dinner. I wasn't expecting to hear from him."

Chris Whittle asked if he could come to New Haven and see the Yale president.

"I assumed," says Schmidt, "he wanted to come up and just get some general advice and counsel from me on how to go about thinking through the strategy for this project. And to talk more generally about my sense of education and what the problems were in the country, and what the opportunities were."

When Chris arrived, Schmidt was in the midst of a busy "sort of dentist-style day," rushing from one meeting to another. Schmidt took his visitor to the celebrated Mory's for lunch. At the table, Chris got right to it.

"I know you are going to think I'm crazy," he said, "but I want to persuade you to leave Yale and to join this new project, because nothing like it has ever been done before."

Benno Schmidt was taken totally off guard. The offer came in what he remembers as "a most friendly, engaging way." His eyebrows shot up, and his mouth fell open.

"Yes, you are! You are crazy!"

The Yale president smiled, dismissing the offer about as casually as he would a five-dollar bet on tomorrow's weather. "I said, 'I think your project sounds very intriguing, but there is no way I could think about leaving Yale.'

"And then he said, 'I expected that would be your response, but let's talk about it anyway a little bit.' So he laid it out a little bit at lunch. I said, 'Look, I really think you mustn't waste your time thinking this is something that I could possibly do. I've got things at Yale that I'm in the middle of that just have to be carried out. This seems a worthwhile project. I'd be happy to give you advice. It's interesting and fun—but there's no way.' "

Chris said, "Well, okay. I understand. But I'd like to talk with you some more about it."

"Okay, okay," said Schmidt. "Just give me a call whenever you're up in this neck of the woods and we can sit down again."

They had no further contact for weeks. But right after New Year's 1991 Chris returned to New Haven.

"I heard," Schmidt recalls, "more of his conception of how the project would be organized and conceived from the beginning, what his strategy was for thinking that it could be accomplished, what his public purposes were in doing it. This was really intended by him as an effort to kind of open up a system of education that he felt was closed and increasingly moribund and failing. And his view that opening it up to innovation and competition and choice was probably the best way to bring about change that was crucial."

Chris Whittle conceded he would have to raise an enormous amount of venture capital—$2.5 billion!

The first step, at a cost of $60 million, would be to create a think tank of experts to thrash out the model for the new schools. Once that was done, his basic scheme called for a network of two hundred profit-making schools that would open their doors in 1996 for children as young as one year old through the sixth grade. Grades up to twelve would be phased in one year at a time. This would require $2.5 billion from large investors to acquire land and build facilities equipped with computers and audio-visual aids. By the year 2010 there would be one thousand Whittle schools.

As he told Schmidt, on the same $5,500 that American taxpayers currently spend per student annually, the schools should turn a profit of 12 to 15 percent. Later the Whittle enterprise would make money by selling the educational software and other services it would have developed to public schools. "We can reduce costs in many ways," Chris told Schmidt. "Elimination of bureaucracy, introduction of technology . . . We see parents and students doing many things that would lower tuition. Not just cafeteria and janitorial work, but students teaching students, for instance."

On his yellow notepad, Chris indicated that his number one priority would be the hiring of one hundred innovators from education, business, science, and other fields to staff the design effort. For this he set an annual budget of $7 million for salaries, plus $2 million for travel, $2 million for overhead, and $7 million for research.

Schmidt was curious about the name—Edison Project.

"Edison did not tinker with candles to make them burn better," says Chris Whittle. "Instead, he created something brilliantly new: the light bulb. In the same fashion, American education needs a fundamental breakthrough, a new dynamic that will light the way to a transformed educational system."

Said Schmidt: "Chris said, 'I have been thinking a lot more about this. I really want to try to persuade you that as important as Yale is, that taking on this project would make a much more important contribution to the country, that it would be much more creative and interesting, much more fun, much more constructive, than being the best president Yale ever had.'

"He then actually asked me to think about a concrete offer. At that point I didn't say to him out of hand, 'You're crazy!' Because we had talked enough about it and I found myself in my daily work at Yale generally thinking more and more about this project and its potential."

Chris's offer held undeniable appeal. But before giving it more serious consideration, Benno Schmidt sought his wife's opinion. "Her view at that point," he says, "was that it was the wrong time to leave Yale." Schmidt certainly could understand Helen's reasoning. In his fifth year as Yale president, he "was up to [his] ears" in half a dozen university problems—crucial, challenging, and mostly controversial. He would not leave them half done.

Schmidt was having to make fifty or sixty trips a year to raise $500 million as the nucleus of a $1.5 billion fund to reconstruct the crumbling New Haven campus. With Yale's budget badly awry, he was forced to slash faculty, major programs, and all expenses. Unhappy graduate students and the university employee union both threatened strikes. He was busy recruiting deans for five schools and replacing the provost, the university's number-two leader, besides watering down strife between the campus and the "townies."

Schmidt's life was so frantic he returned phone calls from his car while driving to Manhattan on weekends. Now, about eight months after the Two Barns dinner party, Benno Schmidt had acquired a much better picture of Chris Whittle's background and meteoric rise to become a multimillionaire entrepreneur in publishing, only to switch career lanes to barge into education with his controversial Channel One broadcasts.

Given his extremely modest background, Chris Whittle seemed cast in an unlikely role. Born in 1947, son of a small-town physician, Chris became a campus politician at the University of Tennessee at Knoxville. There he met and bonded with another student leader, Phillip Moffitt. In 1969, in an offhand way, they published a free campus guide for freshmen called *Knoxville in a Nutshell* and loaded it with advertising. Chris and Moffitt discovered this was a paying business; with two partners they created *Nutshells* for a hundred other colleges. The entrepreneurs moved quickly—and amateurishly—and promptly fell $1 million in debt. In the process, however, they created a million-dollar idea—a formula that permitted advertisers to directly target college and high school consumers.

Their idea paid off gradually but enormously when they chanced to hit on the idea of "print specials," where one advertiser dominated an entire issue of one of the many youth-oriented magazines they developed under the banner of The 13–30 Corporation, named for the age group they addressed.

Within ten years, 13–30 publications, issued from Knoxville, were grossing $10 million a year. Whittle and Moffitt, brash, young, and unseasoned, kept expanding their scope on campus, adding to their profits by signing up health and beauty aids manufacturers to distribute samples of their wares to freshman dorms at two hundred colleges.

Their remarkable success attracted the interest of the Swedish publishing conglomerate Bonnier first and then of Lord Rothermere's Associated Newspaper Holdings of London. When both companies invested, Whittle and Moffitt purchased the ailing *Esquire* magazine in 1979, made a heroic struggle to beat the odds, and turned it profitable. In 1986 they had a falling out and parted, Moffitt keeping *Esquire* and Whittle taking Knoxville's 13–30 Corporation, which he promptly renamed Whittle Communications L. P.

Schmidt was impressed that in 1988 Time Warner had bought half interest in Whittle Communications for $185 million, $40 million of which Chris personally pocketed. He was also well aware of the Channel One controversy. Whittle Communications had proposed providing $50,000 in cable equipment, VCRs, and television sets free to all high schools willing to let students see a daily twelve-minute news and features broadcast that contained two minutes of advertising.

While this innovation was welcomed by hard-up school boards in many states, it triggered a general roar of protest from the national educational establishment. Bill Honig, California's superintendent of public instruction, banned Channel One. "They want us to sell access to our kids' minds and we have no right, morally or ethically, to do that," Honig said. Other states and cities blocked the Whittle newscast, chiefly because it included commercials. Protested one parent, "We'd create Kentucky Fried Children."

But Channel One was an idea whose time had come. In little more than twelve months it was being beamed into 8,700 schools in forty-seven states, and generating $100 million in advertising revenue for Whittle Communications L.P. The Yale president could clearly see he was not dealing with a dullard who lacked ambition and guts.

———

Even while he said no, Benno Schmidt left the door open a crack. Chris took advantage of the fact that they both spent their weekends in New York. Chris resided in the Dakota, an historic luxury apartment building on the edge of Central Park, with his rooms adorned by $10 million in paintings. The Yale president lived within walking distance, across Central Park on East 95th street. Helen Whitney, fiercely independent, retained her own name after their 1980 marriage, (Schmidt's third) and refused to live on the Yale campus in New Haven.

The Yale president and the Tennessee entrepreneur talked a lot in the spring of 1991, one time at Chris's place, the next at Schmidt's.

"I was very impressed with the positive potential of the project for America," says Schmidt. "And in talking with him in our meetings, I had really been increasingly impressed with his vision and his creativity. And the more we talked, the more I liked him. I thought, 'Gee! This would be a great guy to work with. This is a really interesting, creative guy, with genuinely constructive and civic-minded purposes.'

"So I told him again that I had taken it seriously and that I had thought it through enough to say to him that I really did hope he had success with it because I thought it was very promising. But I was just in the middle of things that had to be carried through at Yale, so I just couldn't do it. I told him, 'I'm not at all sure that there is anything that would persuade me to give up Yale at this point, short of some major public job in government, like getting appointed to the Supreme Court.' " (In one of our interviews I suggested Schmidt wanted that. "No, no. But everybody assumes that I do. That's just kind of an assumption that was around.")

Chris accepted the latest turn down philosophically. "Well, I'm sorry," he told Schmidt. "I understand. I've got a lot out of our discussions. You've helped my thinking a lot about it. Would you mind if I sought your counsel from time to time about other people I might consider to take on the leadership of this, or other questions about how to proceed?"

"Oh, no," said Schmidt. "Be great. I'd love to be of any help I can because I really think it's a great project."

Once again the Yale president put the Edison Project out of his mind and turned his full attention to his duties in New Haven.

However, Chris Whittle did not intend to surrender his quest. He was certain the boyish but tough Benno Schmidt had precisely the right qualifications, connections, and stature, to give credibility to the new school network. Graduating from Yale law school in 1966 at twenty-two, Schmidt clerked one year for Earl Warren, chief justice of the Supreme Court. He then spent two years as an assistant United States attorney general and began making a name as a constitutional scholar. In 1969, at twenty-seven, he became professor of constitutional law at Columbia University law school. Highly regarded, Schmidt was appointed dean of the law school in 1984 at the age of forty-two. He promptly showed skill as a fundraiser by bringing in $9 million in a single year, a university record.

In the second year of Schmidt's deanship, Yale lost its president. A. Bartlett Giamatti had held the office since 1978 but then succumbed to a lifelong yen to get into major league baseball. In late

1986 Giamatti accepted the presidency of the National League, becoming baseball commissioner in 1989, only to die unexpectedly at fifty-one, five months later.

Yale's search committee, headed by alumnus Cyrus Vance, the noted lawyer and former secretary of state, tapped Schmidt. At forty-three he became president of his alma mater.

═══

Even without a leader or any of his one hundred brain-trusters in place, Chris Whittle surged forward relentlessly. On May 16, 1991 he presided over a press conference in Washington D.C. to announce the Edison Project. Though he still had his heart set on Benno Schmidt, Chris did not mention this pursuit publicly. The Yale president had to be persuaded to head up the Edison schools.

During the summer of 1991 Chris kept in touch with Schmidt. Several times he went to New Haven specifically seeking counsel on people suitable for the core team of Edison's research and development. Schmidt, for some reason not as buoyant as before, seemed tense and depressed. He felt he was "beginning to see daylight" in conquering his Yale problems. He had found five new deans, brought in $300 million, and made concessions that staved off walkouts by graduate students and university unionized employees. He had calmed the faculty by cancelling or delaying certain staff cuts.

Even so, he remained the target of animosity and some ridicule. The university's social leaders grumbled that the president's wife was never on his arm at official functions; Helen Whitney, busy in Manhattan with her own career as a filmmaker, showed utter disdain for their resentment. Students took derisive note of Schmidt's frequent absences from campus; T-shirts appeared saying SCHMIDT HAPPENS. Faculty gossip surged around the president's somber moods and seeming distraction. Critics privately speculated that he might be on his way out.

Schmidt concedes that period of his presidency gave him some feeling of burnout. In one of our interviews he said, "One of the very frustrating things is you spend an awful lot of time going to endless receptions, listening to endless complaints because university presidents are sort of a complaint bureau. . . . A lot of it is just ceremonial and not really very creative and quite frustrating, because universities are very fractious places about things that aren't very important . . . and a lot of people are just hell-bent to fight because controversy is very energizing for them."

In the fall of 1991, Chris, aware of the wobbly tightrope Schmidt seemed to be walking at Yale, once more undertook a hard sell. He wrote Schmidt a heartfelt seven-page letter. Neither would release the text for this book. Schmidt says, "Chris just reiterated the arguments he had made to me, in a very powerful way." Chris agrees the letter was primarily a reiteration of points of view the Yale chief had already shared with him.

"More than anything," Chris says, "I stressed the importance of Edison, noting that its success had to be more important than that of a single university in three respects: One, an immense problem existed in our country that needed solving: the difficulties within our K-12 schools. Two, Edison would set an example for thousands of schools across the United States and lead the way for Edison 'lookalikes' to follow. Three, Edison could, over a ten- or fifteen-year period, have several hundred thousand students enrolled, so even within its own walls it would touch many children.

"There was nothing 'magic' in the letter. It simply stated the importance of the Edison mission and compared that to his then-current post."

Undeniably, reading the seven typed pages prompted Schmidt to seriously reevaluate Yale vis-à-vis Edison. During the winter months, Schmidt began bouncing this latest Edison offer off close associates, including his friend and lawyer Floyd Abrams, while he continued frequent weekend meetings with Chris. "Floyd thought it was extremely interesting but that people in the New York–New England establishment would find it odd that anyone would give up being president of Yale to take on something new and unprecedented and something that was bound to be controversial."

Nonetheless, Abrams sent one of his partners, an expert in corporate take-overs, to Knoxville to check Whittle's books. Schmidt says, "I just wanted to make sure it was a company with a good reputation and a strong financial base. It was. And fast growing! It had a 30 percent annual growth rate for twenty years. It's amazing!"

Schmidt also went for advice to his Texas-born father, the prominent New York lawyer and financier who coined the phrase "venture capital" and handled investments for the scion of one of America's most distinguished wealthy families, John Hay "Jock" Whitney. A financier, diplomat, and philanthropist, Whitney (1904–1982) is remembered as publisher of the *New York Herald-Tribune* and owner of a Hollywood movie studio. Benno Schmidt also took it up with one of his father's partners, Mike Brooks.

"My father's main reservation was that this is a risky venture in terms of getting it financed. He had very little doubt that we could come up with a new design for schools that would be a radical improvement, and very little doubt about the depth of the public need."

The president of Yale gradually grew enthusiastic about Edison possibilities. In 1992 Chris convinced him that corporate investors to provide the financing would be forthcoming.

"I felt," says Schmidt, "that we would have the necessary resources to do a very thorough research and design effort. I concluded that with those resources in hand we would be able to demonstrate that there is an enormous need for revolutionary change in schools and an enormous demand for a better model. Current schools are so out-of-date and so anachronistic. The time is so right for change in new technology of just designing schools in terms of schedules, daily and yearly, as far as parents are concerned. All the things that one could do if we got there first with a revolutionary new model . . . We could be a catalyst for change, with the whole politics of education and school choice just taking off."

He conferred in confidence at Yale with Dr. Henry Broude, a long-time faculty member who had been adviser to several Yale presidents, including Giamatti. "I remember when I showed Chris's seven-page letter to Henry Broude and Floyd Abrams, they both said, 'Wow! this guy is really persuasive. But it's basically the power of the idea. This is an idea whose time has come. Yes, it's visionary. It's risky. It's large. A very powerful idea.' "

In March 1992, still waffling, Schmidt went to an education conference in Hawaii with Helen Whitney and their eleven-year-old daughter, Christina. "Helen and I told each other we really had to decide this thing. We took off for about a week and went to Lanai and really talked it through."

The parents and daughter took long, pleasant walks on the sunny beach, Schmidt felt his vision lengthen. It was good to escape "the frenetic Yale environment." He recalls, "Things got into perspective. Yale is not the only thing in the world, the way it sometimes seems when you are in New Haven. . . . But I was still uncertain when I got back in April."

Schmidt went to Floyd Abrams and said, "I think I'm serious enough about this—although I'm not completely sure. . . . Let's see if we can get the contracts in shape, and dot the *i*'s and cross the *t*'s."

Chris Whittle had placed a lucrative offer on the table. Published reports later indicated it gave Schmidt annual compensation of $800,000 to $1 million, plus an interest in the new schools. The money was attractive; his Yale salary was reported to be $187,000 a year. In April 1992 Schmidt flew to Knoxville and spent a Sunday talking to Chris Whittle, looked over his facilities, and met one of his executives, Hamilton Jordan, the former chief of staff to President Jimmy Carter.

Chris Whittle drove Schmidt to the airport for his evening flight back to New York.

"Do we have a deal?" he asked. "Want to shake hands on it?"

The president of Yale screwed up his moon-shaped face, rubbed his jaw, and looked thoughtful.

"Well, Chris, before I give an answer, I believe I'd better go back to New York and sleep on it."

2

IN LOVE IN MEDICAL SCHOOL

In the spring of 1943, Herbert Pitner Whittle Jr., a twenty-one-year-old medical student, sat with his girl in the front porch swing of her Memphis home trying to get up the courage to ask her to marry him. Alice Rita Cockrell, nineteen, had long brunette curls and cat eyes and weighed about ninety pounds—"the prettiest girl I ever saw," Herb Whittle said. Fifty years later he would volunteer, "And she still is!"

They first met on March 6 at a fraternity dance; she was there with a blind date. Herb Whittle took one look at the petite stunner and cut in. Rita found him handsome, bright-eyed, and more fun than the boy she had come with. "We danced the night away," Herb recalls. The fraternity jukebox poured out the romantic rhythms of Duke Ellington, Tommy Dorsey, and other big bands—songs like "Serenade in Blue," "I've Heard That Song Before," and "Who Wouldn't Love You?"—a title Herb thought applied perfectly to Rita.

Nearly every Saturday night Herb and Rita cuddled in the swing on the front porch of the house on Forrest Avenue where she lived with her mother, Ruth. Occasionally they took in a movie—*Woman of the Year,* with Katherine Hepburn and Spencer Tracy, *This Gun for Hire,* with Alan Ladd and Veronica Lake, or *Casablanca,* with Humphrey Bogart and Ingrid Bergman. His worry was not whether she reciprocated his love. Rather, Herb wondered if it was fair to ask her to marry a struggling medical student.

His future could be secure once he became a physician, but at the moment Herb had no car, no time, and—worst of all—no money. Every two or three months he sold a pint of blood, pocketing fifteen dollars. He was midway in his thirty-nine-month University of Tennessee Medical School course at Memphis General Hospital. Occasionally he moonlighted as a hospital orderly—at fifty cents a shift.

Herb Whittle knew he was suffering along with other millions from the Depression's lingering pinch. America was now well into its second year of World War II, which brought new sacrifices. For several weeks he weighed the down side of his dim financial prospects against the alluring promise of immediate marital bliss. He finally resolved his dilemma by saving his money and renting a car. On a Saturday night in June, he took Rita out to dinner at the famous Memphis barbecue joint, the Pig 'N Whistle on Madison Avenue—and asked her to marry him. Rita said yes.

Actually, she said more; she was willing to continue working to help support them until he could finish medical school and become a physician. They set their wedding date for the last day in July and arranged to rent a small, one-bedroom apartment in Memphis.

On July 31, 1943, they were married at her parents' home in Trumann, Arkansas. Since Herb Jr. had no car, his parents drove over from Knoxville to Memphis and took them on to Trumann for the wedding.

Night had fallen by the time Herbert Sr. and Louise returned the new bride and groom to Memphis and their little honeymoon apartment. It was too late for them to start out on a night drive of nearly four hundred miles back to their own home in Knoxville, so his parents decided to stay the night, and the newlyweds offered them the only bed in the apartment.

Rita looked at her bridegroom and rolled her eyes. "Where will we sleep?"

Herb Jr. glanced around the tiny, almost-bare living room. "Well . . . I suppose on the sofa."

Early in the honeymoon Herb brought home a package from the butcher shop and opened it in the kitchen. Rita took a look and gasped. "What is that!"

"Liver," said her husband. "Haven't you ever seen raw liver?"

"No! I told you our family always had somebody to do the cooking. That stuff looks—oh, ugh!"

Herb recalls, "Neither of us knew a darn thing about cooking. I got out a big pot and tried making spaghetti. What a mess! Wound up with about eighteen pounds of the stuff."

As the war in Europe and the Pacific wore on, the army commandeered all students in United States medical schools, thus impressing Herb as a thirty-two-dollar-a-month private, but they allowed him and the others to continue their education, subject to call at graduation.

The Whittles followed the 1944 Presidential campaign and were not surprised President Roosevelt was reelected, with Harry Truman as vice-president. Herb noted new medical advances, the first successful "blue baby" operation, and the discovery of the miracle antibiotics streptomycin and penicillin.

The war front took dramatic turns in 1945 with the deaths of Mussolini, Hitler, and F.D.R. Herb graduated from the Memphis medical school, was promptly sworn in as a first lieutenant in the army medical corps, and was released at once to take his one-year internship at Knoxville General Hospital.

Their early days are now bittersweet memories. They were poor and had to scrounge. "Fifty cents a day," Herb recalls. "That's what interns made. It was thirty-six [hours] on and twelve off. Rita had put away some of her paychecks. I don't know how, but we made it."

The young intern delivered babies for a busy "old" doctor and did insurance medical examinations at night. "The cops helped us," he says. "We didn't have a car. We'd have to call in, and the guy on patrol at the hospitals knew what the call was. In fact, they'd come get me in the morning and take me to work. Regas, which is now a great Knoxville restaurant, had a little place at the corner of Magnolia and Gay streets, and the cops would take the interns down and Frank Regas Senior would give us anything we wanted to eat and wouldn't charge us. He knew we worked our cans off, and he was a good friend of the police."

Despite the drudgery and hardship, Dr. Whittle says it was the making of him as a physician. He recalls, "I learned everything I knew as an intern. We delivered babies, did surgery. We had no choice. There were no residents. We had five interns for about 490 beds. When you were seeing 60 or 70 patients a day, you saw every-thing—diphtheria, smallpox, gas gangrene, things you don't even see or hear of anymore. That was back before the days of antibiotics."

V-E Day came May 8, 1945, followed by the atomic bombs and V-J Day, August 14th. After six dreadful years and millions of casualties, 290,000 of them Americans, the war was over. But First Lieutenant Whittle still would have to serve two more years when he finished his internship.

Rita was pregnant and her baby was due in November. Because of Rita's tiny size, the baby would be delivered by cesarean section. Their obstetrician was Dr. Lou Hefley, on the staff of Knoxville General and one of the few female physicians in Tennessee. Their first child, Karen Ruth, was born November 14, 1945.

On June 30, 1946, his intern days over, Dr. Whittle was shipped off like an ordinary G.I. for thirteen weeks of army basic training at Brooke Medical Center in San Antonio, Texas, to endure the usual marching, rifle practice, potato-peeling, and barracks-scrubbing. "But it wasn't too bad," he says. "We made a comedy out of it. We were a group of about three hundred doctors. You know what three hundred doctors could do. We drove 'em crazy."

From basic training he was sent to a military hospital in Augusta, Georgia. The Whittles were still struggling financially. He bought an ancient Plymouth for $150 to make the commute between Augusta and Knoxville. On a mountain road the car died. Transportation was an important item, because Rita was pregnant again and staying in Knoxville so that Dr. Hefley could deliver this baby as well.

Rita was closely following the kaleidoscopic events of 1947 in the Knoxville dailies, the *Journal* and the *News-Sentinel*. Henry Ford died. Sugar rationing finally ended. Jackie Robinson broke the color barrier in major league baseball. *A Streetcar Named Desire* opened on Broadway starring Marlon Brando. Polaroid film was invented. Congress overrode President Truman's veto of the Taft-Hartley law, which prohibited secondary boycotts and other "unfair practices" by labor unions.

On August 23, 1947, Rita Whittle was rolled into the operating room for her second C-section delivery. This time it was a boy, seven pounds and three ounces, twenty-one inches long. "I thought he was beautiful," she recalls.

Rita was determined to name him for his father, but she was stuck on picking a middle name. She didn't like "Pitner" and wanted to avoid "the Third." Her quandary continued for several days and became Topic A in the maternity ward.

"One morning Dr. Hefley marched in," says Rita, "with that certain look in her eye, and said, 'We are going to name this little boy Herbert Christopher!' And I liked it. She never told me what made her think of Christopher."

Although Rita had been kept in the hospital twenty-one days after Karen was born, Dr. Whittle said, "they got real modernized, and when Chris was born she had to stay only fourteen."

In June 1948, finally discharged from the army, Dr. Whittle was four months shy of being twenty-seven and was eager to begin practicing medicine. He scoured the state of Tennessee for just the right location. Specifically, he had in mind (1) a small town that would be a good place to put down roots and bring up his two babies away from the big-city environment, and (2) people who would welcome a "country doctor" who was flat broke.

3

ETOWAH, JUST THE RIGHT TOWN

Halfway between Chattanooga and Knoxville—about fifty miles either way—sits the railroad town of Etowah, Tennessee. It was nonexistent at the turn of the century; the site then was muddy bottomland at the foot of Starr Mountain. In 1906 the Louisville and Nashville Railroad was scrambling to lay new tracks and win a race to link Cincinnati and Atlanta. Needing a division headquarters, the L. & N. rushed in and erected repair shops, turntables, switching yards, and topped it off with a handsome, Victorian fifteen-room depot of yellow pine.

Laborers lived in boxcars and twenty-five-cents-a-night rooming houses—fifty cents with sheets. Then L. & N. civil engineers named the town and laid out its grid adjacent to the depot, with avenues named for states and the streets given numbers. By 1907 there were ten brick buildings on the main drag, Tennessee Avenue, and railroad families living in Etowah's first one hundred fifty houses. The town even had a baseball team, with "Steel Arm" Dickey as pitcher.

Four decades later, when Dr. Whittle arrived in the summer of 1948, it was still a backwater town—although located on a busy north-south highway, U.S. 411, with adequate paved streets, water, and electricity. Etowah had grown little since the first world war, its population remaining between three and four thousand. The railroad, wounded by a local strike in 1922 and subsequent interstate truck competition, still ran passenger trains.

Learning that Dr. Hollis Miles was leaving Etowah to study psychiatry, Dr. Whittle arranged to buy Dr. Miles's equipment for a thousand dollars and rent his office. Banker Tom Cantrell let him sign a note for the amount. The new doctor in town rented a small house on Ohio Avenue and went to work. His office hours were eight-thirty in the morning to five-thirty or six at night, six days a week.

"It was a great little town," he recalls. "It wasn't long before I was seeing forty to sixty patients a day. I skipped lunch rather than keep them waiting. Back then office calls were one dollar. It was hand-to-mouth for a long time. Sometimes you got paid, sometimes you didn't. Obstetrics, from start to finish—prenatal and delivery—was thirty-five dollars."

In 1948 President Truman was reelected, *The Ed Sullivan Show* started on television, and the new movies included *Key Largo* and *Fort Apache*. Etowah was on a sudden boom.

"Everybody got back from World War II and our churches were full of young families," recalls Nancy Cantrell Dender, a judge's wife and longtime friend of the Whittles. "And there was work at Alcoa and Oak Ridge. And in a few years at Calhoun, a thirty-minute drive, Bowater started up—the largest paper mill in the United States. The railroad was still running strong and hiring those young people back from the war."

Etowah then had no hospital, and most sick people were kept at home. But for births or surgery, patients were taken to the hospital in Athens, ten miles distant. Dr. Whittle made house calls, driving a sturdy little Volkswagen, the first one seen in McMinn County. "I had four VWs and drove them twenty-eight years. I just liked the car; it could go anywhere. Back then there weren't many paved roads in the mountains. In fact, there weren't any. You got off Highway 411, you were in mud. Even to go to East Etowah, the road wasn't paved. Wish I still had a Volkswagen today."

The Whittles made an instant hit in Etowah, said Mrs. Dender. "Here was this cute young doctor and his wife and babies. They joined our church, the Wesley Memorial Methodist Church. He had charisma, you know—just bursting with it. Everyone wanted him to deliver their babies because he was interested in family, and he doctored them from cradle to the grave."

Rita wore her brown hair pulled back and was stylish enough to "set a standard" for Etowah ladies. Said Mrs. Dender: "When I think of her back then, I see her walking fast. She was into a lot of things. Always helping with the scouts, the church, the schools. They were accepted by everybody."

Soon there was one more Whittle for Etowah to welcome. On March 6, 1950, another daughter was born, delivered in Knoxville by Dr. Hefley. It took courage to have three babies by caesarean surgery. "We talked them into the last one," says Dr. Whittle. "Back then it was two—and that's it. I told Lou, 'No, that's not it.' " Rita says, "We would have liked more. I'd be having one today, if they'd let me."

The new daughter was named Rita Camille, and called Camille. By that time Karen was four-and-a-quarter years old; Chris was two and a half.

About a year later the local lumber yard started a small, speculative house at 1330 Pennsylvania Avenue. For a week or two Rita watched the two-by-four framing go up. The Whittles took out a loan, bought the house, and had it completed the way they wanted it.

"It was just a little cracker-box house," says Nancy Cantrell Dender. "But it was on an attractive lot. They could still make changes, and turned it into a precious Cape Cod house, and painted it barn red! Rita was very frugal. I don't believe they ever had a brand-new freezer. They bought an old one the drug store kept ice cream in. They really did not throw money away."

———

Rita demonstrated remarkable prescience in insisting on settling the family in a small, neighborly town. The Whittle children matured in an idyllic environment; Etowah High School somehow escaped the burgeoning wildness that plagued teenagers in the early sixties.

Said Jim Alsip, one of Chris's closest schoolday friends: "Those were good honest times—drug free, alcohol free, tobacco free. We were incredibly straight guys, compared to today. It was like [television's] Mayberry, best way I know to compare it to anything."

Kay Derrick Keller recalls, "We were a good group of kids. We had fun. Nobody was doing drugs; nobody was in alcohol. I'm so fortunate to have grown up then."

Chris's parents were kind and loving but attentive and strict. Children were expected to work and behave. "They worked, or else," said Dr. Whittle. "Back then we had two words—yes and no, and that was it. And we didn't have disciplinary problems."

At age six Chris began to display a flair for enterprise and "salesmanship." Near his home, he observed an elderly woman in a hospital bed looking out her front window at children playing on the sidewalk. One afternoon Chris rode his bike up to the door, knocked, and explained to the invalid's daughter that he'd seen the bed-fast woman through the window.

"I just wanted you to know," Chris said, "that my father is a doctor, and we live over there at the end of the block. If you will call him, I'm sure he can help her. His name is Dr. H. P. Whittle."

That impressed Nancy Cantrell Dender; the invalid was her grandmother, who had suffered a stroke. "Aside from being a sweet story of a child's concern, my mother felt it showed a very keen awareness of needs of other people, coupled with a genuine desire to help," she said.

That winter Chris went out to sell mail-order Christmas cards. Mrs. Edgar Johnson, who lived two doors away and owned Etowah's ladies' ready-to-wear store, told him she already had hers. Politely, Chris persisted. "Mrs. Johnson, you just stop and think a minute. You run that store down there and just think of all the people who come in and buy things. Don't you think you ought to send them a Christmas card and tell them how much you appreciate them coming in?"

Mrs. Johnson bought three boxes. "That boy is a salesman-plus," she told neighbor Kathleen Frost. "You can't turn him down."

The barn-red Cape Cod house at 1330 Pennsylvania Avenue became the central gathering place for children growing up near the Whittles.

Camille's father bought her a parakeet when she was two, and when she was five a pony. "She had a love for animals," he said. "We always had cats and dogs and birds. The pony, named Blaze, acted up and threw her. A trainer had a barn about a block away— Camille loved him to death. I bought her one of his old nags, a walker, and everything was all right then. That trainer would go in a stall to give a horse medicine and they'd try to rough him up. He'd make Camille do it. Horses, she could talk to. They didn't bother her. She could do anything with an animal—and still can."

When Chris was two his mother hired a housekeeper, Mary Lou Harris. "And he was just mine," she says, "from then on till he got grown. He was too small to play football or basketball, but he was too proud to complain. He was so smart. I knew when he was little he would be head of something big. He just didn't want to be out-done."

Not even in family games of checkers or cards. "If we beat him," says Mary Lou Harris, "he would sit there and cry. And I said, 'Christopher, if you gonna cry, I'm not going to play. That's not a good sport.' He said, 'I just don't want nobody to beat me!' "

In grade school he showed courage and self-reliance. His friend Jim Alsip came running in to get a sofa pillow. "Chris needs it," he told Mary Lou. "He hurt his arm. If he can just rest it, he says it will be okay." Chris had taken a fall—from a tree, horse, or swing (not even Chris remembers which).

Dr. Whittle came. "Dad, I think it'll be okay." His father examined the arm on the cushion. "It will, son—in a splint. It's fractured."

=====

Etowah learned from the outset that Dr. Whittle had a gruff and direct manner but possessed humor and first-class medical expertise. As an Etowah pharmacist, Dave Murphy filled prescriptions for his patients and could tell by the medicine ordered how up-to-date and competent the physician was.

"Herb knew his stuff," Murphy said in an interview. "He was a very, very, very good doctor. He had a wonderful bedside manner. They missed a bet not having him teach that alone in some medical school. And he always went. One winter we had terrible flu; Herb was making a dozen house calls a night in atrocious weather."

His humor sometimes had a sharp bite. The Methodist minister, who was not at all good looking, brought his wife to Dr. Whittle. Said the preacher: "It seems like every time we eat a meal she develops stomach problems."

"Well," said the doctor, "if I had to sit at the table and look at you, I would, too."

He felt free "to say that sort of thing," said Mrs. Dender. "Everybody just loved him. And even today, though he's long since retired, when somebody's child gets sick they call Herb for advice."

Kathleen and Jim Frost played canasta with the Whittles, and he was their family doctor. When Kathleen thought she was pregnant she went to his office in trepidation for a pelvic examination. She acted embarrassed. Part of his charm was how simply he put her at ease.

"Kathleen," he said, "I'm going to walk out that door as your friend Herb and come back in as *Doctor* Whittle. Now relax."

The pregnancy developed complications, and the baby was a seven-month "preemie" named Mike, born August 2, 1955. His condition was desperate.

"Herb said if we can get him through the first seventy-two hours we can save him," Jim Frost recalled. "He came every hour on the hour and pumped out the baby's throat to keep mucus from choking him. Mike's weight fell to three pounds, but he made it!"

Dave Murphy recalled that Dr. Moore, one of the physicians who had preceded Dr. Whittle, had only charged twenty-five dollars to deliver a baby. Friends urged him to raise the price to fifty dollars, but Dr. Moore shook his head. "I can't afford it. They don't pay me now. If I went up to fifty, I'd lose twice as much!"

The pharmacist estimates that Dr. Whittle provided "thousands and thousands of dollars worth" of medical care for which he collected not one cent. "But I never heard him complain about it."

An avid outdoorsman and crack shot, Dr. Whittle went hunting for quail, dove, boar, and bear with Etowah men. Rita was a hunter too. In the sixties she braved a two-day mountain blizzard while hunting deer at North Lake, and was the only woman in the Etowah party.

═══════

Chris often rode along in the VW when his father made house calls. Sister Karen says, "Chris says he learned how to deal with people watching Dad. I guess that's right; it's easy for Chris to get in a crowd and start talking to people."

Chris recalls his boyhood highlights as joining the Boy Scouts and building forts with Jim Alsip in the woods in back of his house. Their clubhouses were built with log slabs thrown out by the downtown lumber yard. Jim Alsip says, "They were shacks, but we called them forts because we had battles, fighting off the enemy—imaginary, of course. We had wooden pistols with a clothespin trigger that fired rubber bands cut from an old inner tube."

Chris threw himself into scouting with a vengeance—and the goal of winning its highest honor, Eagle Scout. "They said he was too young," recalls Dr. Whittle, "and he could never pass the life-saving test. That required rescuing a swimmer—and Chris was a small kid. But he did it, at age fourteen. You didn't ever tell Chris 'no.' "

Chris carried two paper routes and worked after school at Hamby's Gulf station in Etowah. Jim Alsip recalls, "Ask him about the time he left the nozzle in a '58 Buick as it pulled out, and Tennessee Avenue was awash with Gulf Supreme!" Does Ernest Hamby remember any such funny incident? "Heavens no! Chris was so far ahead of me, when a customer drove in for gas, he had them waited on and gone before I could even get out the door!"

Chris showed no interest in music, but his mother insisted he take piano lessons, which cost seventy-five cents. "I hated it," Chris recalls. "I quit after two or three lessons." He learned to play the saxophone in the high school marching band, and later taught himself to play piano by ear. With Karen he organized a musical group called Five Hits and a Miss that played at student dances. In the summer of 1965 he and two friends, Tom Holt and Doug Merrill, performed as a trio at a Gatlinburg nightclub while Chris also worked the day shift as a Holiday Inn waiter.

As an adolescent, romance was not high on his list. He had a third-grade sweetheart, Karen Wear, though pretty Janet Elrod later caught his eye. Janet, five feet four and a half, was his date for the eighth grade banquet. She recalls, "I had to wear flats. I didn't want to be taller than Chris. I knew he was sensitive about his small size." They never got serious; Janet married Shadd Newman, one of Chris's closest buddies.

———

On Saturday, August 13, 1960, the Whittles held an outing for some of Chris's pals from Scout Troop 74 at their cabin on an island in Lake Ocoee, twenty-five miles south of Etowah. Lacking a road, the young guests had to be ferried in the physician's motorboat, a sixteen-foot Crosby with outboard engine. It took several one-and-a-half-mile trips across the water to transport them, a few at a time.

That evening Dr. Whittle shuttled the Etowah-bound group of Boy Scouts back to the dock at Parksville, making his last trip at about ten P.M. Then he turned the boat back toward his cabin. Also aboard were Rita and two of their children, Karen, three months shy of fifteen, and Chris, who would be thirteen in ten days. Camille was in Memphis visiting her grandmother.

Patches of light fog were drifting over the river. That didn't worry Dr. Whittle; he knew the lake well. By ten-twenty their craft was about halfway home.

Suddenly, out of an inlet roared another motorboat—heading straight at them. Dr. Whittle had no time to turn. In an instant the motorboats collided. The second craft struck the Whittle boat amidships, peeling back the windshield and deck, hurling jagged shards of fiberglass and plastic into the four occupants, mauling Dr. Whittle's face. The optic nerve was severed in his right eye, and both sides of his jaw were broken. He fell unconscious into the bottom of the cockpit.

Karen was badly hurt, her throat crushed. Rita sustained broken ribs and a minor lower vertebra fracture. Chris's broken nose gushed blood.

The Whittle boat began sinking, but flotation devices lifted it back to the surface. Its propeller was racing, sending the crippled craft around in wild circles. Chris saw the new danger and started crawling across the twisted deck. He seized the jammed throttle and killed the motor.

Alerted by the noise and cries for help, two boaters—Sam Lattimore of Etowah, one of the Whittles' closest friends and lake neighbor, and Paul B. Abel of Cleveland, Tennessee, sped to the rescue in their motorboats. The injured were taken to the dock and rushed by ambulance to the nearest hospital, Bradley Memorial in Cleveland. All needed immediate attention.

Two teenagers were in the second boat, William F. Johnson Jr. and Jill Davis, both of Cleveland. They escaped with only lacerations, bruises, and broken ribs.

In the Cleveland emergency room, Karen underwent a tracheotomy—insertion of a tube in her damaged throat so she could breathe and take nourishment. She was admitted to the hospital along with Rita and Dr. Whittle, who was in a coma. Chris was treated and released, as were the pair in the second boat.

In critical condition, Dr. Whittle was taken to a hospital in Chattanooga, where surgeons repaired the fractures on the right side of his face, wiring his jaw together. He was not lucid for six days. At not quite thirty-nine years old, he had taken a drastic blow to his career; with the loss of sight in one eye, he would have to abandon surgery because of the resulting lack of depth perception. His blind eye was removed a year later.

The Lake Ocoee accident was traumatic for the Whittle family. Chris, still in his bloody shirt, went from the hospital to Jim Alsip's home. "He was scared to death," Jim Alsip remembers. "With all that blood flying around, he thought he was dying."

According to Karen, the boy driving the second boat had turned around to help the girl hunt for a lost tennis shoe. Their boat, a fourteen-foot Glaspar, belonged to Joseph McCoin, a Cleveland physician. The teen boaters were on an outing at the Dixie Products Company's cabin.

Dr. Whittle filed a damage suit and was eventually awarded a meager settlement. He bought a new boat and returned to Lake Ocoee as soon as he recovered.

———

In his cluttered office at the weekly *Etowah Enterprise,* sixty-four-year-old R. Frank McKinney, editor and publisher, squirmed under a rapid-fire sales pitch from Chris Whittle. Now in his last year of high school, Chris wanted to be a part-time sports reporter.

"I don't know," McKinney said. "Hmmmm . . . Well, okay . . . I can't pay you. But you'll get a byline."

Chris jerked back, blinking, disappointed. He had expected money. "Thanks," he said, sighing. "Okay if I start this week?" They settled on a weekly column, "Looking Things Over At E.H.S., by Chris Whittle," which first appeared on January 14, 1965.

"Has your son or daughter shown you his grade card?" was the lead of his first column. Chris then typed out a lengthy explanation of the Etowah High School grading system and followed with items about homeroom fashion shows, a barn dance, an upcoming Tellico bus trip—about five hundred words in all.

In an interview in Etowah a few months before his death—in 1993 at age ninety-two—McKinney recalled Chris favorably. "His copy was comparable with the other kids. He was pretty good on sports."

Chris's avid interest in school athletics prompted him to volunteer to be the official statistician for Etowah High. Everyone credits him with doing a superb job. Chris, slender and about five-four, would have gone out for football and basketball had he been bigger, says Jim Alsip. "Too bad that's all we had back then. If we'd had golf or tennis teams, Chris would have been a championship player. But we didn't."

Chris's second column in the *Enterprise* contended that only 10 percent of his classmates had "school spirit" and exhorted them to "get some." He wrote: "Take an interest in your school, attend its activities, help out when and where you can. . . . A family, not a house, makes a home; students, not a brick building, make a school."

His February columns dealt with a four-day shutdown of schools due to snowfall, Vicki McMahan becoming valedictorian with a 97.4 grade point average and Charles G. Smith Jr. salutatorian with 96.7, praise for the hard-fighting E.H.S. basketball teams, and the selection of Ricky Flowers as a National Merit Scholarship finalist.

Chris received a page-one byline under a four-column headline when Etowah High's girls basketball team, the Piledriverettes, went to the district finals against Polk County.

Chris reported the pressing question as the May 25th graduation approached was, "Where do I go and what will I do?" Term papers on the future were required. Chris wrote: "Students were able to choose topics from a wide list of fields: hypnosis, many types of sports, musical instruments, heart surgery, occupations, dreams, hunting, and types of government. . . . An FBI agent visited E.H.S. (not because we stole a Civil War cannon), talked to students on job opportunities in the FBI."

Conflicting emotions—reveling in the past and disturbed about the challenging future—almost overcame Chris when he ended his newspaper career with this comment in his final column on May 27, 1965:

A PERSONAL NOTE

Some feelings simply can't be expressed. Just to say there is a lump in my throat and tears in my eyes isn't adequate. Regardless of the description of these feelings I do know why they are there.

There are two reasons: (1) I can't grasp that high school is over. I've been too involved in it to think about it until now. But EHS will always remain close to me because it's given me more than I can ever repay. (2) I have a feeling of obligation also. Everyone at EHS has been so great to me. I feel that it's now my responsibility and obligation to do well in the future. But with the help of that "voice behind my ear" and more generous souls, I'm going to give my all.

To end, let me say that even though I have often written lousy columns, I have enjoyed writing for the *Enterprise,* and I hope you've enjoyed it.

I'd also like to thank my teachers, friends, principal, editor, and family for their understanding, patience, and guidance that they've given me. May God bless them all.

So. . . . World, here I come!

4

FOUR PARTNERS IN COLLEGE

The portal through which Chris Whittle made his promised assault on the world was the University of Tennessee, in the fall of 1965. The sudden leap from friendly, rustic Etowah into the bustle of Knoxville and an academic community of twenty-five thousand students did not daunt him.

Following his father's footsteps, Chris embarked on a pre-med course. Having just turned eighteen, he appeared in coat and tie on what had traditionally been an ultraconservative campus now beginning to be touched by the hippie culture. He observed other freshmen in jeans or khaki pants, sneakers without socks, and a few braless girls. Chris sensed the bafflement of university administrators over the emerging "flower children," and in particular the first coffeehouse on campus, called the Mad Mouse, which was known as the meeting place for beatniks.

Of more than 4,000 entering students, Chris was among 709 chosen for fraternities. He pledged Phi Gamma Delta, perhaps the most influential on campus—the same chapter to which about four decades earlier his great uncle "Bob Doc" Layman had belonged.

The football stadium towered over the southwest corner of the venerable riverside campus, five minutes from downtown Knoxville. On autumn Saturdays Chris sat facing the sun in the student section and joined sixty thousand other fans cheering the Volunteers. But to be an athlete was still not an option for the boy from Etowah. "In my junior year in high school I grew about a foot," he says, "but at U.T. I was still small." Chris stood five feet seven.

Early on, Chris decided he had chosen the wrong career. It would not be medicine. "I had saved my money, but I don't think I had the bucks," he recalls. "You really have to be dedicated—and I wasn't." The threat of socialized medicine, with Congress having just enacted the Medicare system, troubled his physician father, and Chris too.

His pre-med life ended abruptly in the college biology laboratory when he was assigned to dissect a frog.

"I had to stick the frog," Chris recalls. "Next thing I knew I had collapsed on the floor!"

That fainting incident did not disappoint his father. "He stuck his foot in the water," Dr. Whittle says, "but it didn't last but one quarter. We never pushed our kids. Let them do what they wanted . . . as long as they stayed in the right path. But doctors are born, not made."

Switching to liberal arts, Chris came under the spell of several excellent professors who inspired and challenged him with vistas into history, philosophy, and logic. They were impressed, in turn, by their student's intelligence, demeanor, energy, and optimism.

The two destined to have the heaviest influence on his education were Richard Marius, a history professor, and Anand Malik, who taught a popular course called The Philosophy of Education. These teachers came from totally dissimilar backgrounds and cultures, but both were dubbed "troublemakers" by their academic superiors for their open and vocal advocacy of change and greater student input in university policies.

A native Tennessean who grew up in Loudon County's Dixie Lee Junction, Marius had whizzed through the university in three years and received his bachelor's degree in 1954. Intrigued by foreign service, he passed the State Department exams but finally chose an academic career and started teaching at the University of Tennessee. However, in 1959 and 1963 he spent his vacations overseas in a program called Experiment in International Living, which sends college students abroad for the summer.

As an undergraduate, Marius had been appalled that his geology professor had to skip chapter three in their textbook because teaching evolution was banned by the Tennessee legislature. "We all devoured chapter three," he recalls. Professor Marius also looked askance at the emphasis placed on athletics at the expense of academics, and said so unhesitatingly. That made him no friends on the board of trustees.

Born in India, Malik had taught in several foreign universities, including Kenya, before coming to the Knoxville campus. Students loved him—for his classroom brilliance, marked by pixieish humor, for how he challenged their imaginations, and for his friendliness, demonstrated by lunching not at the faculty club but in the student cafeteria. Most student leaders, whether enrolled in education or not, took his course.

Malik was a marked man to the administration, however. Workmen marched in and took down the bulletin board on which he habitually posted items that ridiculed the dogma of the chancellor; thereafter he posted them on the wall with Scotch tape. "I would have been fired," he says, "but the university couldn't. The students had elevated me to Mace Bearer, the school's most respected honor." Chris was so much in the professor's thrall he would visit him at his home, sit by the fire, and talk about the meaning of life.

In thirty years of teaching, Marius remembers Chris as among his five or ten favorite students. "I liked Chris enormously," he said. "Just from sheer sharpness, he's very smart. He was such a delightful person when we were young—always laughing. He was of a ruminative mind; he was profound and always wonderfully adept at dealing with people. And I remember to this day his coming in and sitting down and having that wonderfully wry smile and just being so charmingly humble without being obsequious in any way."

This professor was not stuffy. Once when he was grading papers on his back porch, a large bird flew over "and made a large deposit" on one student's paper. Marius tried to clean it off to make the paper legible but to no avail. He returned it to the student, saying, "God is the judge of this paper."

Feeling his Tennessee future stymied because of his outspokenness, Marius moved to Harvard University in 1978 to conduct a creative writing course. In December 1992, he had just published a novel and was perhaps vindicated by being invited back to the University of Tennessee to address the 1,500 winter graduates.

"Don't ask me why," Chris says, "but in Philosophy of Education we spent a good bit of the course on *Notes From the Underground,* by Fëdor Dostoevski. And that was an influential work. I remember reading that book rather quickly, and I haven't read it since, but the thing I remember most about it is that it deconstructed the kind of obvious order of things. It made you think about how the world was put together differently. I thought it did a great job of bringing all conventional things into question, and I enjoyed it. And if you took that work, and have a wide path of existentialism that I read after that, there was a body of literature that had an impact on me."

=====

Chris's first campus sweetheart was a pretty majorette named Becky Nanny. Chris quickly realized that courting a college girl was more time consuming and expensive than walking eighth-grader Janet Elrod to the Gem Theatre in Etowah and scrunching down with Cokes and popcorn to be terrified by *Godzilla.*

Chris and Becky dated for a year, going to campus dances and fraternity parties, and lunching together. It was not a serious romance. "We were mainly just good friends," she says. "I don't know if you would call it greatness or whatever, but there was always something there. You could look at Chris and know that someday he would be head and shoulders above everybody else." She foresaw his future in "his whole manner. His confidence in himself."

Later he dated a cheerleader, Jeannie Gilbert, described by his sister Camille as "real cute with beautiful brown hair."

Another college flame was a strawberry blonde named Becky McGlacklin, a student from St. Louis who had her eyes on Hollywood with ambitions to be an actress. "He really liked her," says Camille. "She went with us, the whole family to Aspen one year. And I remember that we went on vacation to the beach another summer. Chris again took Jeannie Gilbert along."

Becky McGlacklin pursued her dream and eventually landed bit parts in a few movies. For years Chris kept track of her Hollywood career.

=====

The first handshake that brought together four University of Tennessee students in the partnership that would launch the Chris Whittle business saga occurred during rush at the old Phi Gamma Delta fraternity house in the fall of 1965.

"Hello, I'm Brient Mayfield, from Athens," a young man said, introducing himself. "I'm pledging. Are you? They tell me you had a great uncle or somebody who was Phi Gam. My dad was too."

Chris smiled at the good-looking, dark-haired freshman, a stranger from Etowah's nearest neighboring town, Athens. They hit it off at once. Both Brient and Chris lived in the student dormitory across Melrose Street from the Phi Gam house, and when a handsome new house was completed on "fraternity row" in their sophomore year they moved in as roommates.

Son of the owner of a large regional dairy in Athens, Mayfield had been dabbling in science and electronics since age thirteen, when he got a "ham" radio operator license. At sixteen he became a pilot—his father flew his own company plane. In the summers he delved into the Mayfield Dairy Company's computers and talked knowingly about trying to rig up software to calculate the intricate mix of ingredients for making ice cream. Around the U.T. campus Mayfield was called "that techie."

As roommates their friendship strengthened. "Chris has one of the most wonderful personalities you can imagine," Mayfield recalls. "Gracious. Incredibly funny and clever. He was a caring person, ready to help anyone with something. As became more apparent later, Chris has a different way of looking at things. Chris is able to relate things that are not obviously related. He is beyond convention."

Though he had rebuffed his Etowah piano teachers, Chris became a better-than-average musician and taught Mayfield to play both the guitar and the piano. "It was an incredible gift to me," Mayfield says. "Music is just intuitive to him—and without lessons. He just explained, 'Here's the way music works. This is the way I play it.' I just picked it up from him. Chris became involved in two university programs—Carnicus, which is where you put on plays, and Allsing, an outstanding chorus competition."

In the students' *UT Daily Beacon* and in the Knoxville newspapers, they read about the battle over civil rights, which exploded with the Selma march, the Watts riots, the shooting of Malcolm X, and the assassination in nearby Memphis of Martin Luther King Jr. In these years Bobby Kennedy was also killed and "yippies" disrupted the Democratic convention in Chicago. At dozens of colleges students rose up in protest over the Vietnam war and the doubling of the draft call. "We all had friends who were getting killed in Vietnam," Mayfield remembers. "It was upsetting—even though at first the turmoil seemed a long way from Knoxville."

Not every day was grim for the Phi Gam friends. About once a month they would relax with a weekend in Etowah or Athens. "It was great fun with Doc and Rita—and Camille," Mayfield recalls. Chris brought his younger sister to university weekends, fraternity dances, and football games; two years behind him, she would enroll as a freshman as he started his junior year. Karen was then at the University of Chattanooga, bent on a music degree.

In this period, the world beyond Knoxville, of course, had not come to a halt. The first commercial communications satellite went aloft. Dr. Christian Barnard successfully transplanted the first human heart, and Drs. Michael DeBakey and Denton Cooley followed with others. Lyndon Johnson declared he would not seek reelection and Hubert Humphrey and Richard Nixon fought for the presidency. And on the immediate horizon were the first men on the moon and the Woodstock love-in.

On their guitar and piano, Mayfield and Chris attempted to harmonize the hit "Lara's Theme (Somewhere My Love)" from the movie *Dr. Zhivago* as well as John Lennon's and Paul McCartney's "Yesterday" and "Michelle." They cheered when Mickey Mantle hit home run number 500, stood in line to sample Diet Pepsi, and took dates to see Dustin Hoffman and Anne Bancroft in *The Graduate.* They hardly noticed when five-cent, first-class postage went up a penny.

The other two student-partners, David White from Madisonville and Phillip Moffitt of Kingsport, were also Tennessee natives. Initially they were not well acquainted with each other or with Chris or Mayfield. What drew the four together was their mutual interest in campus politics, both in getting elected to leadership positions and then eradicating the entrenched cliques and "backroom" dealing. They began working closely together—not in any business venture but in student government elections—in the spring of 1967.

White, who had come to the university three years ahead of

Moffitt and four years before Chris and Mayfield, had served as president of the Student Government Association (SGA) his senior year, getting an insider's look at the dirty politics that stemmed from $50,000 in campaign slush funds raised by assessing fraternity and sorority members. On a smaller scale, campus politicians copied election tricks from Tennessee's "good ole boy" courthouse pols, down to stuffing ballot boxes.

Ironically, White was president of the Phi Gamma Delta chapter when Chris and Mayfield pledged but knew them only casually, as the fraternity was large and he had many other major interests. But everyone in the university knew of David White—and looked up to him.

"David was absolutely phenomenal," Mayfield recalls. "He is brilliant. He is probably the most-read person I know in terms of a person who reads books. He just devours them. David was gifted in most every way you could imagine. He was very articulate, funny, handsome, incredible athlete, singer—he made outstanding grades and ended up being the leader of everything he got involved in. He had an intense interest in politics and philosophy."

For all of White's achievements and sterling qualities, with his liberal arts degree he admittedly had no clear idea of what to do with his life at graduation.

"Back then nobody knew what they wanted to do," he later explained. "That was the late sixties, and so the people that were graduating from college at that time were really totally torn between the old images of what a life was supposed to be like and the wave of enthusiasm that was sweeping the country in terms of black music and drugs and free love and drop-out-and-have-fun. Those cracks were all through the college generation of that time, and a lot of people didn't know what they were going to do. How to relate to the old images versus those new currents and images."

White decided to postpone solving his dilemma, at least temporarily. He reenrolled for a graduate degree in history and philosophy, supporting himself by taking a one-year job as assistant to Winston Martin, dean of students. White's father, owner of a small-town appliance store, also continued to help defray college expenses.

Moffitt, medium sized but striking because of his untamed mop of dark ringlets and brush mustache, went around campus with a crinkly smile. He, too, felt confused about the future and shared White's spiritual bewilderment.

"From the time I was a little boy," says Moffitt, "I have always wanted to know what life was really about. I think some people are just born that way." In Kingsport his father was an electrician at the Eastman Kodak plant; the son vowed to rise above his blue-collar heritage. From age seven he saved his money for college, intent on becoming a lawyer "like Estes Kefauver or Clarence Darrow. I was going to go off and right wrongs."

But near the end of college, he changed his mind. Ironically, he took the standard law school entrance exams and his score "blew through the roof." He says, "Three more years of school—oh, God! I just desperately didn't want to go to law school!"

As a reporter for the *UT Daily Beacon*, Moffitt wrote about campus politics and attracted the eye of nonfraternity student leaders who talked him into running for a minor office, which he won. On his beat he interviewed White, and they gradually developed a philosophical rapport and friendship.

"At U.T. there were elaborate political parties in those days," says Moffitt. "It's hard to grasp that student elections could be so sophisticated and involve so much money. But they were. Mostly the parties were organized around the fraternities and the sororities because they were the biggest voting blocs. But gradually there developed an independent student voting bloc so therefore it began to have more power."

Moffitt occasionally asked White's advice. "We weren't best friends or anything," Moffitt says, "just people who knew each other through campus life. But I really admired him because he stood for something. He was trying to do away with back-room politics on campus, and I wanted to help him do that."

The real world of politics, too, was much aware of White's savvy on issues and campaigns. He was visited in 1966 by Howard Baker, a Huntsville and Knoxville lawyer who had graduated in 1949 at age twenty-four from the University of Tennessee. Baker was running for United States senator and needed a college campaign coordinator. Would White take it on? He accepted with alacrity—and the subsequent November victory propelled Baker into a long and distinguished career in politics that saw him serve as both Senate minority and majority leaders, make an unsuccessful race for president, and serve as White House chief of staff before returning to practice law in his home state.

On the U.T. campus, Chris's star rose dramatically. In addition to making the dean's list, he was named outstanding freshman in a class of about five thousand and elected president of the sophomore class. It dawned on him that the voting blocs were essentially "handing out class officers as political allotments." Turning maverick, he got himself elected senator representing the College of Liberal Arts and then surprisingly engineered a unanimous senate vote to banish all class officers except senior class president, axing his own position.

On February 9, 1967, the *UT Daily Beacon* quoted Chris as saying that the senior president was retained only because he had specific duties, being on the Knoxville mayor's council and in charge of the class reunion. "The others serve no useful purpose. People simply don't know why they are there." The student newspaper called this a "significant revamping" of the university administration and student associations, adding, "Computer registration will soon replace the old 'walk-through' method."

In this climate of change, Chris decided he could run successfully for Student Government Association president. He sat down with White to talk about it. White frowned. "I don't know, Chris. Phillip Moffitt tells me he's going to run."

"Good Lord, Dave! Phil's not a Greek! They won't elect somebody who's not a fraternity man!"

White leaned back, looking thoughtful. "They might, Chris, if you manage Phil's campaign." Chris blinked. "Then," said White, "you could run next year."

Chris agreed and joined the campaign to buck tradition and elevate an "outsider" to student president. Fortunately, Moffitt's running coincided with the first wave of the women's liberation movement coming south. Moffitt recalls, "It had just started to hit that women could have careers and separate lives, as well as be good wives and mothers. I was an idealist. They understood. Some of them were sorority presidents, and they believed in the kind of change I stood for—more than any other single factor."

The candidate and his manager were only casual speaking acquaintances. They quickly gained huge respect for each other. "Chris was an effective organizer," says Moffitt, "and I was good at arguing for what I believed in, and unafraid. I stood for what my values were, take 'em or leave 'em! You must remember this was the sixties, and that all counted for something. People would stop me on campus and hand me a one-dollar bill or a five-dollar bill and say, 'Put this in your campaign kitty.' And it would bring tears to my eyes."

Moffitt recalls that election campaign as one of his greatest experiences. "Having people believe in me, people who weren't going to get anything, people just expressing their beliefs in me. Huge thing!"

Any convertible, of whatever make, age, or color, that passed on the street caused Moffitt to stop and stare enviously after it. As a child he had been taken for a spin in a neighbor's car with the top down; that fired his determination to one day own a convertible.

Moffitt was helping pay his way through college by playing in a blues band, and most of the gigs were back in Kingsport, a hundred miles away. He scraped together enough money to buy his first convertible—a Ford Thunderbird, black with red leather upholstery, with broken windows and a top that had to be manhandled up or down.

"I loved it," Moffitt says. "Mostly I drove late at night, on the back roads. The carburetor was three deuces. And I would fly. I could be in Kingsport in the wink of an eye!"

His Thunderbird did not always fly. One day he parked at the Knoxville post office to mail a letter and the convertible wouldn't move. It was the transmission. Moffitt threw up his hands. "I didn't have two hundred dollars to fix it," he says. "But I talked the Aamco guy into rescuing it with his tow truck, putting in a new transmission, and letting me pay a little at a time."

Five students were running for student president. On April 19, 1967, when the ballots were counted, Moffitt squeaked through on a razor-thin margin of thirty-three votes. The vote: Phillip Moffitt, 1264; Keith Peterson, 1231; Bill Pickard, 882; Jim Smith, 449; and John H. Kleinerman, 1.

White beamed and congratulated the winner and his campaign manager. "Chris," he said, "it will be your turn to run next year!"

=====

In July 1967, nearly five thousand miles from home, Chris carried his suitcase into the railroad terminal in Brussels, Belgium, and boarded a train for Czechoslovakia. "It was a shock," Chris says. "I had just stepped off a sleek, modern train. That Czech train looked like it was left over from our Civil War."

The boy from Etowah, still a month shy of his twentieth birthday, was en route to Prague to spend the summer in the people-to-people Experiment in International Living program. Professor Richard Marius picked Chris for the adventure. Two other U.T. juniors also wrote winning essays and were sent abroad, to Poland and Argentina. Each paid his own way—about twelve hundred dollars. Before flying overseas all took crash foreign language courses at the project's Vermont headquarters.

Going behind the Iron Curtain was an eye-opening experience. Most everyone in Prague lived in apartments. "The Czech economy was very strong and capitalistic before the war," Chris says. "At war's end, most of its industry was gone and its land was in bad shape."

On his return in mid-September, Chris told the *Knoxville News-Sentinel:* "After the war, the communists decided to put all the money into industrialization and for twenty years they just forgot about housing. So most of the houses you see are shoddy and ill-built."

His host in Prague was a thirty-three-year-old engineer, a college graduate who spoke fluent English. His wife, twenty-five, was also an engineer but knew little English. With two small children, a boy and a girl, they occupied a three-room apartment. For six weeks Chris lived with them.

"I found the people in Prague seem to be happier than they have ever been before," Chris reported. "They are all very optimistic. The Czechs are a very lively people. They have lots of family parties. We went to several operas and ballets." At a Prague university, Chris attended two lectures daily—on economics, political science, sociology, and history.

The Czechs told the visitor from Tennessee how much respect they had for John F. Kennedy and how they "out and out disliked" President Johnson. On his way home Chris traveled to Budapest, Hungary, and found it very depressing as a result of the 1956 revolution. "Every other building was filled with bullet holes," he said.

As a youngster on his first trip out of the country, Chris made one major false assumption. He recalled that his visit behind the Iron Curtain did affect him.

"It did impact on me," Chris says. "What is interesting is about five years later a lot of that impact just disappeared. And let me quickly tell you why. I was in Prague for most of the summer and it was the first time I'd ever spent time in what I'd call a larger city. Compared to Knoxville it was an urban environment. I was confusing urban life with Communism. I was looking at it and going, 'Oh, this is what Communism is!' And some of it was. But in reality a lot of it was urban life. And the next time it really hit me was when I was in New York City. But I hadn't had the experience of being in large cities yet. And I sorted it out."

David White pushed Chris into a front-row seat in the real-life political arena by recruiting him as vice chairman of a program called Youth in Government, devised in Senator Howard Baker's Washington office. The object was to recruit thirty of the "best and brightest" high school seniors in Tennessee, escort them to Washington, and let them spend a week observing the secretary of state, Supreme Court justices, and others. The first year Chris helped White recruit the seniors; the next year he did it himself and accompanied them to the capital.

"It was heady stuff—top of the heap—national politics," says White. "I could see Chris's mouth watering for a real taste of it all."

Chris's creative flair also took off on a scheme to promote the University of Tennessee in high schools throughout the state. He recruited sixteen classmates as "U. T. Ambassadors." They periodically fanned out over the state giving ten-minute humorous slide shows boosting the university in an unorthodox and slightly zany style. Knowing well the inattention of typical high-schoolers, Chris directed his "ambassadors" to sit in a window, stand on a ladder, or perch on the edge of the stage as they talked. When the travel bills came due, a clear precursor of the future entrepreneur also arrived: Chris let the university pay.

In the winter of 1967–68 Chris, not yet twenty-one, decided that in the spring he would announce his candidacy to succeed Phillip Moffitt as head of the student government. The two men rapidly grew closer. Says Moffitt: "And that despite being quite different in background and life experiences. I'm an introverted person and he's an extroverted person. I knew who I was philosophically and what I was interested in. Therefore, at least in experience, I was more than just one year older than Chris. I was like an older brother, but it was more than that."

White and Mayfield could see Moffitt assuming the role of Chris's mentor. "But not politically," Moffitt rejoins. "Politically he was way beyond me. Chris is a natural—a politician-salesman-promoter by nature."

Chris remembers sitting one night in the Thunderbird convertible in front of the Phi Gamma Delta house chatting with Moffitt. "He had a lot of interesting ideas about a lot of interesting things. I don't know where he got them, but he did. Well, it was starting to get late, and we were just, you know, sitting there in the car. And I looked at my watch because I wanted to see how late it was. But Phillip saw me, and he said, 'Don't look at your watch while I'm talking to you!' And you know what? I stopped looking at it."

Moffitt was also on a much faster romantic track than Chris. Moffitt began dating a girl named Susan, who worked for the university. "In my senior year," said Moffitt, "we moved in together. This was a very, very big deal. First, it was still in the student handbook that members of the opposite sex weren't supposed to be living together. And the fact that she was on staff added to the tension. And we were scared to death!"

They were frightened not only that the university would discover their liaison but that Susan's landlady, Helen Nybert, would evict them from her apartment on Clinch Avenue.

"It was a wonderful little apartment," said Moffitt, "with a small sitting room, a pretty large bedroom, a shower off the hall, and a pullman kitchen, all on the third floor. Gradually it became apparent that I was living there—the Nyberts having to come in to fix the plumbing or something. But Mrs. Nybert was very good to us."

For some reason Moffitt was slow to become involved in Chris's campaign, which began with behind-the-scenes maneuvering in mid-February 1968. Chris, learning that a popular fraternity man, Jim Thurston, might run against him, hurriedly tried to recruit him as campaign manager. Thurston, who had curly red hair and the nickname Fuzzy, declined and jumped into the race. Chris, a Phi Gamma Delta, broadened his appeal to independent voters by getting a non-Greek affiliate, Gary Blackburn, as campaign manager.

In April the race was on, and it was lively. Chris was backed by the SAM party—Student Action Movement. It was not until April 17th that the *UT Daily Beacon* carried a top-of-the-page banner: MOFFITT ENDORSES WHITTLE CANDIDACY. Moffitt now says the delay in making the endorsement was a secret ploy he and Chris devised to guarantee a page-one headline.

The newspaper quoted Moffitt: "I had hoped to remain neutral during this campaign because I feel that it is very important that SGA continue to represent the student interests to its best ability during spring elections for otherwise SGA loses all dignity as a governmental body." Moffitt was also quoted that although he endorsed Whittle, he would not be active in the campaign. The same issue of the student newspaper carried a full-page ad signed by the Student Action Movement, which said:

EXPERIENCE MAKES THE DIFFERENCE

CHRIS WHITTLE...UT's Outstanding Freshman (1965)
CHRIS WHITTLE...President of Sophomore Class
 (1966)
CHRIS WHITTLE...S.G.A. Senator (1967)
CHRIS WHITTLE...Author of I.F.C. Rush Handbook
CHRIS WHITTLE...Studied Abroad in Czechoslovakia
CHRIS WHITTLE...Omicron Delta Kappa Honorary
 Fraternity
CHRIS WHITTLE...Creator of UT Ambassadors
CHRIS WHITTLE...Dean's List 5 Quarters
CHRIS WHITTLE...Homecoming Advisory Board
CHRIS WHITTLE...Director of Experiment in
 International Living for UT
CHRIS WHITTLE...Man of Responsible Action
CHRIS WHITTLE...S.A.M. Presidential Candidate.

The ad included two photos of a studious-looking Chris in jacket and tie with neatly trimmed hair, his hands hooked in his belt.

For the first time in University of Tennessee politics Chris's cohorts rented a circus tent—paid for by assessments on his fraternity and sorority supporters—and erected it centrally on campus near the student union. The tent contained refrigerators filled with free Cokes and snacks—and appropriate Chris Whittle propaganda.

Because of the Vietnam unrest, *Time* magazine included Knoxville in a nationwide collegiate poll called Choice '68 that would coincide with the student government balloting, and the hoopla was destined to bring out a record vote at the University of Tennessee.

The initial Student Action ad in the *UT Daily Beacon* was followed a week later by another full-page ad featuring five photos of Chris, and proclaiming: "Chris Does Nothing . . . but discuss ideas and issues with students who visit S.A.M.'s tent . . . but write letters to students, faculty, and administrators . . . but think about ways in which to better our educational system . . . but put together the most representative movement in UT's history . . . but speak to groups of students . . . But Think and Act Responsibly. STUDENT ACTION MOVEMENT."

The election on Wednesday, April 25, 1968, brought a record number of students to the polls—5,811, compared to 3,500 the previous year. Chris received 3,086 votes to Fuzzy Thurston's 2,725.

Turmoil over national politics played a significant role in the election on the Knoxville campus. The Vietnam war, the draft, and the threat of a protest march on Washington distressed and divided U.T. students. Chris's SAM party seemed to represent a more conservative and mature agenda than did Fuzzy Thurston's POP—Party of Progress.

That is the recollection of a 1968 student candidate, Ron Leadbetter, now associate general counsel of the University of Tennessee. "Chris campaigned harder," says Leadbetter. "And we spent money. I was running for the senate. All thirty-five candidates had to kick in thirty dollars apiece. My father was a New York City fireman, and I didn't have thirty bucks. I went to Cas Walker, a Knoxville folk hero and ex-mayor. I told him I was the only conservative running. I requested a contribution. While I was at it I asked for an extra thirty. He wrote me a check for sixty dollars."

As the new student president, Chris Whittle would be involved in one of the most violent periods of unrest in University of Tennessee history.

5

FOOZBALL AND THE WHITE KNIGHT

Two men and a young woman rattled the locked back door of the University Center. It was spring 1968, about midnight. Chris Whittle emerged, key in hand.

"What's on for tonight?" he asked.

"Foozball!" said Mayfield, with Moffitt and his girl Susan muttering, "Yeah, yeah!" The four trooped downstairs to the bowling alley and game room.

As a sort of de facto "night watchman," Chris slept in the building in a "dreadful" small room and bath. He had no duties guarding the building, though as student president he also had an office in the University Center. Chris says, "For some reason if a student lived in the building the insurance rates were lower. One of the unwritten perks of the job was that after the student union closed at eleven or midnight, I would often let my friends in a back door, and we would basically have the run of the center."

Mayfield recalls," We all were crazy about foozball. It's a kind of tabletop soccer. You have these 'men' suspended on bars with handles which you twist and kick the ball. You aim for the goal at your end. Two people can play, but it's better with four—faster. We stuffed socks in the return slots so the balls could not drop back under the table; that way we could play all night on one quarter. Our other favorite game was Ping-Pong. We often battled each other until dawn and then walked to the Fort Sanders Hospital cafeteria, the only place open at that hour, for breakfast."

In their long foozball encounters and in Chris's SGA office, the nighthawk companions spent long hours discussing politics and campus unrest. Big topics were the "stupid" Vietnam war and the hated draft. They inveighed against "dinosaurs" in the university administration who were ignoring student complaints about "locking up" the women's dormitories at night, and who were much too conservative in allowing controversial speakers on campus.

Chris brought up a money-making idea. He had heard about a series of student study guides called *Cliffs Notes,* started in 1958 by a Lincoln, Nebraska textbook agent. They were selling fast in West Coast college bookstores. Why not undertake something similar in Knoxville? Mayfield was interested. They brought Moffitt into their scheme.

Moffitt recalls, "Television classrooms had come to the University of Tennessee, and so for the first time you had fifteen hundred people taking a class and the professor giving the lecture once and then the rest of the day they show it on video tape. The student's ability to understand his textbook would be greatly helped if he had intelligent notes as a guide."

Chris, Mayfield, and Moffitt located a dozen graduate students who had copies of old exams, lecture notes, and a clear overview of the current textbooks. The grad students were hired to write guides similar to *Cliffs Notes* for a few U.T. courses, including basic English, some math, history, and so forth.

Wisely, the three entrepreneurs talked the off-campus Orange and White Book Store into making advance payment for an exclusive contract to handle their guide, titled *Time Saver Test Analysis.*

"These things were okay," says Mayfield. "They had a lot of information in them. A freshman really wouldn't even have to attend class. The bookstore would simply put a *Time Saver Test Analysis* on every stack of textbooks and tell the student customer, 'And here's a study guide to go with it.' Most of the freshmen would just take whatever they were offered. I think the bookstore charged four or five dollars for each *Time Saver.*"

To cut their costs, the partners met in Chris's office and personally assembled and stapled the *Time Savers.* They also kept inventory low by printing only the number of copies presold to the bookstore.

The venture proved so successful that the three partners gave themselves a name—Collegiate Enterprises—and later added an impressive but pseudo *Inc.*

"*Time Savers* was profitable," says Mayfield. "I think we made one or two thousand dollars on the first set for the fall of 1968. And we divided up the money. To us it was not like really being in business. It was simply a college version of mowing lawns or going out and washing cars. It was a project. It had a beginning, and it had an end, and we got some money out of it."

They realized they could earn much more money while simultaneously attending college. On occasion they brought the more experienced David White into their entrepreneurial discussions, but at that time he did not become a partner. Chris and his friends looked around for creative ideas and spent nights brainstorming a variety of schemes. Tiring of *Time Savers* after two issues, they sold their rights to the idea to another student group.

Their next venture was the "Box Brigade," a stunt whereby they would lure more students to the Orange and White Book Store, farthest from the campus.

With Mayfield and Moffitt, Chris built seven fifty-pound wooden boxes with a harness inside, and peep holes so one could climb in and walk around the campus handing out bookstore coupons and candy.

For the Box Brigade's leg power, Chris hired a guerrilla theater group called Big Orange for a Democratic Society (BODS), known for zany stunts such as luring several hundred students to try to catch fifty Alabama-Tennessee football tickets they tossed from the Administration Tower, or dressing up in military gear, "shooting" each other, and falling down "dead" on campus.

All went well with the parade of the Box Brigade until an overzealous collegian saw a BODS man clumsily descending some stone steps in his wooden contraption. The zealot shoved the box, sending the trapped student rolling twenty feet down the steps. The student was unhurt, but his fall inspired the theater guerrilla to enlist his fellow students. Looking out onto campus from his lunch table, Chris saw the seven BODS men in boxes suddenly attack each other, splintering their containers. He rushed out to stop the combatants—but it was too late.

"Every one was wrecked," Chris says. "They cost seven hundred dollars to make. True, the Box Brigade had just ended, but we were going to park the boxes in a warehouse and use them the next year." Collegiate Enterprises later tried a similar stunt with giant cans, but the high winds toppled them, sending dazed occupants on a dangerous roll.

It took at least two years for the Knoxville campus to emerge from its ultraconservative cocoon and let its passions be ignited by the wave of Vietnam-spawned anger that had already triggered explosions at scores of colleges. So parochial were U.T. students that in a mock election they gave Richard Nixon a big margin over Eugene McCarthy, the liberal Democrat and presidential favorite at most campuses. Even the official U.T. historian, Dr. Milton M. Klein, recorded that the Knoxville collegians were "conservative and apathetic."

The University of Tennessee remained out of the loop. A visiting reporter from the *Los Angeles Times* wrote that while campuses from Berkeley to Columbia seethed with antiwar turmoil, the Knoxville school was embattled over whether to choose the Tennessee walking horse or Smokey, the blue tick hound, as the football mascot. Eventually both were used—the hound the most. The *Times* described U.T. as "another world, a place where kids listen instead of shout, where coats and ties have scored a smashing victory over beards and bare feet, and where the university president always gets a standing ovation."

But that was not quite true. The university president, Dr. Andrew ("Andy") Holt, was in disfavor on campus. And if Chris Whittle could manage it, Dr. Holt had to respond to the undergraduates' demands or face continuous criticism. In the fall of 1968 serious protests erupted at the University of Tennessee. As student president and as an individual fighting President Holt's policies, Chris was drawn into controversy.

On September 25, 1968, in a "State of the Campus" speech to the student senate, Chris challenged "great numbers of students" to become more active in pressing for "needed changes in every area of University life."

He conceded that getting "the establishment" to listen to student concerns would be difficult. "In many areas students are regarded as necessary evils. Some administrators say we only criticize and have no alternatives. My response is this: 'We're not asking to run the University; we simply want sincere consideration of our position within it.' " He said the university should establish courses "more relevant to our lives," especially for freshmen, and "should try to maximize privacy while minimizing loneliness" in the dormitories.

Chris's latter comment referred to an unsuccessful student-led campaign to extend "hours" in the women's dormitories and permit female students to stay out beyond the midnight curfew, or eliminate it entirely. Another ongoing controversy began when chancellor Charles H. Weaver barred "radicals" Timothy Leary and Dick Gregory from speaking on campus but permitted Dr. Sidney Cohen, an antidrug crusader, to address a student assembly.

Chris and others argued that U.T. students were being denied their constitutional right to free speech and asserted that speakers were paid from student activity fees not university appropriations. Their protests were directed at President Holt, Chancellor Weaver, and Dr. Robert G. Gordon, vice chancellor for student affairs.

With tension growing, the arguments simmered through the winter and finally erupted just before midnight on February 4, 1969, at the university's Clement Hall. One hundred fifty coeds rushed from the eighth floor to the dormitory's lobby five minutes before midnight and charged the front doors—which were already locked. "Let us out! Let us out!" they cried. "No hours! No hours!"

The melee subsided when the head resident agreed to let the girls outside if they did not exceed their four-minute grace period. Mary Ann Flemm, the protest leader and an art education senior, agreed. Fifty women stepped out on the patio for four minutes and then returned to their rooms.

The walkout, born out of two years of frustration by leaders of the Associated Women Students, immediately drew Chris Whittle and his Student Government Association into a heated new "war" against President Holt's oppression of student liberties.

The following night Clement Hall residents again came out and paraded to four other dormitories, assembling a thousand coeds in the U.T. Presidential Complex. They voted to stay out until one A.M. and demanded that within twenty-four hours university officials cancel the midnight curfew.

Climbing atop the base of a statue in the campus plaza, Chris addressed the milling throng, praising the women for their courage and urging them to continue the protest for the next ten nights. He waited until twelve-thirty A.M., and spoke again. "You have proved your point, and your resolve. Now you should all go back quietly to your dorms. And stand ready to walk out again every night—until we get action!"

He singled out one of the coeds and hugged her affectionately—his sister Camille, then in her second year at the University of Tennessee. "We had probably our strongest relationship in college," Camille says. "He did seem to take care of me. When I came to Knoxville as a freshman, he helped me get to know people and just get into the swing of things. And I was the sort who would have done anything for my brother."

No further walkouts were needed. The next afternoon Vice Chancellor Gordon called in leaders of the Associated Women Students and the Student Government Association. He announced that an experimental program would start the next quarter permitting women over twenty-one and others with parental permission to set their own curfew hours. The experiment would be evaluated by a student-faculty committee before permanent approval.

"Again we have proved that it is impossible to stop an idea whose time has come," Chris asserted. "We have met the issue of equality for women—and we have won." He was joined in approving the concessions by Ann Alexander, president of Associated Women Students.

Chris and the women cheered too soon. Although Chancellor Weaver had devised the "no-hours" policy, President Holt would not ratify it. Holt insisted on excluding freshmen and sophomores, even if they had parental permission.

When this revised policy was announced late in February, Chris angrily demanded the administration "publicly explain its deceit." The president and his men, Chris told the *UT Daily Beacon,* "did not think that an administrator should grant or 'concede' on an issue following a demonstration or protest—regardless of the validity of the request."

In the end the coeds accepted their halfloaf. Later in the spring the *Beacon,* the campus newspaper, reported that the assistant dean of women considered the scheme "working beautifully," with few eligible students rarely staying out past two in the morning.

Historically, the skirmish resulted in lifting many restrictions in U.T. residence halls, but not all. Freshmen coeds are still denied visits by members of the opposite sex except in dormitory main lobbies.

During the spring of 1969, Chris carried the "war against the establishment" off campus. He was invited to address Knoxville civic leaders at a Civitan Club luncheon. He closed his stirring speech by saying, "After all, how would you feel if someone told you Chris Whittle couldn't speak at this meeting? It would probably bug you!"

With a wide grin, the twenty-two-year-old student president sat down. His remarks won support from editor Ralph L. Millett Jr. in the April 1, 1969, *Knoxville News-Sentinel:*

OPEN SPEAKER POLICY
A STITCH IN TIME

Some of the best sense yet made in controversy over an open speaker policy at the University of Tennessee was made the other day by Chris Whittle, president of the Student Government Association, in a speech to the Civitan Club.

It wasn't so much that new ideas were advanced in favor of an open speaker policy, it was the emphasis he properly put on the potential danger of radical and militant leaders finding encouragement in a policy of suppression. "Militants," he said, "can act only in time of crisis. And we want to get rid of the issue before it causes a crisis." Such a crisis, he pointed out, will fester in the squelching of responsible individuals who want their proposed reforms carried out within the framework of administration control.

U.T.'s administration should listen to and heed the admonition of this young man, who is one of the "responsible individuals" on campus. He and his fellows want to hear both sides of issues, not just one as was the case when Dr. Sidney Cohen was permitted to speak but Timothy Leary wasn't on the subject of LSD usage.

The sole issue is about as simple as taking a stitch in time to maintain the orderly process followed so far on U.T. campus in fine contrast to the tragedy of disorders and violence of so many other campuses.

University administrators watched the rising tempo of student rebellion warily. They gave ground grudgingly, appointing a study committee that wouldn't report for months. They further delayed decisions by "changing the rules," according to the *UT Daily Beacon*. In Nashville seeking legislative appropriations, President Holt stood firm, but Professor Marius and other faculty members took up the students' cause. "Holt was a spineless coward," says Marius.

Rumors swept Knoxville that the governor "intends to call out the National Guard if Leary is brought to our campus," the *Beacon* reported, adding: "The mere fact that many doors of the administration were chained and padlocked shut last week shows that in many instances the administration is indeed over-reacting."

Dr. Jack Reese, then assistant graduate school dean who in later years rose to U.T. chancellor, watched Chris "get caught in a difficult position" between the warring factions. Did Dr. Reese help him get out of it? "I'm sure I did. I just counseled him to be honest. Those were not the easiest of times; there was a good deal of animosity around. And Chris displayed qualities of leadership, like patience, persistence, dignity, and a wonderful kind of tough-mindedness."

The two-faced behavior of Dr. Gordon, the vice chancellor for student affairs, aggravated Chris's predicament. Dr. Reese said in an interview, "Chris's chief troubles were with a guy named Gordon who was frankly incompetent. . . . Gordon would go out to the alumni chapter and talk about student unrest and disruption and how there needed to be a lot of discipline. Then he would come back to the student group and tell them what great kids they were."

Dr. Reese retired as chancellor to resume teaching English. He said Dr. Gordon was ultimately fired. "Gordon moved back to California. He was going to open a craft shop so he came back to our Smoky Mountain resort at Gatlinburg and bought a truckload of candles. Then he took off across the desert and by the time he got to California all he had was a mass of melted wax. A lot of us rejoiced. I'm sure Chris did."

Ron Leadbetter, now the university's associate general counsel, recalls serving as an SGA senator during Chris's presidency. "I was a law student. I still chuckle when I think of the problems we tried to solve in student government. I've kept copies of bills we brought up—subjects like the Vietnam war, and poverty and world hunger and things like that we would vote to abolish."

He didn't agree with Chris on the Vietnam war. "Chris was very much with the majority—against it. I wasn't for the war. I just thought we were trying to do a worthy job over there, and the military deserved our support. . . . I always called him a well-dressed hippie. Hippie is out of date now, but he really always dressed very well, wearing bow ties and was very polite, a nice fellow."

Leadbetter remembers Chris "always seemed to carry a lot of burdens on his shoulders. He wasn't what you would call a bubbly and happy and cheerful individual most of the time. I think a lot of it had to do with his views on the Vietnam war and government in general."

When university officials continued to waffle, Professor Marius filed suit in federal court with other faculty and two SGA councilmen, Jim Smith and Gary Blackburn, challenging the speaker policy as unconstitutional. Judge Robert L. Taylor in Knoxville ruled on May 1, 1969, that the U.T. policy violated the First and Fourteenth Amendments.

Eventually Timothy Leary and Dick Gregory were given permission to speak. Marius says, "Leary was crazy. I was asked to sit on the platform with Gregory and refused. I was interested in the First Amendment issue and not Gregory himself."

That might have resolved the conflict over the open speaker policy, but an uglier blot was in the making. After Chris Whittle had graduated and was no longer involved, Richard Nixon spoke at Rev. Billy Graham's crusade in the U.T. football stadium on May 28, 1970. It was Nixon's first public appearance since national guardsmen shot four Kent State students. Outraged Tennessee students demonstrated in the stadium. Two professors and forty students were arrested for disturbing the peace at a religious gathering. Most were let off with fines, but one coed was jailed. Professor Charles Reynolds, fined twenty dollars, appealed to the U.S. Supreme Court, which refused to hear his case. There were brief cries of outrage over the arrests. Dr. Klein, the university's historian, wrote: "A *Daily Beacon* editorial opined that the events of May 28 would remain for a long time in the memories of those who witnessed 'the spectacle in Neyland Stadium,' but the paper's own news columns belied the editor's opinion; there was only one story in the next year on the fate of any of the protestors."

As soon as the original entrepreneurs for Collegiate Enterprises Inc.—Chris, Moffitt, and Mayfield—received their diplomas, they were due to serve in the armed services. David White, a fringe partner as an unpaid consultant to Collegiate Enterprises, also faced the draft. In 1969 American forces were still engaged in bloody fighting in Vietnam that would continue until the 1973 cease-fire, leaving a U.S. combat death toll of 45,958.

White joined the Tennessee National Guard as a pilot candidate. He spent four months in basic training but had to wait for an opening in flying school. Restless and eager to utilize his political skills in the 1968 presidential campaign, he joined New York governor Nelson A. Rockefeller's staff to work on college strategy. Rockefeller's bid failed, but White became acquainted with his foreign policy adviser, Henry Kissinger, and earned his respect.

Phillip Moffitt reported to draft headquarters in Knoxville, filled out personal history questionnaires, and stripped for his medical exam. The last doctor in line took his papers and studied them with a frown.

"What's this mean?" he asked, pointing to an answer about feet.

"Oh, I wear shoes with little bars attached. Orthopedic problem with my ankles. Had it all my life."

"Go get your shoes."

Moffitt came back with them. He told the doctor, "I just assumed the army would put these bars on my boots."

The physician examined the shoes and shook his head. "Son, I can't let you join the army!"

Moffitt recalls, "I'll never forget this genuine look on his face. I didn't do anything. I thought I was going to be drafted. But I didn't want to go to Vietnam; I desperately didn't want to!"

His girlfriend Susan was leaving Knoxville to work for a university in Illinois. To stay near her, Moffitt won a last-minute fellowship at Southern Illinois University at Carbondale. He sensed himself heading into a career as a clinical psychologist. After four months he gave up his fellowship—and Susan—and returned to the University of Tennessee to enroll for a master's degree in economics.

The threat of being drafted was a gamble that Brient Mayfield accepted philosophically. Like hundreds of other graduates, he was not eager to go to Vietnam. He patiently waited for his call, but he received a low number—thirty—and the war would end before it came up. Chris's problem was related to chronic asthma that was destined to classify him, like Moffitt, 4-F.

Thus, instead of fighting in Vietnam, the manpower of Collegiate Enterprises Inc., was intact in 1969.

At his desk in Dean Charles Burchett's office, Phillip Moffitt thought about how to improve freshman orientation. From his own experience he knew how lost an out-of-town high school graduate felt coming to Knoxville. How could he help these neophyte students?

To finance his graduate studies in economics, Moffitt had taken on the job of assistant dean for students. Now he was a mere sideline spectator to the protests erupting over the open speaker and no-hours policies, but he cheered when Chris Whittle and others triumphed in both confrontations.

Moffitt concentrated on his orientation dilemma. When an idea struck him eagerly he took his proposal to Dean Burchett, "a really Southern character who cared deeply" about the students. "I told him," Moffitt recalls, "that I was arranging to put out a little magazine to hand out to freshmen to tell them some helpful things about Knoxville. Dean Burchett said that sounded like a good idea to him, but he'd have to check with his boss. So his boss said, 'It sounds like a good idea to me, but I've got to check with my boss.' You know how that goes.

"So I find myself with Dean Burchett sitting in the office of the university's number-two guy, me telling him my idea. And he said, 'Well, this is a university publication.' I said, 'No, it won't be a university publication. I'm going to have students put it out, and it won't cost any money because they'll sell ads.' He said, 'No, if you distribute it, it's a university publication.'

"I said, 'Okay. It's a university publication. What do I do?' He said, 'You've got to get it approved by the university publications committee.' I said, 'Fine. I'll do it. When do they meet?' He said, 'They've already met.' Typical bureaucracy. And I said, 'Never mind.' "

Moffitt thought of his ace in the hole—his Collegiate Enterprises partners. "I went to them and said, 'Do you guys want to make a bunch of money?' and that's how the magazine was started." Chris came up with the name: *Knoxville in a Nutshell.*

They decided on a page size of eight and a half by eleven inches, and created a forty-four-page "dummy" with separate sections for dining, the nearby resort area of Gatlinburg, men's clothing, women's clothing, entertainment, services-shops-stores, an index, and map. And plenty of space for paid ads—thirty-four pages!

They hired student solicitors who sold the ad space easily. They found a printer and contracted to publish five thousand copies for free distribution as the Fall 1969 issue. "I was editor—nobody else wanted that job," Moffitt says. "The whole thing was a breeze. We made a couple thousand dollars on it."

The first issue of *Knoxville in a Nutshell* deserved high marks for volume of paid advertising, but the editorial content was mundane. The introduction said:

> Since part of the anxiety and frustration of the first months of college results from problems of not knowing where to eat, what to wear, where to go, or how to find things you need, this book provides an introduction to these four critical areas of college life—clothing, dining, entertainment, and services. It is designed to help you understand the UT community and to serve as a handy reference source. . . . Bring the **Nutshell** to school with you and refer to it each time you are confronted with the need for a particular product. . . .

The section on dining plugged thirty restaurants—all advertisers.

> The individual student's dining pattern varies greatly. . . . The vast majority of new students have made no particular provisions for eating. . . . For breakfast many students will use the vending machines in the dormitories, the University Center cafeteria and grill, or Strong Hall cafeteria . . . The cost will vary; a typical breakfast might be milk and a sweet roll for 35 cents or ham and eggs costing up to $1.65. . . .

The magazine's longest article was on men's clothing:

> The past two years at UT have shown a marked trend to-
> ward more liberal wear as evidenced by the frequency of
> bell-bottoms ("bells"), wide leather belts, neck-tie scarves,
> trench, army, and safari coats, and fly collar shirts with
> french cuffs. However, the overall campus style would still
> be classified as slightly conservative.
>
> College dress is a deliberate, bright, well thought-out
> casualness. . . . For late November football games, a stadium
> blanket, a muffler and gloves are invaluable.

Barely half as much space was given to women's clothing:

> Your goal should be a wardrobe which is well suited both
> to Knoxville's climate and to UT's general dress trends, yet
> one which avoids the stereotyped (round-collared, print
> shirtwaist) college girl image. You should always strive for a
> look that is unmistakably your own.
>
> Coeds will begin the football season with three-piece cot-
> ton suits and bright knit dresses accessorized by scarves,
> long gold chains and small heeled shoes (loafers don't go to
> UT football games!). An absolute must is a good pair of sun-
> glasses, for students sit directly facing the hot afternoon
> sun.

In sum it was a serviceable, if not spectacular, "Guide for Students," as the cover proclaimed. The partners in Collegiate Enterprises Inc. were satisfied; they had made some money on another
project they equated with washing cars or mowing lawns. Getting
their five thousand copies from the printer in late summer, they
made arrangements for distributing the magazines to freshmen in
the fall, collected for the ads, and split their profits. They visualized
this venture as a one-time enterprise.

6

THE LAW AND MUD
AND POLITICS

Walking across Columbia University's campus toward the law school building, Chris Whittle could easily see why students called it "The Toaster." Tall and thin with prisonlike horizontal strip windows, the concrete building had balconies extending from each end of the final, eighth floor that somehow did make it resemble a gargantuan kitchen toaster.

Chris had arrived in New York City in September 1969 to pursue a law degree. Yale was his first choice, Harvard his second. Both rejected him. "I was very upset about that," he says. "I wanted to go to Yale." His application had been accepted also at Georgetown, but he finally settled on Columbia for its greater prestige.

What he encountered inside "The Toaster" was considerably more disagreeable than its ugly exterior. Everything was regimented. First-year students were assigned places, with their names and seats displayed on wall charts. Chris could not hide; the professor would spot him: "Mr. Whittle, will you please stand and explain *Stubbs* v. *Jones*."

I have made a *big* mistake, Chris thought. Somehow he had expected law school to be easier. "I thought I was going to do law school the way I did college," Chris says. "For the last couple of years at U.T. I really didn't go to class. I just didn't have to."

Columbia still bore the scars of the 1968 student uprisings triggered by the Vietnam war and racial strife. The campus had been gridlocked and exams suspended. But the aftermath of those riots had little bearing on the difficulties Chris faced. Professors intentionally piled on work for beginning law students, in part to test their resolve and determination. The work load, everyone told him, would begin to ease up toward the end of the three-year grind.

Chris was startled to discover how misogynism dominated Columbia law school. The first-year classes contained few women, and they were shunted to second- or third-class status. By protocol they could be asked to respond in class to questions from a professor only on the one day a week designated as "Ladies Day." Usually, Chris observed, instructors only posed questions about sex crime law in an obvious attempt to fluster or embarrass the women students.

Although Chris lived in a graduate dormitory on the Morningside Heights campus, he did most of his studying in the New York University law library near Washington Square in Greenwich Village. But his desire to become a lawyer soon ended.

"I think I realized two things," Chris says. "One, going to law school was going to be a big commitment in time and energy. And two, that it was not going to be like my college days at U.T. when I could kind of go do whatever I wanted to do. It was going to be an enormous grind."

Chris quit attending classes at Columbia after only three weeks, but he stayed on in New York City for three months, living in his dorm room. However, he continued to spend most of his waking time in the NYU law library—"working on some interesting assignments they gave out at Columbia"—and loafing in Greenwich Village coffee shops.

His sister Camille came to visit him on her winter break from the University of Tennessee, and he decided to drive her back to Knoxville. Late at night, Chris's GTO convertible was barreling down a highway in the Shenandoah Valley with Camille at the wheel. Chris was asleep in the back seat. A state trooper came up with blue lights flashing and siren wailing and pulled the car over.

"I was going too fast," says Camille. "The cop had me nailed. But Chris woke up fast and that brain of his began conjuring up some ploy to get us off the hook. While the trooper was standing there getting ready to write a ticket, Chris started yelling at me about how he had warned me not to go over the speed limit and how he could never trust me and would never let me drive his car again—ever! Just all kinds of yap like that. I think the cop felt sorry for *me*. Anyhow, he let us off with just a warning."

Chris's return to Etowah that Christmas disappointed his parents. He says, "I think they were very upset when I quit law school and had no plans. Nothing."

Dr. Whittle was philosophical. He recalls, "Chris would have made a miserable lawyer. He's totally honest. In fact when he went to Columbia I said to myself he'd be home by Christmas. And he was."

His mother says, "It was very difficult for us to send him. I had never worked, but I took a job in Herb's office when he needed some help. Every cent I made I saved to send Chris to school."

Chris was unaware that his mother's paychecks went to meet his New York City expenses until that subject came up during one of our early interviews in Knoxville, in October 1992.

═══

Depression had seized Chris during the New Year holidays. It was now 1970. He was twenty-two and a half years old and totally lost as to his future course. That question had plagued him in college, but he had been so caught up in the university politics and confrontations that he had, without realizing it, avoided a decision. The embarrassment of dropping out of law school—perhaps the only significant failure so far in his young life—now intensified his dark mood.

In the tenor of the times, conventional wisdom on campus was that to get a college degree and just go into business was a disgrace. Chris agreed. "My friends would look down their noses at me," he says. "Somewhere in the back of my head I had a feeling—remember the times—that the only moral work was manual work."

His frustration and aimlessness brought him back to Knoxville, where he rented a small attic apartment from Helen Nybert in the same university district building where Phillip Moffitt, assistant to Dean Burchett, was living.

At length the days and nights of anguish over this impasse drove him to a decision: He would get a job of manual labor, and it must be the hardest, meanest, dirtiest he could find. He didn't know exactly where to seek that kind of work, but he thought he knew someone who did—Bob Hanggi, the student Camille was dating.

Chris looked on Bob Hanggi, only a year or two younger than he was, as a sort of husky "muscle guy"—and a personable and handsome one at that—because he spent his summer vacations working on highway construction jobs. Hanggi was taught blasting techniques by a friendly dynamiter on a bridge job and often obtained high-paying work blowing up rock.

"What I'd like to do," Chris told Hanggi, "is see an entirely different side of life, the hard-working side of America."

"You mean that, Chris?"

"I do. I do."

"Well, about the hardest job I'm aware of is offshore oilfield work," Hanggi said. "The way the system works is you are typically out on a rig for two weeks working twelve hours a day, and then you get two weeks off, and do it over again. It pays good money. I have an uncle over in Louisiana whose company supplies all types of workers for offshore rigs. His name is William Haygood."

"Could you help me get a job?" Chris asked.

Within a few days Chris was bound for Morgan City, Louisiana, the principal port for boats and helicopters transporting men and material to the oil drilling platforms out in the Gulf of Mexico.

"Chris bought his steel-toed boots," Hanggi says, "and I lent him a hard hat I had from a construction job. He got his rain slicker and his blue jeans and denim shirt. He was all set and expected to be out there wrestling steel pipe and lifting those big chains. It was going to be quite an experience for him, just being with these offshore drillers and roustabouts. My uncle told me the majority of these guys would come in off the rigs and spend time in the bars. Then he would have to round them up and get them back out on the rigs where they worked like dogs, and then again in two weeks they'd come back for another round in the bars. Later on Chris told me, 'It was a great experience, but I found out I don't want to be doing that the rest of my life.'"

The work Chris landed in Morgan City was nothing glamorous like helping the drillers and roustabouts out on the rigs in the Gulf, but mere pick-and-shovel duty as one of many men who reported every daybreak to the casual labor pool.

"What you did," Chris says, "you showed up every morning

and a truck would pull up, and the driver would say, 'Give me six.' And six of us would hop in the back. You had no idea of where you were going or what you were going to do that day.

"One day I asked a fellow in the truck, 'What are we doing?' He said, 'We are going to do a mud run.' And we pull up beside a box-car, and hop out. The boxcar is filled with hundred-pound bags of stuff they called mud, which they pour down the wellhead to lubricate the drill.

"It is a powder, and it started raining and some of these bags were broken. And they got wet, and they became slick and so the whole boxcar became slick and greasy—a terrible mess. By the end of the day I could hardly stand up!"*

Chris was living in a room over a Morgan City bar.

"One day the saloon owner called upstairs and said I had a long distance call on the pay phone," he says. "It was a guy calling from Washington—and this is a very funny thing—he wanted to know if I would go to Connecticut and work for a guy who was running for governor. And I said, 'I'll be on the next flight!' "

———

When Chris abandoned his mud-run career and started his trip to Connecticut, back in Knoxville dormant Collegiate Enterprises Inc. was beckoned, oddly and out of the blue, to begin operating again. In February 1970, the phone rang at Phillip Moffitt's desk, where he was still working on freshman orientation for the University of Tennessee dean. Economics professor George Anthony "Tony" Spiva was on the line.

"I am looking at your *Nutshell* magazine," Spiva said. "It's got promise. I assume you intend to publish more issues. I would like to be an investor. Perhaps this could be expanded to other universities."

Moffitt was pleasantly taken aback. He knew Tony Spiva fairly well, having taken his course. Everyone seemed to think he was a pretty savvy guy. So Spiva thought *Knoxville in a Nutshell* had profit potential? Moffitt wondered if the other partners would be interested. Mayfield was working in his family dairy business in Athens.

---

*From this lifting and grunt work, Chris developed a hernia that gave him discomfort until he underwent surgical repair in 1992.

David White, still waiting to enter flying school, had taken an interim job at the White House helping Henry Kissinger monitor foreign policy directives. As far as Moffitt knew, Chris was still a grunt laborer in Morgan City, Louisiana.

"Sure, Tony," said Moffitt. "Let's get together and talk about it."

They did.

What Tony Spiva offered Collegiate Enterprises Inc. was not only capital, but office space and his business expertise—along with his confidence that it would be a money-making venture.

Spiva was in his mid-forties, round-faced and stocky, healthy and energetic, well versed in business practices, and anxious to make use of an inheritance recently received from his father that ran close to seven figures. Virtually shooting from the hip, Spiva had taken a wild gamble, backing a Knoxville man who had an idea for making foam rubber pillows to sell to airlines.

The professor bought machinery and foam rubber, hired workers, and leased an abandoned, run-down warehouse in West Knoxville at 1005 Maryville Pike S.W. that became his two-thousand-square-foot pillow factory. His pillow entrepreneur couldn't make a go of it and soon fled town, leaving Spiva with an inoperative factory. He found another entrepreneur who also tried and failed.

Spiva was already $20,000 in debt when he decided the pillow factory would make a good site for the *Nutshell* magazine operation. He gave Moffitt a tour, introduced him to his banker, and wrote a personal check for several thousand dollars as his initial investment. "I didn't see this as a situation where I would gain much of a profit," Spiva recalls. "I just wanted to help them get started."

In a rush, Moffitt contacted his partners with a proposal that they revive the magazine and expand it to other college campuses. "Tony believed in us," says Moffitt. "That made a real difference." Mutual financial obligations still bound the partners, created by Mayfield who, then twenty-one, cashed in a $10,000 trust fund set up by his father. Brient then invested the money into the business and took a $2,500 note from each of the other partners, who still regarded their venture as a sideline. With Chris and White far from the new scene of operations in the pillow factory, the heaviest burden of restarting *Nutshell* and invading new territory would fall on Moffitt, in Knoxville. But Mayfield could also help, since his hometown was only an hour away.

"We went into the pillow factory one weekend and threw up some dividers," Spiva recalls. "They moved in before the pillow making actually stopped. I set up an office there for myself and mainly tried to introduce Phillip and the guys to people who could help their business."

The technique for expanding was not very scientific. "We just looked at the map," David White recalls, "and tried to find schools that had a fairly large population and were somewhat similar to U.T., and relatively close geographically." The first new deal was struck at the University of Kansas at Lawrence. In need of help, Moffitt culled the roster of outstanding seniors in the University of Tennessee English department and settled on Laura Eshbaugh, a sober, diminutive brunette who would soon attend the University of Florida on a full graduate scholarship. Her goal was to become an English professor.

"It was very strange," says Laura Eshbaugh. "I didn't know him, but I had run for student body vice president and he knew about me. He asked if I would be interested in a summer job. He described it in a way that I would now think was very pejorative—Girl Friday, basically assistant editor. We went out and looked at the pillow factory and then went to Sears and bought a desk and a filing cabinet. I got five hundred dollars a month—seemed like a lot at the time.

"From the start I was heavily responsible on the creative side for coordinating with the people who were writing copy for all our different editions of *Nutshell*—because we were gradually expanding to twenty separate editions. We all did a little bit of everything, even sweeping the floors. Because the staff was a very, very small group of people."

Disaster lurked in every foam-littered corner of the pillow factory. Moffitt and Laura Eshbaugh did not realize until later that they were in over their heads. Students were hired to do freelance articles from the other colleges. "We should have set rigid standards," Laura Eshbaugh says. "The articles would come in different lengths, different quality levels, the punctuation and grammar would be horrid. Often some fundamentals were missing. We pulled a lot of all-nighters at the pillow factory fixing copy."

That was not enough. They faced a bigger problem. The Knoxville printer who had produced the first *Nutshell* had given a set price to turn out all twenty new editions, but he lost so much money printing the University of Kansas issue that he quit.

"He left us high and dry," says Laura Eshbaugh. "It was a nightmare scrambling from Chattanooga to Johnson City, Tennessee, to find new companies to do our printing. Someone even wrecked my car when he was taking stuff to the printer after working all night. We finally got the *Nutshells* out—but all were late!"

However, they were well received by college administrators, students, and advertisers. The new *Nutshells* were vastly more professional, polished, and interesting than the Knoxville debut edition. The layouts had been executed by freelancers from the U.T. art department. Cutting and editing by Moffitt and Eshbaugh sharpened the articles.

The sixty-page *Lawrence in a Nutshell* carried a $1.25 price tag, though it was distributed free. The smoother introduction boasted it contained "eleven editorial articles written by students from your campus, combined with messages from local merchants, to give you the 'inside' information on nonacademic facets of college life. . . . [and] three national articles . . . to give you a better idea of the situation you face as a student in 1970."

According to the article on women's clothing, whether University of Kansas coeds would be called on to choose mini, midi, or maxi hemlines remained to be seen—"or not seen (depending, of course, on the direction her hemline takes)."

The *Nutshell* article on men's clothing poked fun at all the college men who said two years ago they would not buy bell-bottomed trousers. "Raise you hand—or rather your leg, and show off the flared slacks you're now wearing!"

Of the K.U. edition's three "national" articles, the most pertinent was by Phillip Moffitt, titled "What You Were Afraid to Ask (And They Were Afraid To Tell)." He wrote, "Many freshmen find so much difficulty adjusting to college life, they may flunk out or attempt suicide." To get started right, he offered thirteen tips, among them:

BEATING THE SYSTEM

During your first week many upperclassmen will be eager to give you "helpful hints" on shortening the registration process or avoiding hard work in a particular class. Watch out for these people! You can cut corners and get away with it. But the "expert" who is telling you how . . . may simply be on an ego trip and giving you a lot of misinformation. . . . Play it straight until you learn the ropes. . . . You might cut a corner and run into a stone wall.

BEING AGGRESSIVE

If you sit in your dormitory room waiting for other people to come along, you may sit there your whole freshman year. Get out and meet people. Do not hesitate to be aggressive; it's expected of freshmen. Even if you are shy, force yourself to go places and meet people. . . .

ALCOHOL, DRUGS, AND SEX

You probably suffer from many misconceptions concerning college students and their use or participation in alcohol, drugs, and sex. Your social acceptance depends on where your *head* is, not on your level of intoxication (from any of the three sources). You can find stimulating people with whom to associate, no matter what your views are on these three.

The long hot summer of frustrating, arduous, nerve-wracking, sleepless, and disagreeable labor stretched on into the early weeks of September. Everyone connected with Collegiate Enterprises Inc. was exhausted. But at last it was over. All twenty *Nutshell*s were out and had been distributed. They had won against huge odds.

Then Moffitt and Tony Spiva sat down to check their ledgers. They had lost $60,000!

The *Nutshell* publishers had exhausted their financial resources, which were minuscule from the outset. Collegiate Enterprises Inc. was essentially bankrupt. What happened next depended entirely on Tony Spiva. The professor's banker and his CPA were already warning him that he was gambling too heavily in a shoot-for-the-moon enterprise. Spiva played a lone hand, guided by almost child-like optimism and confidence.

Not only was he betting on the intellect, imagination, and energy of these outstanding college leaders, he was also struggling—personally—to turn his pumpkin of a pillow factory into a Cinderella's coach.

"I had done some venture capital investing prior to that," says Spiva, "so I was not completely a neophyte in the area. And the thing that appealed to me was that I knew Phillip personally because he had taken a degree and a master's in economics. And I knew Brient Mayfield's family, the Mayfield Dairy people down in Athens, very big family, and he was very prominent here on campus.

"David White was one of the brilliant students in the history department, and Chris was an outstanding fellow. They were all well-known names on campus, and I knew them to be bright. When they explained to me the concept behind the *Nutshell* series, I said, 'Hell, that does sound like a good idea.' And they were so bright and so enthusiastic that I just had a gut reaction that they would make the damn thing fly. They worked like absolute dirty dogs."

In this period, Spiva was often absent as an economic consultant to third world countries. In Knoxville he hovered around *Nutshell* as though the publishers were his children.

"When I was here," he says, "I went out to the office every day trying to lend guidance and mostly moral support. It got really tough. Everybody was working hard. They'd be there until midnight, two o'clock in the morning. Sleep there sometimes. After attending a social event I'd drive by and if there were lights on, I'd just automatically turn around and go back to the pizza place or Arby's and get a bunch of sandwiches and Cokes, knowing they probably hadn't taken time to eat, and bring them out to the pillow factory."

Terrified by the $60,000 deficit, Moffitt and his partners felt they had no choice but to shut down operations. If Tony Spiva had agreed, the drama of what was to become one of the outstanding entrepreneurial episodes in the history of American business would never have achieved its sensational multi-million-dollar climax.

"We'll have to keep going," the professor said. "Figure it out. Make it work."

Spiva led Moffitt to the office of a young banker he knew, Laurance Frierson, president of Knoxville's Volunteer State Bank.

"Most bankers would not touch this kind of proposition with a ten-foot pole," Spiva recalls. "But I had a feeling that my friend Frierson would take a chance on these kids. He was the type of banker who went on gut reaction rather than purely on numbers. He agreed to make a loan against the wishes of his own board of directors, and even though Collegiate Enterprises Inc. then had a negative net worth."

With Tony Spiva cosigning the note, Volunteer State Bank loaned $100,000 to keep the *Nutshell* enterprise operating.

Due to individual circumstances, the involvement of the partners in the Knoxville operation kept changing. It was still merely their sideline, all of them being otherwise committed to full-time careers. At this time Chris was totally out of the loop, having abandoned his colleagues to try his hand at offshore oilfield work. Moffitt, who was in Knoxville, could not escape daily work at the pillow factory. Brient Mayfield took an oblique turn away from *Nutshell,* devoting more time to the family dairy business. Also, he was toying with a computer invention that was destined to become very important to the *Nutshell*s. David White became more involved, leaving Washington to come back to Tennessee.

On a summer junket, Mayfield had visited White in his National Security Council (NSC) office in the Executive Office Building next to the White House, and came away with the impression that David White, "at only about twenty-four, was in charge of American foreign policy in half of the world." His government job was impressive for someone so young, but even as a minor protege of Henry Kissinger, chief of the NSC, White did not have the clout his friends mistakenly credited.

"The national guard never could get me a slot in flying school," says White, "so they said I could go ahead and get a job. So I went to Washington and talked to the secretary of the White House foreign policy staff and asked for a job as his assistant, and got it.

"Three or four months later under Kissinger, they decided to reorganize the NSC to try to figure out what was happening to executive orders that had been issued. Often nothing was happening. So they assigned a foreign service officer and me to start reviewing all the executive orders issued by Nixon or Kissinger and then go to all the meetings where decisions are supposed to be made regarding those executive orders, and to read all the policy papers in regard to those orders written by the State Department, the Defense Department, or any other agency.

"Our task was to write reports, usually monthly, on where those actions stood. The White House had discovered that often they would tell the bureaucracy to do something and nothing would happen. So it was our job to keep up with what had been decided and what was being done about it.

"There were two of us, and we each took one-half of the world. Nobody asked for our opinion about what to do. I kept thinking they should, but they didn't. It was a fascinating assignment."

A year later, in midsummer 1970, White had been lured back to Tennessee to work with Lamar Alexander, a popular young lawyer who was manager of Winfield Dunn's successful campaign for governor. White took the job as Alexander's deputy and chief strategist. Thus Dave White was again able to serve as a nearby consultant on *Nutshell*.

Alexander was to emerge a legend in Tennessee politics, becoming governor himself, and later president of the University of Tennessee before going to Washington as George Bush's secretary of education. In 1995 Alexander declared himself an active Republican candidate for president.

Mayfield startled Moffitt and White with a proposal that their partnership—now called Collegiate Marketing and Management Inc.—branch out into computers.

"What the dairy industry desperately needs," Mayfield told them, "is a device that will efficiently calculate the proper mix of ingredients for making ice cream. I think I can build a computer that will do that! We would make a barrel of money."

White liked the idea and promptly telephoned his brother-in-law, Pete Cowling, a University of Tennessee engineering professor. "Find us the two top electrical engineers in graduate school," he said. To the pillow factory came Jon Schaffer and Ross Duncan, who were promptly hired to work with Mayfield. Within weeks they had built a prototype. It was a crude box about the size of a typewriter with thumbwheels for entering data and flashing lights to display answers. It worked.

Mayfield borrowed his father's airplane and flew the gadget to Beloit, Wisconsin, where he had an appointment with Dale Seiberling, a former employee of Mayfield Dairies and now an engineering technician with Economic Laboratories. He set the computer on Seiberling's desk and plugged it in.

"Okay, let's have a race," Mayfield announced. "We're going to formulate some ice cream. Here's what we are going to make and here are the ingredients we have. You tell me how you'd put them together, and I'll solve the same problem on this computer."

Mayfield punched in some numbers and flipped a switch or two. He recalls, "In ten seconds I had the answer. Dale was still trying to figure out what the problem is, much less getting started on it. To solve this manually, even at best, takes three to five minutes. You had to write down intermediate calculations, and it was nearly impossible to get the best-cost answer."

Seiberling, bowled over, invited Mayfield to demonstrate the device the following month in his booth at the national dairy show in Houston.

"We were the first thing at the show that was electronic," says Mayfield. "We had crowds standing around looking at this thing. But it was kind of dicey. We had two hand-built prototypes. What would happen was in about fifteen minutes the circuit boards would heat up and short out and the lights would start flashing, and go crazy.

"We'd plug in the other computer, and by the time the engineers got the first one fixed the one that was on the stand would fail. What was going on was really comical. We were presenting this as a finished product and seeking orders. We knew we could correct the overheating. The big thing was that it did work!"

The enthusiastic response at the dairy show so impressed Dale Seiberling that he ordered 110 ice cream calculators at $4,500 each and put down a deposit of $100,000.

"When I took that check back to Knoxville," says Mayfield, "they cheered so loud the walls shook at the pillow factory!"

———

Chris Whittle drove his decrepit '59 Beetle into the little town of Farmington, Connecticut and parked in front of the Wally Barnes-for-Governor headquarters. He stepped out carefully, for the Volkswagen had no floorboards.

In his office, Wally Barnes, a forty-four-year-old wealthy industrialist and lawyer, shook hands warmly but was taken aback. This was the astute campaign expert the Rockefeller people in Washington had sent to help him in a tough election? The visitor was rumpled and scruffy. But worse, he looked like a high school kid.

On the other hand, Chris found Barnes looked aristocratic, standing six-three, a trim 185 pounds, with black receding hair and dark, blue gray eyes. The candidate was not a dramatic speaker but came across earnest, intelligent, and very likeable.

Hired to be number-three man or "the scheduler," within ten days Chris was number one—and running the whole campaign. He was twenty-two-and-a-half years old.

"Chris just had a talent," Barnes recalls. "A way with people. Very persuasive. And we just woke up one morning and Chris was running the whole show. There was very little backlash. One or two of my old men left. Nobody really went away mad. I enjoyed working with Chris immensely."

The phone call to the Morgan City, Louisiana bar that brought Chris to Connecticut in March 1970 came from Robert Bonatiti, a political consultant to Senator Howard Baker and a former assistant dean at the University of Tennessee, where he had seen Chris in action.

Barnes had impressive credentials. He was CEO of a precision spring manufacturing plant founded in 1857 by his great-great-grandfather to make rings for women's hoop skirts and watch and clock springs. He had degrees from two colleges: economics from Williams, where he won a Phi Beta Kappa key, and law from Yale. An avid flier since sixteen, he held a professional pilot's license, and flew across the Atlantic in 1967 in his twin-engine Beech Baron with his teenage daughter Jarre Ann. Barnes had been a Connecticut state senator for ten years. The family company had plants worldwide and annual sales of $125 million.

Even so, Barnes was in awe of the campaign manager half his age. "Chris worked fifteen, sixteen, seventeen hours a day. I don't know when he slept or ate. I'm not sure he lived anywhere. He may have lived in that VW. Or with friends."

With unexpected bravado, Chris told Barnes his campaign strategy of trying to steamroll the upcoming state convention for the Republican gubernatorial nomination was wrong. "I told Wally he couldn't do that," says Chris. " 'There are one thousand delegates. The most you can get are three hundred, as I see it. So write off seven hundred, don't even talk to them. We'll spend all our effort on the three hundred, and count on getting at least two hundred.' "

Chris knew that if Barnes got 20 percent of the delegates—two hundred—he would qualify to run in a primary election, where his chance to win would be considerably stronger.

"I told Wally, 'It's your only chance. You don't have much time, just ninety days.' I showed him a list of our three hundred, basically the outs, the disaffected. Wally Barnes said, 'No one has ever primaried—done it this way.' And I said, 'We will never win unless you agree to primary!' And so he agreed. It was very bold on his part because nobody had ever said they were going to primary if they got 20 percent.

"And off we went. For ninety days I drove every back road in Connecticut in my '59 VW and just talked to delegates. The night before the convention at Hartford a reporter asked how many votes we would get. I told him two hundred thirty-one. Missed by one. That's why I've often said that sales and politics are similar."

That was Chris's first use of a strategy that was later to become one of his mainstay gambits in business, which he declares as: *Concentrating your power where your efforts or your energy against a smaller group of circumstances yields greater results than dissipating it across a wider front.*

Chris now says: "The idea of focusing your energies is something I try to get us to do. Some people in life will play what they call the numbers game. They'll say, 'Let's put a lot of things in play, and surely something will work out.' I'm not a believer in that. I think you put less things in play, focus tremendously on that group of things, and you'll get a greater result. And the Barnes campaign is the first example I recall of my using that strategy."

Barnes's 230-vote tally threw a scare into his leading opponent, Congressman Thomas Meskill, who decided about midnight to send a man to ask Barnes to withdraw and join the Meskill ticket as candidate for lieutenant governor.

The offer was tempting. Barnes huddled in his Hilton Hotel suite, within walking distance of the convention hall, with wife Bonnie, Chris, and two or three others. "We debated and debated," Barnes recalls. "We actually kept the convention waiting. It was a very dramatic thing. Chris told me, 'If you run for lieutenant governor, I think I will move on.' He meant he didn't want to be part of a campaign for a conservative like Meskill. So I decided to turn down the offer, and we primaried."

When Chris talks now about the primary election, he just shakes his head. "He asked my advice and I gave it. I don't think I realized what I was doing to his career. Here he had turned down the lieutenant governorship, and in the primary we were slaughtered. And the other guy went on to be governor."

Looking back on the campaign twenty-three years later, Wally Barnes is both charitable and philosophical. "I think that in retrospect Chris thinks he unduly influenced me, and I don't view it that way. I still think today that it was the right decision for me. I'm not sure that I would have been comfortable in the role of lieutenant governor."

Ironically, if Wally Barnes had accepted the offer he would have become governor of Connecticut because Governor Meskill was appointed a federal judge and his lieutenant governor finished out his term.

"So I would have been a sitting governor at the next election," Barnes says. "Be that as it may, I came back to my company and it has done very well. I find that satisfying. I really don't regret the decision that I made back in 1970."

His Barnes Group is a *Fortune* 500 company, listed on the New York Stock Exchange, and manufactures precision springs and custom parts for automobiles, aircraft, appliances, and space vehicles. His achievements fill forty-four lines in *Who's Who*.

Perhaps with his candidate's wealth in mind, Chris Whittle attempted to interest Wally Barnes in the *Nutshell* business down in Knoxville.

"After the campaign was over," says Barnes, "I got a little grumpy with him. He was trying to raise money from me and at that point I was pretty heavily in debt as a result of the campaign and I just didn't have any money that I was willing to throw at some of his investments. And he is a very persistent salesman and I felt that he pressed the sales pitch a little too far, so I got a little cross."

Barnes felt he was being asked for a loan without being offered any equity. "I told him, 'Chris, this is nuts. This doesn't make any sense at all.' That's what I thought, and I'm sure it showed. But that was the reason for it. It wasn't that I thought he had given me bad advice on the primary. I had a lot of respect for his political advice. I felt that his business request as a business proposition was out of line."

An oblique encounter in Connecticut that had nothing to do with politics seriously impacted Chris's life and headed him toward an entirely new career path.

Near the small town of West Simsbury, not far from the Barnes headquarters, a private alternative high school had been built in 1968 on Westledge Mountain. Louis Friedman, a thirty-five-year-old Hartford school teacher who raised $7.5 million in start-up capital, named it Westledge School because of its location. Many blacks from the Hartford inner-city were among Westledge's three hundred students.

Chris was introduced to Westledge by going there with Wally Barnes, who was on the school's governing board. Friedman recalls that Chris was instantly captivated by the school and its progressive, "open" campus, where students were not required to attend class and could call their own shots regarding their life-style and discipline.

"He was a fascinating young guy," says Friedman. "I can't tell you how many times he came out to Westledge. He kind of hung around and kept saying you ought to do this and do that. Whenever he was there, he loved it.

"I saw incredible talent in him. He was wonderful with the kids. I will say he looked scruffy. One wouldn't have assumed the brain that was contained in that head just by looking at him. But the minute one started listening, you got the feeling this is someone to take notice of."

Listening to the youngster from Tennessee gave Friedman sudden inspiration. "You've got to come here and teach," Friedman told Chris. "You are a natural with the kids. You love this environment. I don't have any money to hire you right now. But possibly you can help us raise some money. . . ."

Two decades later Friedman recalls how Chris stood and frowned, thinking over the offer. Friedman says, "I was trying to get my hands on him because he had so much imagination and vitality and everything."

Chris, at length, nodded affirmatively. "I think I'll do that. I'd like it a lot. Right now, I am thinking about something that could tie me up several months. But later we'll give it a whirl. . . . I'll stay in touch."

When Chris got in his '59 Beetle and took off for Knoxville, he had every intention of returning to Connecticut to teach school.

———

Two weeks later Chris sat with Camille in the departure lounge of Knoxville's McGhee Tyson airport. It was late September 1970. He was no longer involved in the *Nutshells* and hadn't been in months.

"You are traveling light," his sister said. "Are you sure you're taking everything you need?"

Chris smiled and patted his backpack. "Two shirts, an extra pair of jeans, this windbreaker," he said. "The books Dave White picked out for me." He pulled out his wallet, and Camille recalls it looked astonishingly fat. "I don't remember," she says, "if that was because of the money he had to carry, or the size of the ticket."

Boarding for the New York flight was announced. Chris stood and hugged his sister. He tried not to show his emotions, which were tangled in knots that he could not unsnarl. He felt at a crossroads, unable to fix a suitable course for his life and career. Somehow he must come to grips with his dilemma and work everything out. His father bought him a $1,500 airline ticket, and with the money he had saved from Connecticut and a little he had borrowed he was all set. He gave Camille another hug, said a choking goodbye, and strode down the boarding ramp.

Chris Whittle was leaving home to spend a year traveling around the world—while trying to decide how he wanted to live the rest of his life.

7

LESSONS FROM
RUSSIAN NOVELISTS

On a winter morning in early 1971, Chris Whittle trudged up the mountain road out of Katmandu, the capital of Nepal. In the thin air, his breathing was labored and his pace slow. He hiked toward the border of Tibet, gazing at his first vista of the Himalayas. The scenery was stunning, but he was a hundred miles from the world's tallest mountain, 29,141-foot Mount Everest, too far for a clear view.

As a teenager he had several times hiked to the top of Tennessee's Mount LeConte, but that was a mere 6,500 feet. On this Katmandu road, he calculated giddily, he had already reached an altitude almost twice that high.

Chris loved mountains and snow, but he was by no means foolhardy. Not for a moment did he contemplate climbing Everest. Only trained mountaineers with Sherpa guides dared undertake its treacherous ascent. The most Chris desired was to actually see this monarch of mountains—a look that would last him a lifetime. I will never make it here again, he thought. Limiting himself to this daytime walk, he would return to his Katmandu hotel before dark.

During the last six months his around-the-world journey had taken him to several places off the beaten track. He was glad he had come to Nepal; this ancient kingdom wedged between China and India was certainly not a routine stopping place for the average tourist. But strange places and different peoples fascinated him. In letters to his parents, he logged his impressions and his experiences. He also was spending hours reading.

When Chris departed from Knoxville, Dave White had loaded him down with books by Ayn Rand, Dostoevski, Tolstoy, and other authors. "I think it's the only time in my life that I basically had a year to do anything I wanted to do without any agenda," Chris says. "What I had was a knapsack filled with books. I had an extra pair of jeans and an extra sweater and the rest of it was all books. And what I did that year was I traveled, and I read. That's all I did."

For a few hours on the road high above Katmandu, Chris studied the ice-capped landscape. The day was windless, and he was aware of an eerie stillness in the mountains that pressed heavily on his psyche and prompted him more than ever to ponder the meaning of life, the question that had triggered this global journey. Occasionally a vehicle would pass along the road, its engine grumbling if climbing uphill or its brakes squealing if going down.

Not long after noon he saw a truck coming uphill in the direction of Tibet. The vehicle slowed down and he noticed that the men aboard surveyed him curiously with hard eyes. Abruptly the truck stopped and several rough-looking men leaped out.

"Basically," says Chris, "I got shook down by a truckload of Tibetans. But I didn't get hurt."

They took his knapsack but not his books.

"I didn't have books with me. I was just on a day trip out of where I was staying and I had left them there. I wasn't in any danger, ever."

This was the scariest experience of his world journey, but he didn't recount it in his letters home. "He didn't mention things that would worry us," says his mother, Rita. "His letters usually asked me to send him books. And money."

When Dave White put *The Brothers Karamazov* in Chris's knapsack he felt certain Dostoevski's classic work would have an impact on the traveler. It did. But Chris's introduction to the life and works of Tolstoy, especially *War and Peace* and *Anna Karenina,* made a much deeper and more lasting impression. And when Chris read of Tolstoy's experiments in adapting education to the individuality of the pupil he was sharply reminded of his commitment to return to Connecticut and teach at the alternative high school in West Simsbury. An aristocrat and a famous author, Tolstoy had become a humble teacher of peasant children and for nearly two years taught singing and drawing.

In reading the Russian's literature, Chris discovered that he himself currently struggled for answers to the identical questions that one hundred years earlier had plagued Tolstoy—*Why do I live? How should I live?* As he went about among strangers in unfamiliar lands, Chris had yet to resolve the confusion about his own career goals and aims in life. His thinking began to be guided strongly by the sincerity, thoughtfulness, sympathy, and stern justice he recognized in Tolstoy's writings. In Tolstoy's view, man's aim in life was to achieve happiness by doing right and avoiding all forms of evil. Chris could go along with that, but the novelist's denunciation of the wealthy and all forms of capitalism gave him pause. Of course, Chris mused, being rich was not a problem he had to contend with at present.

He traveled on the cheap. "In Morocco," he says, "you could live very well for fifty dollars a month. Of course I was living on a rooftop. I was in Iran, in Afghanistan, Kashmir, Thailand, Japan. Even in those sections I would try to go to the out of the way sections, to the northern islands of Japan, for example, not the big island."

When Chris finished a book, he gave it away and wrote home for more. "I read a lot of very long works," Chris says. "I read everything Rand wrote. I wish I could go back and read those books now."

At American Express offices he periodically collected his mail and kept up fairly well with what was going on back home. Chris was only mildly surprised when he learned that his three college partners had finally taken the plunge into *Nutshell* as a full-time venture. That's a real gamble, Chris thought, but they should pull it off.

Back in Tennessee, David White certainly had much trepidation. He recalls:

> In the early summer of 1970 I had talked Lamar Alexander into managing Winfield Dunn's campaign for governor of Tennessee, and he insisted on me becoming his deputy. Winfield won, and they wanted me to join his administration.
>
> At that point Phillip and Brient and I had our heart-to-

heart talk about whether to go forward with all the projects under our CEI umbrella. During the year Phillip had been in charge of doing the twenty *Nutshells* and Brient was making sure the computers were worked on.

I had tentatively agreed when all this was ready to become a full-time business I would come back and manage it. After the election, the three of us went to dinner in Knoxville, and they said, "Hey, this is getting too big. We're already in debt. We've either got to do this or not do it." And I said, "I want to stay in Nashville [the state capital] for a year." And they said, "That won't work. Either we all make this happen, or it's not going to happen."

So I thought about it for a week and came back and said, "All right, if you will both quit your jobs—Phillip in the dean's office and Brient at Mayfield Dairies—I'll come back and we'll all go full-time and do the company."

That night after dinner we drove out to the pillow factory. We walked in and there was still foam through the back part of the old warehouse and in all the corners and crevices. The twenty *Nutshells* had been finished and all the summer workers were gone; the engineers were still working on the computers, but just part-time. We had a woman who came in half a day and answered the phone.

I sat there and looked around. It was a pretty dramatic moment. The three of us had just committed our full time to running a debt-ridden company that had just one half-time employee. I remember thinking, *there is not much here!*

The excitement of his foreign travels kept Chris from pondering the uncertain destiny of his old comrades back at the pillow factory, and also helped subdue occasional homesickness. But he could not escape twinges of nostalgia about his family, especially when some American Express clerk would hand over a letter with an Etowah postmark.

Camille wrote that she intended to marry Bob Hanggi on May 29th, and asked him to please come back for her wedding. His sister's letter gave him several uneasy hours of indecision.

In his mind's eye Chris could picture his mother busy with preparations for the wedding, which would take place at the "house on the hill"—the beautiful, large residence his parents had built in 1965 on secluded upland acreage a few miles west of Etowah. Although he had a bedroom there, Chris realized that, being away in Knoxville and elsewhere, he had spent barely one night in his room. But he considered it home; in her roomy attic his mother faithfully kept his old toys and books, Boy Scout mementos, high school and college yearbooks and photos, extra clothes, as well as his sisters' things. To this collection Rita was now adding the letters from his travels, though the foreign stamps were torn off the envelopes for the sizeable collection his sister Karen took over from their dad. Nothing had been overlooked at the "house on the hill"; for Camille's horses the Whittles had even built a large barn and fenced in a pasture.

Camille wrote that Rita was having a gazebo built so the marriage ceremony could take place outside. That news brought a smile to Chris, remembering Karen's wedding at home. She had deserted music entirely and earned a degree as medical technician. While serving her internship at Grady Memorial Hospital in Atlanta, Karen met and became engaged to a young physician, Eric Patrick Ellington.

From her extensive flower garden Rita had picked roses and wound them around the bannister of the stairs Karen would descend from the second floor to the altar in the living room. "You look so much better without these," Rita said, taking off her daughter's glasses. Karen started downstairs, not seeing too well, and missed a step. She grabbed the bannister and cried out in pain. "I can still remember getting a handful of rose thorns," she says.

In the end, Chris decided against returning for his baby sister's wedding. Instead he sent a letter, postmarked "Turkyie," in which he had block-printed:

DEAR CAMILLE AND BOB,

ALL THINGS ARE THE SAME IN THAT THEY ARE VERY

DIFFERENT FROM OTHER THINGS. AND SO IT IS THAT

MY BEING THERE AND MY BEING HERE HAVE SIMILAR

QUALITIES. REGARDLESS OF WHERE I AM, I CAN BE WITH

YOU. JUST REMEMBER THAT I AM REMEMBERING.

MAY YOUR PATHS ALWAYS BE PARALLEL.

CHRIS

Camille was deeply touched by his message. She keeps the letter in her safety deposit box. Chris recalls, "On that trip I was reading a good bit of Zen literature. I think I actually wrote this from India. In that stretch I was also into a lot of Buddha, and the letter certainly sounds like it."

About three months later the newlywed Bob Hanggis were driving in Knoxville off North Broadway, crossing the McKinley Street bridge.

"We were going in one direction," says Camille, "and we passed this guy on a bicycle going in the opposite direction. Bob said, 'That's Chris!' And I turned around and looked and said, 'No, it's not!' And Bob said, 'It's Chris!' I was still expecting him to be overseas, and we turned the car around and sure enough it was Chris!"

On his twenty-fourth birthday, Chris had indeed terminated his world travels and returned to Knoxville. "I spent three or four thousand dollars," he says, "and then I ran out of money. That's why I came home."

Chris stopped in Knoxville just to pick up his clothes. His soul-searching was over; he had chosen his next work. He was going on to Connecticut and join Headmaster Lewis Friedman's faculty at Westledge High to teach history—and help raise money for the school.

Of course, he went out to the pillow factory, where he was greeted like the prodigal son. "Come back and join us!" said David White, excitedly. "We need you—very badly," Brient Mayfield exclaimed. Phillip Moffitt put his hand on Chris's shoulder and gave him a sober look. "Come back," he said, "and take over marketing and national advertising sales. You are just the guy to pull us out of the hole!"

Once again Chris was in a career quandary and torn by indecision. In one way he felt honor-bound to go to Westledge School, but on the other hand these were his closest and dearest friends, and they *needed* him.

The four sat on rickety chairs in the pillow factory and talked for several hours. There were financial stumbling blocks; Chris had sold his one-fourth interest and thus could not come back immediately as a full partner. But David White concocted a scheme where Chris would gradually buy back a major stake. "From an ownership standpoint," Chris says, "I would be fifth or sixth player on the team."

Chris wouldn't take their bait. That evening at a restaurant over dinner they pressed him—to no avail. They wouldn't let up and haggled with him at several meetings in the next few days. Chris recalls, "If you cut right through it, I was very fond of the group. The idea that we were all going off on some adventure was very powerful. If it had been that alone, I wouldn't have done it. But they dangled the prospect of making millions of dollars right in front of my nose." Finally, Chris agreed to rejoin his old partners.

As Chris remembers it, when he telephoned Lewis Friedman to declare that he was not coming to Westledge School, "the headmaster was very angry." Chris felt bad, too, but later through his own business experience came to see both sides of such a rift. "The headmaster was right, but he was wrong. I didn't really understand this until later because many times in my career people have walked into my office and announced they were not coming, or they were leaving. Even if it is inconvenient, you've got to look at what it means to them and whether it's right for them. It's troublesome and disturbs your plans, but that's not the only thing in life. Yet I went back on my pledge to the headmaster." (Lewis Friedman doesn't recall becoming "angry" over the broken pledge. "I will say it was a great disappointment." Westledge School closed in 1980; the buildings are now used by another prep school.)

Professor Spiva dropped by the pillow factory and saw Chris for the first time—and was underwhelmed. "I told my wife that night this business was never going to work, that I had just met the national sales director, and he was so laid-back that he'd never be able to sell anything."

At the time of Chris's return, the whole pillow factory was tumbling downhill faster than ever. The partners even stubbed their toes trying to come up with a name. Initially they called the operation Collegiate Enterprises Inc., and from that formed two subsidiaries, Collegiate Marketing and Management Inc., under which the *Nutshell* editions were produced, and Computer Concepts, the division that manufactured ice cream formula machines. In one of their late 1970 brainstorming sessions, Moffitt and White came to the realization that their entire effort was targeting young men and women—from teenagers to those just finishing college graduate courses.

"In fact," mused White, "we offer advertisers an approach to the thirteen-to-thirty age group."

"That's the name," Moffitt exclaimed. "Approach 13–30!"

The name was formally adopted on December 7, 1970—in signs, logo, and letterhead. But it lasted less than a year. As soon as Chris Whittle started making sales calls he saw at once that the name was confusing to receptionists, advertising agents, and business managers. Puzzlement often showed on their faces, and some could not repress a snigger.

"That name is stupid!" Chris came back and told his colleagues. "What seems to throw everybody I call on is the word *Approach*. They don't get it! We'd be better off just calling ourselves the 13–30 Corporation."

Everyone agreed. Thereafter the pillow factory was synonymous with 13–30.

Coming up with a simple name, however, was not the answer to 13–30's plight. Nor did Chris Whittle have the magic that would immediately stem the constant flow of red ink. White, Moffitt, and Mayfield had calculated that bigger would be better and expanded the 1971 edition of *Nutshell* from twenty to sixty college campuses. Once more it was a madhouse getting the ads sold, all the articles written, pages laid out and printed. Finally all the *Nutshell*s were delivered, but some were late.

The partners checked the ledgers, and gasped. They had lost another $160,000. Again they were bailed out by Tony Spiva and banker Laurance Frierson. The professor added to his growing investment in 13–30, and the bank provided a straightforward—but risky—loan. Tony Spiva never lost faith in the ultimate success of 13–30. And despite his poor first impression, he warmed up quickly to Chris.

In a 1993 interview, Professor Spiva explained that the entrepreneurs simply did not comprehend their project's time and money requirements. "I told Phillip and Chris and David White they had to be aware of what I called the *pi* factor—*pi* has a value of what? Three point one four, something like that. And I said you have to figure in these ventures everything is probably going to cost *pi* times as much, and take *pi* times as long. I don't know that I had any sort of idea as to how much money I was going to put up, but the thing escalated pretty quickly. Quite soon I was either putting up or guaranteeing pretty substantial amounts of money."

That really did not worry him.

"All four of those young guys," said Tony Spiva, "were just very bright and they were very highly motivated and they were success-oriented, however you want to define that. And they were all of them so damn smart it was a foregone conclusion that they were all going to be successful."

He added, "You and I know that you could walk into any high school in Kentucky or Tennessee right now and out of the junior class of one hundred people there will be two or three who are just really bright and outstanding. And I simply don't know what causes that kind of thing. But all these guys were that kind of a kid. Plus they had all done very well in the University of Tennessee."

David White concedes there was no fully thought-out plan or road map for embarking on the 13–30 adventure. However, there was something that he thought helped offset that deficiency—the camaraderie of the crew of ex-collegians that had been assembled in the pillow factory. The atmosphere struck him as perhaps about midway between D'Artagnan and the Three Musketeers and the "Lost Battalion."

"During those years," White recalls, "we lived the dynamic of 13–30 night and day. We were all working every moment. Not sleeping very much. A great sense of taking on this challenge together. Everybody doing whatever they could to make it work. And a very great sense of cooperation. Trying to solve the problems, trying to do whatever was needed."

Occasionally a belated order came in for pillows, and Tony Spiva would summon a crew of his ex-workers and start up his idle machinery. Dust from the foam rubber shredder flew through the air, choking the artists and editors working at their 13–30 desks. They had to rush outside. "I admit it got a little ripe in there," Tony Spiva recalls.

David White recognized two glaring weaknesses in their *Nut-*

shell scheme that contributed to their inability to turn a profit. Most serious was that even though the small, permanent and part-time staff in Knoxville could be directed efficiently, the freelancers hired on other campuses lacked close supervision.

A fraternity brother, Ed F. Smith Jr., had just returned from army duty in Vietnam. White lured him into joining 13–30 as "a sort of general of our field division," taking charge of all the campus representatives. "If you were going to do a magazine on each campus," White says, "you had to have several people selling ads, writing copy, and making contact with the bookstores or whoever was going to distribute it. He took over all of them."

And with gusto. "Ed had this open space office right as you came in the pillow factory door," says White, "and you couldn't come in without going by his desk. I remember he was always there, always on the phone. Night and day. He would stay very late talking to California, and get up early in the morning and start making calls first thing."

Financial records were a mess, so the second biggest problem needed its own "general." Another U.T. graduate, Garrett Pierce, was hired as 13–30's vice-president of finance.

"He was a real good financial person," says White. "Once he got involved and saw what desperate condition we were in, he just couldn't handle the pressure. So he left, which was probably the wise decision for him. He was married and the rest of us were not. At the time the only reason the pressure didn't kill us was that we didn't have any obligations. Nobody was depending on us to be home at night. Nobody was depending on us for money. We weren't taking much salary. For three years, I didn't take any. We just drew what money we had to have."

Gradually the 13–30 staff grew to about twenty-five. Half a dozen busy technicians soldering together and shipping out the ice cream computers also toiled at the Computer Concepts workbenches.

In addition to Laura Eshbaugh, who returned from her year in graduate school at the University of Florida to be a *Nutshell* editor, 13–30 hired two additional University of Tennessee graduates, Judy Mizell, who had been editor of the U.T. *Beacon,* and Wilma Jordan, picked by White as the company's first full-time secretary.

With the intention of expanding *Nutshell* to at least one hundred colleges, 13–30 needed a trained professional as managing edi-

tor. Moffitt and White were impressed by the resume of Pat Ti-
chenor Westfall, a graduate of the University of Illinois who was
attending Columbia University in New York while writing for a
book and movie review magazine. They interviewed her in New
York.

"I was sick of New York," Pat Westfall recalls. "But I didn't think
much of the magazines they showed me. They were just plain
tacky, and I thought, ugh, I don't want anything to do with these
people.

"But Phillip really impressed me. He was so bright, and so articulate, and so interested. We had a long talk and the thing that persuaded me was that Phillip seemed to be definitely interested in
quality. I was real blunt. I said, 'These books don't look good. They
don't seem to be well edited.' He said, 'That's why we are looking
for someone. We need someone who knows.' "

Oh, hell, what's a couple of years, Pat Westfall thought. I'm just
twenty-two, and it will get me out of New York.

She had no inkling of the mountainous task awaiting her in
Knoxville. "It was more work than I have ever done in my life," she
says. "My experience up to then was basically writing and working
with one or two editors, and I knew my stuff. The one thing I didn't
know was management and I suddenly find myself with twenty-
three people reporting directly to me. Management textbooks say
no more than six should report to you. It was absolute hell.

"I was their first trained editor, the first who really knew how to
write and edit, knew the technology. But it was too much. Many a
night I spent all night in the pillow factory. People were sleeping on
cots, just trying to meet the deadlines.

"We were all pretty good friends. I liked Phillip. He told me
once, 'There are two people here, who if they left, I don't think I
could keep going—one is Chris and one is you.' The thing that was
interesting about Phillip for me was that he just wanted to know
everything. He would just haunt my bookshelf looking for titles he
didn't know: 'What's this? What's that?' And he just read vora-
ciously: 'Who's this author? Why are they important? What do you
like about them?' Anything I knew, he wanted to know. I guess he
saw me as more educated than him, like he kept seeing me as a
teacher. And that was kind of charming. He was just so curious
about the world.

"One of the editors who came later, Pam Beaver, once tried to put her finger on the magic of 13–30. She said, 'Chris and Phillip made us all believe that we were special. We were all just ordinary people, but they made us think we weren't. Made us think we were extraordinary, so we did things that we really can't do, we don't have the ability.' And I think she's right."

But the stress of the pillow factory madhouse never let up. Pat Westfall related one crisis:

> One night we were really having trouble getting a *Nutshell* edition finished. It was about three in the morning. We were pasting up the page flats. They had to be on the five A.M. plane for our printer in Hannibal, Missouri. Finally Phillip said, "We gotta go, ready or not."
>
> I got in his car and we took off on one of his amazing one-hundred-mile-an-hour runs to the airport. We missed the plane. Phillip said, "They've got to be on the next plane, and you're taking them." I said, "I'm not going; we've been up all night!"
>
> And he said, "You're not on that plane, we're shutting down the company. Because the printer will take our time on the press away from us—he's got to keep it running. We'll be sunk!"
>
> "Oh, all right," I said. "Take me home and let me pack a suitcase."
>
> "There isn't time for you to go home," he said.
>
> I'd been up all night. I had on a stupid little dress. "I'm not going," I said, "unless I get a shower." And so, in his wisdom, he didn't argue with me. He found someone near the airport who'd let us in before dawn to take a shower and so I got on the plane. I had to carry a suitcase that weighed ninety pounds. A whole bunch of pages. On the flight to Missouri I just fell sound asleep.

But that kind of pressure finally wore her down. Now a journalism professor at Ohio University in Athens, Ohio, she has vivid memories of how she became a cropper in the pillow factory.

"Remember how Chris and Phillip told us we were extraordinary? That myth sort of fed on itself. And I think that's maybe one reason I kind of snapped. I never really believed it. I knew I was ordinary. And I couldn't face it anymore.

"I could tell you the moment when I snapped. I was alone in the building. Night and alone. Trying to finish a magazine. Knowing there's no way to get this finished. And I kind of blacked out, but I didn't faint.

"It was just like my mind went blank for a minute, and when I came to I'm holding a Coke bottle in my hand about to throw it through a window. I came to my senses. I realized I was about to do something crazy. I just got up and went home. I was terrified. It's awful. Next day I quit, and went straight back to New York. The next six months are a total blur. All that pressure at the pillow factory was just too much for me."

———

On December 30, 1971, the twin-engined Aero Commander 500 owned by Mayfield Dairies taxied down the runway at Knoxville's McGee Tyson Airport to take off for New England. Brient Mayfield was at the controls. He had borrowed the aircraft for the weekend from his indulgent father.

Six passengers were aboard—Chris, Moffitt, White, Ed Smith, and two young women who were the New Year's weekend dates of Chris and Ed Smith—"the whole 13–30 Corporation," in the pilot's words. The Aero Commander lifted off into the cloudless Tennessee sky with laughter and easy banter echoing among the passengers, tempered by unspoken hope and trepidation, especially for Chris, about the success of their mission. They needed money to keep 13–30 going, and Chris knew a potential investor who might provide it.

"You have to understand," recalls Mayfield, "we were just hanging on, trying to survive. It was awful. It was terrible. And had not David White been at the helm of this thing and controlling the money, we'd have never gotten through it. But it took a genius like David to keep the doors open. And truly, for about two-and-a-half years David figured on a daily basis how to solve that day's crisis. And that was an awful job."

Capital had been raised in a chaotic fashion. The 13–30 principals, being just out of college, had no real resources. They begged and borrowed from their families—a total of $300,000 to $400,000. David White's father cosigned notes that if called would have wiped out his appliance store. Herb and Rita Whittle scraped together more than $100,000 to loan Chris, mainly from the doctor's retirement policy. Moffitt managed to encourage his family to dip into their modest savings. Brient Mayfield was able to come up with substantial money. Tony Spiva dug so deep into his pockets that eventually he would own 23.5 percent of the stock.

The young entrepreneurs bombarded their friends and colleagues at the University of Tennessee, painting a bright scenario for what was going on in the pillow factory, and managed to get ten or twenty of them to invest around $10,000 each. Ed Smith inherited a share of his grandmother's Tennessee farm; when the land was sold at probate he invested his bequest.

"We would do anything to get money," says Mayfield. "We had no idea how much we'd have to raise to stave off disaster. Would you believe a million and a half dollars!"

At an altitude of 9,500 feet, the Aero Commander streaked north at 180 knots. They were flying to Burlington, Vermont. Mayfield felt he had been lucky to find a holiday when his father's dairy would not need the plane. Chris had made an appointment to offer a financial proposal to Wally Barnes, the man whose campaign he had run for Connecticut governor in 1970. On a ski vacation with his stepdaughter, Barnes was at the Mad River resort near Waitsfield, Vermont, expecting the 13–30 party for dinner at his chalet.

For about three hours the flight was uneventful. But north of Buffalo, New York the weather suddenly changed.

"We flew into freezing rain," Mayfield recalls. "The windshield was quickly coated with a thin layer of ice. I couldn't see out. The plane, since normally it was flown only in the South, did not have deicing equipment. Being unable to see out did not harm my ability to fly. But that certainly created a problem for landing."

Chris, who had already logged a lot of miles on commercial flights and had a good sense of engine noise and in-the-air vibration, occupied the copilot's seat. He didn't like the sound of the right engine, and mentioned it to Mayfield, who brushed off his concern.

Mayfield considered changing course and flying out of the weather, but he was afraid they might run out of fuel. Talking to controllers on the ground, he debated landing in Albany, New York or some other nearby airport to refuel before going on to Burlington. Because of the icing, landing in one place would probably be as hazardous as any other. Mayfield decided to go straight on to Burlington.

"I had the defroster on full blast," says Mayfield. "It did nothing to clear the windshield but the hot air hit my four-inch square side window, and melted a little glaze. That gave me a porthole to see out. We reached Burlington and I circled the field and lined up the runway for our approach.

"All my passengers were excited, and I suppose scared. The whole airport was covered with about five inches of snow. I had to land. I considered opening the little side window and reaching out to try to scrape ice off the windshield. But at one hundred miles an hour that easily could turn into a disaster.

"I started down. They told me later Ed Smith opened the passenger door and stood there yelling out our altitude as we descended. I don't recall that. We landed okay, but with everything covered by snow I could not see a taxiway to get to the hangar. They sent out a truck so I could follow it in."

Chris recalls the episode as extremely dangerous. "The first time we shot our approach we broke out of the clouds about fifty feet over the parking lot, not anywhere near the strip; it was very frightening and we were very lucky that night. Basically the airport was closed, but Brient had nowhere else to go. It is true about Ed Smith. We couldn't see out the front; he had to look out the side door to have any sense of where we were. It was quite a night."

The pilot and his shaken passengers piled into a rental car and began the forty-mile drive to Wally Barnes's place outside Waitsfield. Barnes was pacing the floor in his ski lodge, fretting about the supper he and his stepdaughter had prepared. "I just remember we were worried about what to do with this meal," says Barnes, "because it was getting late and we hadn't heard from them."

Darkness had fallen when the Knoxville contingent finally reached Barnes's chalet. They had a late supper.

"Chris had been calling me on the phone and making a rather persistent sales pitch," says Barnes. "He wanted me to meet some of the other players, and that was at least one of the reasons for their visit."

The little banquet was fine, but once again Barnes could not accept the deal Chris and Moffitt spent a couple of hours that evening laying before him.

"His reaction was like 'How dare you!' " says Moffitt. "We were devastated."

"They weren't talking about an investment," Barnes says. "They were talking about a loan. I don't remember the amount, but it seemed like a lot at the time, because I still had substantial debts left over from the campaign."

Leaving Vermont, the disappointed Knoxville party broke up at the Burlington airport. "I don't like the sound of that engine," Chris told Mayfield. "I'm not flying back with you." In their rental car, Chris and Moffitt drove to New York City to try to sell *Nutshell* advertising while the Aero Commander took off for Knoxville with the other five. But a jinx still rode the borrowed airplane. Over Johnstown, Pennsylvania, the right engine began running dangerously rough. Mayfield promptly shut it down and made an emergency landing at the Johnstown airport, where he was held up twenty-four hours getting spark-plug wiring replaced. Chris's ear for trouble obviously had been true.

Instead of waiting for the repairs, David White and the two women also abandoned Mayfield and his ill-fated Aero Commander. They took a commercial flight back to Knoxville—where they were grimly confident some new financial crisis would urgently await them at the pillow factory.

8

TENNESSEE
ACCENTS
AND LONG HAIR

Every morning a troubled Chris Whittle would open his eyes with dread. "Everybody who saw our financial statements told us to give up, that we were finished," he remembers. He would get out of bed and mope in his little rocking chair. *You are going to face this day,* he told himself. *You are not going to quit. You are going to go in there and do your job, and you are going to do it well.*

He was by no means alone. His colleagues, too, were all valiantly struggling to prevent their teetering little company from plunging into the abyss.

Ironically, the more 13–30 grew, the further behind it fell. Expanding the *Nutshell* editions to one hundred campuses, their losses soared by another $550,000. "We were all freaked out by the amount of money we owed," Chris says. "It was a staggering sum. After the first three years we were one million dollars in debt. We didn't know what was coming. Our funding was patched together from a huge network of mainly private sources. They were more than investors, just people loaning us money. As we lost money, we relied on these people and anyone else to keep us going. We would literally have weekly meetings on Friday afternoons where each of us would sit down and determine where we were going to get the money to pay next week's payroll."

"We were scared to death," says Moffitt.

Expenses were held to a minimum. The staff remained small, their pillow factory rent was "dirt cheap," and the partners tapped the red-ink treasury for little more than actual living expenses. Moffitt recalls, "I was living in a basement apartment out in the middle of nowhere. It was something like $110 a month. I don't believe in those first days I drew more than $250 any month."

Getting finished copies of *Nutshell*s delivered to campuses around the country on time proved a constant struggle. Because of deadline screw ups and production delays the magazines often ran late. Only air shipment would get them to a designated college on time, and that was an expense 13–30 Corporation could not afford.

"We desperately needed to get the magazines there," says Moffitt, "and one of our people discovered this obscure airline regulation that said for each piece of excess baggage that you carried with you when you were flying you were charged one dollar per bag or box.

"We didn't have money to air-ship these magazines so we would fly a person to the campus and they would go to the airport with like twenty boxes and register them as excess baggage. And the airline people were furious with us. And rightfully they should have been.

"I was at the Knoxville airport a couple of times when it happened and our guys would have to carry copies of the official regulation because a lot of airline agents would say. 'I'm not going to do this!' And the worst example was when they didn't have room in the baggage hold for the boxes, and they strapped them into seats in the first-class cabin."

Trying to keep afloat in the money quagmire, Dave White tapped another University of Tennessee graduate and fraternity brother, Mark Medley, as chief financial officer. Medley took over a desk piled high with overdue bills, and his telephone rang constantly with creditors screaming for payment.

The most threatening noise came from a printing company in Atlanta where 13–30 had run up a $85,000 bill, which had been guaranteed in advance by Professor Spiva. Collections for *Nutshell* advertising were slow. Consequently there was scant money to send the printer. Finally, the printer demanded immediate settlement of the bill.

"Oh, come on, guys," pleaded Tony Spiva. "Be reasonable. The money's coming in. Give us another thirty days."

"No way," said the printer. "Now!"

Spiva, his lawyer, White and Mark Medley flew to Atlanta and met with the printer and his lawyer.

"I learned then," says Spiva, "that if I ever got in trouble in Georgia and wanted the meanest son of a bitch in the western world for my lawyer, I knew exactly who—their lawyer! They did agree to a thirty-day extension but only when I, in effect, had to sign over everything except the fillings in my teeth. They even took a lien on my ski boat and my wife's jewelry!"

Within a month the debt was paid and 13–30 continued to do business with the Atlanta printer for a while. "It is somewhat ironic," says Spiva. "Later the printer fell on hard times, and came begging us to do business with him again. We didn't."

Fresh from his year of carefree backpacking around the world, Chris was a distinct anomaly when he set out to lay siege to the headquarters of corporate America. His appearance did not blend with the blue pinstripe suits and white shirts at staid Procter and Gamble, and was in sharp contrast to the upscale grooming at IBM. Chris was still the laid-back hippie, wearing corduroy pants and tweed jackets, with his now abundant hair flowing almost to his shoulders. His saving grace, perhaps, was that he did not have a beard.

"When I came back my partners told me my role was to sell advertising," Chris recalls. "I said, 'Fine. What do I do?' And they said, 'You call on advertising agencies.' The interesting point is that my next question was, 'What's that?'—meaning I had no idea advertising agencies even existed. The level of ignorance I had in the business was extreme. I'd never taken any business courses.

"And I quickly realized I had to get appointments—General Motors, IBM, Procter and Gamble, big companies. I was supposed to go in and sell something. How am I ever going to get to the right people? So I came up with the idea of instead of writing a letter I'd send something entirely different."

Chris dispatched a long slender cardboard carton to his prospect. Inside was a leather case containing an elaborate parchment scroll, done up in "Olde English" style, rolled up on two gleaming oak rods capped by hand-carved finials. When opened, the scroll—in antique hand-lettering—tried to pique and capture the CEO's attention by proclaiming, "Hear ye! Hear ye! Now, throughout this land, let it be known that . . ."

Then the scroll's text went on to tell the CEO that the 13–30 Corporation of Knoxville, Tennessee could effectively carry his advertising message to America's college market, reaching some 300,000 students at 200 colleges and universities.

"Was it a marketing success?" says Chris. "Actually, no. It didn't work. The scrolls didn't get through. There was a reason for that. When big companies receive things in the mail they don't understand, they send 'em back. They are afraid maybe there is a copyright. At any rate my scrolls didn't work. We sent out seven or eight. That was it. Around Knoxville they are fondly known as the Dead Sea Scrolls."

When Brient Mayfield saw the 13–30 scrolls being hand-lettered, he rushed to steal the technique to reach customers for the computers he was offering to the dairy and food industry.

"I thought ours was pretty clever," says Mayfield. "The theme I used was to play it off of being hillbillies. It was a different style. We depicted ourselves as a bunch of hillbillies, and bragged that we had put together a moonshine whiskey operation and were using all these computers to control the processing, and taking care of the money, and finding the best booze recipes.

"Chris made his look like an ancient manuscript. Ours looked like it had been printed on toilet paper. Isn't that what you'd expect hillbillies to do? We were making fun of all this technology coming out of the Smoky Mountains, because Knoxville, Tennessee, is not exactly Silicon Valley, and neither is Knoxville exactly Madison Avenue.

"All we got was good laughs—no computer orders."

Chris Whittle felt comfortable with his hippie appearance, and did not give it up. In Detroit, Chris and Phil Moffitt entered an elevator in the General Motors building with a bearded young man in jeans loaded down with packages from the mail room. The hippie leaned over and whispered to them, "Hey, man, it's good to see another freak in the building."

On the road trying to lure national advertisers into the *Nutshell* editions, Chris was spending very little time in Knoxville. In fact, he was off on such a travelling jag he would later estimate that for a stretch of four or five years he spent no more than three straight weeks in the same city.

He came to not particularly care for flying. Once he was startled when the passenger in the next seat told him about an airplane crash in which he claimed to have been the sole survivor. Months later, another flight companion horrified Chris with an identical story. Gritting his teeth, Chris kept booking flights. He had to; no other way could he make the rounds of potential *Nutshell* advertisers.

"I have flown so much over the years," Chris recalls, "I developed a great sensitivity to noise tone and vibration of airplanes—and still have it. I literally have told the captains of airlines that they have problems, and they have confirmed it. I was on the Concorde once and I said to the stewardess, 'I'm reasonably convinced there is some problem over here in your right wing. There's a sound that's just not right.' She went up and told the captain. We were already in flight, and the captain came on the intercom and said, 'One passenger back there really knows airplanes, because we do have a problem.' And it was exactly the sound I had described. He said, 'It's a fuel pump that's malfunctioning.'

"Another time I was on a Delta flight from Chicago to Knoxville, and I told the crew I thought one of the baggage compartment doors was open. We landed and the captain said, 'You were right.'

"I was on an Eastern flight about to take off and I looked out the window and saw a jagged piece of metal stuck all the way through the wing. This was a dangerous problem. I told the stewardess, 'You can't take off!' and showed it to her, and of course we didn't."

In their tinkering and soul-searching, the partners came to realize that perhaps their most substantial achievement was the solid development of their access to the college campuses, which they dubbed "the pipeline." They had created a unique college distribution network by cleverly circumventing a law that prohibits the free distribution of commercial literature on campus.

"There's a legal requirement," says White, "that we had to have official sponsorship. So we would go to a college or university and negotiate an agreement with an on-campus organization or the school administration, such as the dean of student affairs, or student housing office, student life, student government, bookstore, or union. It's illegal unless you have a sponsor."

No money changed hands in these deals. The sponsor's only responsibility was to assist in distributing the magazine on campus, usually under supervision of a 13–30 field representative, who also provided campus newspaper ad copy and radio announcements about the magazine, to be paid for by the sponsor.

Many bull sessions at the pillow factory were devoted solely to considering additional ways to exploit the pipeline. Why not create another magazine to serve the college crowd, graduating students for instance? The idea began to jell. Moffitt and his editors and writers created a dummy edition containing feature stories on careers, job hunting, practical living, travel, working life, graduate and professional programs, and other topics of interest to graduates.

Titled *The Graduate: A Handbook for Leaving School*, it was jammed with about 40 percent advertising, launched into the pipeline, and delivered in bulk to colleges and universities throughout the United States for redistribution through alumni associations, offices of student activities, and student placement offices. Some copies also were distributed through banks.

As soon as *The Graduate* proved itself, it was promptly replicated in a publication targeted on the seventeen- and eighteen-year-olds getting out of high school. Named *18 Almanac, A Handbook for Leaving High School*, the magazine carried feature articles on college, the working world, and day-to-day realities of living independently. Likewise there were stories to help students make post–high school decisions in three primary areas: college, careers, and practical living. Through the 13–30 pipeline, *18 Almanac* was distributed to college admissions officers, who employed it as a recruiting tool for prospective freshmen by passing it on to high school guidance counselors from September through February. A debate inside the pillow factory was whether all troublesome local advertising could be eliminated and enough national advertisers found to support and make *Nutshell, The Graduate,* and *18 Almanac* profitable.

"I've got a good friend who's an executive at Procter and Gamble," said Tony Spiva. "Let's scoot up to Cincinnati and try it on him."

They did. The P & G man was intrigued, but not impressed enough to advertise. "He told us we weren't quite big enough for them," Spiva says. "But to come back—when we had grown some." Not many years later Procter and Gamble would be among the largest 13–30 accounts.

On Wednesday, June 7, 1972, another tragedy struck the Whittle family—and the aftermath of the calamity would ironically help ease the financial pinch at 13–30 Corporation.

At their beautiful "house on the hill" outside Etowah, Dr. Whittle was on the telephone about six that evening. It was difficult to hear because a severe thunderstorm was raking the countryside, rattling windows.

Suddenly a bolt of lightning flashed over the house, came inside along the telephone line and knocked the receiver out of his hand, leaving him shaken with a slight burn on his throat, but otherwise unhurt.

Several minutes later Dr. Whittle smelled smoke and realized the house was on fire. He rushed upstairs and saw flames crawling up the wall where the phone line came in near the attic. He ran out, unreeled his garden hose, and dragged it upstairs. The fire was still small and spreading slowly. Dr. Whittle began spraying with his garden hose and felt certain he could extinguish the flames.

The phone still worked, but he knew it was pointless to take time to call the fire department in Etowah; the town council had voted to prohibit Etowah's fire trucks from answering calls beyond the city limits, pressuring rural areas to develop their own volunteer fire-fighting companies. Nor, for the same reason, would the nearby Athens fire department come. So he summoned the Etowah rescue squad.

The physician was winning his one-man fight against the fire. "I got it down to a dull glow," he said later.

Then lightning struck again, knocking out power to his pump and water system. The garden hose went dead. Flames again began crawling up the attic wall with Dr. Whittle now helpless.

Volunteers from the rescue squad arrived at the scene along with neighbors and Etowah friends like Jim Frost. "If we'd had water, the house could have been saved," says Frost. "Lot of people were there. We all rushed in and stripped the house as best we could. Took down the chandeliers, the drapes, the doors, the rugs. It was a slow-burning fire, and we stayed one room ahead of the blaze. It was like a bunch of ants, going back and forth, people putting things in their cars and pickups, saying, 'I'll take it home and save it for them.' "

It took two hours for flames to consume the house. Lost in the attic were scores of family keepsakes: the wedding dresses of Karen and Camille, some of Camille's wedding presents, along with the journals Chris had sent home from his world travels and his mementos from high school and college days.

The *Etowah Enterprise* ran a page-one photo of the burning house and quoted Dr. Whittle: "The power went off too soon. I could have stopped the fire with fifty more gallons of water."

Privately, the Whittles were bitter that no fire trucks came. "After all, he delivered half the town," said Karen, "probably delivered half the firemen who didn't come." Their housekeeper, Mary Lou Harris, was upset, too. "Oh, for shame!" she says. "That town owes him a million dollars in unpaid bills."

In a letter to the editor of the *Enterprise,* Dr. and Mrs. Whittle mourned the loss of what they had hoped would stand as a "home place" for their children, and thanked "friends, neighbors, and the Etowah Rescue Squad [for] working tirelessly and dangerously to save our material possessions."

More to the point, the letter said: "We hope that from our loss attention will be called to the great need of fire protection in the surrounding area and that consideration might be given some movement which would help other families in the future caught in similar circumstances."

The letter pointed out that the Whittles had rented a house in Etowah, it gave their phone number, and asked "anyone giving care and protection to our belongings since the fire" to call to have them picked up. Friends say it was quite a while before all the furnishings hauled away from the burning home were returned. Weeks after the fire the Whittles drove up to the site just in time to frighten away intruders who had come with a truck to jack up and haul away the untouched gazebo.

Even in ruins the "house on the hill" was destined to make a second contribution to keeping the 13–30 Corporation afloat. Initially, Herb and Rita had mortgaged their new house to acquire money to loan Chris for his investment. Now they collected their fire insurance, paid off the mortgage, and handed the several thousands remaining to Chris for 13–30.

=======

In the face of unrelenting deadline pressure and an ominous bottom line, the 13–30 colleagues needed an occasional break—

and took it. They were all young and spirited, still in their twenties, and had just graduated from a Knoxville campus that had been liberalized by the Vietnam college rebellion. On sunny weekends they gathered for picnics about a mile from the pillow factory at an unusual place called Log Haven, an in-the-city nature park of Smoky Mountain trees and shrubs and a collection of real log cabins.

They had good outings at the two-room cabin Chris had purchased from Bert Vincent, a famous columnist on the *News-Sentinel*. One added dividend of the picnics was that fresh ideas for "growing" the business emerged, becoming valuable projects.

Every time Chris, Moffitt, and White sat down together, methods not only to pull 13–30 out of its financial quagmire, but to expand the scope of the business were discussed. To them it was clear that they had an exclusive niche in the publishing world—the college market. And being students fresh from the campus themselves, they felt they understood the collegiate mind, certainly much better than the removed advertising executives on Madison Avenue. Not only could they fashion an effective advertising message for students, the pipeline that 13–30 had created would deliver it to these young, potential consumers directly, with a speed and economy that was impossible for television or general circulation publications. Unfortunately, they kept running into a stone wall when they attempted to get corporate America to buy into their product.

In a weird but rather significant way, concepts derived from the published works of psychiatrists Sigmund Freud and Carl Jung helped fashion ammunition that 13–30 used in trying to breach the ramparts of Big Business. As teenagers, Chris, Moffitt, and White had read Freud in high school, and at the University of Tennessee, Chris and White were exposed to courses that further explored Freudian theories.

"When I was in college," says Moffitt, "I was very interested in philosophy and spiritual studies and religion—and psychology. From the time I was a little boy I have always wanted to know what life was about. I think some people are born that way because my friends weren't. I was reading Freud in high school. It wasn't until in my mid-twenties that I read Jung's biography or autobiography *Memories, Dreams and Reflections,* and I was shocked and amazed.

Up to that time the person who had impressed me most was Maslow, who had created this idea of the hierarchy of needs, and that once you fulfill your basic needs you get more and more interested in more civilized needs and then more spiritual needs. And all communities and all individuals go through this.

"As a boy I was really interested in the religious feeling and the religious philosophy of the Judeo-Christian tradition. The thing is, the way I look at it is: 'What is the story?'

"I always want to know the detail of the story. You know, there's a factual level of the story, and the psychological level, the symbolic level, and finally the spiritual level. All of these are entwined at any given moment on any given episode of a person's life or even any kind of a community life. I think of a business as being a community and being a culture."

In discussing psychology and human motivation, the partners developed what they termed their "Principles of Business," which Moffitt considers the cornerstones of their eventual success.

"We spent a lot of time," says Moffitt, "developing our assets of what we did, so that our people were really well trained. The thing that we emphasized was that in marketing you don't start selling. You start with your research, not selling.

"You want to go out and understand what their needs are. We developed a technique which we called the 'probe.' The first meeting was always to understand the person you hoped to sell. Another principle we had was that you never waste anybody's time. You don't have a meeting unless you have something that the client is going to perceive as valuable.

"Another rule was that if you had a meeting then there has to be something that deserves a good follow-up letter, or else you shouldn't have had the meeting.

"And every account was a managed account—there was no such thing as just calling on somebody. You had to have a specific goal, and you worked toward that goal.

"And all of this came from just having to learn under very difficult circumstances at 13–30 when we were selling the college market and not many of the major corporations realized the dimensions of the college market and our avenue for entering it.

"The fact of the matter is we invented this market by starting *Nutshell* and expanding it nationwide.

"So we had to do all of this education, and then we had to find ways to sell our market."

From a rash of brainstorming in 1973, a fresh scheme emerged that offered the promise of rescuing 13–30 from its constant deficit. Yet 13–30 backed quite slowly into its discovery.

Two key events took place on separate stages almost simultaneously. A corporate executive in a New York office, thumbing through a *Nutshell* edition while listening to Chris's sales pitch, mused, "Too many ads in here. Maybe you ought to get one advertiser to sponsor the entire magazine." Chris's eyes lighted up. He said, "We can handle that!"

Back at the pillow factory he relayed the idea to his partners, explaining, "It would be like a TV special, only a print special!"

"Yeah, oh yeah," agreed Moffitt. "Like those shows by Hallmark, or General Electric—just one sponsor."

Only days before they had hit on the idea of launching a travel magazine for college students. There wasn't anything else like it, and they thought collegians would be very interested since many spent a lot of time traveling around.

Attracting a single sponsor—some company willing to buy all twelve to fifteen advertising pages to turn the travel magazine into a "print special"—was appealing. If the concept could demonstrate sufficient potential the advertiser would essentially pay in advance, thus removing the risk that the entrepreneurs would lose money. This would be in sharp contrast to the struggles they encountered in launching *Nutshell, Graduate,* and *18 Almanac,* which were still in the red, although close to breaking even.

"Let's take a stab at Chevrolet," Chris said. "They're getting ready to bring out a compact called the Vega."

"They ought to consider us," Moffitt agreed. "One of their primary markets has to be the college market—a lot of young first-time buyers who can't afford anything but an inexpensive vehicle. Our new magazine would be a perfect way to reach that audience. It also happens to be very compatible with their manufacturing message—economical small automobiles. Not that all travel has to be done that way, or that our new magazine would promote the idea of traveling only by automobile, but the whole idea of travel, adventure, fun, freedom is pretty compatible with their Vega idea."

With high hopes, Chris and Moffitt rushed to Detroit. For once they were in the right place at the right time. General Motors bought their print special. They settled on the magazine's name: *The Vega Student Guide to America*. Writing a check in advance, General Motors agreed only to a limited test run, a western edition targeted primarily at California.

The magazine's cover proclaimed it offered articles on "Student Camping In The West," "How To Have A Weekend Adventure," "Practical How-to's For The Outdoors." "The Great Spring Breakaway & More." The Knoxville editors were still winging it. Laura Eshbaugh wrote the camping-out piece, but now admits, "I had never been out West in my life."

The travel magazine was a success; the Vega wasn't. Sales of the compact car were so disappointing GM pulled the plug on *The Vega Student Guide to America*. However, the Detroit executives were so impressed with 13–30 they commissioned the Knoxville publisher to analyze their Vega launch and report what went wrong.

"Chevrolet gave us their quantitative research," says Moffitt. "Reports from outfits like J. D. Powers, ownership of cars, things like that. We were making the qualitative analysis. Chris and I went to California and visited campuses and talked to students."

They prepared their report and returned to Detroit.

"The meeting was set up in the old General Motors building, around a horseshoe table," Moffitt recalls. "The room was full of people, extra chairs had been brought in and there were gobs of folks around the table's perimeter."

The size of the throng caused the Knoxville pair to roll their eyes and glance apprehensively at the reports they laid on the table. They had brought only five copies. Nobody seemed concerned.

"We told them they had a problem of a whole different proportion than they understood," says Moffitt. "We said, 'Basically, you're worried about selling to kids in California. You've already lost them. And you're going to lose kids across the country, and if you are not careful you are going to lose them for an entire generation. They'll never buy American cars!'

"Now it is amazing that we were so right on, so ahead of the change here. And we said, 'There are three things you can do. The first is to immediately change your advertising message. Then you must change your accoutrements—your radio, get a good hi-fi system, your packaging so that it's right for this emerging generation.

The third thing you are going to have to do is retool.'

"You know that's pretty presumptive. But if they had paid attention, they would have been far better off."

Their audience listened attentively. Chris and Moffitt came to the end of their discussion and looked around GM's horseshoe table.

"I asked if they had any questions," Moffitt says. "No one asked a question. Not one! This whole room full of people. We said, "Thank you, very much,' and left."

Instead of returning to Knoxville they sped back to California—and luck rode with them.

From researching the auto industry they knew that since 1960 Nissan Motor Corporation USA had been importing a pickup and three models of a small Datsun to the American market. Sales were not robust. Why not urge the Japanese company to try to improve its market share by stepping into the Vega void as sole sponsor of the travel magazine?

Chris and Moffitt had earlier approached Mayfield "Mayf" Marshall, advertising manager for Nissan, who had his headquarters in the Los Angeles suburb of Carson. They made sure he was in his office and rushed over a letter. It intrigued him.

"That letter told just enough to whet your appetite," recalls Joe Opre, who was then Nissan's assistant advertising chief. "Then they came in and struck us as inadvertently humorous just because of their looks. They wore long hair, were not well dressed at the time, but clean. And very articulate, obviously very smart, and, again intuitively, we felt very honest.

"They had done the thing for Vega, and we had some empathy for them because they probably thought they were going to continue with General Motors and when that fell through, it wasn't hard to figure out talking to them they were kind of on their last gasp. As a company and as entrepreneurs, they really needed a sale badly.

"But you know, looking past all that, it was just a good property at the right time. I don't recall the dollars, but it was fairly priced. It was just something that fit where we felt our company needed to grow."

As their visitors departed, Marshall and Opre exchanged amused glances. "We kind of chuckled," says Opre, "about the way they talked, with the Tennessee accents, and the way they looked—like caricatures of the times, sixties and seventies. But we took an instant liking to them. They were easy to work with, very accessible, and open, as we tried to be also. It was just a good partnership. We both wanted the same thing. We wanted the magazine to succeed, and of course it did."

At the Parker Advertising Agency on the other side of Los Angeles, Mike Collins, manager of the $25,000,000 a year Nissan account, took the surprising call from Marshall.

Collins says,"Mayf told me these kids from Tennessee had just sold him a magazine, and to find $590,000 in my budget for it. I was pissed!"

But Collins had come to expect the unusual from Mayfield Marshall. "He was smart, but a very weird guy. Weird in the sense that he was terribly bright but terribly willing to do off-the-wall, unique things. It certainly would not have been that way at, say, Ford. Chris and Moffitt never would have got past the reception desk."

Understanding Marshall's quirks, Collins just listened. Collins says, "I didn't say to Mayf, 'You're out of your goddamned mind!' But behind the scenes I really was upset. Because it didn't make any sense. How in God's name would you, number one, buy out an entire magazine? Number two, that nobody knew!"

Thinking it over later, Collins reversed his opinion and decided it was a master stroke for Datsun cars. "It came to me," says Collins. "It was first of all a very keen understanding of perceived needs, that the logic was quite good, meaning that if you can capture a share of interest—a disproportionate share of interest—of a group of young people who are at most four years away from their first major purchase, which is always a car, why not? The logic was very, very strong. And Mayf said, 'Yeah, that makes a lot of sense.'"

Not to take anything away from the 13–30 entrepreneurs for "inventing" the project, Collins decided Marshall deserved a lot of credit. Mayf had the guts to say, 'Hell, this is a great idea and I'll trust you guys,' and sign off on it."

The think tank at 13–30 was off and running on a hot streak. On the heels of the travel magazine, which was renamed, *America: The Datsun Student Travel Guide,* quickly came two new ideas that were easy sells.

To cash in on the surge in 35 mm photography, an expert, Rick

Smolan, was commissioned to produce *The Beginner's Guide to the Single Lens Reflex Camera* for distribution on college campuses through the 13–30 pipeline. Nikon snapped up the sponsorship.

The pillow factory drawing board created a magazine devoted to hi-fi music. That struck the fancy of another Japanese company pushing its sales on this side of the Pacific—Sony quickly agreed to sponsor the publication, called *Sound: The Sony Student Guide to Music*. How that deal was closed right at the end of 1973 became a 13–30 Corporation legend—and perhaps for the Sony Corporation as well.

One December afternoon in New York the final terms were worked out between Chris and Dan Gallagher, Sony's vice president for advertising. They had their formal handshake, and then Chris said, "We need to get this all done today."

A perplexed look crossed the Sony executive's face.

"What?"

Chris didn't bother to explain that he wanted to get back to Knoxville in time for the 13–30 Christmas party and celebrate the deal, the third big profitable contract executed in 1973.

"I mean sign the contract—now," said Chris.

The Sony man again blinked. "Well, you know, this is a long contract. It's not finished, there are these revisions to put in, I won't be able to get it typed today."

Chris picked up the contract. "Don't worry, I'll type it."

Somewhat awed, Dan Gallagher led Chris to a secretary's desk. A fast typist, Chris knocked out the contract in a couple of hours. He took it to the Sony officer and said, "Okay, we need to get this signed."

Chris knew that required a trip upstairs to the senior executive suite.

"Can't we let it wait?" said the Sony veep.

"No," said Chris, "Let's go up there now."

And they did. With no delay, the contract was signed. As they left the floor, Gallagher gave Chris a smile and said, "Thanks a lot."

"Wait," said Chris, "there's one final step. We need a check."

His companion began to get exasperated. "You know," Gallagher said, "the check will come in due time from our financial office."

Chris, thinking of the serious cash-flow problem at the pillow factory, gave him what he hoped was a winning, as well as pleading, smile. "But, we need it now!"

"The check place is out on Long Island."

"That's no problem. I can go there."

The Sony official, obviously in awe of such persistence, just shrugged and gave in. They went to the Long Island financial offices and the check—for $100,000—was written.

Says Chris: "And he physically gave me the check, and I went from there to La Guardia [Airport], and got back for the Christmas party, check in hand."

The sequel to that episode is that later Dan Gallagher left Sony and spent three years working for 13–30 in Knoxville.

9

"YOU MUST BE WILLING TO DROWN"

From the dining room table they watched the spectacular sunset. The dying Pacific sun scattered crimson shafts across the ocean and the tree-studded Palos Verdes hills. Chris Whittle, sporting worn jeans and a rumpled sweater, had driven down from the Los Angeles airport in his rental car to have dinner with Mike Collins and his wife, Christine.

"Chris always looked like he'd slept on the plane," she remembers with a grin. "He never brought wine or flowers. Just Chris. That was enough, really."

Since the advent of *America: The Datsun Student Travel Guide,* the Collinses had socialized a good deal with Chris on his business trips out to the Parker Advertising Agency. The three had become close friends; only her husband and Chris called Mrs. Collins "Chris." To others Christine was "Christy." This evening was one of several when he was their lone dinner guest.

Sitting on one side of the table with host and hostess at each end, Chris began fidgeting with the silver and acted uncomfortable.

"May I rearrange the table," he said, "so I don't have to twist back and forth talking to the two of you?"

Christy laughs at that memory. "So one of us moved. Typical Chris thing."

The Collinses never tried to fix him up with any of the girls they knew. "We assumed he was in a relationship back in Knoxville," Christy says. "And I think he was."

Christy Collins discerned deep emotional currents in her Tennessee guest. "One time Chris said to me, 'Why is it that you like living here in Palos Verdes?' It was just the way he asked, or something, and my answer came out without thinking. I said, 'I have a sense of place, and I am kind of on the edge of a continent.' Which is true because I can practically see the ocean from my window. I had never thought of that before and that was not bullshit. That was true, but I was amazed that the question from him would cause me to be really thoughtful about myself."

On another evening, as the three sat out on the back patio, Mike Collins began talking about the phobia that seems to haunt every Madison Avenue ad man—that he'll be washed-up or burned out by age forty. It was too soon for him to harbor such thoughts. Mike and Christy were sweethearts at Ohio State University, got married, and went to New York's Madison Avenue for six years before Mike's adman career brought him west to the Parker agency.

Christy recalls, "Mike was afraid of being a forty-year-old advertising man. Fear that you can't stay in the business. At that time Mike was only in his early thirties. But he was thinking of doing something on his own. I don't remember what it was.

"Mike was using Chris as a sounding board, as a friendly counselor. With friends, Chris seems comfortable being that. He has a way of what I call attending to people. And he readily gave Mike advice. I'll never forget it. Chris said, 'You have to be willing, Mike, to drown. You have to be willing to be at the very bottom. You have to be willing to take risks, and to be to the point where you feel you are never going to be able to come back up for air. That's how I do it.' "

That ultimate risk-taking formula which Chris espoused in an offhand way in the seventies made a lasting impression on Christy Collins. She thinks he has not wavered from it.

"And that's how Chris has continued even to today," she says. "He gets himself into ventures or projects that are so overwhelming that he really has to work so intensely to turn them around, to get them to be successful, that it is a factor—I'm not saying that is how Chris became so successful—but it definitely is a factor, and it probably does have something to do with his character."

This easy social friendship was in marked contrast to the rocky beginnings of the Collins-Whittle professional relationship. His feelings already ruffled by the brash way the deal sprang up, Mike Collins was suspicious of the ability of 13–30—a company he had never heard of—to deliver. He also confessed having something of a provincial bias; after all, Knoxville, Tennessee, was not exactly a world capital.

"This was a large sum of money on a very weird venture," he says. "They didn't really have a lot to show for what they did. They had a magazine called *Nutshell,* which in my opinion was not a very impressive book. My recollection was when Chris took me through it I kept saying to myself, Maybe this is how college kids are these days. He showed me their other publications. I think what struck me was that graphically they were very crude."

However, from the start Collins was taken with Chris's personality. "I was extremely impressed by his maturity, his bearing, his demeanor, how he chose to handle himself. He was very quiet, calm, and very logical and rational and clearly much beyond his years in terms of intellect and maturity. I just fell in love with him."

Collins adds, "He dressed in those days more like a tweedy young college fellow, usually in corduroy pants and something like a tweed coat or sports jacket. Corduroy was a big part of his wardrobe. His hair was flowing to his shoulders."

In an indirect way, Collins came to understand that possibly the Datsun deal was "a real miracle" for 13–30, that it came at a life-or-death juncture in the road, and that it saved the Knoxville entrepreneurs from going bankrupt.

"I got a call from their banker—Frierson," Collins says. "He asked if we had signed the Datsun contract, and I said yes. I immediately called Chris telling him this was very odd, but I thought he should know this banker just called me. As it turned out, he was calling to confirm, because if they had not signed—so the legend goes, which I'm about ninety-eight percent sure is accurate—they were going to shut 13–30 down."

Mike Collins was in for more hand-holding than he expected. "Basically they were learning as they went. And I was the instrument in that process, meaning they didn't really know how to deal with advertising agencies, particularly on such a close basis—a full basis of relationship of one agency and one advertiser. So that required a set of disciplines they weren't accustomed to."

In their ignorance of these protocols, Chris and Moffitt were very rigid and naive at certain levels of the magazine deal. But there was never any doubt that Parker Advertising and Datsun held the upper hand.

"I can remember phone calls," Collins says. "They might say they were not going to change some particular thing in editorial, and I would say 'Yes, you are! Either that or you're gonna get yourself in deep shit trouble and I'll cancel the contract!' In the end, everything worked out."

After they had worked together for a couple of years on the Datsun project, Chris flashed Collins a warm smile over the dinner table in Palos Verdes, and said, "Mike, we'd like you to join us in Knoxville. You've said you'd like to do something different. Here's your opportunity."

The offer didn't come as a surprise. Chris and Phillip Moffitt already had made subtle hints that 13–30 urgently needed an experienced and successful advertising executive—someone they had never had—to bolster their ranks of self-trained amateurs. Collins said he would have to think about it. Doing the right thing ethically, Chris notified the Parker executives he was trying to hire their Los Angeles man.

"I was thirty-five or thirty-six and I had been going through the whole process of saying to myself, What am I going to do when I grow up?" Collins said. "And here came Chris offering me a chance to have a real shot at something."

Collins made up his mind. He sold his beautiful Palos Verdes house for $165,000, left Christy to pack the furniture, and as soon as she could, follow him to Knoxville with their two sons, nine and seven.

What the Californian found on arrival staggered him. "Basically," Collins says, "what the company was then was a very, very uptight, extraordinarily serious group of young people. I had never been in an environment which was so quite—stultifying is the wrong word—but it really said, *My God, these people take themselves way too seriously!* And there was an almost kind of cult feeling around the place."

On his first day Collins came into what he called "this wretched, cinder-block pillow factory" casually dressed, wearing a "very tasteful" Mexican silver bracelet and neck chain. "That sort of thing was perfectly okay on the coast at the time. But I never wore them again. It just didn't play in that building full of all these young but terribly serious people—at that time about thirty of them. And I recall vividly the first night saying to myself, *What in the hell am I even doing here!*"

The incredulity Collins felt was the same commented on by others who found they had to make an adjustment to the 13–30 culture, a curious blend in which counterculture casualness coexisted with an uptight sense of mission. Beyond doubt, the company resembled a commune more than a business, with Phillip Moffitt looked upon as the guru and spiritual adviser to the young staff. To newcomers, the mood could be unsettling.

In leaving Parker, Collins had given up $50,000 a year and a car to sign on with 13–30 for $40,000. "It gave Chris and Phil nosebleeds to pay me that much," he says. "During my relocation to Knoxville I was staying in a twenty-eight-dollar-a-night motel near U.T. Then Chris comes in and kicks me out because it's costing too much. I end up staying in a furnished apartment and paying for it myself."

In fact, Collins's debut in the pillow factory was, he says, "a very, very scary situation" because his new colleagues were so "serious" and "everything was critical."

"There was no real time for reflection," Collins recalls. "Everything was on a kind of basic crisis—'We got to get this next deal moved!' "

Moreover, Collins discovered a side of Chris Whittle's personality that he had not seen before—one that stemmed from the Californian's new status as hired hand. Without rancor, Collins learned to live with—and actually profit from—their altered roles where Chris called the shots.

In retrospect, Collins feels that Chris unintentionally used him as a guinea pig in learning how to deal with people one-on-one more effectively. "There were a number of very, very terrifying instances where I thought I had done a very good job of making a presentation, or something I thought went fairly smoothly, etcetera, and he would be very quick to tell me how it didn't go well, and this is how I should have done it differently."

These humbling episodes caused Collins to wonder about himself and his own abilities—even though both Chris and Moffitt were aware that Collins had been the only person permitted to make presentations for the Parker agency because he was "the only one who did it right."

At this stage, Collins believes Chris had a strong need "to control," and thus would tell him, "I don't want to tell you what to do, but here's how you do it." Collins recalls finding this quote quite paradoxical. "Chris does it the way Chris does it," Collins says. "And the fallacy is that other people try to emulate him. As a result of that, they would sometimes fail because you can't do it the way Chris does it. The point is that at that point Chris didn't quite conceptualize."

Memories of those struggles at the pillow factory in the mid-seventies come flooding back to Collins two decades later. He gets up and stares out the window, sees his boat at anchor in the river behind his Knoxville house and ducks swimming in the Tennessee sunshine.

"I must tell you," he says, as he returns to his desk chair, "Chris is the most absolutely incredible presenter I have ever witnessed!"

If so, what are his secrets? Collins smiles, wagging his head in admiration.

"Chris gets you in a position of a little series of agreements which are very hard, if not impossible, to refute. And with each slight affirmative nod of your head, he tightens the grip just a little tighter and tighter until you finally think, Of course I'm going to buy off on this. And it is because of his logic. There's no razzle dazzle. He comes off in large groups, perhaps just the opposite. His strength is in small groups. I don't think he has a challenger in small group dynamics."

Collins casts another look at the ducks while meditating on his twenty-year association with a colleague he now attempts to characterize in the present day.

"That doesn't mean other people aren't good like Chris. He's a very charismatic person. I don't think that's practiced at all. He's just been blessed with a gene pool. And to that you add an extraordinarily high level of intelligence, and a real wonderful ability to move something from point A to point Z, with no interruptions. He is just spectacular."

Collins has often seen another of Chris's salesmanship strengths

ABOVE: Seven-year-old Chris Whittle (*standing*) with Louise Witt, wife of Chris's future scoutmaster, and her children on McCamey Lake, Etowah, Tennessee, July 1954. (Courtesy Eugene Witt)

LEFT: Chris, 14, (*far right*), receives Eagle Scout medal from Fred McGhee in Etowah in 1961.

Chris (*left*) with fellow U.T. student Barton Haynes upon their return on September 24, 1967, from a summer in Czechoslovakia. (Courtesy *Knoxville News-Sentinel*)

David White, Chris (*center*), and Phillip Moffitt at their pillow factory office during the early days of their *Knoxville in a Nutshell* venture. (Courtesy David White)

ABOVE: Seven-year-old Chris Whittle (*standing*) with Louise Witt, wife of Chris's future scoutmaster, and her children on McCamey Lake, Etowah, Tennessee, July 1954. (Courtesy Eugene Witt)

LEFT: Chris, 14, (*far right*), receives Eagle Scout medal from Fred McGhee in Etowah in 1961.

RIGHT: Chris as a senior at Etowah High School, 1965. (Courtesy Janice Elrod Pickens)

BELOW: Chris (*right end, third row from bottom*) played saxophone in the combined eighth-grade and high school bands in Etowah. (Courtesy Janice Elrod Pickens)

Chris campaigning for president of the Student Government Association at the University of Tennessee. On April 25, 1968, he won with 3,086 votes to his opponent's 2,725 in a record turnout. (Courtesy University of Tennessee)

Chris (*left*) with fellow U.T. student Barton Haynes upon their return on September 24, 1967, from a summer in Czechoslovakia. (Courtesy *Knoxville News-Sentinel*)

David White, Chris (*center*), and Phillip Moffitt at their pillow factory office during the early days of their *Knoxville in a Nutshell* venture. (Courtesy David White)

Phillip Moffitt (*left*), David White, and Chris confer at their pillow factory office. (Courtesy David White)

Chris began wearing his trademark bowtie at the pillow factory. (Courtesy David White)

RIGHT: Chris's parents, Dr. Herbert and Rita Whittle, at a 1991 party in Knoxville. (Courtesy *Knoxville News-Sentinel*)

BELOW: Whittle Communications employees examine architect Peter Marino's model of the new Historic Whittlesburg headquarters in downtown Knoxville. (Courtesy *Knoxville News-Sentinel*)

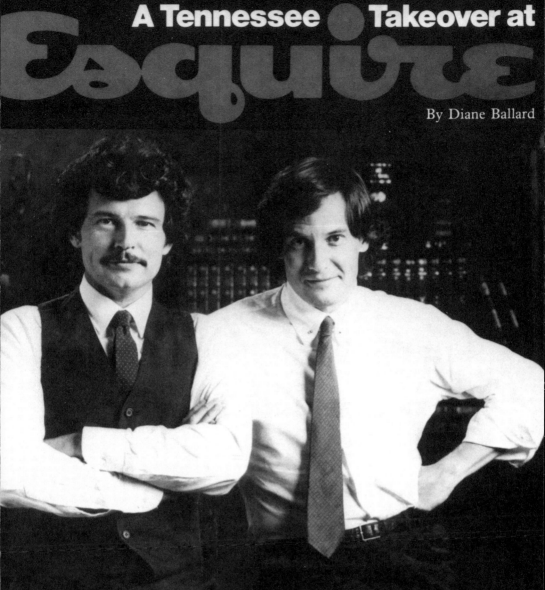

A Tennessee Takeover at Esquire

By Diane Ballard

T graduates Phillip Moffitt and Christopher Whittle, itor and publisher respectively Esquire magazine

A write-up in the University of Tennessee alumni magazine paid tribute to Whittle and Moffitt's takeover of *Esquire* magazine. (Courtesy University of Tennessee)

RIGHT: Younger sister Camille's photo on the society page, February 14, 1971, announcing her engagement to Bob Hanggi. (Courtesy *Knoxville News-Sentinel*)

BELOW: Construction underway on the Whittle headquarters building in the heart of the Knoxville business district. (Courtesy *Knoxville News-Sentinel*)

in action. "He can go with the flow if the agenda changes midstream. Chris can adapt to that instantly and redo the deal linearly. Suppose Chris expects reaction with X and it winds up being Y, it doesn't rattle him. He can reconstitute the deal while he's standing there."

When the Knoxville company began attempting deals involving millions of dollars that ability was often called into play because, as Collins recalls, not one of the negotiations went flawlessly on the original agenda. "The Chris Whittle way of opening a presentation is to basically say, 'Vance, I'm going to show you some things. I've got three things to talk about today.' And somehow or other it would always work out to be three. It would never be seven because that's too complicated. 'That's too many things to talk about,' he would tell us. And he's absolutely right in that regard. And he'd say, 'Now, if you please, Vance, let me go through these with you, and then we'll come back. If you've got any questions we can talk about them.' "

Some sixth sense alerted Chris to the critical importance of having the proper setting that would provide his sales team the very best advantage in any meeting. Collins says, "He was the king of reorganizing rooms and redecorating rooms. He would go into a board room and literally move the furniture around if it wasn't suitable for his presentation. So many times we have moved conference room tables, credenzas, chairs, everything. Forcing a certain person, even on that person's turf, to be in Chris's world."

The focus of the Whittle presentation always was the decision-maker. "Even though there might be seven people in the room, there is only one who counts. Two, at the most. And they would be organized in such a way—'Bill, I want you to sit right there.' And Bill would sit his ass down right where Chris told him to sit it. In a way it became Chris's turf. Bill's not going to say, You can't do that! So you've got him right where you want him."

It became a standard rule of Whittle procedure to redo the furniture in any company's offices, and to make certain the 13–30 people scheduled their arrival with the client's secretary half an hour prior to the meeting so they could create their desired set up.

"Another thing," explains Collins, "if our meeting was supposed to be at two o'clock and the guy shows up at two-thirty looking at his watch and saying, 'Look, I've only got half an hour. I have another meeting at three.' Why, we'd just pack our bags and leave. Our meetings were rarely less than an hour, and Chris would just say, 'I know you're pressed for time. This would not be appropriate. It's important enough that we reschedule and do it some other time.' I've seen Chris do that a dozen times. And he may have come all the way to New York for that meeting, and cancel because it wasn't going to come off right. Why? He was losing control."

Part of Chris Whittle's technique appears to be instinctual, but was it also developed by trial and error?

Collins laughed. "Certainly there's a level of trial and error in it because some of their efforts were so crude in the beginning. Someone may have shared with you the first Dead Sea Scroll he did as a direct mail piece. It was ridiculous. It was a hand-rolled piece of parchment trying to sell single pages of space in *Nutshell*. It was amateur night. It was just terrible. They will go back and laugh about how funny it was, but they didn't know what the hell they were doing. So they learned through their own trial and error process, but as you so aptly said, I think so much of it—with Chris at least—was terribly instinctive."

In our interviews, Chris singled out one presentation he made over a twenty-year span as "a very funny story." As he tells it:

> I had given our pitch to the president of a spirits and beverage company. I'm not going to tell you any of the names. The president told me, "We need to show this to our chairman." I said, "Fine." He arranged a meeting for the three of us in their company board room.
>
> The president and chairman were seated on one side of the long conference table with me opposite. I had about seventy or eighty charts that I was going to go through, a substantial deal. It was about ten-thirty in the morning. I got through about the first three charts and the chairman's chin hit his chest, and he literally began snoring.
>
> And I don't mean he was nodding. He was gone! And I'm sitting there. It's me, the president of the company who has seen the presentation, and the chairman who is sound asleep. I've got about seventy-five charts to go. And I didn't know what to do.
>
> So I didn't do anything except keep presenting! For forty

minutes I presented to a sleeping man. Just rolling through those charts. And I couldn't look at the president; it was too embarrassing. So I kept presenting. There were lots of visual aids. I was uncovering a lot of different things.

Forty or forty-five minutes later the chairman wakes up, and I am right at the end. He looks at the president and says, "It looks great. How much is this?"

And the president says, "It's about five million dollars."

"That's peanuts. Let's do it!" And the chairman gets up, shakes my hand, and leaves.

I look at the president and say, "What does that mean?"

He says, "You got a deal."

═══════

The transition from struggling start-up venture to a modest, small publishing company came while Chris, Moffitt, and their partners were still in their late twenties.

Five years after the first *Nutshell* made its debut on the University of Tennessee campus, the 13–30 Corporation ended 1974 with a profit of $30,000. "And that thirty thousand was so important," Moffitt notes, "because it certified that we knew what we were doing. It reassured me that I wasn't just fooling myself." And 13–30 was no longer living on hope and dreams and sunshine; the following year they earned $300,000. The entrepreneurs were getting wise.

"There were two big decisions in terms of the formation of a profitable company that made a difference," Moffitt says. "One was to realize the gargantuan task we had in selling local ads and to give up. We were handing one hundred editions of *Nutshell* all around the country in which we hired local students to write local articles and then we hired students to sell ads—and for only one time, so we never developed a skill base. And in many instances we had to design the ads."

Even so, those clearly had local value and represented a large part of 13–30 Corporation's revenue base. "There was a lot of debate about that, and we were afraid," Moffitt says. "But we were losing a lot of money, and had to make the move. And, of course, the second critical decision was to develop the print specials."

Once local ads were abandoned, all the *Nutshell* editions carried the same national advertising, thought they retained local editorial for each individual campus. The print specials were paying off handsomely; the Knoxville publishers figured a 15 to 20 percent profit margin into every deal. And they kept making deals—springing up with ideas for new magazines to be distributed through their solidly entrenched pipeline.

Throughout the uphill climb, Brient Mayfield's computer operation had grown. On many occasions profits from the Computer Concepts division were the difference between meeting the *Nutshell* payroll or shutting down the whole pillow factory. In 1975 Mayfield hit a big score: a $300,000 contract to design computers to totally automate a dairy in San Leandro, California.

Recalling how they all worked eighty- and one-hundred-hour weeks up until mid-1974, Mayfield says it would not have been possible except for their youth, energy, and dedication. "We had a culture here that was fun. We were young and everyone who worked for us was young. In the beginning there wasn't anyone over twenty-five. Seems like all of a sudden we went from ten employees to twenty to forty to sixty—maybe one hundred. And we still looked like college kids. And it was really bewildering when anyone would come to visit us. Let me tell one particular story."

After we started the print specials, one of the problems we had was getting people to take us seriously. We did not look like slick young entrepreneurs. We looked more like aging hippies.

Chris had been working with the U.S. Army and their ad agency to get them to buy into a book that would be for high school students on how to make decisions on their careers. The army wanted to get individuals interested in the army, because the draft had been abolished and instead of the army just going out and getting whomever they wanted, they had a marketing problem. They had to interest people in signing up for the Army.

And right after Vietnam this was a difficult marketing problem. So Chris had talked to them, the agency, and the people in Washington. And they were very excited about this book that we would do for them for high school students where we would present one of the options as being enlisting in the army and letting the army send you to college if you stayed in a certain number of years.

Finally, the army folks decided they wanted to come to Knoxville, Tennessee and figure out if we were real or not. This was fairly alarming because we were in this abandoned pillow factory. On one side of us, a liquor warehouse, behind us a railroad track, and literally if you are on the phone when a train went by you had to get off the phone.

On the other side of us a junkyard and later we determined—it has been published—it was just loaded with toxic waste. It had nuclear waste material. We always used to speculate what might be in that junk yard. Turned out it was worse than we thought.

And we were in the poorest part of Knoxville. We used to joke that Vestal was the official training grounds for hoodlums. It was a pretty bad place. I remember that these high school dropouts used to come by and steal Chris's car every afternoon. At this time he was driving that Volkswagen that didn't have a floor. But those hoods would bring it back in the evening.

Anyway, the army's coming to town and we knew we had a real sales problem; convincing them was going to be difficult. But even back in those days we knew how to make a presentation. So the people from the ad agency, and a couple of colonels and a few lieutenants come down.

Our building is a disaster, but we made our presentation to them and we were very compelling in terms of all the logic. Chris did a fine job, and the editors did great in talking about how they could communicate better with students than could the army because we were in sync with the college and high school worlds and they weren't.

Well, Chris had this neat plan how we could convince them we were for real. It came time for lunch and we set up a little buffet. On our buffet we had basically fruits, nuts, and juices to drink—and yogurt. And one of the colonels didn't even know that yogurt was a member of a food group. They were meat and potato types.

This was a real turning point for them. For they saw how out of touch they were with what was going on in high schools and colleges. This was more the diet of the day than their familiar meat and potatoes.

Our lunch relaxed everything. It changed the subject. We went from talking about marketing and financing and details to talking about people and their life-styles and how they were thinking. It's one thing to put up a chart; it's another to kind of see and experience. First of all there's kind of the reaction: What's this? Do you eat it? But, second, it enabled a transition: Hey, this is what your audience is interested in! Of course, not everybody was a hippie back then, but certainly a significant number of the people were living that way.

Anyhow, we were always coming up with ways to work around our handicaps.

From the yogurt luncheon came a contract with the U.S. Army to use two 13–30 publications: *Sourcebook,* designed as a senior year planner, was distributed free to high school seniors every fall through guidance counselors, and *On Your Own,* distributed in the winter, contained feature articles dealing with the high school student's future after graduation. They premiered in 1975.

As the staff expanded to accommodate the growing volume of work, there was no longer enough elbow room in the pillow factory. "There was some sort of a wholesale distributor next door," says Moffitt, "but they wouldn't let us have any of their space. So what were we going to do? No landlord would have thought in advance to prohibit you from knocking holes in the side of the building. So we found two cheap house trailers, knocked out cinder blocks, and hung the trailers on the side of the building. Chris moved his office into one front bedroom."

To give the editors and artists more breathing room at the pillow factory, Mayfield looked around for new quarters for his twenty-person computer staff and moved them into a building on Martin Mill Pike. But with the magazine work load constantly growing the pillow factory was still too cramped for efficiency.

The 13–30 Corporation scouted downtown Knoxville for suitable office space and quietly leased two and a half floors of the Arnstein Building at the corner of Market Street and Union Avenue. The move was made with no fanfare; the average local citizen knew nothing of the Knoxville outfit struggling to become a major success in the publishing world.

"I was opposed to any kind of publicity," says Moffitt. "We didn't need it. Why should we give anybody ideas? We didn't want competition."

In finding a new use for their pipeline, the 13–30 brain trust, scanning the scene for new and profitable ventures, struck gold again. Their first scheme that did not involve publishing was a national college student sampling program that distributed free samples of personal care items to dormitory residents. Dubbed "Good Stuff" the program was launched in 1977 and sponsored by fourteen manufacturers of toothpaste and the like who provided free kits of their products, and paid 13–30 handsomely to deliver them through residence hall associations.

"By this time," Chris Whittle says, "the company was finally healthy. We were about a five-million-dollar company, gross, in 1977–78. We were making a good solid profit but we were still relatively small."

With the annual profit on that gross calculated at about $1 million, the 13–30 Corporation paid back most of the debts incurred in the miserable red-ink years. Professor Spiva was phased out over a span of about a year. "As soon as they started making money," Spiva says, "they wanted to pay me back. I was agreeable because my sole interest had been just getting them started. I didn't need to make any money out of it. So as quickly as they could they started buying my stock back, and we amicably sort of parted company and they went on their way. I was tickled to death."

Several backers, including Dr. and Mrs. Whittle, elected to remain investors, taking stock in the company in lieu of repayment. Chris's entire family owned shares in his holding company, WC Inc. Investors who remained for the long haul profited handsomely. Mayfield and others calculate that $10,000 invested in 13–30 in 1970 escalated in value to about $1 million by 1986.

———

Not surprisingly, the commingling of frisky young women and men for long hours in the confines of the pillow factory spawned a goodly number of office romances. Not even Chris Whittle and Phillip Moffitt were immune.

Crediting the "do your own thing" ethic of the sixties, Clay Shwab, one longtime executive, says the atmosphere was laissez faire and counterrevolutionary. "We all loved one another anyway, so it was like, do whatever you're going to do." Laura Eshbaugh believes it was the long hours that drove coworkers into each other's arms. "We didn't have time to socialize with people outside the company, so dating came to feel perfectly natural." And Michele MacDonald, research chief, observes, "When you were married to or dating someone here, you felt your family was around, and it gave you an incentive to work even harder and stay longer."

In the early days David White ruled that employees were not supposed to date coworkers directly in their chain of command, but nothing happened when love-struck couples defied the ban. The rule would have been difficult to enforce anyhow, when everyone knew that Moffitt and Chris were as guilty as they looked.

Both of them—rule or no rule—over many years openly dated various young women who worked for 13–30 while also squiring around several not associated with the company. Chris and Moffitt remained bachelors until past forty, and despite constant overtime, both still managed fairly active social lives.

Tony Spiva felt sorry for the 13–30 colleagues. "They really didn't have time for romance," he says. "One girl who dated Chris [Lisa Bruner, who sold Jaguar and Porsche autos] told me Chris would be sitting in a chair talking to her and abruptly fall asleep from exhaustion." Chris told me he wanted to get married in his twenties but never met the right girl at the right time.

The first 13–30 girl to whom Chris's name was linked was Ellen Barrentine, a freelance illustrator who became close to the Whittle family, and is described by Dr. Whittle as "a wonderful, wacky girl, a free spirit who woke up every day in a whole new world."

Daughter of an air force pilot who fought in Vietnam, she came to Knoxville to attend the university because Tennessee was her family's home state. She was in Chris's sister Camille's sorority. In college Ellen was briefly married to another student and gave birth to a daughter named Blue. She was hired at the pillow factory as a designer and dated Brient Mayfield for about a year. Then she took up with Chris and was identified in a company publication as his "current girlfriend."

The extent of their romantic involvement is not easily ascertained. "I didn't date Chris," Ellen Barrentine said in a 1992 interview. "I knew him. He was just always a good friend of mine. I've known Chris a really long time and I know almost everything there is to know about him."

When she inherited some money, Ellen Barrentine opened a small restaurant near the university, helped by Chris and Moffitt, who eached loaned her $3,000, but the restaurant failed when she was unable to obtain a liquor license. Later she married 13–30 executive Clay Shwab, bore two sons, and resumed her painting career.

"Chris lives in the future," she says. "He probably doesn't give a lot of thought to today, because it's of no interest any more. He's probably living in the year two thousand right now. He is single-minded in his drive. You just have to understand that he's not a nostalgic-type person."

What has been her observation of how he approaches a problem or develops an idea?

"He writes everything down, and keeps copious notes. I guess that is part of it. I think it is a combination of his ideas being implemented, and also he takes other peoples' ideas and implements them. He is like people say, the greatest salesman of all time. If he intends to do something, and you are against it, he can usually talk you into it somehow."

Another girl staffer in whom Chris took an interest was Shelley Williams, who joined the 13–30 layout department in 1972, right after graduation from U.T. at age twenty-three.

"One thing I remember he was always a man of his word," she says. "My job was to arrange the magazine space for editorial matter and advertising. Chris might give me a number for the ads he was going to produce that seemed impossibly large. But he always did it.

"Several years I lived on Log Haven, half a block from his cabin, and we did a lot of things together—just good friends. At the pillow factory we all felt wonderful. We hung around together in large or small groups. That was our life.

"I can remember being at my house, like a Saturday afternoon about six o'clock when any person with a normal life would already have plans—date night. Chris would just pull up in my driveway and say, 'Let's go to a movie.' And we would do that."

Had Shelley Williams been impressed by Chris's brilliance or thought processes?

"He has an amazing ability to put his finger right on something. I can't ever imagine him saying he couldn't do something. He always finds a way—he just thinks so optimistic. I don't believe he knows the word *can't.*"

Did she ever see him down or defeated, on in failure of any kind?

"Not that I can remember. I can't imagine that would last very long. I don't think he dwells on that. If something comes up in his face, he just turns in another direction, or goes around it. We used to play video games together, and he's very good. He's so quick! His reactions are really quick, and I have to think it applies. . . . It doesn't matter if he's got a bunch of space ships shooting at him. He's going on, they're not going to hit him. He just knows they're not. He'll find some way to get through!"

True love brought Ed Smith, "inventor" of the campus pipeline and Pam Beaver, an early editor, together at the pillow factory in the mid-seventies. But their romance was so discreet that few people in the very small company—only about fifty at the time—knew they were dating before they announced their wedding plans.

That item was a highlight in a feature "Dates and Mates," written by senior editor Hope Dlugozima for the twentieth anniversary edition of the company house organ picaresquely known as *Fred,* a highly candid and aggressive magazine. It concluded:

Stories of [13–30] marriages may inspire our romantic senses, but company wags also tell stories of sizzling affairs and torrid quickies that got our hormones cooking. Oft-told tales (which may or may not be true) include the couple who, *ahem,* intertwined in their natural state on the Arnstein Building roof and were spotted by several people meeting in the top-floor boardroom of the building next door. The shocked observers promptly called to complain.

The same rooftop deck saw action two years later when four employees decided to get in a little nude sunbathing only to have their boss discover them. And an art director who engaged in a little late-night hanky-panky in her carrel alerted other late-working employees when they heard a "rhythmic, pounding noise coming from the floor above," says one witness. The mortified art director took corrective action—she bought a plush rug for her carrel floor.

Former editor [Peter] Moore recalls an even more scandalous incident: "I remember the time when some couple supposedly had sex on the couch in Phillip's office and made a real mess. There were rumblings around the building next day that they were going to find out who did it. As far as I know, they never did." [*Fred* knows, but will never tell.]

When that concluding item was mentioned to Phillip Moffitt in an interview, he laughed. "That's one I never heard. Looks like my old couch got put to good use."

10

THE STOCKHOLM CONNECTION

Arriving from Knoxville on a 13–30 selling mission, Bob Hanggi, Chris Whittle's brother-in-law, deplaned one midnight in 1977 at Chicago's O'Hare International Airport. Tired and weary after a trying day, he remembers being in a "blind stupor." He walked along the concourse toward baggage claim in "really a daze—just staring at things, not really seeing them."

Suddenly he woke up.

"I got excited. They had big lighted display signs. At O'Hare they're bigger than most airports. It gave me a great idea. I couldn't wait to get home and try it out on Chris and Phil."

Next day back at his office in the Arnstein Building, Hanggi drafted a memo outlining what he thought was "absolutely a brilliant flash." Even though he was married to Chris's sister Camille, Bob Hanggi had no privileged status in 13–30 Corporation. When Moffitt had offered him a job in marketing and sales, Hanggi had taken it, abandoning his intention of studying veterinary medicine.

"Chris and I reached a very firm understanding," says Hanggi, "that the fact we were related was never to play a part in our business life. And, if anything, he was tougher on me." Initially Hanggi was regional marketing director, later moving into other executive positions. By investing over the years, he became one of several limited partners.

Hanggi wrote his memo and gave it to Phillip Moffitt. After scanning it Moffitt scowled, crumpled the paper, and tossed it in his wastebasket.

"What Bob had suggested," says Moffitt, "was that we put a sheet of advertising on the walls of student unions around the country. My first reaction was, Sure that would be like printing money, but the student unions would never let us do that. And I pitched his memo!

"But then I said, Oh, no! Wait a minute! and dug it out of the trash and straightened it out. I said, If we can put editorial matter with those ads, that becomes a buyable publication. That's how wall media was invented. Bob had identified an opportunity but hadn't seen the way to shape it. Had it not been for Bob suggesting one thing, I would never had thought of it on my own."

It did not happen overnight, but what emerged from about a year of research was a two-by-three foot poster called the *Wallpaper Journal*, containing student-oriented news, useful information, entertaining features—and advertising. By using the same college organizations that sponsored *Nutshell*, 13–30 managed to get the poster authorized at three hundred fifty campuses nationwide, about ten locations at each school.

Even then the 13–30 approach to corporate advertisers was still rather haphazard, almost shoot-from-the-hip. The first pitch for the *Wallpaper Journal* was made to Honda Motor Company in Los Angeles by *Nutshell* salesman Bill Longley, one of four others teamed up with Chris on national accounts.

"Imagine this!" recalls Longley. "The night before going to Honda all I had was a mock-up of the poster. It was supposed to be displayed in a glass case, but that hadn't been made yet. I needed something to show Honda."

Longley walked into an art shop near UCLA and saw an impressive travel lithograph of the S.S. *Normandie* under glass in a chrome frame. He bought it for $60, removed the steamship print, and replaced it with his poster.

Alan Greenberg, a 1972 University of Tennessee graduate who spent five years in marketing at Procter and Gamble and Johnson and Johnson before joining 13–30, flew in to join Longley in the sales pitch to Honda.

"We've been trying to think for a long time of how to get billboards on college campuses," Greenberg told the Honda advertising director. "Of course you can't just go on a college campus and erect a billboard, so we've come up with this hybrid form of media that has the readability and newsworthiness of a newspaper, and the constantly exposed advertising of a billboard. The colleges will permit us to put these up to give their students quality information. This has never been done before." Greenberg pointed to the bottom of the poster. "Your ad here will be bigger than a spread in *Life* magazine!"

Honda was asked to become one of ten corporate sponsors which would have an exclusive ad on one poster of the ten displayed on campus. New posters were to be put up every two weeks, and rotated to different display cases, meaning that over a five-month cycle the Honda ad—and the other nine—would have appeared in each separate campus location. At a cost of about $180,000, Honda signed up.

"We had a nice display case built," says Longley. "But they made a mistake by putting the lock in the middle. College kids would pry it open at an edge, crack the glass, and put something in there, like 'Car for Sale.' "

Even so, as a strictly campus vehicle, the *Wallpaper Journal* was destined to become an astounding success and a big money-maker. But more importantly, the principle of placing this kind of news-and-advertising poster on a wall where people congregate was eventually to be expanded to other fields and professions. One classic example is in physicians' lounges in hospitals. Wall media thus became a 13–30 revenue mainstay.

Not to be overlooked as a key element in the *Nutshell* success was that national salesmen were carefully picked from the ranks of recent collegians—because they would be attuned to the magazine's audience and were men of aggressive ambition. Longley, having attended Hillsdale College in Michigan and the University of Arizona, fit the mold; he had also bought and sold antique cars to pay his tuition, and later sold Steelcase office equipment.

At his job interview with Chris and Moffitt, Longley was offered the job selling all *Nutshell* advertising west of the Mississippi. He questioned whether 13–30 would deliver on promises he made to clients.

"Tell me, if I sold one thousand ads, would you print them?"

Chris started, and then grinned. The biggest number of advertisers ever signed up in the western territory had been eleven. "You can stake your life on it, Bill! We'd print 'em all!"

Longley felt pressure from Moffitt and Chris. "They were probably wondering: Since I was going to live in Los Angeles, would I spend all day at the beach surfing on their nickel?"

Moffitt, apparently anticipating that prospect, was blunt. "If you don't make your quota, we are going to treat you like you have a social disease. Then we expect you to quit."

They had nothing to worry about. In his first year he sold nineteen clients, earning $51,000 in salary and commission, and winning the bonus of a trip to Europe. He gave those tickets to his parents.

"The money was great," says Longley, "but at 13–30 there was tremendous competition. You really weren't working for the money. You wanted to win, not be in second or third place. I wanted to fly back into Knoxville and say, 'Hey, I sold more pages than any other guy!' "

Later he could brag when Twentieth Century-Fox brought out *The Rose,* a 1979 movie based on the life of Janis Joplin in which Bette Midler played a down-and-out rock singer whose comeback becomes embroiled in booze, drugs, and aborted romance. Bill Longley sold the studio on inserting a fold-up poster into *Nutshell.* "It was the biggest deal in the history of the magazine," Longley recalls. "Kids got that *Rose* poster at the start of school when their dorm walls were bare, and it went up just everywhere!"

═══

When gross annual sales climbed to around $5 million or $6 million in late 1977, 13–30 Corporation reached a crossroad. The partners who had started out so enthusiastically a decade earlier were changed people. The strain and strife, the bone-numbing long hours had taken a toll. No longer did they see the business world with the naïveté of untried college graduates. They had grown up and, in the process, altered their goals for the future. The first split came when Brient Mayfield decided the computer end of the business was not really compatible with the publishing end, and not harmonious either. Mayfield and Mark Medley, the 13–30 treasurer, engineered stock swaps with the other partners that permitted them to go off on their own, each with a computer company in Knoxville.

David White was also eager to leave. He had borne the burden of juggling the razor-thin financial structure too long. He still had nightmares recalling such incidents as the I.R.S. calling and threatening to shut the company down in two days if it couldn't come up with a sizeable withholding tax deposit, past due because it was news to 13–30 Corporation that the I.R.S. had changed the schedule. (White got the money. "I found the best way to get more money out of banks is to already owe them a loan you can't pay.")

On weekends the remaining 13–30 founders scooted into their regular booth in the Copper Cellar in the university area, spread their papers on the big table, and struggled to chart their future course.

"Essentially," says White, "we all were doing two jobs. Running the business by day. And trying to be creative by night. But we were young, and we didn't need a lot of sleep."

They searched for wrinkles or schemes they could turn into magazines—"properties" they called them—and they came up with several.

Moffitt, White, and Chris spent hours considering options. They could sell out and take the money and run. Or locate another publisher willing to invest and help their little company expand, and then, from such a new capital-sufficient mode, purchase an established national magazine and get into traditional paid publishing instead of throwaways.

To Chris and Moffitt the magazine industry's center in New York was an alien environment; they knew they would need an experienced guide to make successful deals. Already they had an acquisition target in mind—a magazine both had grown up with that was now rumored to be in financial straits—*Esquire.*

They felt certain their hard-won skills would enable them to take over a magazine that was struggling with sagging advertising revenue and circulation and turn it smartly around. They were brashly confident they would succeed. But of course, they would first have to acquire capital for expansion. A stock offering seemed inadvisable because the 13–30 Corporation lacked the recognition needed to make that move successful. Therefore their best bet would be to interest another publishing company in buying part of their firm, and utilize the new partner's capital, expertise, and facilities. They would go forward without White, who wanted to sell off his share of the company and retire to a simpler life where he could study philosophy and do some writing.

Though still little known nationally, at that point 13–30 had paid back most of the debts incurred in the first starvation years. "We were finally healthy," says Chris. "We were making a good solid profit but we were still relatively small. We were about a five-million-dollar company (gross) in 1977–78. A way for our shareholders to take some of their money off the table was through the sale of their shares. They had invested, hoping that would occur. That included all of us. The only way you can reap rewards in an entrepreneurial situation is through the sale of your stock."

In their Copper Cellar brainstorming sessions, Chris and his partners explored not only publishers who might be interested in teaming up with 13–30 but also whether to venture outside their traditional college campus marketing niche.

Their sales pitch to national advertisers had always been built around the idea that 13–30 offered an edge in "transition marketing." In other words, the 13–30 publications reached young people when they were going through life transitions, such as graduating from high school or finishing college, times in their lives when they needed information about coping with change, and were beginning to form brand loyalties.

Their first off-campus "transition" publication was *New Marriage,* an annual magazine for newlyweds that would be sponsored primarily by banks and distributed through marriage-license bureaus across the country. It was a sprightly publication dealing with such topics as preparing family budgets and adjusting to married life. It looked promising—but was destined to fail.

"Some marriage clerks wouldn't distribute *New Marriage,*" says Jim Omastiak, a salesman. "Where that happened, we copied the names from the license books and mailed out the magazine. But the main reason it didn't work was we caught the newlyweds too late. By the time they were getting a license they usually had much earlier decided on a bank, for instance."

However, they had a winner in a print special, *Insider,* a college newspaper supplement developed for the Ford Motor Company and distributed three times a year to 2.5 million students. But Ford would discontinue *Insider* after three years because of deteriorating economic conditions in the automotive industry and a desire to try an alternative advertising media.

Over time at least two partners—Chris and David White—were able to work in other pursuits to relieve the nose-to-the-grindstone boredom. White again dabbled in Tennessee politics, organizing a citizens' committee for the gubernatorial campaign of Lamar Alexander in 1974. "It only took about one day a week," White says. "I could manage that." The candidate was defeated, but in 1978 White again would be involved in another Alexander campaign for governor of Tennessee, this one a success.

For Chris it meant refreshing himself in two divergent ways—through trips to the solitude of snowy mountains and by again courting the musical muse that had inspired him in high school.

"Every summer for about ten years," Chris says, "I would go to the Swiss Alps for two to three weeks. I would go alone, and just kind of walk around in the Alps. And I would just kind of refuel, rethink. And that was in my twenties and thirties. And I really miss it. I don't know what happened, but I stopped doing it."

Early in his career as West Coast salesman, Bill Longley got first-hand exposure to both Chris's musical ingenuity and of his adventurous love of mountains. These facets of the Whittle personality surprised him.

"I was back in Knoxville for a sales meeting. Chris took us down to his cabin at Log Haven for a beer. He put on his stereo a tape that played some of the most beautiful music—not haunting—just beautiful, very instrumental with piano, flute, guitar. Sort of unconventional. I said, 'This is absolutely fascinating!' And Chris said, 'I wrote this, and then I recorded it.'

"He had a little recorder and he would do the piano, and then the flute, and the guitar, and it all came together on the tape. This is a really gifted guy. This certainly was not amateur music. I never even knew Chris was into music, and here is this beautiful composition coming through his stereo. Just like, Oh, yeah. I did that."

David White recalls when Chris bought a four-track recorder and began taping several compositions, combining at least four instruments—piano, saxophone, guitar, and panflute. He created one tape as a gift for his mother. "It is very beautiful," she says, "quite different. I would call it haunting music. He can play several instruments, and loves to compose. When he went around the world, he took his panflute with him."

An episode in which Chris impressed Longley with his daring

occurred in Aspen, Colorado, where Alan Greenberg organized a ski weekend for the sales crew.

"I've been skiing since I was four," says Longley. "So here's Chris Whittle. I figure I'm going to be able to out-ski him as well as all the other guys. After all, they're from Tennessee. But he puts on skis and away he goes. I just couldn't believe it. And he'd only skied five or six times. He's just an uncanny person.

"So he and I leave the others and go off and do more challenging things. We go up on the lift and I said, 'Hey, we ought to race down this thing.' He said, 'Okay.' Chris is a pretty competitive guy.

"So we got off the chairlift and took off down the mountain just like a couple of maniacs. We got going faster and faster and faster. We were side by side coming around corners, hitting jumps, and flying through the air. There were other skiers and we were flying by them.

"Finally both of us hit this big jump, and we must have flown twenty or thirty feet through the air. As each of us landed we came to a full-scale stop. It was interesting. Neither of us wanted to back off, and we knew we were going to get killed. We looked at each other after that big jump. And I thought, That's it for me. If this guy wants to keep going, he wins. He's the boss anyway.

"At the same moment his instincts told him that's enough. There were trees out there, and that was pretty scary, and frankly I think we waited about twice as long as we should have."

═════

The "magazine doctor" finally selected to lead the 13–30 Corporation into "big-time" publishing was highly respected—and high-priced—James B. Kobak, a cheerful silver-haired New York business consultant known for making million dollar deals. He was also a sartorial renegade. Chris and Moffitt gulped when he arrived at the Knoxville airport in summer 1977 wearing Bermuda shorts, a pink sweatshirt, white socks, penny loafers, and an English bowler.

"My purpose in going to Knoxville," Kobak recalls, "was to tell them whether they were doing a good job publishing, and second, to find out what their company might be worth at that time, and what methods there might be to pay off the old investors. I studied everything they did—which was quite clever, of course. I wrote a business plan which meant a description of the company and projections for the future. I then got in touch with a bunch of what I thought were potential buyers."

Kobak's hourly rate was $300. His new clients felt that would be money well spent if he could work the same magic for them as he had for other magazines, including Hugh Hefner's *Playboy* and several hundred others.

Summoned to Hefner's legendary Chicago mansion, Kobak found the *Playboy* publisher wrapped in a dressing gown, his usual work attire. "Why," snorted Hefner, "you're wearing *shorts!*" Kobak laughed. "And *you're* wearing a bathrobe!" They got along fine.

The Tennesseeans were impressed, too, that Kobak found their operation a success and their prospects bright. He suggested they propose deals with the New York Times Company, Ziff Davis Publishing Company, Capital Cities–ABC, or Whitney Communications.

"We went first to the Times and talked to Sydney Gruson," says Kobak. "We developed a plan where 13–30 would become the magazine acquisition agent for the New York Times Company. We did projections for the next five years and what would happen if we made X amount of money, and then they would get so much for their company. Chris and Phil were betting on the come, as to what percentage they would own, what their salaries would be and things of that kind. This was all very complicated."

Before he invented a computer business plan that pinpoints and forecasts each financial step in magazine publishing, Kobak did these calculations by hand. "But that's hard on the eyes and fingers."

His model, later sold to 3-M for $11 million, is quite simple in concept, but enormously sophisticated in detail. For a monthly magazine, the model provides start-up costs for promotion, production, printing, personnel, and even petty cash for each month over a five-year period. The cash flow along the way is detailed, plus cumulative profit and loss, and return on investment. Rises or declines in advertising pages to be sold (and revenue generated) are detailed; peaks and valleys of capital infusion are pinpointed; and even break-even dates are determined.

"We spent a lot of time at the *New York Times,*" says Kobak, "made a lot of calculations. And we really never got very far with them."

Kobak next led his Tennessee clients to Harlequin, in Canada, the romance novel publishers owned by the Toronto Star. "We met with Larry Heisey and Bill Willson, and some of the other executives. We made I don't know how many calculations, probably fifty. We worked out projections for the next five years. In the end I thought it was a lousy deal."

Kobak didn't think Harlequin was offering enough money. "I'd been through a million of these things, and I just didn't think this was good enough. But Phil and Chris were anxious to do it. They never had had any money in their pockets. What happened? I talked long and impressively. Fortunately I'm bigger than they are, and I almost had to beat on them with my fists. I finally got them to turn it down."

And the let's-make-a-deal odyssey continued. Kobak huddled with Chris and Moffitt at his home in Darien, Connecticut, at his office suite in the Drake Hotel in Manhattan, and finally they met in the fall of 1977 at his vacation home on St. Croix in the Virgin Islands.

When they flew down from Knoxville they found the magazine guru in his traditional shorts, high-spirited and optimistic.

"I think," he said with a roguish wink that indicated good news, "I have found your man—Lukas Bonnier. He's quite anxious to get a beachhead in the United States. I think you can cut a deal. Let's fly to Stockholm and find out."

Kobak had done some consulting for the fifty-five-year-old Bonnier, whose family not only dominated magazine, book, and newspaper publishing in Denmark, Norway, Finland, and Sweden, but also had operations as diverse as filmmaking and ferryboats.

"The Bonnier family is the Rockefeller family of Sweden," says Chris. "They are the Time Warner of Scandinavia. Lukas is quite a guy. Very charming, handsome. He doesn't like to fly, so we used to joke that if a business crisis developed, we'd call and he'd say, 'I'll be on the next boat!' " (Moffitt amended that: "He would fly in an emergency, but he'd have to get boozed up first.")

In 1976 the Bonnier Group reported overall annual sales of $600 million. Lukas Bonnier was managing director of Ahlen & Akerlund, the group's magazine flagship, which had earnings of $8.6 millon on revenues of $110 million.

In looking for an opportunity to expand into the American market, Lukas Bonnier had told Kobak, "I am more interested in finding the right people than the right property. I am looking for people who might appreciate that we have learned a little. And I'm just not one to sit on my tail. I don't want to be a sleeping partner."

Chris and Moffitt were elated to discover that the Swedish publisher wanted no more than a fifty-fifty deal—an equal partnership. "I'm convinced that you boys will take advantage of our many mistakes, and go much further than you would otherwise."

Sealing an alliance with such a powerful publishing empire would put Chris and Moffitt in a position to launch their own general consumer magazine for twenty-one- to thirty-five-year-olds—with the intention of moving ahead with their own youth market at a start-up cost of $3 million to $5 million.

Chris told Kobak, "We'd get equity for our stockholders, meaning our staff, family and friends, as well as strong financial backing, expertise in launching magazines, and international connections."

One question remained—how much was one-half interest in The 13–30 Corporation of Knoxville, Tennessee, worth to Scandinavia's biggest publisher?

While the answer was being determined over dinner discussions, the Americans were introduced unexpectedly to one of the business and social mores of Sweden. "The three of us went over there," says Kobak, "and we got along wonderfully with Lukas and his people. In Sweden, the custom is that after dinner you go out with girls. I didn't know this. But I'm a older person and I didn't have to do this. And I saw the stricken look on their faces when Lukas said, 'Now I've got these two girls for you.' I don't know what happened. I went back to the hotel and went to bed. It was funny at the time. I don't know whether they went out or not. I never asked." (Chris says he does not recall such an episode.)

After some discussion, they agreed on the price Bonnier would pay for a half-interest in 13–30 Corporation—$3.2 million!

Signed and sealed before Christmas 1977, the deal contained one unusual and friendly provision. Chris and Moffitt insisted that their new Bonnier partnership be kept secret until they could return to Knoxville and surprise their staffers with the special provision.

Setting the stage for the revelation, all 13–30 employees were invited to Knoxville's Lord Lindsey restaurant on the night of January 4, 1978, for a "company dinner." As master of ceremonies, Chris gave a general report on 13–30 Corporation's achievements. He did not mention Bonnier at all, but as he rambled on his audience began to get the impression he was working up to a big announcement.

"I know we ask a lot of you," he said at last, and paused. "But we have another big project in the works. . . ." Another pause. "And we need each of you . . . next May . . . to drive out to the airport . . . " Again he stopped, and surveyed the room with a mischievous look. "And get on a plane to Sweden!"

That was how he led into the announcement not only of the partnership, but also that all fifty-four men and women of 13–30— "from the mail room to the top"—had been invited to fly to Stockholm en masse to spend three days visiting the Bonnier publishing plant and headquarters.

Michele MacDonald, the Knoxville research chief since 1974, recalls the thrill and joy of that night at the Lord Lindsey. "It was really a unique thing for us. Our company has always been so modest, and all of a sudden we were having this great extravagance."

Knoxville got the news next morning in a *Journal* story under the headline: 13–30 MERGES WITH EUROPEAN PUBLISHER; WILL KEEP MAGAZINES FOR YOUNG READERS, EXPAND. David White would retire in June, the article said, and Chris Whittle would become chairman and publisher with Phillip Moffitt continuing as president and immediately becoming chief executive officer.

The *Journal* said:

> Concerning 13–30's future, Mr. Moffitt said, "We are only one of three young publishing operations that have found success in the 70's. In the next few years we will continue our current operations, but you can also expect a whole series of new magazines from us. And that will mean more jobs and more dollars flowing into Knoxville, for we plan to keep our headquarters here."
>
> Mr. Whittle, 30, pointed out that a partnership with an internationally known company provided 13–30 with the capital it needs for growth as well as publishing opportunities in the U.S., England and Canada that it would be difficult to achieve independently.

"The Bonnier management is counting on Phil and me to take 13–30 from a successful medium-sized publishing company to a successful large publishing company. We are gearing toward becoming a $50 million operation in the early 80's," he said.

Asked about Bonnier's view of the partnership, Mr. Moffitt quoted the absent Lucas [sic] Bonnier as saying: "One thing is for sure: It will be an adventure."

The $3.2 million payment from the Bonnier Group made instant "almost millionaires" of White, Moffitt, and Chris, the three holding most of 13–30's stock. Others received lesser amounts, determined by the level of their individual partnerships.

Virtually the first use Chris made of his newfound wealth was to write a check at the Saint Paul United Methodist Church in Maryville, Tennessee, for $10,000 as a youth ministry endowment in honor of his parents.

Ironically, the weeks spent on the Stockholm deal prevented Chris and Moffitt from pursuing their dream of buying *Esquire,* the literary icon which had fallen on hard times and had just been taken over by British publisher Lord Rothermere.

"We were just a week away from closing our deal with Bonnier," Chris said later, "when the Brits sold *Esquire* to Clay Felker."

Word on Madison Avenue was that *Rolling Stone* magazine could be bought for $20 million. With Kobak, the 13–30 partners called on publisher Jann Wenner, who coldly rebuffed them. They kept looking.

=====

The May excursion to Stockholm did not go off without a hitch. The party boarded two chartered planes at Tyson McGee airport for New York, where they would switch to overseas flights. The first charter took off without incident, but the second plane developed engine trouble, stranding half the group. It took so long to bring in a backup plane its passengers reached New York too late to make their Stockholm connection. After some confusion in New York, the delayed passengers caught a flight to Toronto to wait overnight for the early morning plane to Stockholm.

"Most of us had never been overseas before," recalls artist Shelley Williams, "so it was all very exciting. In Stockholm, it was great to hang out with professionals in another country who were doing what we were doing back in Knoxville. We were so impressed. Their production process seemed very advanced to us."

After their fun-filled junket, it was back to Tennessee and a new challenge. The 13–30 Corporation, girded by Swedish capital and modern publishing expertise, was again bursting with fresh ideas for more new magazine projects.

11

TWO YAHOOS HIT
THE BIG APPLE

With cat burglar secrecy, Chris and Moffitt tried to tiptoe onto the New York magazine scene. It was late March 1979. They had finally snagged a prize. They were bursting with pride and wanted to announce their triumph with a splashy press conference—and a full-page ad in the *New York Times*.

To do that they needed the help of a New York advertising agency. They retained Altschiller, Reitzfeld and Jackson, the one that handled Polaroid and some General Mills products, on promise no word would leak in advance. "It may take three or four weeks to wrap up our deal," Chris cautioned. "A leak could blow it."

Partner Bob Jackson interviewed Chris and Moffitt, who explained why they were buying a national magazine. Jackson shaped their words into copy for the $25,000 *Times* ad. He swore his agency staff to secrecy, but had to send out his copy to be set in type. The typesetters might talk.

"To keep it hush-hush," says Jackson, "I sent out the copy in unrelated pieces, and on separate days to our typesetter. I didn't include the name of their magazine, just left spaces. The one-hundred-twenty-point headline read: 'Why We Bought . . . blank.' In the body of the ad, spaces were left to later insert the name of the magazine."

The next day, on a supposedly different job, Jackson ordered identical headline type reading, "Establish the requirements." One day later he got a long list of magazine names set in the ad's body type.

With an exacto knife in the privacy of his office, Jackson's artist cut the *Es* off *Establish* and the *quire* out of *requirements*. These were pasted together in the *New York Times* ad, making the headline now read, "Why We Bought Esquire." The word *Esquire* also was stripped from the body type lists and inserted where needed. Now the ad was ready to go, and the secret remained intact, waiting only for the 13–30 partners to wrap up the deal and spring their big surprise.

———

From his high school years Moffitt had read, admired, and kept up with *Esquire*. Chris was not such an avid magazine reader. *Esquire* was already a decade and a half old and a landmark magazine before they were born. It was launched the winter of 1932–33 by Chicago advertising man Arnold Gingrich, a twenty-nine-year-old literary fireball, and two backers. Gingrich met and charmed Ernest Hemingway, and got him to write a piece for the first issue for two hundred dollars. He acquired stories for half that amount from Dashiell Hammett, John Dos Passos, Erskine Caldwell, and Ring Lardner Jr. The debut issue of *Esquire*, intended to be a quarterly, also contained golf champion Bobby Jones's illustrated putting tips as well as forerunners of the classic Petty Girls.

Despite the Depression, the first issue sold 100,000 copies at fifty cents when a nickel would buy the *Saturday Evening Post*. Gingrich, seeing he had a magazine that was a standard for class, quality, and good taste, promptly launched *Esquire* as a national monthly. Within three years it was a profitable literary magazine and a style-setter, with a 550,000 circulation, and he could now pay authors and artists top money.

Under Gingrich's urbane editorship, the magazine regularly attracted big-name writers, and is remembered for Hemingway's "The Snows of Kilimanjaro" and F. Scott Fitzgerald's *The Crack-Up*. Gingrich cultivated luminaries like H. L. Mencken and Theodore Dreiser, who both wrote for him. *Esquire* also published articles and fiction by William Faulkner, Dorothy Parker, John Steinbeck, and scores of other famous writers.

While national weeklies including *Liberty*, *Collier's*, and the *Saturday Evening Post* dwindled and died because of hard times, Gingrich kept his monthly alive by gracefully adapting to America's changing social climate. From its beginning it gave middle-brows a sense of sartorial and literary style, with a dash of what Gingrich called "uptown sex." During World War II quality declined but circulation rose as the magazine catered to G.I.s, with adventure stories and blatant cheesecake. In the late fifties and throughout the sixties, quality returned under Gingrich's chief editor, Harold Hayes. The magazine again blossomed as a major outlet for mainstream writers, and cultivated a new generation of journalists like Thomas B. Morgan, Gay Talese, Tom Wolfe, Norman Mailer, and Garry Wills. By the 1970s circulation peaked at 1,250,000.

In his student days in Tennessee, Moffitt had fallen in love with *Esquire* because "it was big and fat and juicy" with great articles and fiction. "Gingrich's original intention," observes Moffitt, "was to create a magazine whose name stood for quality in thinking, in living, and in writing. It was a simple and brilliant idea." At the university, Moffitt secretly dreamed of one day becoming the magazine's editor.

Hayes resigned in 1973. Gingrich died in 1976, just after going into semi-retirement. Meanwhile *Esquire*'s management discovered it had artificially pushed the magazine's circulation beyond its natural level; it began to lose money at a frightening rate.

To the rescue came Clay S. Felker, at fifty-two perhaps the decade's most innovative magazine editor. Felker acquired *Esquire* in August 1977 with the financial backing of friend Lord Rothermere (Vere Harmsworth), head of London's powerful Associated Newspapers Holdings Ltd. *Esquire* claimed 875,000 circulation, but Felker ruefully discovered it was "mostly garbage. [Meaning subscriptions were sold at heavy discounts.] Ninety percent of it was literally given away." Felker gambled with major changes, chief of which was to go biweekly, a costly error. The *New York Times* said he converted the magazine, "into a much slicker publication, plump with news of business, law, politics, Hollywood personalities and travel. It had more sports coverage and the latest in expensive gadgetry."

To no avail. Readers deserted. Madison Avenue found other places to spend its advertising dollars.

Though Felker hired a big staff and spent lavishly, he couldn't

capture the reader he was after—"the savvy-but-sensitive professional managerial man of the post-macho era." Lord Rothermere
had pledged $5 million to carry the magazine for three years. Felker
spent most of that in a single year, 1978, when the magazine sank
deeper in debt despite revenue of $8.6 million from advertising and
$3.4 million from circulation. To get more capital from his British
backers, Felker surrendered his own stock to Associated. Still, *Esquire* kept hemorrhaging red ink, careening toward an anticipated
1979 loss of $5 million.

In late 1978 word went out on Madison Avenue's bamboo wire-
less (Chris's term for street talk among magazine and advertising
agency insiders) that Lord Rothermere wanted to bail out, to dump
Felker, and to sell *Esquire*.

That news spurred Chris and Moffitt into action. They had long
wanted to own this magazine. They would make any sacrifice to get
it. But they feared the deck was stacked against such small-time
suitors like themselves.

At New York's Pierre Hotel they opened negotiations with two
of Lord Rothermere's top executives from the *London Daily Mail*,
McGregor "Mick" Shields and Charles J. F. Sinclair. Guardedly, the
two British executives conceded that Lord Rothermere was dis-
pleased with *Esquire's* staggering losses. Indeed, there was a chance
the magazine might be sold.

Walking to the elevator, the Knoxville men considered whether
to press on. Chris, flush with the million bucks he had taken off the
table in the Bonnier deal and happily splurging, was departing almost immediately for one of his mountain excursions—a month's
hiking in the Himalayas in Nepal. His backpack was ready. Riding
down, Chris said, "Phillip, I think we ought to do this!"

"I spent the next month convincing Mick Shields we were for
real," says Moffitt. "Lord Rothermere was undecided, but Mick said
if they did sell it he would see that we got it even though we might
not be the best in all-around terms of paying them the most
money."

With consultant Jim Kobak, Moffitt flew to Stockholm to get the
blessing of Lukas Bonnier, 13–30 Corporation's fifty-fifty partner.
"On the eight-hour flight," says Kobak, "Phil talked incessantly
about how he would revive *Esquire*. He had a great longing to edit a
major magazine."

Lukas Bonnier was not enthusiastic about buying *Esquire*, but gave tacit approval. At that time 13–30 Corporation was on a boom, with annual revenue of around $10 million. Chris and Moffitt calculated it would take them three years to make *Esquire* profitable. During that period they proposed to subsidize the New York magazine with profits generated by 13–30, just as the Computer Concepts earnings in the lean early days had propped up the budding *Nutshell* empire.

For weeks transatlantic negotiations continued secretly with Associated Newspapers. Jim Kobak sat in, helping to convince Lord Rothermere. "My guys decided they would become New Yorkers," Kobak says. "Moffitt bought a place at Sutton Place and Whittle at Ritz Tower. These are two very expensive and very high class coops. They couldn't get in because they were unknown. I wrote letters, explaining what wonderful people they are, and thank goodness, they got in. It is very interesting the way they changed from being little country boys, wanting to be in the best places in New York."

Finally the Knoxville partners won over Lord Rothermere by convincing him they possessed the editorial and advertising know-how, fresh ideas, and stamina to turn the magazine around. They flew to Paris where the British publisher had an apartment on the Ile de la Cité in the middle of the Seine. There, at midnight, they uncorked champagne for toasts all around, and shook hands on an agreement to acquire a two-thirds controlling interest in *Esquire*. Chris and Moffitt rushed back to New York.

"One of the most unusual aspects of the purchase," says Moffitt, "is that we bought, as they phrased it, 'What's in the bag.' We really didn't know what was in the bag. They never allowed us to examine the books."

Even so, lawyers on both sides began drafting documents to seal the bargain. The prospective new owners plunged into preparations with the Altschiller, Reitzfeld and Jackson advertising agency for their splashy announcement.

By the last weekend of April 1979 Chris and Moffitt were ready to take over *Esquire*—and tell the world about it.

The sale came as a jolt to Clay Felker. Lord Rothermere had kept him in the dark until the last minute. "I didn't even know negotiations were going on," Felker later told reporters, "and all of a sudden I hear I'm going to lose my magazine to two guys who arrive out of the blue from Knoxville."

On Thursday, April 26, 1979, Chris and Moffitt plunged into a five-day scramble to nail down final details. They were either on the phone or scurrying all over Manhattan by taxi getting ready to make the announcement at a press conference scheduled for Monday, April 30.

Their brash entry onto New York's magazine scene was destined to set off a flurry of confusion—as well as anger—not only in the media but among the literati and the staff of *Esquire* itself.There was no advance inkling that two young interlopers from Tennessee who nobody had ever heard of could inspire such a commotion.

"Didn't know it was coming—that people would be upset," says Moffitt now, with a chuckle. "We were two pretty confident fellows."

They began Thursday evening with a courtesy call on Felker at his East 57th Street apartment. "We talked about an hour," Felker says. "It was friendly. They wanted to know about personnel and so forth, the usual things. I never saw much of them afterwards."

On Friday top executives at *Esquire* and Byron Dobell, the managing editor under Hayes in the sixties and briefly editor in chief before Felker bought the magazine, were summoned to a conference at Moffitt's Sutton Place apartment, where they were informed of the changing ownership.

"They were all dubious," says Moffitt, "about who are these new guys, and what's what. I told them that my view of *Esquire*, from day one, was that Arnold Gingrich had the correct idea, and I was not going to do my magazine, I was going to do the magazine Arnold Gingrich created. I had dreamed of owning *Esquire* for years and I had always thought he created a wonderful combination of a literary magazine and a commercial magazine, one that could survive. My job was simply to refurbish a great literary institution in America. It wasn't my job to create a new magazine."

Moffitt announced that he would be the new editor, and Chris would be publisher, overseeing the advertising and circulation departments. That news shocked Dobell.

"I was very wary of Moffitt," says Dobell. "He had just come in and bought the magazine and named himself editor. That's perfectly legitimate in capitalist America, but I didn't like it. He didn't have the background or experience. If he had come to *Esquire* asking for a job, we wouldn't have hired him. I told him so, not angrily but as a matter of fact. I think he was a little stunned, but he accepted it."

Looking back on that meeting, Moffitt says, "I remember two or three people on the staff saying I should make them editor instead of me. But the fact is I would never had done it except to be editor. That was the whole point. I didn't think the magazine was ever going to make any money to speak of. I was in it because I wanted to be editor. Remember when Luce started *Time*. It wasn't that he was so well qualified. He had the guts, he had the vision, and it turned out. In my instance, I had the same thing. So it worked out."

Near the end of the meeting Moffitt inquired about upcoming issues of the magazine.

Dobell recalls, "He turned to me and said, 'All right, the urgent thing is to give me a list of the inventory so I know where we are and what the next issues will have.' I gave him a look. 'There is no inventory!' He didn't understand that the magazine was operating very much on an issue-to-issue basis, with stories coming in at the last minute, which was the way Clay used to operate *New York* magazine. There was no inventory in the sense of major pieces that could be cover stories or lead stories. Phillip's face fell to the floor."

A moment later Moffitt was called to the telephone—to receive another jolt.

"It was our lawyer," says Moffitt. "And he was saying the British were balking at some item in the contract, something I felt we had to have. I don't remember now what it was. I said, 'We've just got to have that, so stick to your guns!' So then I walked back into the meeting as though nothing was wrong. But for all I knew this was all going to fall apart at the last minute. I had to keep this cheery face on, and I didn't even tell Chris we had a problem until after everybody had left."

Their lawyer held out against the British, and won. On Saturday all parties signed the purchase contract. Moffitt also conferred with Byron Dobell at his East 69th Street apartment, and got him to agree to take on his old job as managing editor.

Esquire was already in turmoil. For years its office had been in the old *Look* magazine building at 488 Madison Avenue. The landlord raised the rent, so Felker leased new quarters on the twenty-fourth floor at 2 Park Avenue. The move had just taken place. The new space—a barn-like "newsroom" with a few private offices—was still a "war zone," cluttered with stacks of brown corrugated boxes containing circulation and advertising records, equipment, manuscripts, files, typewriters, adding machines, and the like. It would take weeks to untangle the mess.

On Monday, April 30th, they held their press conference in the Boardroom Club, 280 Park Avenue. About one hundred showed up—newspaper and magazine reporters and photographers, television crews. They snatched up and burrowed into the four-page press release. All arrived curious, most skeptical and suspicious, many sarcastic and sneering. Who were these yahoos from down in Tennessee, young "lads" nobody had ever heard of daring to take over a giant of the literary world, even a fallen one? The New York press was dumbfounded and affronted.

Chris and Moffitt stood together at one end of the room in front of a wall display on which were 13–30 growth charts and *Esquire* covers. They already had seen a proof of their full-page "Why We Bought *Esquire*" ad that would appear Wednesday morning in the *Times*. They hoped it would impress Madison Avenue. It made the point that Chris Whittle and Phillip Moffitt "grew up on *Esquire*" and thus were the magazine's "target audience," and as a result could interpret what effect the seventies were having on the post-Vietnam male.

"In the midst of all this unsettling change," said the *Times* ad, built around a suit-and-tie portrait of the two smiling 13–30 Corporation partners, "a man is still expected to know which wrench to use, what to wear for each occasion, what wine to order, how to make important decisions about his life, how to entertain a woman, where to vacation, and how to buy a stereo system that sounds like a concert hall."

The new *Esquire* would bring all that information to its readers. The ad concluded:

> We have always believed in Esquire.
> That's why we have bought it. That's why we are about to put an additional $5 million in it.
> And why we are so excited, we couldn't wait to tell you about it.

The new owners of *Esquire* looked over the press mob and felt ready to field questions, expecting many to be repetitious and several impertinent and rough. Normally in their offices they favored casual dress, jeans and sweaters; Chris was especially noted for his studied, rumpled look. Jim Kobak and their new ad man would blink when they saw them occasionally kick off their shoes in business conferences. Chris seldom wore socks with his Adidas sneakers. Under stress, he bit his nails. But both shopped at Barneys and Bloomingdale's in New York, Britches in Georgetown, and at elite haberdashers when in London.

For their press splash, they dressed up. Chris wore a neat, dark blue suit, white shirt, and brown-and-white-checked tie, with his normally tousled hair blown dry and in place. Moffitt who would be characterized in newspaper accounts as Muppet-like because of his dark curly hair and trim mustache, wore a dark brown suit and maroon tie.

They were center stage. It was their day of glory—and the media's opportunity to fire a harsh barrage.

Charlotte Evans of the *New York Times* asked about *Esquire*'s future. Moffitt answered that the magazine and its staff would stay in New York and revert to being a monthly. The 13–30 Corporation would pump in $5 million and hope to attract 100,000 new readers in two years, and get *Esquire* in the black in three.

"Our aim is to combine the classic aspects of *Esquire* tradition with relevant editorial for the new American male," Moffitt said. "We'll gradually phase in a new editorial focus, which will be exciting to readers and advertisers. Today's twenty-five- to forty-five-year-old man, the prime *Esquire* reader, has, in effect, been abandoned by the print media. He has a changing life-style and changing values. In a real sense he's a man without a context and no magazine is adequately helping him find his identity. We don't want to preach but to explore with him, to make *Esquire* the book that speaks to the realities of his life."

One reporter yelled out, did that mean it would be a skin magazine? "Never," responded Whittle. "We intend to start a column on male heroes, and a guest column by women writing about their experiences with men—at dinner parties, on the street, or in bed."

Betsy Carter, covering for *Newsweek*, remembers it was a "very un–New York presentation. They were both very hyper. They showed many, many charts. They had every minute figured out. It was all very New Age when New Age hadn't even blossomed yet. Phil spoke in a language that most New York people didn't get."

The *Times* reporter tried to nudge Chris into telling the purchase price. "We're not disclosing it," he said, "by agreement of all parties." (*Newsweek* reported it was $3.5 million.) She pressed on, asking who assumed the magazine's debt, said to be $7 million or more. Chris chewed on the question for a minute. It struck him she would be flabbergasted if he could just blurt out all details of the deal. He sighed, and smiled at the reporter. "I can respond that all creditors and liabilities have been handled in some shape, form, or fashion."

Chris did not reveal that Associated Newspapers, unable, as a British firm, to take a legal tax write-off on its American property, had in effect given control of *Esquire* to 13–30 at no cost, with the Knoxville company agreeing to assume its debts. Lord Rothermere felt that where Felker had failed, Chris and Moffitt could somehow succeed.

When Betsy Carter went back to the *Newsweek* office she told her editor, "These guys are going to get creamed by the New York press. Mark my words. It would be easy for us to do the same thing. But I think they are smart." *Newsweek*, she says, ended up doing the most fair story, "and everyone else ripped them to shreds."

This did not escape Moffitt's notice. He later invited Betsy Carter to lunch and begged her to critique issues of *Esquire*. She did, and Moffitt, impressed by her skills, hired her as a senior editor. Later he would launch *New York Woman* and name her its editor. In 1993 she was named executive editor of *Harper's Bazaar*.

Following the press conference, Chris and Moffitt assembled all *Esquire* employees in a meeting room at the Waldorf Astoria hotel to introduce themselves and their plans for the future. They got a chilly reception. One of those present was Lee Eisenberg, a former *Esquire* editor in chief whom Felker had brought back to the magazine as a consultant.

"They said things that made many of us apprehensive," Eisenberg recalls. "There was a lot of muttering that they were contemplating 'a male *Cosmopolitan*.' On the other hand, that they were intent on repositioning the magazine for a new reader and a new time was something I personally applauded. It was similar to what I was trying to do a few years prior.

"Still, they made some mistakes in how they chose to characterize the changes they had in mind. They seemed to imply that there was a formula that struck some people as overly formulaic: this much fashion, that much travel, and so on. It seemed too simplistic to a number of journalistic and literary insiders in New York. The grander traditions of *Esquire* seemed to be at risk."

However, most such concerns were groundless, Eisenberg now says, ironically from Knoxville, where he became a core team player on the Edison Project.

"Phillip is a profoundly interesting and complex person. But his style and delivery weren't what the New York editorial world was used to. Having now lived elsewhere, I can attest to how provincial New York insiders can be. They largely underestimated Phillip and Chris's creative abilities. They certainly underestimated their tenacity.

"Frankly, I am now a bit appalled how parochial New York is, and how divergent are the personalities and sensibilities of people who come from places like Tennessee and people who live in New York. I hear it all the time now. And they were victimized by it then. There was just no understanding. America has changed a lot since then. Now we understand that not everything starts in New York. We understand that full well. I think we are beginning to understand that New York, with many bad habits and a lot of demoralization, actually is a counterforce to innovation and new ideas in all fields. But back then we hadn't quite worked all that out yet in New York, and we really felt if it didn't happen in New York it didn't matter or count."

Not unexpectedly, several *Esquire* staffers took public potshots at their new bosses. National editor Richard Reeves told *Time* magazine bluntly, "I've never heard of these people. They could have landed from Mars." Later Reeves warmed up a trifle. "You have to say one thing, these guys appear to have done what everybody fantasized about in college: starting a campus publication and expanding it into a real national money-maker. Maybe they have the secret and it's stored away in a computer in Knoxville. I'm still a little numb, but a lot of greats in *Esquire*'s past have come out of the South."

In a harsh article in the *New Republic,* Harold Hayes, the magazine's former editor whose twenty-year stint ended in 1973, attacked what he considered the impending pedestrianization of *Esquire.* Later Hayes softened his criticism, but still maintained that

Whittle and Moffitt refused to be editorial risk takers and that some of the articles were "puerile . . . sappy, and image-gratifying as a kind of journalism." He did concede that *Esquire* might be developing a new audience.

The *Village Voice* got in a dig. Its press critic, Alexander Cockburn, lamented that *Esquire* might be turned into a "male *Cosmo*," and asserted the new owners had never displayed "the talent required to transcend the literary achievements of a cornflake packet."

Negative feedback was bad enough; but the "Gold Dust Twins"—as they were derisively dubbed on Madison Avenue—weren't fully prepared for the realities of life at a sinking literary icon. "Every time they opened a desk drawer they found new problems," one staffer told an *Atlanta Journal* reporter. "It really ate away at them. They had to completely restructure the magazine."

Being strangers in New York compounded their takeover. Moffitt had delved into library files and catalogued just about every byline that had appeared in *Esquire.* But he needed to personally get acquainted with the top-flight writers. Moffitt initiated a friendship with one of them, Gay Talese, who was just finishing his book *Thy Neighbor's Wife.* Though he hadn't written any articles under the Felker regime, Talese began writing for Moffitt. They toured the Manhattan bars where writers hung out and had long dinner conversations.

"Here was this young unannointed prince," Talese recalled in a 1986 article in *Manhattan Inc.* magazine, "who had come up to New York from the provinces, and I saw myself in this guy, the openness, the receptiveness. It was like when I had first come to town. [Talese, a native of New Jersey, is a graduate of the University of Alabama.] Phillip has a sense of wonder, a tremendous curiosity, and he's not governed by anyone else's ideas. He felt he belonged here, and he *does* belong here. Anyway, I felt right away that I wanted to work for Esquire again."

The *Manhattan Inc.* article gave Talese considerable credit for taking "the eager young Southerner" under tutelage, including him in his social life, and advising him what to do with the magazine, viz: " 'Take the staple out, for one thing,' Talese said that first night to Moffitt, referring to the *Esquire* binding. Moffitt did." (In 1993, Moffitt does not give Talese that much credit. "Everybody said take out the damned staple and go back to square binding!")

Chris and Moffitt began the *Esquire* chapter of their partnership on a harmonious and equal footing that brought wry comments from New York journalists. They were, observed one reporter, like overgrown puppies scampering around the living room apt to knock over the table lamps. The serious-minded *Wall Street Journal* tabbed them "Southern lads." They were "Muppets" because of their youth and abundant hair, which reminded one imaginative writer of Davy Crockett coonskin caps without the tails.

On Madison Avenue they were regarded as sort of Siamese twins, perfectly matched halves, joined at the hip. They shared a mutual vision; when one began a sentence, the other could—and often did—finish it. But they had distinctly separate roles.

Moffitt held the reins of design and editorial content. He was well prepared. As publisher, Chris took charge of advertising and circulation. It was a challenge. He was a bonafide supersalesman, but this new territory was foreign and somewhat frightening to him, especially magazine circulation. He had learned giveaway distribution with *Nutshell* and their other "controlled circulation" publications, but was flustered by finding that paid subscriptions for *Esquire* were lumped into a promotional grab bag with other magazines where the low or nonexistent renewal rate was scandalous, amounting to a rip-off of their new property.

Chris was more than a little frustrated by his mission. He felt the magazine had lacked a distinct focus. Moffitt had corrected that, and Chris made strides on the advertising side but admittedly not with as much success. Trapped in the circulation swamp, he felt like giving up.

To overhaul *Esquire*'s advertising, circulation, and finance departments, Chris imported some trusted lieutenants from Knoxville headquarters—Mike Collins, Alan Greenberg, and Wilma Jordan. They thinned out the business staff, brought some of 13–30's star salesmen to beat on the closed doors of ad agencies, and worked furiously to upgrade the magazine's circulation.

To their horror they found a Felker-originated subscription circular poised to go out to a million and a half people. "It cost half a million dollars," says Moffitt. "But they said it had to go out or we'd miss the rate base, and so forth. So we sent it out, and got almost no response. It was like throwing money in the fireplace." However, in a matter of months they tripled newsstand sales.

The reborn *Esquire* was off to a rocky start. Chris and Moffitt felt optimistic. At least they had a shot—at long odds—to make it with their first big-time magazine.

=====

The New York adventure had a profound effect on 13–30 in Knoxville. Initially it spawned pride and celebration, but within a short time it would evoke two dark sides, creating dismay and potential danger.

News of the *Esquire* purchase was announced by Mike Collins to the Knoxville media at the same hour the press conference was held in New York. That same evening Chris and Moffitt flew home from Manhattan and hosted all employees at Barrentine's restaurant near the university. It was a glitzy, upbeat dinner where wine, praise, and good wishes flowed freely at every table.

The merciless ridicule the New York media had heaped on the pair of upstarts from Tennessee—who thought they could succeed where legendary editors had failed—was shrugged off by the 13–30 troops.

"There was so much media attention," recalls research chief Michele MacDonald, "and we had all the news clips posted in the hallways outside our offices in the Arnstein Building. We got so much enjoyment out of the New Yorkers guffawing over the country bumpkins in east Tennessee who thought they could take on the New York publishing companies."

The euphoria in Knoxville soon began to evaporate for two reasons. Those lucky enough to be transferred to New York to work on *Esquire*—a handful of ad salesmen, production, and circulation-distribution people—were thrust into glamorous Big Apple excitement. Those left at home felt they were somehow regarded as second class.

The second, and far more detrimental, effect of conducting publishing enterprises simultaneously in Knoxville and New York was that neither Chris nor Moffitt could be in two places at the same time.

Turning around *Esquire* and extricating it from the financial quagmire was, of course, indisputably their first priority. The publisher and the editor normally labored in their 2 Park Avenue quarters until Thursday evening, then hurried to catch the Delta flight—which was direct at that time—to Knoxville. In Tennessee they worked through the weekend on 13–30 affairs. In two hours on Monday morning they were able to fly back to their *Esquire* desks.

But this paradoxical attempt by the Gold Dust Twins to run two separate shows provoked subtle changes in the previous one-for-all, all-for-one climate at 13–30. A management vacuum in Knoxville began to take shape, asserts Frank Finn, a 13–30 editor. It was unnerving, and noticeable. Concerning this period of the company's history, Finn wrote:

> Part of the shift was a natural consequence of the fact that Moffitt and Whittle were rarely "home." A catch phrase of the time was "swoop management."
>
> Managers in Knoxville would work away on a project, making decisions they thought Moffitt and Whittle would make. Then the two would swoop into town and hold marathon management meetings at which many of those decisions would be reversed.
>
> Many managers resented the fact that Moffitt and Whittle were running 13–30 at 30,000 feet without the input of the workers in the trenches in Knoxville. The two seemed unable to delegate genuine authority, insisting on keeping their hands in at both operations.
>
> Some of the consequences of Moffitt's and Whittle's visits to Knoxville were more comical. [Laura] Eshbaugh remembers a plan to prop silhouettes of Moffitt and Whittle up at their desks. Then those going by could look in and at least imagine that "the boys" were home.

Stress was heavy on the two bosses. Says Moffitt: "The process of our commuting back and forth went on for me many years. I split my time trying to be at both companies as needed. And I carried manuscripts. I never had time during the day to read manuscripts. I essentially gave my life over to making a success out of something that turned out to have been in much worse shape than we imagined.

"Our biggest problem was that nobody was renewing *Esquire*.

The subscribers were just saying, 'No, I don't want to renew.' This had been going on for some time, and we didn't know it. So we walked into a situation where our subscription base was disappearing. It was a real mess."

Chris and Moffitt were badly frightened.

"It was really a tough time," Moffitt recalled in 1993. "It looked as though we might go broke. We had three and a half million dollars in the bank and a million and a half line of credit. We went through that in, I think, eight months. Maybe it was the whole five million in five months. I can't remember all that.

"Money just flew out the door. We were losing twenty-five thousand dollars a day! We used to make this joke that we gave as many holidays as possible so we could close shop and save the twenty-five thou.

"It was really terrible. We couldn't get advertising salespeople to present a sales pitch that was the vision of the magazine I had. They were trained in another way of selling, and they were just very resistant to change.

"I trotted all around the country speaking to advertisers as editor. The ad salesmen were not telling what I believed was going to happen. And if what I was saying was going to happen wasn't going to happen we had a dead magazine. So there was no choice. *Esquire* was just in deep, deep trouble."

The best thing about owning *Esquire* at that point was it gave the 13–30 shop in Knoxville a higher level of credibility.

"So we were able to get even larger ad sales contracts," says Moffitt. "And the other thing that we did was really fantastic. We did what they call multi-year contracts. This is almost unheard of in the advertising world. We were able to sign contracts for like twenty-five million dollars, which was five million over five years.

"This gave us a lot of cash up front. I've said this before, if it wasn't 13–30 continuing to grow and prosper we would have run out of money in New York. So 13–30 supported *Esquire* until it reached break-even."

But that glorious day was yet to come in 1979, when the *Esquire* bookkeeper's ledgers steadily dripped red ink.

Chris and Moffitt were concerned about the predicament into which they had drawn their partners from Stockholm.

"We had put Lukas Bonnier in a situation where we were very

uncomfortable," says Moffitt. "It all wasn't working very well. Lukas's family was sort of looking at him and saying, 'What have you done to us? We're going to kill one of the great prestigious magazines in America!' And Lukas kept saying, 'No. These boys are going to get it done.' Fortunately we had a buy-back clause which gave us the option of reclaiming their fifty percent ownership in 13–30."

The wise course would be for the men from Tennessee to buy back the Bonniers' share of their 13–30–*Esquire* conglomerate. But where would they obtain the $3 million the Scandinavians had paid—as well as the considerable sum the Bonniers would be entitled to as profit on their investment?

They devised one of their brilliant schemes, and rushed to JFK airport for an overseas flight. First they would visit Lukas Bonnier, and then call on Lord Rothermere. Chris explained: "The Bonniers thought we were going to drive the company right into the ground. There wasn't any hostility or anything. They were just going, 'Guys, don't do this!' And we went to them and said, 'Look, we have to do this. If you want out, we'll get you out.'

"And the Brits, Associated, were very impressed with how we were doing. They thought we were doing great, compared to what they had done [with Clay Felker]. So we basically said, I'm simplifying this immensely, 'Would you like to take the Bonniers' part, and buy back into what you have just sold us [*Esquire*] and our other company [13–30] as well?'

"And they said yes, and agreed to basically buy the Bonniers' position for about $4.2 million dollars. So the Bonniers made some money, not much. . . . The Bonniers were happy, they didn't lose their money. But they're unhappy now. Their 3 million stake became worth around 400 million dollars."

In the new transaction, Associated bought only 42.5 percent of the combined company, leaving Chris, Moffitt, and a handful of limited partners with control—57.5 percent.

The new deal was executed December 17, 1979.

As the year ended, back in New York Chris stared glumly across the desk at his equally grim-faced partner. Neither had to verbalize why they faced 1980 with so much dread. It was *Esquire*. In the eight months since they took control of the magazine they had been unable to turn it around. And *Esquire* still devoured money as fast as the "tacky little magazines" in Knoxville could make it.

12

LOOKING FOR A
WIFE

In Ellen Barrentine's restaurant near the University of Tennessee campus on a spring noon in 1980, Chris Whittle appeared unusually tense. His three companions, Moffitt and 13–30 executives Alan Greenberg and Frank Finn, bantered small talk and looked over the menu.

Chris, brow furrowed, stared out the window and squirmed in his chair. He was deeply concerned about the speed with which *Esquire* burned money. Somebody had to whip up the creative horses in Knoxville and quickly drag in a ton more cash. Otherwise the magazine would sink.

That daunting challenge was the reason for lunch. Chris wanted to talk about engineering a quick fix. He saw bright prospects in their new wall-media concept—the *Wallpaper Journal,* the Bob Hanggi idea that Moffitt had rescued from his wastebasket and which had just blossomed on one hundred fifty university campuses as an educational and dramatic poster. They should move beyond the customary college environment and create newsy wall posters that would appeal to different fields and audiences. To Chris that looked like the surest and quickest way to accelerate 13–30 cash flow.

It was essential to find wall-media locations with a high volume of foot traffic. And they needed to get cracking on locking them up in order to preempt possible competition. Once a poster case was installed, he theorized, the proprietor would be unlikely to allow a second case. Their quick action might thus freeze out any rival.

"Let's move," Chris said. He grabbed a napkin and unlimbered his pen. "We'll make a list. Our contacts at our top advertisers." He scribbled names of executives at companies like Ralston-Purina, Johnson and Johnson, and Procter and Gamble.

Frank Finn, vice-president and executive editor of 13–30 magazines, was taken aback by this incongruity. Everyone was much aware of Chris's meticulous lists on yellow legal pads and his pristine coordination of props for sales pitches. Now Finn watched a business strategy being scribbled on a flimsy napkin in a cafe.

"We made another column on Chris's napkin," Finn recalls, "and wrote down places where people are trapped with nothing to do but scan old magazines—doctors' offices foremost among them. Finally we plugged in the editorial concepts—pet care, dental health, child care, and so on.

"By the time lunch was over, a grand wall-media strategy was scribbled on the napkin. The scary part was that virtually all of the plans came to pass, and then some."

Discussing the episode later, Chris says, with a broad smile, "Oh, I've made a lot of plans on napkins. The *Esquire* deal, for instance. I laid all that out on a napkin in an airliner tray."

The lunch at Barrentine's proved a success. The hieroglyphics on Chris's napkin inspired a string of new "properties," a dozen or so of which would be launched by the middle of 1982. They would bring in millions in new revenue, with the lion's share going to prop up *Esquire*.

Chris and Moffitt, with the most at stake, carried the heaviest burdens. Their work ethic stunned their new colleagues at *Esquire*. "Few people in New York," said Lee Eisenberg, who quickly settled in as part of the *Esquire* inner circle, "could fathom their intensity, how hard-working and determined they were."

Managing editor Byron Dobell, initially skeptical of Moffitt and Whittle, feared they would junk up the magazine. "They didn't. They put a lot of stereotypical zip into it. There were things I didn't much love, but they didn't make it into some shameful product."

Dobell later left to become editor of *American Heritage* for eight years, after which he resumed a second career as successful portrait painter.

Moffitt, he recalls, "was afraid that *Esquire* was seen as too smart-ass. I remember he said at one point, 'Let's not be too funny.' He didn't like the idea of being too sophisticated. Listen, I think they were both terrific businessmen. They did take a magazine that was in a lot of trouble and they saved it. And they saved it so that some-day a great editor can come along and make it a great magazine, which has yet to happen."

―――

The vaunted twinship which gave Whittle and Moffitt the pub-lic image of a strikingly sharp New York team began to come un-glued. Moffitt settled comfortably and effectively into his role as editor. Chris, on the other hand, was miscast as *Esquire*'s circulation and advertising director. He was well qualified, especially in adver-tising, but he still was saddled with his salesman role at 13–30. He could not do both, scampering back and forth between New York and Knoxville.

"It was a very difficult stretch for me," Chris recalls. "And the early days of that I remember as relatively unpleasant because I didn't feel like it was working the way it should. And it was one of those situations you get into in life where you are working as hard as you can, but it's not working.

"What that tends to indicate is that there's some kind of struc-tural problem, meaning it wasn't that I couldn't do the job or that the job couldn't be done. There was nothing magical about what had to be done, it wasn't physically possible."

Fairly rapidly, Moffitt assembled an active stable of older writers such as Gay Talese, Truman Capote, George Leonard, and Adam Smith, along with newcomers like Guy Martin, Harry Stein, and Donald Katz. A top designer was brought in to perk up *Esquire*'s typography, and bring back the familiar logo.

In one monthly editor's column, Moffitt conceded: "As you ex-pect, the magazine has aroused controversy at times on such topics as politics, sports, social issues, and sex. While it has been accused of being sexist, irreverent, left-wing, and right-wing (the same charges that have been made, by the way, throughout most of its history), it has not been accused of being dull, stereotyped, or unin-telligent. Like all products of human striving, *Esquire* sometimes stumbles; but we are ready to learn from our mistakes."

As publisher, Chris learned from his mistakes, too. He corrected his number-one error by elevating his key Knoxville business executive, Alan Greenberg, to full-fledged vice president of advertising and marketing. Though he was rarely seen there, Chris kept his *Esquire* office at 2 Park Avenue and moved his actual base of operation back to his "hometown" Arnstein Building. Both in Manhattan and Knoxville the situation improved almost at once.

Daniel J. O'Shea, one of *Esquire*'s top financial officers, recalls Chris went in thinking "it would be simple and easy" to get the magazine in the black in eighteen months. "He became very frustrated. Chris is a master salesman, but his style is much better used in a whopper contract with, say, Federal Express than selling a six-page *Esquire* schedule to Chrysler. Selling pages takes a lot of blocking and tackling. There's not very quick return, not instant gratification, versus going out and selling P and G a five-million-dollar program. To get five million dollars of advertising revenue at *Esquire* would mean roughly four hundred pages. The most any single advertiser would buy would be maybe forty-eight."

O'Shea viewed the culture of 13–30 as "a neglective one"—for lacking the best employment of resources and personnel for the best gain. "And Chris could make a bigger impact by going out and selling programs that were worth three, five, ten million dollars. Being something of a social scientist, Chris was a master at strategic selling, finding the decision makers, probing to determine their needs, creating a program to fill them.

"Phillip and Chris were very, very good together. Chris would come back and say, 'I've been to R. J. Reynolds. They want to reach this certain age group. They want to have an impact X amount of times a week to this audience, and they are not really getting it. What do you think?'

"Phil would brainstorm and he would come up with ideas. For instance, the concept called *Sports Page,* a wall media of sports stories with RJR brands advertised on the bottom that was posted monthly in sports bars and taverns. What made them great together was that Phillip was the creative person and the person in control of the business. And Chris was the salesman. Chris could sell snow to Eskimos."

Looking back on the *Esquire* adventure, Chris said in one of our interviews, "To be fair to all involved, my role in *Esquire*—there are a few things I did that I think matters. And all credit goes to other people. The one thing I did, I did the Associated-Bonnier transaction. And then the second thing I did, I spent the next five years increasing sales at 13–30 to fund *Esquire*.

"But the two people who really fixed *Esquire* were Moffitt and Greenberg. And I played the role of cash provider, but Moffitt was really the editor and Greenberg was really the business man. And Wilma [Jordan] did circulation. So I was really involved as a support system."

In the vast solitude of the Swiss Alps, Chris Whittle is a lonely figure silhouetted against the high-domed blue sky. He sits with a seven-by-ten-inch hardbound personal journal on his knees. He has come here, to majestic snowy terrain that both challenges his endurance and recharges his creative batteries, to think. At age thirty-three, Chris is undergoing a sea change of emotions. His pent-up uncertainties about what he should really do with his life, how to maximize both purpose and happiness, have finally brought him to a personal crossroads.

Chris Whittle, wanting a wife, is writing down his requirements for a mate. They are not yet precise. Still in formation, his ideas are broad, warm, generous, and ambitious.

She must be attractive, not necessarily beautiful in the Barbie doll sense, but a woman other men will also consider appealing. With good looks, energy, and enthusiasm, Chris jotted down: "life."

Dark-haired and slender. Unpretentious, a Smith College type. He wrote: "depth." He would not insist on an intellectual, but a woman who knew herself and formed her own opinions about people and the world. It would be a disaster, Chris felt, if she had to look on him as an idol or teacher. She must have respect for who she is and be honest with herself.

Passion. To Chris that word did not mean sex, exactly. He was thinking more of chemistry, of enjoying being together, like wanting to hold hands at every opportunity. He had been with attractive women, in fact, beautiful women, when he felt he would cringe if he had to hold their hand.

Chris's hands at this moment were fondling the crisp pages of the journal he always used for personal matters, as opposed to his yellow pads for business. He really loved making lists—the positives and negatives, even of romance. He felt he could think best when he wrote notes so that he could review them and reconsider alternatives.

With close friends and colleagues he had been candid and rather open about his relationships with women. Back at Etowah High he was not much of a swain; being shy, short, and skinny, Chris was hardly the Galahad vision of any of his female classmates. At the University of Tennessee it was a different story. A busy campus activist, bright, somewhat taller and good looking, he dated many coeds, especially as a junior and senior.

In the pillow factory days he had been guardedly and deliberately casual about women. Both he and Moffitt dated some young women who worked at 13–30, but apparently not with matrimony in mind. Even then Chris held the institution of marriage in highest esteem, doubtless because of his parents' influence on his upbringing. He wanted to be sure of a wife; it would be a lifetime marriage.

Now he looked up from his writing and searched the Alpine horizon as if for an answer to his dilemma. Chris mulled over his options and decided he had at least four. He could remain a bachelor all his life. He could sleep around. He could continue to get involved in live-in relationships, even though he expected them to come unglued sooner or later. Or he could get married.

There had been one. . . . Thinking about her, Chris frowned and uttered a little moan of regret. She had come into his life too early, when he was not ready for marriage. Later, reflecting on lost loves with a confidant, Chris lamented that she was the one he should have married. Why not marry her now? Chris shook his head. *If you miss it, you just miss it. You can't go back.*

"Now that you've decided you'd like to marry, what will you do until she comes along?"

The answer emerged slowly, thoughtfully. *A difficult question. I've reached the point at which sleeping around brings little other than feelings of guilt. I find myself opting for occasional stretches of celibacy. Not for any moral reason, but because when you sleep around, you mess up other people's lives. You lose your integrity. Celibate, I think I will be better able to know this woman when she appears.*

In the early, busy days of *Esquire*, Chris was too pressed for time to engage in a deliberate search for a wife. However, his never-ending 13–30 and magazine chores did not prevent him from looking.

The crucial elements he observed about any new woman who entered—or almost entered—his life ranged widely. The curve of her neck, the shape and taste of her lips, the feel of her hair to his touch. Her taste in shoes, gowns, jewelry, and books, art, and movies. Her grasp of the day's news. Her health.

Until he could be dead certain, he would be a most cautious suitor.

—————

The advent of 1980 sent Chris Whittle plunging into three new, spectacular emotional involvements. Two were mad, adventuresome, and expensive obsessions with new homes—an historic picture-postcard farm in New England, and a famous apartment building huddled alongside Central Park in Manhattan.

The third was a real love affair with tall, smart, and pretty Tricia Brock that blossomed from total happenstance.

A 1971 journalism graduate of the University of Missouri, Tricia Brock had started her career in New York at the Doyle, Dane and Bernbach advertising agency. As associate producer of television commercials, she worked chiefly on the Polaroid account. When Candice Bergen did a live Polaroid commercial on *Saturday Night Live*, Tricia became enamored of the show. "*SNL* had stupendous energy," she says. "I knew I had to write for it. Advertising was too boring."

She wrangled a job writing for the specials that aired when *Saturday Night Live* took a break, an assignment that lasted two years. Then she raised $150,000, went to the University of Mississippi in 1979, and produced a documentary about sorority life called *Rush*.

A preview of the film, which was entered in the 1980 New York Film Festival, was shown that January at Doyle, Dane, and Bernbach. Ted Voss, a Polaroid executive, took his friend Chris to the screening and introduced him to *Rush*'s producer.

Chris observed that she was blond with cropped hair, small (a size six), with strong features: high cheek bones, a slightly pointed nose, and green eyes. Her dynamic personality definitely impressed him.

Tricia Brock says, "Chris showed up because it was a screening about the South and sororities and fraternities. I thought he was great. He complimented me on the movie, and gave me some advice on marketing it. Which I was totally ignorant about. I just barely knew how to get a film made."

A few days later he phoned her. They began a slow courtship.

"Slow was the only way Chris could court anyone," says Tricia, "given the demands on his time. Weeks would go by. Then he might call from some bizarre hotel. Now and then he would take me to dinner.

"I really admired him, and he was an inspiration to me because he believed that anything was possible. I used to tease him about being the new American cowboy riding the plains, or planes in his case, to carve out this niche for himself. But he was very lonely a lot of the time. So much energy went into his work. He would screw up and get his hand slapped by Phillip. But Phillip was far too hard on him, and Chris was no longer willing to be the student and sit at Phillip's feet."

Tricia became enmeshed in Chris's life. She was more than a front-running entry in what some friends called the "Whittle Matrimonial Sweepstakes." She rapidly became a confidant and trusted adviser.

About the time he met her, Chris began to get passionate about acquiring a mountain retreat to augment his log cabin in Knoxville and his Park Avenue apartment at the Ritz Tower. He had an idea where to look. From the Wally Barnes's gubernatorial campaign he had become well acquainted with Vermont's mountain resorts, having done cross-country skiing out of Stowe.

He engaged real state agent Peggy Macdonald Smith of Stowe. "He didn't know where in the Vermont mountains he wanted to be," she says. "He had a yellow pad with specific notes on what he wanted—open meadows, a lot of land, a winding drive up to the house, a scenic vista, and privacy."

Chris came up from New York nearly every weekend to look at farms with her. "We walked nearly every foot along the ridge from Johnson to Stowe and on down to Moretown," she says. "Once my car's clutch went out. 'Don't fret,' he said. 'I can make it go.' And he did. He was a sparkling personality, and fun. Often he brought along a girlfriend, mostly different ones. They were agog about him, but I think he had a different agenda. None of them impressed me."

These weekend searches covered about three fruitless months. "He asked me to keep looking. To hire a plane and survey the Waitsfield area from the air."

When he arrived the next weekend Peggy Smith's eyes were flashing. In her car they sped down the Mad River valley and halted on a dirt back road three miles south of Waitsfield, a town of about three thousand.

Seventy-five feet up the slope sat a large, rambling nineteenth-century white clapboard farmhouse with three porches and a dozen terraces behind thick stone walls. The ancient red barn was flanked by twin meadows, pastures, a large sugar maple grove, and mountain shrubbery. They stepped on the porch facing Scragg Mountain and Chris gasped at the stunning panorama.

Peggy Smith excitedly threw her arms wide. "Three hundred fifty acres, the house and barn. They're asking six hundred thousand."

Chris was ecstatic. This farm offered solitude, privacy, and a million-dollar vista of meadow, valley, and ridge.

The farm, handed down in the Joslin family for one hundred years, was famous. Its 1940 owners, the Perry Joslins, were selected the typical farm family to represent Vermont at the World's Fair in New York. Chris decided to buy it and insisted on handling negotiations personally. "I didn't mind, but I believe I could have got it for him for less," says Peggy Smith. The sale was recorded December 4, 1980.

Even without a winding drive, the Joslin farm suited Chris. His long-range plan was to design and build a large mansion in the woods on the higher elevation. First he would remodel the farmhouse for temporary weekend use; later it could house his caretaker. He started looking for a Vermont architect.

His other obsession was a curious case of love at first sight with New York City's fabled Dakota, the dowager queen mother of apartment houses. Not until he was taken there in 1977 by a real estate agent did Chris know anything at all about the pale yellow, brick Victorian fortress on Central Park West at 72nd Street.

Built in 1884, the Dakota was the forerunner of latter-day luxury apartment buildings, and in 1961 was converted to ninety co-ops—ranging from one-room studios to twenty-room apartments. The Dakota became a tourist attraction in the late 1960s when its nine-story exterior was featured in the film *Rosemary's Baby*. Chris was in New York when famous Dakota resident John Lennon was gunned down in December 1980 at the building's doorway. Many other celebrities have lived there, including Boris Karloff and Lauren Bacall.

Its style was derided as "Brewery Gothic Eclectic" or "Middle European Post Office," and the flats were expensive. Nevertheless, Chris dipped into his first million to buy a six-room apartment. It was dilapidated and badly needed renovation.

Tricia Brock, who knew her way around New York, put him in touch with Peter Marino, the most sought-after architect and interior designer on the international axis, who had a studio at 150 East 58th Street and a staff of eighty. "He's very, very expensive," Tricia warned, "but he's very, very good. They call him the designer's designer."

Two years younger than Chris, Marino grew up in the New York borough of Queens and became a protégé of Andy Warhol while attending Cornell University. He vaulted into the big time after graduation in 1971, when Warhol commissioned him to renovate the pop artist's townhouse and the Factory.

That led to commissions for Yves Saint Laurent's apartment in the Pierre Hotel and a country house in New Jersey for Fiat heiress Margherita Agnelli. Later he did the Park Avenue apartment of her father, Fiat chairman Gianni Agnelli of Milan, Italy. Marino was off and running, with a growing list of celebrity clients: Calvin Klein, Giorgio Armani, Philip Niarchos, Carla Fendi, and Valentino. Meshulam Riklis and Pia Zadora had commissioned him to renovate Hollywood's fabled Pickfair. "I didn't deliberately go out and say, 'I want only the world's richest people as clients,' " he told a *House and Garden* magazine interviewer. "The fact that they happened to come along was very lucky."

Marino went with Chris to inspect the run-down apartment and was intrigued by the superb detail of the Dakota's carved marble mantels, elaborate stone friezes; arched and beamed, floors three feet thick, and paneled oak-and-mahogany walls.

Chris learned Marino totally subscribed to opulence, and even brought artisans over from Europe to finish wood paneling and stenciling by hand, to do gold and silver leafing, and to craft drapes, rugs, and furniture which he designed.

The architect-designer saw the renovation as a challenge. "Appropriateness is the central point of architecture," Marino said. "A palace should look like a palace, a loft should look like a loft, and a hot dog stand should look like a hot dog stand. And an apartment in the Dakota should look like an apartment in the Dakota, not a sheik's spread in the Olympic Tower."

That's exactly what Chris wanted to hear. He took an instant liking to Marino and commissioned him on the spot.

By Etowah standards, Chris Whittle might have seemed to be foolishly splurging for the good life which he had not even remotely imagined as a kid. Even his colleagues in Knoxville and at *Esquire* were startled by his abandon. "Chris lives on the cusp," said one. "I've never seen anyone so young spend so lavishly—money he doesn't have yet, at that."

Fixing up the six rooms in the Dakota would take Peter Marino and his European handcrafters nearly four years—and the cost would be hundreds of thousands of dollars. That didn't bother Chris Whittle. He wanted only the best. He could not bring himself to abandon his humble Tennessee roots, but as Lee Eisenberg observed, "Chris *needed* the accoutrements of New York."

Buying and decorating the Dakota apartment did not result in a loss. "It was not unwise," Chris says. "When I sold it, I got back everything I invested in it."

———

It was another introduction which Tricia arranged that began an important chapter in Chris's life—intensive and enduring psychoanalysis. He revealed to her that he was confronted by what he now describes as "personal and professional problems." She gave him advice: See a psychiatrist. He agreed, and she introduced him to one located near her Madison Avenue apartment in Manhattan. Tricia knew the physician because he had treated a couple of her friends. Chris began seeing the doctor, and liked him immensely.

Chris Whittle first publicly revealed—in an offhand way—that he was in therapy when the *Knoxville Journal* wrote him up in a

1988 interview as one of that city's movers and shakers. Privately he had earlier discussed visiting a therapist with a few company colleagues.

In response to a question in our interviews, Chris readily asserted he is an "unabashed advocate" of psychotherapy. "I think there are many different ways you can benefit from it. The gentleman I have been with for over ten years is a Freudian. I've learned a tremendous amount, and he's been through a lot with me."

Chris says a "mixture of personal and professional problems" prompted him to seek psychiatric help, but declines to give details. Half a dozen of his friends believe the problems basically stemmed from a struggle to escape Phillip Moffitt's dominance over him, especially in controlling *Esquire.*

Chris identified his therapist as Dr. Joel Markowitz, whom he has seen hundreds of times. Initially they consulted two or three times a week. Chris says, "Then it evolved into something different. Now I would call him a very trusted adviser. He knows me well. He knows how I think, how I feel. He has a very great sense of all the players in the company. Now [in 1995] we talk twice a week. Most of the time over the phone."

Dr. Markowitz, son of a successful furrier, attended Cornell and received his medical degree in 1953 from Columbia University. He is on the faculty of Mt. Sinai Hospital in New York.

Dr. Markowitz described his relationship with Chris as "not a typical therapist-patient relationship." He explains, "It is more than just a friendship. It requires a certain flexibility, which some patients don't have. How would I describe this relationship? You could say that each of us goes into this as something of a specialist. Each of us has a different expertise. Chris and I come from different vantage points, of course, different perspectives. My work is to illuminate situations from my deeper vantage point, psychodynamic thinking, which simply means to get closer to the root of issues, the deeper machinery of human processes. The source material. The more primary levels. Which is what I have been doing all my life. I'm sixty-six years old and I really am deeply invested in this.

"Chris is coming from a much more worldly, more externalized vantage point. So between the two of us we encompass quite a wide range of thinking. It's a very extended perspective, and the reason we have done it for thirteen years so far is because it works so well.

It leads to some very good problem solving."

Do they delve into both personal and professional problems?

"Well, yes. We approach every aspect of his life from these two vantage points. Professional, personal, company. Whatever problems come up, we will both sort of brainstorm. And I think that's what therapy is going to be in the future. I think in the twenty-first century you are going to have psychiatrists not sitting in their offices dealing with immediate emotional problems from the vantage point of 'I'm the expert and you are just the patient.' I think there will be a kind of working together partnership. Different specialties."

═══

The love affair with Tricia Brock grew more intense, but there were frequent separations because of Chris's business travels. They talked a lot on the phone. Judy Trott, dean of students at the University of Mississippi, followed their romance as a friend. Tricia was her guest in Oxford, Mississippi, while on campus shooting *Rush,* and the dean stayed in New York in Tricia's apartment during previews of the documentary, which won awards on both coasts.

"Chris called her a lot, when she was in Oxford," Dean Trott recalls. "I was with them in New York. And saw her other places, such as in New Orleans at a jazz festival."

Tricia was travelling a lot, too. Mary Kay Place, the actress remembered for *The Big Chill* and *Mary Hartman, Mary Hartman,* saw her documentary and was impressed. They met and decided to collaborate on a feature film, *Daughters of America,* based on *Rush.*

Paramount Pictures bought their script for $250,000 but did not produce it. That sale, however, gave Tricia a break in making other Hollywood contacts. "But all the connections in the world won't help you if you're not talented," she says.

Chris brought Tricia Brock to Tennessee to meet his parents. "I was in Knoxville a bunch," she says. She also accompanied the family on an excursion to the snow slopes in Aspen. "That's one girl I was crazy about," says Dr. Whittle.

Tricia took Chris to meet her parents, Allan and Patty Brock, when they lived in McLean, Virginia. Her father was acting undersecretary of agriculture in the transition between the Carter and Reagan administrations. Later Chris also went with Tricia to Missouri to a family reunion for her grandmother's ninty-fifth birthday.

"Chris seemed to fit right in," says Patty Brock. "He was very gracious and talked to people. I thought he was a very intense young man and probably consumed with his work and ambition. All of these challenges lay out there for him, and his vision seemed just kind of tunnelled to all these things."

Tricia's mother was struck by Chris's low-key demeanor. "He took everything with that little shy smile of his. Chris is a very private person. I wish I did know what he thought about that family reunion, but I never found out. I think Tricia did have a lot of influence over Chris in a lot of ways. I'd hate to say what exactly, but I think she did. She opened him up quite a bit."

During their love affair both the Dakota and the Vermont renovations were in progress. "There was a period of time when Chris and I lived together in my apartment at 787 Madison Avenue because he sold his apartment on Park Avenue," Tricia says. "As a transition. Initially the Dakota was something we were going to do together, but it just didn't work out."

———

Like a juggler, Chris successfully managed to keep a lot of balls in the air at the same time. He contemplated his romantic future and tinkered with designs for his Vermont farmhouse and the Dakota apartment. He collaborated with Moffitt to a certain extent, but most of all he almost plunged into exhaustion whipping up the horses in Knoxville.

His chief objective was to think up and launch a wide array of new, one-advertiser, controlled-circulation publications. In their longing to publish a legitimate national magazine, Chris and Moffitt had earlier purchased rights to the name of a defunct publication, *Intellectual Digest,* to serve as a springboard. They converted it to *Successful Business,* but just then came the *Esquire* acquisition, and because of a shortage of manpower and capital *Successful Business* was in the way. After only seven issues *Successful Business* was sold to *Inc.* magazine.

But out of 13–30 brainstorming sessions emerged ideas for other publications. First came *Destinations,* an upscale travel magazine sponsored by BMW automobiles. *Moviegoer,* subsidized by R. J. Rey-

nolds, debuted as a monthly magazine distributed in theater lobbies. RJR also sponsored *Sports Page,* the wall media that was posted
in bars.

Three magazines called the *New Parent Series* were launched
under sponsorship of Johnson and Johnson. And 13–30 broke new
ground with *Pet Care Report,* a wall-media project for pet owners in
veterinarians' offices. In pockets alongside the poster were take-
home booklets, an innovation Chris and his cohorts categorized as
an "information center." At the same time 13–30 brought out a
companion magazine for veterinarians, *Veterinary Practice Management.*

One brainstormer raised the question: Why not wall media for
medical doctors? The staff devised a wall media called *Physician's
Weekly* to be posted in doctors' lounges in major hospitals. The
project was jump-started so quickly the 13–30 salesmen pitched
prospective advertisers with merely a prototype.

"We were walking in to sell a publication in a market we knew
nothing about," recalls Warren Guy, the executive in charge. "But
that never stopped us before. One of our consultants told us we had
a great idea, but we wouldn't sell more than two million dollars in
advertising the first year. We brought in five million."

More importantly, the poster for doctors would serve as the
beachhead for an astoundingly profitable invasion of the medical
field nationwide.

Not every trial balloon was able to stay aloft. Keith Bellows, one
of the principal 13–30 editors, had the habit of photocopying magazine articles to read on his frequent travels. Says Bellows, "I came
up with a wild-brained scheme. Chris was looking for some idea
that we could sell to Procter and Gamble. You know there are about
fifty magazines in supermarkets. What I suggested was taking ex-
cerpts from about sixteen of these, combining them into a sort of
Reader's Digest–type mega-magazine. We even had a name: *Quick.*
We did tons of research. Even devised mini-magazines on single
topics—cooking, health, sports, entertainment, decorating, and so
on. We pitched it at Procter and Gamble. The stumbling block was
it would cost between 160 million and 200 million dollars to
launch."

Among the hundreds of ideas floated informally were many that
were bizarre and ridiculous: putting ads above urinals in public toi-

lets; an 800 information line to Kroger stores; sending new home-owners "yellow pages" listing doctors; table tents in restaurants dis-playing a Hemingway chapter on one side and a beer or wine ad on the other; a "Zap TV" game for bars; an ATM card that would do customer surveys and let them win prizes; a computerized menu planner in grocery stores; during Desert Storm, a newspaper for G.I.'s including a scratch-off centerfold to outwit Saudi Arabian censors; video screens at Burger King drive-ins and over the counter inside showing Joel Siegel's movie reviews; a wall-media poster at self-service gas pumps.

Martha Hume, a senior editor, recalls: "We thought of a whole series of nine hundred numbers. On one, you know you have all those silly decisions in your life, like whether you should wear green or blue today. You call the nine hundred number and they say wear green. The call makes your decision for the day, and that's done. How would we work in the advertising? I guess we'd say, 'Hello, this is One–Nine Hundred Decision. Here's a good decision: Buy some Wheaties!' That's how most of these things work. They put you on hold, and then give you a little ad.

"Then we have One-Nine Hundred Arguments for family argu-ments, where someone can call in from home, and someone at our place will say, 'Mom's right!' You tell them what's wrong and they just settle your family argument. You never know. We have a lot of silly one-nine hundred services we thought up."

———

In the quaint Swiss Alpine village of Zermatt in the summer of 1981, Chris Whittle, now thirty-four, is up early to drink in the spectacle of daybreak. From his nineteenth-century inn's bedroom window he watches the cobalt blue fade from the night sky. Slowly the sun emerges, splashing the lesser crests with red and gold, and finally bursting across the Matterhorn.

The challenge of climbing the 14,782-foot mountain had in-trigued Chris since he first started coming to Zermatt in his twen-ties. The climb is dangerous and exhausting. In 1865, when an Englishman was the first to scale the mountain, a rope broke and four companions perished. Chris had strolled the little Zermatt cemetery counting graves of fallen climbers, finding at least a dozen.

His decision to make an attempt came about when he watched a Japanese woman undertake to scale the mountain's most difficult rocky face—by herself. In awe and admiration, Chris watched her reach the summit. Somehow her bravado affronted, and challenged, his daring and pride. He booked himself for a climb up the backside—the easier route. Roped to a guide, he would not be alone. His climb would require three days—one to reach the base camp, the second to ascend the final face and come back to base camp, and the third to return to Zermatt.

Of all the mountain resorts he had visited, Zermatt, on the Italian border, was Chris's favorite. Whenever possible he had gone there annually for two or three weeks in summer, to hike, ski, think, and recharge. The slopes at Zermatt offer fifty-seven ski runs, of all kinds.

"Zermatt has been a resort for over one hundred years," Chris says. "The thing I like about it is that—and this was particularly true twenty years ago—it has no autos in town. They have little electric carts now. Tourists arrive by train after parking their cars at a station five miles away. Basically it's a pedestrian town, which makes it really charming. Fifty feet out of town you are in an Alpine wonderland. And I know it well.

"I love to walk in the mountains. I hiked all around the Matterhorn. Over many years. I heard all the tales about the Matterhorn. The mountain is smashing. I think it's the most beautiful mountain in the world. It stands alone, very distinctive. Some people say it resembles a sphinx. One writer said it looks like a sea lion couchant, or like a monstrous hooded cobra."

Two years earlier the Himalayas had drawn Chris back to Nepal and Tibet, where he had hiked—and been robbed in 1971—on his around-the-world sojourn. On that second visit his main purpose was to walk from Katmandu to Mount Everest, at 29,141 feet the world's highest mountain.

"That hike took about a month," says Chris. " I went right up to the Everest base camp—actually up to almost twenty thousand feet, which is somewhat above the base camp. It was a memorable experience."

In the thin air, climbers, especially amateurs, are often severely stricken by altitude sickness that can cause eye hemorrhages and serious seizures. "I had one night of altitude sickness when I really was quite ill," Chris says. "And I went down three thousand or four thousand feet to kind of get myself feeling better, and then I went back up."

On the Matterhorn climb, Chris did not anticipate being bothered by the altitude. At less than fifteen thousand feet, it is smaller than a dozen other European mountains.

"There's one thing," he says, with a grim look. "I wouldn't want to be caught up there on the face at night. I went up what is called the easy ridge—and I didn't think it was easy."

But he made it. After struggling to the Matterhorn's summit, somehow Chris felt personally let down. Back at his inn on the Bahnhofstrasse, Zermatt's main street, he summed up his reaction to the climb: "It wasn't exactly exhilarating. It was exhausting!"

———

Hiking over his meadowland outside Waitsfield, Chris came to the conclusion that he needed more acreage to permit easier access from the country lane to the site of his future house. Close by was the old Edward Eurich farm of four hundred acres. Chris bought it for $900,000.

Between him and the Eurich land was another Joslin farm of six hundred acres. Chris wanted to buy that land also in order to consolidate his divided parcels. The owner was a sixty-year-old eccentric named Donald Joslyn. He snapped, "That's how they spelled my name in the first grade—no reason to change it now."

Unmarried, bearded, stubborn, and opinionated, Donald Joslyn raised eighty heifers along with pigs, chickens, and one hundred sheep; the latter sometimes strayed and blocked the dirt road. He scrawled on his mailbox: "Atilla The Hun." "The post office people," he says, "told me I had to have my name or number on the mailbox. I asked why. 'So we know where to deliver the mail.' I said, 'My family has been living in this house one hundred years, and you don't know where I live!' " Propped on the stone wall behind the mailbox is a piece of slate on which is carved "Misery Manor." He collected a splendid Civil War library, keeps an investment account to pay his taxes, and minds his own business.

Despite living next door, Chris made his first contact with Donald Joslyn by sending him a Federal Express letter.

"The Federal Express driver hiked clear up in the field where I was mowing," Joslyn says. "He said he had a letter for me from Chris Whittle. He wanted me to sign for it. I said, 'I ain't going to sign for the damn thing.'

" He said, 'I can't leave it then.' 'That's fine,' I said, 'I don't want to hear from him anyway.' Then he says, 'Can you give me a reason?' And got out a little tape recorder. So I told him, 'Yeah. I think it's bad news.' So the Federal Express fellow went off."

Joslyn says Chris later phoned him and said he wanted to walk their boundary line.

"He didn't give a damn about the boundary line. He just wanted to start pumping me. He came over and it was a wet morning. So we walked it, and on the upper mowing he said he wanted to protect the land and build a house up in the woods. He said he would buy my mowing for twenty-five thousand dollars, something like that.

"I said, 'Well, I cleared this upper mowing in the 1940s with a team of horses and been mowing it ever since. I think I'll just keep mowing it.' Then we came to the edge of my property, and I said to him, 'We got to stop here. See those signs. That land is posted. We can't cross here.'

"He said, 'Oh! Whose land is that?' 'Well,' I told him, 'I do believe it's yours.' "

In Joslyn's opinion a lot of people in the Mad River valley sold their land too cheap. "I hate to see land chopped up. They're putting up houses here and there, and posting every god-damned foot of it."

He tugs at his beard and gets back to talking about Chris Whittle.

"They tell me he didn't own anything anyway. It was all some bank down in Tennessee that owned it. He just had a line of credit with 'em. He was spending their money. I guess they must have trusted him. That's the only time I ever saw him to talk to him. I'll die on my farm. Selling land is like cutting off your fingers. What do you do then? If I'm going to starve, this is as good place as any to starve."

Whatever the source of the money, Chris was pouring a lot of it into his Vermont farmhouse. By the time the renovation was finished, it cost $400,000, including extensive landscaping.

Architect John Robinson of Waitsfield drew up plans in January 1981 to revamp the entire farmhouse. "Chris said, 'Oh, no. I'm going to build up on the hill. Just renovate about half of these rooms.' A year later he said, 'Well, you guys were right.' And we started over."

The landscaping change Chris wanted most was to create a quarter-acre pond to contain a man-made island with birch trees. "So he would have some place to swim to," Robinson says. To supervise new stone walls, drives, and plantings of lilacs, yews, ferns, periwinkle, and day lilies, Terrence Boyle of Burlington, a member of the American Society of Landscape Architects, was hired.

For guidance Chris gave Boyle photos of a pond in Colorado. "I remember it had mountains and blue sky reflected in the water," Boyle says. "In excavating to a depth of twelve feet, we had to take out several boulders. The cost jumped from an estimate of six thousand to about twenty-two thousand dollars. Chris was unhappy, and blamed us." Chris also disagreed on plantings. Says Robinson: "Chris just said, 'No, I don't want that. I want this.' And Chris being Chris, got his way." Boyle recalls that deer ate the yews and they had to be replaced by prickly Mugho pine. The overall result proved successful enough to get a big photo layout in the Autumn 1986 issue of the American Society of Landscape Architect's magazine, *Garden Design.*

On frequent weekends Chris arrived in Waitsfield to check on the work, now usually accompanied by Tricia Brock. "They were very close at that point," says Robinson, "and we thought that maybe she was going to be the one that ended up with him. My image of her was frankly *girlfriend*, uh, perhaps somebody who is becoming a significant other. She had ideas of what she would like in the house. Chris would ask her opinion and she would come back and say, 'No, I think X, Y, and Z.' I do remember that. We'd end up doing it Chris's way."

The real style arbiter was the New York interior designer who had done Chris's one-bedroom apartment in the Ritz Tower. "Liza Lerner," said Robinson, "as in Broadway's Lerner and Lowe. She was Mr. Lerner's daughter from one of his marriages. Marvelous person, really. Lotta fun. Because she was in New York, where Chris was, she kept shipping these objets d'art to Vermont, and we would try to build them into the house."

What was the most unusual?

"A fantastic copper bathtub, probably circa 1800s. It was large, held one hundred and twenty gallons of water. We had to reinforce the floor and put in a special water heater. Placed it so Chris could look out the window across the valley to the mountains. Finding brass fittings was a problem, but we did."

What else?

"She got some lovely rugs and sideboards. Mostly it was just furniture. Talked to her about curtains and colors and tiles for bathrooms. Worked with her. She found this fantastic wicker furniture for the porch. The porch wasn't wide enough. We had to tear it up and build it over."

Liza Lerner had met Chris at a dinner in 1979 while her future husband, Porter Bibb, a journalist and author, was working on magazine acquisitions for the *New York Times* when Jim Kobak was unsuccessfully trying to arrange a marriage between 13–30 and the *Times*.

"Porter said I should drop Chris a note, that he'd probably be moving to New York," says Liza Lerner. "I did and a year later he called me. Wanted me to look at his Ritz Tower place. We did that. He had never worked with a decorator before. He had definite ideas, which is good. It was a small apartment, but we opened it up with French doors between the living room and bedroom. He didn't need all that privacy.

"Then he asked me to do the place in Vermont. It was fun. He kept adding on to the farmhouse. We packed everything up three times—locked all the furniture in the living room—and kept starting over."

Chris paced his porch, fretting about the power lines running along the road. "They blocked his view of the mountains," Robinson said. "He had us take down two poles and bury the lines." He continued, "Had us build a garage and put in a hot tub with sliding doors so he could see out. In the ski country it is not unusual to run into people with a great deal of money who are willing to change their mind and pay for it. Chris certainly had a charming personality in changing his mind. It was always very hard to say no to him."

Robinson and Boyle were surprised when Chris asked them to cut something off their professional fees. They did—several hundred dollars. "Maybe he just wanted to prove he was becoming a frugal old Vermonter," Boyle says.

Architect Robinson, and partners Bruce Wade and Robert Blair, observed Tricia Brock coming to the Vermont retreat through what they called Phase Two.

"Just about the time we were going into Phase Three, which was to start designing the new house, she just seemed to disappear," Robinson says. "That would be sometime in the fall of 1983."

After three years she had been eliminated from the "Christopher Whittle Matrimonial Sweepstakes." The Chris Whittle–Tricia Brock romance was dead.

———

A decade later, Tricia is a respected professional working on television and movie scripts in Los Angeles. Her love affair with Chris is ancient history. "It was just the timing," she says, explaining the end of the romance. "Chris was looking for a certain type of woman. We are still friends. I think it was a true parting of the ways. It wasn't easy. We spent about three years together, and I just think it was time.

"I don't know what to say. Whenever you break up with anyone it's always with a certain amount of difficulty and regret. But the best I can say about it is we are still friends. So no matter how difficult it might have been at the time, it was obviously something that both of us knew was the right thing to do. And that's why we are able to still be friends."

About a year after moving to the West Coast, Tricia married Marc Abraham, an independent film producer. Their daughter, Cleo, was born in 1985. Later they were divorced.

In early 1993 Tricia Brock described herself as "a happy craftsman" who was proud of having written two scripts with Harley Peyton, another writer and producer, for the bizarre *Twin Peaks* television series. They also collaborated on a book adaption for a Disney movie. In May 1992 she and Peyton were married. Peyton was creator and executive producer of *Moon Over Miami,* a weekly television series that ran on ABC from September through December 1993.

"Now," says Tricia Brock, "I am adapting *Due East,* and have optioned another book, *Killer Diller,* which I am writing on spec."

———

Gradually the critical elements at *Esquire* fell into place. Moffitt and Greenberg could see light at the end of a long, dark tunnel. Not so in Knoxville. The stress from the absence of a functioning management proved frightening. Mike Collins got fed up with neglecting his wife and children by splitting his time between New York and Tennessee. He resigned. Chris and Moffitt talked him into coming back, naming him general manager of 13–30 under a three-year contract. That deal, too, was destined to fail.

Ivan Samuels, a financial executive who had managed a growth company in the contact lens industry, was brought in as 13–30's chief operating officer. That move became another disaster.

"One of Samuels's first moves," says Frank Finn, "was to put the company on the management-by-objective [MBO] system. In theory, each employee would write a list of goals for his or her position. A manager would ascertain they were consistent with company aims. Annually Samuels rated each employee on goal attainment. Employees hated it. It was creeping bureaucracy."

For a free-wheeling band of young people who had been unfettered since the gruelling late-nighters at the pillow factory, this "unfair and demeaning" intrusion on the laissez-faire climate would not long be tolerated.

As complaints about Samuels escalated to a near revolt, Chris and Moffitt sent an S.O.S. to Nick Glover, who had just become a freelance management consultant. They knew Glover well and viewed him favorably. As U.S. head of consumer marketing at R. J. Reynolds, with one of America's biggest advertising budgets, he had spent millions on their magazines and wall-media ideas. Glover, a 1965 graduate of the U.S. Naval Academy, joined RJR in 1970 and rose to vice-president of international marketing before quitting in 1982 as the result of burnout.

"Chris called me," says Glover, "and said that 13–30 had reached a watershed, he wasn't sure what was needed to grow the company. 'We're still running this like a college project. We've got to make it a real company, with a real organizational structure. That's not something we know anything about. Can you come spend some time and help us?' I agreed to spend three months analyzing the company and mapping a plan for the future."

It was a shock to Glover, who had become an entrepreneurial expert in working with RJR subsidiaries all over the world, to see 13–30 doing many things right "just by instinct." It was a fun place to work. "There were less than a hundred people," says Glover. "It was a very casually interactive sort of place. I picked up on what was making it work, and put in some of my own pieces, and really tried to institutionalize that attitude."

The COO, Ivan Samuels, says Glover, was smart and competent, but too much a technocrat. "What's been bizarre to me is that Chris and Phillip would hire somebody like that. This was not a technical company, certainly not in those days. It sure as hell wasn't bureaucratic. The poor guy had no chance to succeed. He did the best he could. He was just completely in the wrong place."

Glover essentially psychoanalyzed the business, conducting interviews with every manager, listening to their complaints about swoop management and the growing bureaucracy under Samuels.

Then, in mid-1982, after listening to managers rave about Glover, Whittle and Moffitt announced that Glover would join the company as CEO and that Samuels was out. From that day on, swoop management evaporated. Chris now was free to skitter all across the country on business. Glover, at his desk in Knoxville, became known as "Mr. Inside" while Chris was "Mr. Outside." It was a combination that worked perfectly.

The growth rate of 13–30, measured in revenue, was now climbing around 30 percent a year. The corporate outlook was bright—but not so for the Gold Dust Twins. In the early days Chris Whittle and Phillip Moffitt flirted with disaster by racing each other in their Porsches from Knoxville to Atlanta. Now they were heading toward an inevitable personal collision.

ESQUIRE'S GOLDEN TURNAROUND

In a Manhattan art gallery, Chris Whittle, in the throes of his newest passion, stood in rapt admiration before Richard E. Miller's *The White Shawl*. He wanted the large and magnificent painting for prominent display in his Dakota apartment. It could be expensive; Millers commanded as much as $420,000.

At the moment there was no wall on which to hang the painting. Workmen were still gutting his six rooms on the Dakota's seventh floor. Wheelbarrows of splintered wood, busted plaster, and bricks were trundled by the hundreds down the freight elevator. Chris's inspiration was to fix up the apartment as it could have looked in 1884 to its first tenant.

Thus he and architect and designer Peter Marino were avidly collecting important nineteenth-century art to make the renovation scintillate. For two years Chris would pore over catalogs, bid at auctions and estate sales, and even scour basement antique shops, especially abroad.

Chris debated whether to buy *The White Shawl*. In 1904 Miller had painted a handsome woman draped, of course, in a white shawl. It was large—forty-eight by seventy-nine inches. Whittle and Marino decided it would be appropriate for a certain prominent wall. Chris bought it.

Financially, this was a Chris Whittle light years removed from the oil-field laborer in Morgan City, Louisiana, the political novice tooling a broken-down VW over Connecticut back roads, and certainly from the backpacker exploring the world on the cheap. "Chris spends money with both hands," said an *Esquire* colleague. That was obvious to those knowledgable about his forays into lavish living. But not too many people were aware of his wild spending, because he did not boast about his acquisitions, or announce them. Nor does Chris volunteer much information about his private life, and certainly not about his personal finances.

His art collection grew enormously—dozens of paintings and objets d'art. Chris bought many portraits of museum quality—by John Singer Sargent, William Merritt Chase, Gustave Dore, and others. Scouting for these treasures brought Chris great pleasure, but rebuilding his six rooms from scratch turned into a hellish nightmare. Every room was reshuffled. "My new twenty-by-thirty-four-foot living room was the dining room when the kitchen, which used to be the master bedroom, was where we put the study," Chris says. "Not an inch of the old flat—ceilings, walls, moldings, floors—was kept," adds Marino.

Disaster struck when Chris insisted on relocating fireplaces in the dining room and living room. Workmen accidentally smashed pipes in the wall, flooding several apartments directly under his own. At all hours his Dakota neighbors grabbed their phones to curse him. In one lower apartment a painting was damaged; Chris had to pay to have it restored at the Metropolitan Museum.

Fortunately, at this juncture, Chris had free time in Manhattan. He seldom showed up at *Esquire,* having abandoned the challenge to reinvigorate the magazine's circulation and advertising, opting instead to escalate needed revenue from 13–30 activities. Though Chris surrendered the position of publisher to Alan Greenberg, he clung to the token title of chairman. However, he still contributed importantly to the magazine. For one thing, he was a creative sounding board for both Moffitt and Greenberg. He also applied his vaunted energy and imagination to the 13–30 Corporation—it grew fatter and richer. Thus the Knoxville operation remained a healthy cash cow paying off *Esquire*'s losses, which for the year 1983 still ran about $3 million.

Even on European jaunts, Chris made art finds. In a basement shop he was intrigued by twelve French decorative paintings of Roman emperors. "I recognize Julius Caesar," Chris told the shopkeeper. "And I think that one's Nero—looks like him."

"You must know these belonged to Christian Dior," said the shopkeeper, smugly.

Chris was thinking they would look good in his Dakota dining room. "I like a lot of faces in a dining room," he observed. "It's like more guests for dinner." He wrote a check. His "guests—" in addition to Nero and Julius Caesar—would be Octavianus, Claudius, Tiberius, Titus, Vespasian, Vitellius, Caligula, Galba, Otho, and Domitian.

The object of both designer and owner was a dark, strictly masculine atmosphere. Major rooms, as in the 1800s, were to have strong colors. Oxblood in the dining room, gold in the living room, terra-cotta in the study. In the central windowless main hall, Marino hung Richard Miller's *The White Shawl.* The full-length portrait depicted a woman in a white shawl looking into a mirror set above a commode. Marino created an effect by hanging an oval Regency mirror exactly like the one in the painting perpendicular to it, giving the suggestion that it had been the artist's model.

"Look, the apartment was a dark hole," says Marino. "But it's Christopher Whittle's idea of merry—he's a very serious guy. So I wanted candlelight everywhere, fires in all the fireplaces, ormolu shimmering on the furniture."

The result was a tremendous candlestick collection: Russian, French Empire, Georgian cut crystal, American bronze, seventeenth-century English twirled wood, nineteenth-century English feldspar and jasper. Along with an American architect Frank Furness mantle salvaged from a Philadelphia mansion being razed, topped by a 1645 still life by Paulus van den Bosch, the dining room had griffins on the fire screen and Directoire carpet under a large Flemish chandelier.

Chris kept having to dig deep. Sargents cost $60,000 to over $1 million and important William Merritt Chase's paintings fetch $75,000 or more. Chris does not discuss the prices of his paintings, but art experts estimate his collection was worth $10 million. Was he concerned about security? "No," he says. "I don't want to start worrying and fretting over them. I want to keep it fun."

His most famous acquisition is a double portrait by Sargent. Chris jested if he fell on hard times he could cut the picture in half and sell both pieces.

Among his earliest favorite artists is Chase. From a gallery in

Cincinnati he purchased Chase's portrait of the man who founded the Nabisco company. He found it in a catalog. "I called immediately," Chris recalls. "This is a great find in art because a large one of his works is difficult to come by." Chris missed his second Chase, a portrait of a woman, at an auction and later decided he had to have it. So three years later he bought it from a gallery. "I learned a valuable lesson. The auction price is usually half the gallery price. Although I don't buy art for investment, I found out about investing in art. It's a lot like the stock market. Five years after I bought one particular work I was offered five times what I paid for it."

Colleagues always have characterized Christopher Whittle as an extremely patient man. Awaiting completion of his new quarters at the Dakota, he needed every ounce he could muster. He was demanding absolute perfection—in every detail. Month after month the work continued. To Chris it seemed there was no end in sight.

═══

"This year is *Esquire*'s fiftieth anniversary. What can we do to celebrate? How can we turn it into a marketing splash?"

Expectantly, hopefully, Phillip Moffitt addressed the three men he had gathered for a brainstorming session in his Knoxville cabin in early 1983. With him at Log Haven were Chris, Alan Greenberg, the magazine's business manager, and Lee Eisenberg, the managing editor.

Earnestly, and sometimes loudly, they talked most of the night. Moffitt proposed publishing a special anniversary issue. Chris liked the idea and talked about mailing 500,000 or 1 million complimentary copies. Eisenberg drew up a concept not for one but two anniversary issues—and ticked off a list of possible themes. "We liked his ideas," says Alan Greenberg, "and decided to do them both. They made magazine history!"

Esquire was geared to do something spectacular. Moffitt had fixed editorial. Greenberg had increased business by discharging half the old ad staff and recruiting Bill Longley, Mike Trainor, and Julie Lewit (later publisher of *Mademoiselle* magazine), from the 13–30 ranks to head a sales team of twelve. "It was phenomenal," Greenberg. "They were young, hungry, motivated, and on a mission—they thought *Esquire* was the greatest magazine in the world."

Ad pages jumped from 535 in 1981 to 779 in 1982, the latter figure representing about $13 million in revenue. "Phil, to his credit, worked very hard with me to make some editorial changes that really were important," Greenberg adds. "Together we created a whole series of magazines-within-a-magazine, quarterlies dealing with music, travel, entertainment. That gave my people the opportunity to go out and contact the advertisers in those fields." For example, *Esquire* ran a sixty-eight-page section on bars and drink recipes that included twenty-three pages of full-color liquor advertisements.

To market the two fiftieth anniversary ideas hatched at Log Haven, Eisenberg created a compelling video presentation. With Chris, Moffitt, and Eisenberg also appearing, Greenberg staged this dog-and-pony act about fifteen times in New York, Detroit, Chicago, Los Angeles, San Francisco, and Atlanta. It worked so well that *Esquire*'s advertising revenue for 1983 would rise to a record $24 million on 1,255 pages.

Those ideas were dubbed "print events"—two special issues of *Esquire*. The first fiftieth anniversary issue, "How We Lived," in June, was a fat four-hundred-page compendium of some of the magazine's best writing over the past half-century. The cover trumpeted the edition as an "extraordinary chronicle of American life."

Many media critics seemed to agree; the *Charlotte Observer* declared:

> Without exception, these are wonderful pieces . . . chosen not only for the star status of their writers but because they characterized a particular time and place. There is John Steinbeck writing on the Depression, Ralph Ellison on jazz, Gay Talese on George Plimpton and the Paris Review, Joan Didion on shopping malls. . . .
>
> Whittle and Moffitt have tinkered with *Esquire* and transformed it into a magazine for the success-minded man of the eighties. But the June issue—beautifully designed and skillfully edited—shows they also understand the *Esquire* legacy with which they are entrusted.

The December golden anniversary issue featured profiles of a group of distinguished Americans hailed on the cover as "Fifty

Who Made The Difference." Selected from six hundred nominees, the fifty included both well-known and obscure people, ranging from five former presidents to Elvis Presley and a student Vietnam protestor at Columbia University.

The gargantuan special edition—616 pages, of which 291 were advertising—came out November 7, 1983, the same day *Esquire* threw itself a travelling fiftieth birthday party in New York City. The festivities started with breakfast at Gracie Mansion, the mayor's residence, to announce the fifty honorees, twenty of them living.

All were invited to dinner at Four Seasons restaurant. Those who came included boxer Muhammad Ali, feminist Betty Friedan, broadcaster William S. Paley, architect Philip Johnson, birth-control pill developer Dr. John Rock, pollster George Gallup, polio vaccine pioneer Dr. Jonas Salk, and activist Ralph Nader.

A black-tie gala for two thousand guests at Lincoln Center, where Gay Talese and actress Blair Brown narrated a film about "the fifty" and Sarah Vaughan paid tribute to the last half-century in song, capped the evening.

This time the troops down in Knoxville were not neglected. The 13–30 managers and their spouses were flown up and billeted at the Grand Hyatt. "It was like a high school trip," recalls Mary Eben-shade, who was 13–30 marketing director. "They had us take a bus from the hotel to Lincoln Center. And we were not about to look like a bunch of hayseeds from Tennessee getting off a bus in front of Lincoln Center. So we made the driver park a block or two away, and we walked. Nearly froze, too."

Hearing this comment a decade later, Cindy Still, who as *Esquire* marketing veep coordinated the day's events, was amused. "I don't know why they worried so. I took the honorees from Four Seasons to the gala by bus!" Even using buses instead of limousines, the promotion cost *Esquire* about $500,000.

Other Tennessee friends were present, including Ruthie Ed-mondson Leyen, who as Senator Howard Baker's field representative had recruited Chris and David White as tyro pols during their University of Tennessee days. She encountered White, looking "el-egant" in a gray tux with gray tie and cummerbund, in contrast to the sea of black tuxedos.

"David, why gray?" she asked.

"Can't you guess?"

Her face lit up. "Confederate gray!"

White nodded. "It just seemed like somebody from Tennessee ought to come in gray."

Profile writers at the gala included Kurt Vonnegut Jr., Norman Mailer, Wilfred Sheed, Marilyn French, Tom Wolfe, Frances Fitz-Gerald, William F. Buckley Jr., Ken Kesey, and Richard Ford.

One much talked-about oddity in the list was lumping Ernest Hemingway, William Faulkner, and F. Scott Fitzgerald together as one winner. Ford, who wrote the joint profile, did not consider the three authors demeaned. "I think Faulkner is the greatest writer of the twentieth century," he told the *New York Times,* "but that doesn't reflect the least on Fitzgerald or Hemingway. I don't think they would have minded, because writing is not a competitive business." Lee Eisenberg concurred, saying, "We tried to be provocative, but not perverse."

The golden anniversary issue, priced at $4 instead of the regular $2.50, sold 950,000 copies. The June issue, at $3, also had sold 950,000, and seemed to please most media critics.

Time magazine complained that the whole was less impressive than its parts because the depth and focus varied erratically in the profiles, and some writers marred their pieces by injecting themselves.

"But," said *Time*, "there are some splendid, mildly off-beat entries: Wilfrid Sheed's portrayal of the on-the-field politeness and off-the-field anger of baseball's Jackie Robinson; Ronald Steel's evocation of Cold Warrior Dean Acheson; Alistair Cooke's precise homage to Jazz Composer Duke Ellington. 'The common theme,' says Moffitt, 'is the power of the individual, our wanting it not to be true that institutions are everything.'

"The issue's merits—earnestness, attention to social trends, appreciation of what makes a star in any line of endeavor—are also the strengths of this incarnation of *Esquire*. It may not enjoy the cachet and influence it once did, but this institution has survived."

Newsweek magazine gave Whittle and Moffitt pats on the back, and several shin kicks. "They've finally pulled *Esquire* out of a dangerous midlife crisis—for the first time since 1970, the magazine is turning a small profit. . . . Certainly the anniversary issue contains more interesting articles than a single issue of any magazine in recent memory."

It was both an accomplishment and a hazard, said *Newsweek*, for the Tennesseeans to perceive the aging of readers and subsequent decline in demand for erotic material, and to replace that kind of subject matter with "life-style" stories on health and consumer goods. "Next summer *Esquire* is planning an annual fiction issue. Commissioning names like Talese and Capote is not enough, however. If *Esquire* insists on serving 'contemporary male' life-style at the expense of literary quality, it may never reclaim its journalistic franchise."

Looking back ten years later, Lee Eisenberg concedes that *Esquire* perhaps "overdosed on a special every month," but most were "extraordinary issues" and involved "immense trouble" in bringing together the resources of journalism and the literary world.

Chris played a behind-the-scenes role. "I didn't see Chris a lot," says Eisenberg. "Chris was very friendly and very cordial. He was not active very much at *Esquire*, at least to the naked eye. I think he was probably extremely active holed up with Phillip making strategy.

"I began to understand how truly interesting and effective they were as a team. Wonderfully complementary. They could be disciplined *and* reckless. Reflective *and* spontaneous. They were different in style and substance, and they were combustible."

To brainstorm a sequel to their anniversary-issue successes, Moffitt took two of the magazine's top editors, Betsy Carter and Eisenberg, to a weekend retreat at Chris's Vermont farm. Eisenberg recalls:

> We were walking down a dirt road when Phillip broached the idea for *The Esquire Register*. So startled was I by the earnestness of it that I nearly impaled myself on a cattle fence. Phillip explained that he had in mind a national talent search to find men and women under forty who were making some dramatic difference in their various professional fields—from doctors to poets to geophysicists.
>
> It got very complicated. This search would begin with a lot of regional newspaper supplements in which we would find, for instance, a "Register of the Southeast." We wound up scrapping that part. Then there'd be national winners who would be chosen and profiled in *Esquire*.

Eventually we set up an elaborate search and screening process in New York. There were bureau chiefs set up around the country headed by a remarkable researcher named Burr Leonard. We advertised for nominees in papers around the country, sent out direct-mail solicitations, had an impressive blue-ribbon advisory panel. We soon had a data base of some ten thousand candidates, of whom a couple hundred were honored in the first *Register,* which ran in December of 1984. I've been meaning to go back and look, but I remember that the first issue contained a good many of those who are now holding down important jobs in Washington. Bill and Hillary Clinton were there, Ira Magaziner, and many others.

The *Register* was the kind of big idea we made happen with great regularity back then. In fact, we probably wore the concept of print events out. Still, these issues were key to our turning the magazine around.

———

From about 1984, on the subtle rift between Chris and Moffitt began to perceptibly widen. Moffitt largely stayed in New York City; Chris was all over the place. Now that *Esquire* was making instead of losing money, Moffitt relaxed his hands-on editorship to a degree. The day-to-day decisions were basically relinquished to Lee Eisenberg and Betsy Carter.

Chris, too, had strong daily back-up in Knoxville from his "Mr. Inside," who held down expenses and boosted morale in the rapidly growing 13–30 staff. These brash junior geniuses were encouraged to freely play in their "creative sandbox" and come up with fresh ideas that bolstered the ever-larger flow of cash.

———

With Marino, Chris tramped through dust and ducked under carpenters' and masons' scaffolds to inspect the Dakota renovation. Searching for more suitable art, he discovered a magnificent 1870 rosewood grand piano and a large bronze of Nathan Hale by sculptor Frederick MacMonnies. He bought them both for his living room.

He visited the Vermont farm on free weekends, tinkering with design ideas for his mansion on the wooded higher elevation. With Liza Lerner he prowled some of the New England antique shops, picking up interesting pieces of furniture.

Once more Chris was a freewheeling bachelor. Tricia Brock had gone west to the Hollywood film colony, where she had a number of influential actress friends—and high hopes of launching her own career as screenwriter. Chris got word that Tricia had married a Los Angeles film agent or producer.

Still looking for a wife at thirty-seven, he squired a number of different New York women. In 1984 he chartered a one-hundred-foot crewed sailboat in the Virgin Islands for a month and invited guests in relays to cruise with him. His parents were aboard when Chris's then current girlfriend from New York joined them at Virgin Gorda. Dr. Whittle, who is refreshingly blunt and candid, made a face when asked his opinion of the woman. It was clear the new girl was no Tricia Brock.

In New York, colleagues clearly saw the partnership becoming too tattered to stay intact. "There's a real story there that nobody knows," says Betsy Carter. "The split is so complicated I think you'd need a psychiatrist to explain it."

Bill Longley, who worked with them both at *Esquire* and 13–30 Corporation for several years, made a blunt observation: "In my opinion, Chris's lifestyle essentially didn't jibe with Phillip's. I think he had been carrying Phillip for a long time, to some degree. And I think he didn't want to keep splitting all the dough."

From his vantage point in the *Esquire* counting room, Daniel O'Shea saw the two clashing over business expense, status, and notoriety.

Says O'Shea: "I think this goes back to Phillip being the center, the guy who was in control of the company. When it came to budget time he would say, 'Now, Chris, you can't do that. Let's try to make this cheap; let's not hire those people until we get the contract.' On the other side, Phillip had talents, but he was never a salesman."

Chris wanted each to have his own car and driver, Moffitt was opposed. Says O'Shea: "Phillip would go, 'No, I don't need a driver. I can just raise my hand and get a Yellow Cab.' There were a lot of little tensions building up. Chris kind of wanted to be his own guy. He wanted a lot of P.R. for himself and the company, and Phillip not wanting that. Phillip saying, 'We have a very nice business. We are growing at a good clip. We have a great profit margin. Why ruin a good thing? Why put that under scrutiny by other people?' And sure enough when the split happened it brought a media wave. There were a lot of stories about Chris, about how far the company was going to grow, and there has been a public relations oversell."

In 1985, after working together sixteen years, Christopher Whittle and Phillip Moffitt began talking about buying each other out. Moffitt wanted to get control of *Esquire,* which had $40 million annual revenue and 150 employees. That was all right with Chris; he was more interested in 13–30, with six hundred employees and annual revenue of $75 million.

How to sort out their individual financial stakes? Who owned how much of what? They tossed out figures. The talk turned bitter. At loggerheads, they called in an arbitrator: David White, a man both trusted. Even so, terms were haggled over for months. At one point Chris threw up his hands, threatening to retire altogether. It was not until April 4, 1986, that they announced the breakup.

In simple terms, Chris kept the 13–30 Corporation, buying out Moffitt and other investors for $30 million in cash and notes. Moffitt kept Esquire Magazine Group Inc., paying $10 million for Whittle's shares—which made Chris's net cost for 13–30 $20 million.

Lord Rothermere's Associated Newspapers Holdings substantially retained their same minority interests in the two companies. Chris and Moffitt each held on to some stock in the other's new property, and it was agreed Whittle would be listed as *Esquire* chairman until 1988.

The separation of the old college buddies was also the death knell for "The 13–30 Corporation." That name was out, as of July 1st, when the sales agreements took effect.

Henceforth Chris's Knoxville company was to known as Whittle Communications L.P. Since his enterprises had outgrown the category of merely student and youth-oriented magazines, the new name was more appropriate for a growing, broad-scale media enterprise.

The principals made only halfhearted stabs at explaining their breakup. A *Knoxville Journal* reporter tracked Whittle down by phone at the Atlanta airport and told him that Moffitt attributed the split to "*Esquire* needing Moffitt's creative voice at the same time 13–30 began to rely on Whittle's marketing experience."

"Is that what Phillip said?" Whittle sounded slightly incredulous. "I think Phillip is a very good businessman as well as a very good editor. And I think we both are reasonably well rounded publishers. I think the talents are roughly equivalent."

The *Knoxville Journal* quoted Whittle as saying "the division occurred simply because the time had come for the two interests to go separate ways" if they were to grow faster.

Discussing the breakup after the fact, Tricia Brock found it sad. She said Chris was not good at confrontation. "Rather than splitting," she says, "Chris a few years ago should have said, 'Listen, you asshole. . . . ' But instead he just withdrew and did it through lawyers. Phillip hurt him so badly because at the same time Chris wants nothing more than Phillip's approval. This could be one of the great unresolved emotional issues in Chris's life, although when we talk about it, he seems better about it than he has been before, liberated by it."

The ex-girlfriend said Moffitt, whom she knew well, continued to talk "with a lot of affection" about his former partner. "But if Chris is going to play hardball," she said, "Phillip is going to give him a run for his money. They're fighting old wars now."

═══

Just after Labor Day 1986, the secretary in Knoxville Mayor Kyle Testerman's office answered the phone and told him it was a call from Switzerland. Who could be calling from Europe? Then the mayor remembered Chris Whittle had again gone to the Swiss Alps to recharge his batteries.

"Hello, Kyle. Nick Glover is over here with me. We've been talking about the deal."

"That's good, Chris. Nobody knows any more about our proposition than Nick. I'm glad he's with you."

"Well," said Chris, "I thought we ought to tell you we've had some final thoughts. . . ."

Mayor Testerman caught his breath and waited for an answer. Back in January he and business leaders got a jolt when Nick Glover, Chris's "Mr. Inside," disclosed the company had considered leaving Knoxville. Cramped in the Arnstein building, the growing staff needed much more office space, perhaps its own building.

The company might go to New York, where recruiting top-flight talent would be easier. Even Atlanta or another Southern city such as Charlotte, North Carolina had advantages. They were airline hubs, offering faster travel. Other cities were also being looked at.

Knoxville didn't want to lose a company that annually grossed $75 million and which anticipated its revenue to grow to $500 million in seven years. Tennessee Governor Lamar Alexander, as personal friend and politician, appealed to Chris to stay. To the *Knoxville Journal* Chris said, "It was a private meeting. He's been very helpful and has given us some very good advice, all of which we are taking to heart."

Mayor Testerman had taken Nick Glover in tow. For weeks he led Glover around to potential sites for Whittle headquarters. They looked over land used for the 1982 World's Fair as well as bankrupt financier C. H. Butcher Jr.'s empty Riverview Towers downtown. Chris favored leasing Riverview Towers. Terms were worked out locally, but the Federal Deposit Insurance Corporation in Washington would not approve.

Finally, on April 24, 1986, the *Knoxville News-Sentinel*'s page-one banner read: "13–30 to Stay in Knox Area." Governor Alexander joined Chris at the Chamber of Commerce to formally announce the decision. However, left hanging were two questions: what building and where?

The mayor suggested demolishing the old U.S. pavilion at the site of the World's Fair, replacing it with a Whittle building. An architect drew plans. That scheme didn't quite suit Chris, but he felt a downtown location made sense. "Many of our employees live in nearby neighborhoods and walk or ride bicycles to work," he said. Upgrading aging business district buildings appealed to him. He really wanted to remain in his old college town.

Testerman and Glover undertook a shoe-leather search. "Kyle and I must have walked every square foot and every back alley and byway in a twenty-block area of downtown," Glover told reporters. They tramped through vacant lots on the suburban fringe, but were not impressed. The mayor finally zeroed in on an area bounded by Gay Street, Main Avenue, Walnut Street, and Cumberland Avenue, in the heart of the business district. The two-block site fronted the old county courthouse and was near the post office, Riverview Towers, and the old Andrew Johnson Hotel. "I gave them the idea," Testerman said later, "and they ran with it."

Then came the phone call from Switzerland.

"We're going to do it," Chris said. "We'll build on Main Avenue."

Over the transatlantic phone, Testerman heard Whittle laugh merrily. "You'll be surprised, Kyle, what we've come up with."

The mayor was surprised, and so was most of Knoxville when Chris and his colleagues carried big poster boards into the city council chambers three weeks later to exhibit their design. It was unexpected, and unique. Into the heart of the city, Chris Whittle intended to plunk down the replica of an Ivy League college complete with bell tower and center quad.

The main campus would be a quadrangle of four-and-one-half-story brick office buildings encircling two square blocks, with the open center area maintained as a public park. It was strictly an early American, Ivy League design, with the bell tower rising from a spectacular archway that straddled Market Street, which would be converted into a pedestrian walkway. "There is nothing like this outside of London, England," Mike Collins told the *News-Sentinel*.

Peter Marino had turned out these preliminary, flashy sketches for Chris in a rush. The New York architect was anxious, of course, to get the commission to actually design the complex.

The deal would require the city of Knoxville to buy up $30 million in property in the two blocks, and the city would then sell it back to Whittle at the same price. Whittle would then spend an additional $30 million to $40 million building the 300,000-square-foot quadrangle complex. The mayor mapped a second phase that would expand the redevelopment scope to reach $100 million.

Knoxville, the newspapers said, was agog over the project. However, little enthusiasm was forthcoming from the owners of buildings or lots that would have to go to make room for what soon would be dubbed "Historic Whittlesburg."

Complaints came from the First Baptist Church, the Trailways bus station, a small restaurant, a bookstore, the Appalachian National Life Insurance company, and two leading law firms, both of which had just completed costly remodeling.

One of the lawyers told reporters, "We'll start World War III before giving up our location just half a block from the courthouse!"

It was clear Chris had a fight on his hands if he wanted to go ahead with Historic Whittlesburg.

Knoxville News-Sentinel editor Harry Moskos applauded the project as "good news" and "the most exciting" downtown development in years. The newspaper's editorial took Chris's side against property owners being replaced.

> Obtaining property by the redevelopment process is not new. It has been used in six center city redevelopment projects which Knoxville has undertaken since 1974.
>
> Sometimes it is sad when old, established businesses are uprooted to make way for redevelopment. But, alas, that is a price a city often must pay for progress.

In New York, work drew to a close on the apartment in the Dakota. Chris, curious enough to dig into the history of the Dakota, had been surprised to learn that the architect, Henry Janeway Hardenbergh, was only thirty-four when construction was started in 1881. Financed by Singer Sewing machine magnate Edward Clark, the nine-story building cost $2 million. Nine hydraulic elevators were installed to serve the Dakota's marble-floored, mahogany-paneled apartments with their fifteen-foot ceilings. Chris learned that Hardenbergh became well known for excellence, having designed other monuments such as the Plaza and the old Waldorf Astoria hotels in New York, as well as the Copley Plaza in Boston and the Willard in Washington.

"I believe Henry Hardenbergh would be proud of the changes we have made," Chris told Peter Marino.

In all six rooms artisans, brought over from Europe, made brilliant finishing touches that were elaborate, detailed, expensive, and impressive. For instance, in the dining room thousands of hand-stenciled twenty-two-carat gold-leaf triangles were applied to the ceiling. The borders were individualized, one adapted from a Navaho blanket and the other lifted from an 1800 house painter's design book.

Ironically, the room hid late twentieth-century practicality. Lifting off the French mahogany table's silk-damask cloth, and opening hidden panels to reveal storage cabinets, pads, pencils, and phone, Chris had, at once, a modern conference room.

Marino used a painting to create the illusion of a stairway at the end of the hall to the master bedroom. There he hung a large Chabannes La Palice pastel of 1903, *Portrait of a Young Man,* in which a world-weary French aristocrat in Edwardian attire is sitting at the top of stairs leading to a library. Marino observed, "You feel you can just walk right up the stairs in the picture, that somebody's actually sitting there."

Over Chris's Northern Italian walnut bed, circa 1800, hung a study for a large painting of a Paris church interior and choir by Henry Lerolle. The drapes were thick green wool, which in summer could be flipped over to expose green-and-white cotton lining. Persian pots from the Safavid dynasty served as lamps on both sides of the bed, their mountings glistening with gold filigree and semiprecious blue and red stones.

Chairs in the apartment came from different periods: Charles X and George III, French Empire, including a slipper chair in its original 1865 fabric. Chris also assembled a major pottery collection. His maid innocently took a prized Dirk Van Erp bowl and filled it with detergent in the laundry room. Luckily it was rescued.

The gallery and the living room were separated by twelve-foot-high curtains that were woven with gold thread in Glasgow in the late nineteenth century and had hung in Wardour Castle in Wiltshire. Rich Oriental carpets were everywhere. A deep blue Sultanabad with floating flowers lay in the living room. Four were atop each other in the study-guest room, with two Senneh kilim carpets hung at one end to create an alcove.

The work was finished. Chris moved into the apartment in time to see the renovation featured in the November 1986 *House and Garden* magazine. The ten-page layout was written by Steven M. L. Aronson and photographed by Oberto Gili.

Aronson concluded his story:

> All of this brilliance—every moment of work, every inch of detail, every scintilla of atmosphere—was brought to full effect one recent evening when Marino and Whittle collected a small group of friends to sup in celebration of the apartment's completion.
>
> We ate golden beluga caviar, roast quail, and charlotte russe off imperial Russian porcelain, each plate glittering with its own royal palace in St. Petersburg. Afterward, we gathered round the 1870 massive rosewood piano in the

living room as the Metropolitan Opera baritone Dale Dues-
ing sang Charles Griffes's "Evening Song" and Edvard
Grieg's "Ein Traum"—songs in fashion at the time the Dakota was built.

For a moment the time clock had stopped. Suspended in
the dazzling anachronism Marino had created, where not a
thing was out of resonance, I knew that when I left there to
hail a cab I would be half expecting a carriage and driver.

———

Just as that *HG* issue went to press, the *Esquire* magazine saga
took a dramatic, unexpected turn. Phillip Moffitt, now the controlling owner, was in Florida attending a directors meeting of the Magazine Publishers Association.

"I was sitting there with these guys," he recalled in an interview,
"and suddenly I heard myself saying, 'My God! You are going to be
here when you are sixty-five! You will have done only one thing in
your life!' "

Moffitt had never intended to be a businessman his entire life,
nor, for that matter, an editor. He had been fretting about a change
since 1982. Basically, he wanted to write and delve into philosophy,
especially Jung's teachings.

"I got up from the table and went upstairs and called Bruce Wasserstein, a friend who is one of the hottest investment bankers in
New York. 'Bruce, you've got to help me!' And he was great. In two
or three sentences I told him I wanted to sell *Esquire* and get out. He
said I'd have to do it before the end of 1986 because there were huge
tax implications."

They started from scratch. They didn't have a selling price. They
had no bidders.

Moffitt said, "I was a complete wavering kind of Hamlet. One
day I would think, No, I'm going to keep this magazine. Next day,
I've got to sell it. I've got to. Back and forth every day. Some friends
would tell me, You'd be crazy to do that. And others would say,
'Oh, I wish I had the guts to do that.' "

While this was going on, another Whittle-Moffitt drama was
being played out—a tug-of-war over which one had a claim on Alan
Greenberg, the marketing expert both had credited with *Esquire*'s
advertising turnaround.

When they split, the two partners had agreed they would not raid each other's staffs. Greenberg was the lone exception. He could be bid for. But Greenberg resented being a pawn in their struggle. He hired a lawyer and vowed to make his own decision. For a few months he stayed at *Esquire* attempting to make a deal to take over its "Health and Fitness Clinic," a wall-media poster distributed to 1,400 locations. In the end he couldn't agree with Moffitt and resigned.

Chris asked him to come back to Knoxville. Greenberg said no. Chris told him he could write his own ticket. Still no. Chris said, "Try it for six months." Greenberg said okay.

It took Moffitt and Wasserstein six weeks to sell *Esquire*, just beating the tax deadline.

The Hearst Corporation owned six television stations, fourteen daily newspapers (including the *San Francisco Examiner* and *Los Angeles Herald Examiner*), twelve magazines (*Good Housekeeping, Redbook, Harper's Bazaar, Popular Mechanics, Boating,* and *Sports Afield*), and six cable television systems. Hearst purchased *Esquire* for a reported $80 million.

American Express bought its four-month-old *New York Woman* magazine. Whittle Communications purchased the *Esquire* Health and Fitness Clinic wall media, which had annual revenues of about $5 million.

Altogether Phillip Moffitt shared in total revenues estimated at between $50 million and $100 million. Industry experts speculate his share was close to 50 percent.

Moffitt moved to California, bought a beautiful house with an ocean view north of San Francisco, and set off on a new, two-pronged career. With Rick Smolan, he coauthored two nonfiction books, *The Power To Heal* (1990) and *Medicine's Great Journey* (1992), the latter a collection of photographs covering one hundred years of medical science. He also founded a computer software company called Light Source to market a photographic process used in publishing. In 1992 he married Cheryl MacLachlan, a writer and former associate publisher of *Esquire*. In 1994 he was at work on his first novel.

"Sometimes," Moffitt said, "I think about having had one of the most powerful editorial seats in America. And I miss it at times. But, you know, I have not had one single day of regret."

14

DREAMING OF GREATNESS

Chris Whittle chatted with Bill Connell, a longtime friend from Procter and Gamble's executive suite. The conversation loped amiably along from business success to philosophy to football to classical music to auto racing—Bill's hobby—and finally came to rest on politics. Bill kicked off his black loafers, plopped his shoeless feet on the coffee table, and wiggled his toes. Chris grinned, secretly recalling that he and Phillip Moffitt often did the same in sales meetings in *Esquire* days.

Bill asked, "You are serious about running for office?"

"Yes. Maybe for governor—or perhaps senator. Tennessee, of course."

Warm friends, each admiring the other's verve and talent, they were talking in Connell's home in Cincinnati. At forty-nine, Bill had just wound up a twenty-five-year career at Procter and Gamble, rising to run the $800 million U.S. beauty care division. Chris met Bill in the 1980s while pitching P and G for soap and lotion advertising. They became personal friends and began talking five or six times a year.

"Well, Chris, where would that leave your business?"

"That may be a problem. Bill, you've worked in Ohio politics. Give me some advice."

As their conversation ran on, Bill Connell was quite startled near midnight to discover that being governor or senator was merely a starting point. Chris's real goal was the White House. He had already confided his aims in private to a half-dozen intimates, including Nick Glover.

"Chris has this vision of greatness," says Nick Glover. "I think from the time he was in his teens Chris determined that he was going to be a great national figure in America, one way or another. And in this context the only way he felt he could get there was to do these huge, major, kind of earth-shattering projects that would wind up on page one of the *Wall Street Journal*.

"Obviously he wanted to be successful in the marketplace but that was secondary. He evaluated on the basis of how it's going to read in the *Wall Street Journal*.

"For a long time I think what drove Chris was his ambition to be president. He only talked about it privately and to a very few people. He was totally serious about it. He had mapped out who he would have to run against for governor or senator. And whether it would be better for him to try to get on someone's vice presidential ticket or just make a direct run for president. He actually had the next twenty-five years laid out."

Bill Connell was busy. On his own, he operated day care-learning centers he wanted to expand nationally. He also ran an optical business, and was raising capital to build a high-performance automobile. But he wanted to help his friend achieve his dream of public service.

"Let me tell you about Chris," says Bill Connell. "I have been around some heavy hitters in business. I was chairman of the Cosmetics, Toiletries and Fragrance Association and my board was composed of the CEOs of the largest companies in the personal care industry. So I have known some pretty impressive talent. I can tell you that Chris is indeed a genuine visionary. He is brilliant, intellectually brilliant, and has extraordinary—though narrow—business instincts. The guy is scrupulously honest; he has about as high integrity as anybody I've ever done business with. I have never seen him do a mean thing. He is generous to a fault. So there are a lot of really terrific things about Chris."

In addition to Connell, in 1987 Chris talked seriously—but privately—to other friends. The political dream was growing. Back in college he had thought about making it his career. But he got too busy making a fortune publishing magazines. Occasionally he relived the experience of trying to help elect Wally Barnes governor of Connecticut. That was an exciting adventure, his only real stab at the game.

Now his desire to run for office put him at a crossroads. On his yellow pad he scribbled pros and cons. He couldn't make up his mind. So he went to Tom Ingram for help.

A former Nashville newspaper reporter and editor of *Nashville* magazine, Tom Ingram, just turning forty, had been campaign manager and chief of staff for Tennessee Governor Lamar Alexander, and would later guide Alexander's transition from president of the University of Tennessee to secretary of education under President Bush.

"Lamar sent Chris to me," says Ingram. "I was then a business consultant in Nashville. Chris thought he would eventually sell his business and run for public office. He wasn't sure what office, what party, or really sure he wanted to do it. But he thought he might."

Ingram and his partner Lewis Lavine were engaged to help Chris reach his decision. "We began working with him, questioning him, getting him to think about different things. We went to his place in Vermont, met with him in Nashville, spent quite a bit of time with Chris."

They quickly discovered that Chris was not up to date on economics and foreign affairs. They suggested he take tutorials from experts at three universities. He agreed. At Vanderbilt University in Nashville his instructors were Dr. Tim Smeeding in social services, Dr. Frank Sloan in health care, and Dr. Cliff Russell on the environment. At Harvard he was drilled by two professors, by Dr. Richard Haas in foreign affairs and by Dr. James Verdier in economics. At MIT his instructor in transportation was Dr. Gerard McCullough.

Chris also put himself in the hands of Roger Ailes, President Bush's political adviser, for a course in effective campaigning—public speaking, press interviews, and television appearances.

His schedule was hectic, but Chris stole several days a month to undergo his schooling. For more than a year he prepped to become a politician.

"Some thoughts began to occur to us," says Ingram. "We were dealing with someone very, very capable, and who should not be underestimated when they set their mind to do anything, whatever it was. But for him to set his mind to run for political office in Tennessee in the near future would require either a very radical campaign or a very radical change in life-style.

"At that time he was unmarried. He had not been active in politics. Did not really have a sense of whether he was a Republican, Democrat, or independent. Wasn't sure whether he wanted to run for governor or senator. Was talked out of Congress pretty quickly. Entertained a notion that an appointive political office would be just fine."

His mentors gave Chris the blunt assessment that while he was a capable business man, he was unprepared for Tennessee politics. "We told him that running in Tennessee, a pretty traditional state, a heavily Democratic state, a very conservative state, would have required him to adjust his life-style. He was living in New York, he was living in Vermont, he was living in Knoxville. He was flying around on company jets. He was on a very fast track as a businessman."

For hours at a time Chris talked with his two advisers. He began exploring whether he could take a radically different approach to things. He didn't rule that out.

"There's no rule book," says Ingram, "that says you have got to have been loyal to a party for years and you must have been active for years, and you've got to have voted regularly. Or that you've got to be married, you've got to be a conservative churchgoer. Nothing says all that has to be in place.

"But if it's not in place, you're approaching it radically. So we talked about how he could approach it radically. What it all kind of came down to as far as Lewis and I were concerned—and we were very upfront about it—was: 'Chris, what this would require of you is more than substantial in terms of sacrifice, especially in life-style. But more importantly, if you were successful, we're not sure it would be the best use of you.'"

Chris's ego drove him to start dropping hints to the Knoxville newspapers. The *Journal* published a lengthy profile on May 8, 1988, identifying him as one of the city's dozen movers and shakers. As long as he had the reporter's ear, Chris made good use of it. The sixth paragraph read: "Whittle is even thinking of running for statewide office, although not for another six to eight years."

To other newsmen and friends he also mentioned that he might be interested in running for governor or United States senator from Tennessee, perhaps as early as 1994. But he found that merely talking politics subjected him to criticism. The *Wall Street Journal* reported:

> If he is serious about running for governor in 1994, he clearly has his work cut out for him. One Republican, resentful of Mr. Whittle's waffling about party affiliation, asks, "What does he expect, a draft from the entire state of Tennessee?" Others wonder how a man with such a jet-set life-style and flair for fashion would play in Davy Crockett's state. "He'd have to get rid of the bow tie," suggests James Haslam II, a Knoxville Republican powerhouse.

"There is something deep-seated in Chris," says Ingram. "If you were Freudian about it, you would probably go back to the son of a country doctor. But there is something deep-seated in Chris that says, *I should be contributing. I should be doing something that can pour in the good for the rest of the world.*"

In their many conversations, Ingram heard directly from Chris Whittle that he felt an obligation "to give back and to serve."

Recounting this Ingram said, "I don't discount ego in it either. Chris was attracted to the profile of politicians he saw at the time like Lamar [Alexander] and Howard Baker, whom he knew pretty well. But we reached two thoughts—one: 'Chris, we've been there, and if you got there, you would be incredibly frustrated because the way government works, and the way you work.' Second: 'Don't underestimate what you can accomplish that is a contribution for good for the rest of the world from a business setting.' "

To give Chris a foretaste of actual political life, his mentors lined up a series of experiences in Nashville and Washington. These trips took him directly behind the scenes for a firsthand view of the wheeling and dealing in the statehouse and the U.S. Capitol.

"We wanted him to see what he would have to endure, and be a part of," says Ingram. "Fortunately, we took breaks in all this. We used to go to his place in Vermont and play power croquet. You set the wickets very far apart and literally drive the ball thirty or forty yards. That's exercise that will invigorate your thinking."

The intrigue of life in Washington attracted Chris. "He had

never spent time in those venues," says Ingram. "And was actually fascinated by it. But he also saw the side that involved a lot of meetings, and a lot of staying in one place all day long. Going through a lot of protocol, and going though a lot of mundaneness. But at that point none of us had reached much of a very definitive position about what he wanted to do."

Chris kept waffling. Not even power croquet stirred him to decision. He kept putting off his plunge into politics.

———

In January 1988, with snow a foot deep, Chris Whittle sat before the fireplace in his Vermont farmhouse with Ed Winter and two other Knoxville colleagues brainstorming ways to "grow" his company. Only a few months past his fortieth birthday and no longer the college kid entrepreneur, he now began to keenly feel every tick of the clock. How much time was there left for him to achieve his dream of becoming fabulously wealthy and the renaissance man of his era?

In a sort of frenetic rush, Chris was challenging a big array of mountains yet to climb. He was looking for a girl to marry. He ached passionately to own more (and expensive) paintings of beautiful women, and tramped galleries looking hard for them. He scrambled to complete his Historic Whittlesburg headquarters in Knoxville. He sought out additional homes. In earnest, he pondered starting a political career. To an outsider it might have looked as though he was concentrating on making money—but Chris says wealth really was not on the top of his list.

"At that stretch," says Chris, "I was looking for ways to take the company, which was good and growing, up to a different scale—a medium-sized company. I was interested in transforming the company, but it wasn't just for the money."

Ed Winter, a company division manager who had just taken over education, was reporting to Chris at the farm on research that he and the other two present, his assistant managers Bill Gubbins and Jim Ritts, were conducting. They were delving into possible new school publications, as well as how Whittle Communications could also capture the attention of teenagers in places such as malls and movie theatres.

"Have you found any big ideas?" Chris asked. "Anything really exciting?"

"Yes, I think so," said Winter. "We've been having focus group discussions with teachers in Knoxville. Just last week we had about fifteen of them in the Holiday Inn trying to find out if we should expand our wall media to middle schools.

"One teacher said the reason our publications were so successful with the students was because we bring these TV stars they know so well into the schools on our posters. She said she was not sure schools need any more magazines. She said, 'Maybe what you guys ought to be doing is using these celebrities to do more news. . . . Studies show that students, especially from divorced households, are busy, busy. And with all the running around they do, really don't pay any attention to the news. Honestly, they don't know what is going on. Maybe you guys should be thinking about a news format, about television, because the kids like these stars from television.' Another teacher over in the corner who hadn't said much spoke up. 'I wonder why nobody's ever done like a *Today* show for teenagers in the homeroom?' Now, Chris, what do you think of that?"

Chris Whittle sat up straight. His eyes began sparkling. "That's a big idea! That is a *big* idea!" He touched his finger tips together. Winter heard him going, "Hmmm. . . . hmmm . . . " Then Chris reached for his yellow pad.

Chris said, "Maybe what we ought to do, rather than a *Today* show, is something like *That Was the Week That Was*. Let's do it an hour every week on Friday, and let's bring back *That Was the Week That Was* as a news show and tell students what went on in the world."

Everyone jumped in and began batting the idea back and forth.

"I really don't think any of us had seized the magnitude," Winter says. "It began to dawn on me. We figured on a news show that would either be an hour in length, or we'd send it in by video tape. The more we talked, Chris's intelligence was, 'I'm not sure schools have any technology. Let's run some quick numbers on producing video tapes.' And then he went, 'I'm not sure that makes sense. Has anybody thought if we get a TV show we could literally install the equipment? I'd have to believe we could provide schools with equipment and a TV show that would be an enormous advantage for schools.'

"All we had when we walked into that retreat in Vermont was a notion—a news show for teenagers that could run in schools. It was just a notion. Chris very quickly turned it into a concept: Hey, should we do it once a week? Maybe we ought to be trying to do it every day!

"What he is incredibly good at doing is pulling something out of the air that is a notion, and focussing on it, and turning it into reality. He said, 'I'll bet we could do a daily news show. Why couldn't we do a *Good Morning America* or a *Today* show? Why couldn't we? What do you think of the start-up cost? Etcetera, etcetra, etcetra. It's an exciting idea! Talk to some more schools and see how we do it!' "

Winter and his men did that—promptly. Winter says, "The schools told us, 'Hey, you guys have a great idea. Don't do it for an hour on Fridays. We can't give you an hour. Give us that hour over five days in twelve-minute increments. Homeroom is twenty-two minutes long, and we can spare you twelve.' "

What eventually emerged, after more than a year of secret development, was a satellite program called Channel One that beams a twelve-minute television news and feature program into high schools all across the country. Whittle provided each school with the necessary equipment and installation—TVs, VCRs, cable hook-ups, and satellite dishes. The cost of operation and Whittle's profit came from two minutes of advertising carried by each broadcast.

But nobody at Whittle Communications headquarters had the slightest inkling of the magnitude and duration of the furor that would erupt over beaming TV advertising into high schools.

═══

Even though Channel One had every appearance of a major creative triumph, the Whittleites in Knoxville had already secretly originated another project that seemed even more likely to prove a great success. Alan Greenberg had come back from *Esquire* specifically to try to create a major flagship property for the company. "We centered," Greenberg says, "on the key market in America, which was, basically, Mom."

To find out how to tap into that market, Greenberg's researchers set up focus groups and spent more than eighteen months conducting eleven hundred individual interviews across the country, assembling mountains of quantitative data. One fact jumped out clear and strong: the best place for a magazine to catch mom's eye would be where she waits to see her family physician—the waiting room where she spends on average thirty-four minutes before the doctor sees her.

Chris and Greenberg recognized immediately how they should launch the needed flagship that would rake in new millions from advertisers. They decided to publish a set of high-quality, easy to read, handsomely illustrated magazines exclusively for doctors' offices.

They needed to hire a nationally respected editor in chief, and went after William S. Rukeyser, a top editor at *Time* who had started *Money* as managing editor and moved into the same job at *Fortune*. Bill Rukeyser was surprised when he was contacted by Chris's headhunter. At forty-seven, as *Time*'s director of international development, he was near the pinnacle of magazine publishing. He was also a bit bored.

Rukeyser promptly pulled the Chris Whittle clippings out of the Time-Life morgue and read them. "One quote of his deeply impressed me," Rukeyser says. "Whittle said, 'Growth is inherently embarrassing.' I think what it means and the reason I liked it so much, if you want to really grow you have to be willing to look foolish some of the time. There are many people and a lot of organizations that don't grow much because they are so fearful of putting a foot in the wrong place!"

Of course, Rukeyser was told about the upcoming new venture, dubbed *Special Report Magazines*. "This was going to be the biggest thing Whittle had ever undertaken," he says. "In revenue terms it would be the largest launch in the history of the magazine business. They wanted my ability and experience and credibility. I was happy and highly paid at *Time*. But the possibility of being one of a very small core group who would take this fast-growing company to a new level of editorial prominence was a very interesting challenge to me."

A week or two later the *Time* man met Chris on a Saturday at a New York restaurant near the Dakota to talk terms. "It was a long lunch. We both drank mineral water—a lot of it," Rukeyser says. "I call it our nine-Perrier lunch." Chris laid out a big-money offer with a three-year contract. Between Perrier sips, it is likely Chris mentioned that twenty of the original founders who gambled on 13–30 ended up millionaires.

Rukeyser flew to Knoxville with his wife, Elizabeth, and children, Lisa and James, both students at Ithaca College. Chris gave the family a Knoxville tour and his sales pitch. Rukeyser's son drew him aside excitedly. "Dad, I want to quit school and work for this guy!"

In March 1988, Whittle Communications announced Rukeyser's hiring and at the same time officially took the wraps off their audacious scheme to dominate magazine reading by patients, especially mothers, while they waited in doctors' offices.

Their *Special Report* would be a set of six oversize (14-by-10.5-inch) glossy quarterly magazines in their own six-by-seven-foot oaken display rack. Each would cover a single topic: family, health, sports, life-style, personalities, and fiction. (The first *Special Report on Health* was devoted to relaxation—from ways to combat stress to soothing foods.) Heavy on pictures, each was edited for quick reading, that is, the thirty-four minutes on average patients wait to see their physician. Fresh copies would be put in the racks monthly. Within ten weeks, Whittle agents signed up 16,500 family practitioners, gynecologists, and pediatricians in 125 cities. The magazine debut was scheduled for October 1988.

Special Report offered national advertisers an enormous lure—a large captive audience, primarily women. As an extra bonus, these Whittle magazines would also relieve an advertising problem known as clutter, when ads for competing products jostle one another for attention in the same publication. Each *Special Report* would carry only a single brand in any product category—for instance—one toothpaste, such as Crest, one mayonnaise, like Kraft, and so forth.

It was a great idea, and all might have gone smoothly except Chris and Greenberg decided to take a couple of extra steps. They asked the doctors to pay two hundred dollars a year for their copies of *Special Report*. When many doctors balked and trouble loomed, that idea was quietly buried. Another Whittle requirement was that each physician who signed up had to eliminate all other magazines from his or her waiting room except two, typically a news weekly and a hobby or sports magazine.

That stipulation triggered howls of rage from other major magazine publishers. "Whittle's plan is not far from book burning," said the editor of *American Health*, which sent its magazine free to

Photo from the cover of Chris and Priscilla's wedding announcement, with Anna Kennedy, Maxi, and Zoe Bibb. (Courtesy Jean Pagliuso)

Chris and wife Priscilla Rattazzi look over art from their Manhattan apartment at an exhibit in Knoxville, September 1990. (Courtesy *Knoxville News-Sentinel*)

Jacket photo of Priscilla Rattazzi with her son Maxi (*right*) and daughter Andrea from her first picture book. (Courtesy Priscilla Rattazzi)

executives at Time Inc. made it publicly known that Chris Whittle had a good idea after all—so good, they were willing to bet money on him!

———

Not surprisingly, Chris's budding political ambition led directly to the creation of another Whittle magazine. The idea was triggered at a meeting with Lamar Alexander.

According to Tom Ingram, the former journalist who became prominent in Tennessee politics and public relations, "Lamar suggested to Chris that if he were interested in running, one thing that might help him, and would be very good for the state, would be a statewide magazine." Thus *Tennessee Illustrated* was born.

Started in May 1988 as a bimonthly, it was a glossy copycat of the *Special Report* format, containing well-written articles on Tennessee places and personalities. (One cover story was on Tennessee hero Davy Crockett by Michael Lofaro, professor of English at the University of Tennessee and editor of *Davy Crockett: The Man, The Legend, The Legacy*.)

The magazine was distributed free to fifty thousand state leaders and fifteen thousand Tennessee physicians' offices. Another ten thousand were designated to be sold by subscription or on newsstands or were to be given to advertisers.

Chris Whittle, listed as executive editor, also wrote an "Editor's Note" that featured his photo in white shirt, sweater vest, and bow tie on page three of the magazine. It was his first attempt at writing a column since those he turned out as a high school senior for his hometown Etowah newspaper. His *Tennessee Illustrated* columns were serviceable enough for the role intended—to regularly place his name and picture before a statewide constituency. "I was never much of a writer," Chris says.

One "Editor's Note" argued for keeping Tennessee businesses home-owned. Chris wrote:

> Every year Tennessee businesses are purchased by organizations whose headquarters are outside the state. Though there may be occasional exceptions, we generally experience a subtle loss when these transactions occur.
>
> Outside control tends to make us subject to other peo-

100,000 physicians. *Prevention* magazine railed against "censorship." *Reader's Digest* wrote: "We are not about to roll over." Lawyers for *Parents* and *Expecting* vowed they would "strike back." Some magazine executives contended that removing other magazines from waiting rooms violated the First Amendment and possibly restrained trade. However, no lawsuits were filed against *Special Report*.

Several Madison Avenue advertising agencies attacked the concept and advised their clients not to buy space. One critic called them "nonmagazines—with no heart and soul." Chris Whittle not only shrugged off the threat of lawsuits as "legal-sword rattling," he struck back. In the *New York Times* he attacked his detractors, running a series of "tough, funny, provocative" full-page ads. These ads, wrote one reporter, "seemed to delight in fanning the flames— or blowing on the coals—of the controversy."

Chris obviously knew what he was talking about as far as appeal to advertisers was concerned. The magazines quickly sold out all advertising space (thirty pages in each sixty-four-page issue), not only because of quality editorial content and design, but most likely because they were clutter free. When Alan Greenberg ran his sales totals, it did turn out to be the most successful launch in magazine history. The previous champion was *People*, which debuted in 1972 with annual advertising revenue of $8 million. The *Special Report* launch beat that over five to one, with initial ad revenue totalling $41 million.

Fourteen major corporations, including Procter and Gamble and General Foods, bought thirty units at an annual cost of $2.7 million each, or $41 million. However, each advertiser signed a two-year contract, guaranteeing Whittle Communications a start-up kitty in excess of $80 million. That, of course, really did knock the socks off the old *People* record.

The oddest twist in the *Special Report* brouhaha did not emerge until later. When word leaked about Whittle's waiting room invasion, one of his loudest critics was Time Inc.—Rukeyser's old employer. However, by the time the magazines actually appeared, Time Inc. mellowed a great deal. Reginald K. Brack Jr., head of Time Inc.'s magazine group, looked them over and told media reporters he was "impressed."

And just a few weeks later, the irony came full circle. The top

ABOVE: Chris and daughter Andrea on the beach at East Hampton. (Courtesy Priscilla Rattazzi)

LEFT: Chris (*left*) with Benno Schmidt, the former president of Yale University whom Whittle recruited from to head his Edison Project, a for-profit plan to manage and revolutionize America's public schools. (Courtesy *Knoxville News-Sentinel*)

Members of the core team that designed the Edison Project. *Clockwise from top:* Lee Eisenberg, Nancy Hechinger, Daniel Biederman, John Chubb, Sylvia Peters, Dominique Browning, and Chester Finn.

Lamar Alexander (*left*), president of the University of Tennessee, with Chris, announcing the latter's $5 million scholarship gift on March 30, 1989. (Courtesy *Knoxville News-Sentinel*)

Chris does a selling job on business leaders in Knoxville in 1990. (Courtesy *Knoxville News-Sentinel*)

Chris, circa 1988, with wall media display for which he sold advertising. (Courtesy Whittle Communications LP)

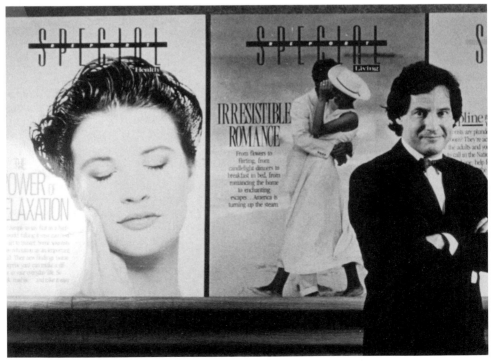

Chris, circa 1989, with blowups of *Special Reports* magazine, which went into doctors' waiting rooms. (Courtesy *Knoxville News-Sentinel*)

Chris, circa 1988, with some of his publications. (Courtesy *Knoxville News-Sentinel*)

RIGHT: Tom Ingram, Whittle's political adviser and head of *Special Reports* magazine, in 1992. (Courtesy *Knoxville News-Sentinel*)

BELOW: Chris (*center*) talking to Mrs. Tom Ingram and Harold Smiddy at a 1990 showing of his art collection in Knoxville. (Courtesy *Knoxville News-Sentinel*)

ple's interests, so it's to our advantage to keep our companies headquartered here, controlled here, and owned here.

Aside from the issue of jobs, the company will be more disposed to construct buildings and make major cultural and charitable investments in a city where its headquarters is located than in a city where it has only a subsidiary office.

Keeping with his philosophy of trying to avoid advertising clutter, Chris launched *Tennessee Illustrated* with only three sponsors—First Tennessee Bank, the Tennessee Valley Authority, and the state's three Baptist Hospitals. Space in his magazine was not cheap. T.V.A., the federal government flood control and electric power corporation, signed up for eighteen color pages in six issues at $40,000 each—or a total of $720,000. The agency's announced rationale was "getting its message out to its ratepayers."

Later the T.V.A. advertising proved to be an embarrassing, or at least awkward, issue for Chris on two counts. One day after *Tennessee Illustrated* debuted, T.V.A. announced it had to start laying off employees to achieve a $300 million cut in operating costs to keep rates stable. On top of that, it later became known that Lamar Alexander, the former governor of Tennessee, accompanied Chris Whittle when he made his sales pitch to the T.V.A. board.

In editorials, the *Knoxville News-Sentinel* criticized the T.V.A. advertising deal and the way it was cut, but the newspaper gave Alexander a chance to deny, in print, that "he peddled his influence to win advertising dollars." At that time the former two-time governor was waiting to assume presidency of the University of Tennessee. "Chris Whittle judged T.V.A.'s advertising campaign in *Tennessee Illustrated* as being in the best interest of ratepayers or he wouldn't have proposed it," Alexander told the newspaper. "I have been notorious as a public person. But since January 1987 I have been a private citizen earning a living." Alexander said he had been a paid consultant for Whittle for more than a year and wanted to continue even after becoming head of the university.

The heat, however, was too much for the T.V.A. board. It cancelled the contract with Whittle's magazine and won *News-Sentinel* editorial praise as "the logical thing for T.V.A.'s directors to do to remedy a situation that should not have happened in the first place."

How was the magazine received? Brient Mayfield, one of the original *Nutshell* partners who had sold out to go into the computer business, came back to be *Tennessee Illustrated*'s publisher. Mayfield said, "We had cards and letters from a lot of people. It was clear Tennesseeans loved the magazine. There were simply not enough companies for whom this was a good advertising vehicle."

From the start, the magazine was on thin ice financially, and T.V.A.'s cancellation proved to be a mortal blow. At the end of the first year *Tennessee Illustrated* showed a loss of $1 million. To save money, it was converted to a quarterly.

Chris's plate was too full of business, and he was still wrestling with the question of whether to launch a political career. He took time to whip out his "Editor's Note" on his laptop instead of having it ghost-written, otherwise he had very little time for the magazine. Except to agonize over its rapidly mounting deficit.

═══════

To experience the thrill of riding a dory through the swirling whitewaters of the Grand Canyon, Chris Whittle flew in from New York, strapped on his backpack and started hiking nine miles from the South Rim down to the bottom. Chris was three months shy of forty.

On the steep trail, he encountered TV reporter Diane Sawyer. They had little time to talk. She was coming up from the campsite at Thunder Falls, the stopping point that was his destination. Both of them were enamored of shooting these Colorado River rapids, a rare adventure that every year attracts a few thousand daring people. Pausing a moment, Diane told Chris she had entered the river at Phantom Ranch in one of seven boats four days before. Her journey, she exclaimed, was "very exciting." That pleased him, because this excursion represented a muscular extension of Chris's continual push to test his physical endurance, whether hiking in the Alps or working out in his home gymnasiums.

Five days later Chris, for the last time, climbed out of the brightly-painted eighteen-foot boat with upturned bow and stern that had carried him, four companions, and a guide nearly one hundred miles downstream. He trudged back up to the South Rim with the same satisfaction and enthusiasm Diane Sawyer had felt about her adventure. Moreover, he emerged from the Grand Canyon with a newfound friend, New York investment banker Richard Holbrooke, whose insightful business conversation as a boat-mate would soon play a major role in Chris's financial career.

In the months following the Grand Canyon episode, which occurred in May 1987, Chris occasionally met for dinner in New York with Holbrooke, who was managing director of Shearson Lehman Brothers Inc. Later President Clinton would appoint Holbrooke ambassador to Germany.

At one get-together Holbrooke asked Chris if he recognized the true value of his company. "Well, not really," Chris said. "What's it worth?"

"Four hundred million dollars."

Chris started. "Four hundred million! You mean it?"

"And I recommend this as a good time to sell part of it," said Holbrooke. "The market's right. It would provide liquidity for you and your partners."

Holbrooke was convincing. Chris commissioned Shearson Lehman to pursue the deal. Holbrooke developed a list of possible buyers, most of whom were in Europe. Chris began a series of meetings with these suitors. It struck him as peculiar that Time Inc. was not on the Shearson Lehman list. Later he learned that Holbrooke was involved in another deal for Time Inc.

"Finally I said 'I'm going to see Time,'" Chris recalls. "I had a very brief meeting with Nick Nicholas [N. J. Nicholas Jr., Time Inc. chieftain who later was ousted when Time merged with Warner]. I told Nick I thought it would make sense to have a partnership. I said, 'Here's what our company is.' And I took him through a very few sheets of paper, and he was intrigued."

A super salesman, the entrepreneur from Knoxville provided a glowing forecast for *Special Report* and revealed to Nicholas his bigger secret—Channel One.

"In a week," says Chris, "we had a much larger meeting. Things moved quickly, and in two or three weeks we had a deal."

And with very little haggling. On October 20, 1988, Time Inc. announced that it had agreed to pay $185 million for a one-half interest in Whittle Communications Inc.

The infusion of Time Inc. money added enormously to Chris's personal wealth. For surrendering half of his personal stake of twenty-two percent in the company he received $40 million cash, retaining eleven percent interest. Until then Lord Rothermere's Associated Newspapers had owned more than half of Whittle Communications. As Time Inc. bought in, the British publisher, of course, sold part of its interest, letting Associated's share fall to about thirty-six percent. Chris's Knoxville partners also received cash payments cutting their individual holdings in half, down to a combined total of 3 or 4 percent.

The headlines gave Knoxville a bad case of jitters. What if the Time executives decided to abandon the Historic Whittleburg complex, which was just a week away from its ground-breaking celebration, and move the whole company to New York? But everyone breathed easier when Chris issued a statement that in his role of managing partner he still was the boss, and the company would go on aggressively in Knoxville as before.

The *News-Sentinel* editorially hailed this as "good news for Knoxville" that allayed citizens' fears the "deal would jeopardize Whittle's business interests in the city." It pointed out that in two years Whittle revenues had jumped from $81 million to $152 million and were forecast to approach $600 million within five years. It added:

> Why is Whittle so interested in Time?
>
> As Whittle explained it, Time "has the major resources vital to our future. They are a major force in the television business and we are going to be in television. They are a major force in book publishing and we will be in book publishing. They are a major force in magazine publishing, but we are already there."

Indeed, it was a happy marriage. Both buyer and seller were upbeat and optimistic. Time Inc. saw the potential for steady growth in the company. So did Chris, but he also had a secret agenda in making the deal. Now he was rich, and could afford to gamble on jumping into politics. So he cleverly wrote the contract to include an option for Time Inc. to totally buy him out in 1994—the year he considered coming out for governor or the Senate.

Media analysts generally liked the connection. According to the Associated Press, the analysts considered it a low-risk way "for Time to share in the rewards of association with a concern that has made its reputation by developing innovative ways for advertisers to reach select audiences. At the same time they said it would give Whittle access to the resources and experience of one of the nation's biggest communications companies."

As the *Wall Street Journal* put it: "For now the agreement gives Whittle a powerful partner to help it expand, and it provides giant Time with a stake in one of the industry's fastest growing and most aggressive young publishing and marketing concerns." On Madison Avenue, ad directors viewed it as "a pretty good match, though the companies have strong philosophical differences at the root."

In fact, the deal was tinged with irony because of the earlier flare-up by Time Inc. against Whittle Communications due to Whittle's heavy-handed invasion of doctors' offices with *Special Report*. Then Time was livid. Now Reg Brack, head of Time's magazine group, downplayed the significance of their old dispute. "Like any marriage," he said, "we're not going to agree on everything."

But at the outset there was peace and harmony between Time Inc. headquarters in New York and the troops in Knoxville. Chris Whittle was the boss. Everything went on just like before, with every Whittleite cudgeling his or her brain for a way to make the company bigger and bigger.

Nor was there much of a ripple in Knoxville less than five months later, when Time Inc. joined Warner Communications to form what was then the world's largest media and entertainment conglomerate, valued at $18 billion and generating annual revenue of $10 billion. The merger creating Time Warner Inc. was announced on March 5, 1989. From Chris Whittle's vantage point everything looked satisfactory. But behind the scenes, in the Time Warner executive suite, serious trouble was brewing, and before many months had passed the internal strife in the New York boardroom began to cast long shadows—some of which would later cause problems in Historic Whittlesburg.

═══

News that Chris had personally come out of the Time Inc. deal with $40 million prompted Lamar Alexander, then president of the University of Tennessee at Knoxville, to call on his close friend.

"With that much money," said Alexander, "have you considered doing something for the university?"

Chris gave him a look, grinned, and nodded affirmatively.

"I have, Lamar. I remember how Phillip Moffitt, Dave White, and I—along with others—practically wore out that foozball machine in the student center." He gave another shy grin. "What I think I'll do is buy you-all a new foozball machine!"

The university president tried to go along with the gag but grunted his disappointment.

Chris held up his hand. "Just kidding. Let me tell you what I'm going to do."

What Chris did was pledge $5.2 million to establish scholarships for academically outstanding students at the University of Tennessee—the largest single contribution for academic purposes the university had received up to that time. The money would fund one hundred five-year scholarships, worth about $30,000 each, with the final year reserved for overseas travel and study. The latter provision, of course, was inspired by Chris's own summer in Czechoslovakia while a U.T. student.

In announcing the gift, Lamar Alexander said: "Even a Vanderbilt graduate [which Alexander is] ought to have enough sense to ask Chris Whittle for money. . . . The Whittle Scholarships will make certain that when outstanding high school students think of college, they'll think of Tennessee. That will keep the next generation of Chris Whittles in Tennessee." Chris specified that 80 percent of the scholarships be reserved for graduates of high schools in the state.

The first year the program began, 1990, the university received 644 applications for the initial twenty scholarships.

15

HOW TO GO HEADHUNTING

Barely three months after Time Inc. came in as major partner, Chris Whittle abruptly seized one-man control of Whittle Communications. In January 1989 the idyllic team of "Mr. Inside" and "Mr. Outside" broke up. "Mr. Inside"—Nick Glover—was out.

They no longer saw eye to eye. But their conflict was papered over in a polite Knoxville press conference. Glover announced he would retire in June to write a book on business management and return to freelance consulting. Chris said Glover was not forced out. "It's just the ebb and flow of business."

Glover said, "There are a lot of lessons I've learned here. It's just time to leave."

"Mr. Inside" had been the architect of Whittle Communications's maverick management style of "disciplined chaos." When he took over as president in 1983, the company had little management structure and was a $40 million firm with 250 employees; when he stepped aside there were 900 employees and revenues of $150 million.

Chris put his best spin on Glover's departure, telling reporters, "He's not going to be easy to replace. It's going to take probably a year to find somebody. It will be a national search. You can't look in traditional places. It needs to be someone who's got an entrepreneurial spirit and has the flexibility to operate this without over-controlling it. I don't think we'd be where we are today without what he did. He's the best I've seen at it."

Not mentioned to the press was the fact that Glover and Chris had sharply disagreed on basic strategy. "Mr. Inside" had turned cautious, warning that disaster lay ahead unless wild spending stopped and fewer expensive schemes were launched. Chris listened, nodding politely, but paid no heed. He kept barging right ahead.

The board did not interfere. All the directors, including Time Inc.'s Reg Brack, had been hypnotized by the chairman's glowing visions of astounding future growth. Glover's resignation shocked Knoxville. The inside story was never told, except to a very few. Glover explained privately to a friend: "The time had come to take the company to a new level or solidify what we had. Chris and I had a basic disagreement, not some big blowup. He wanted to take the company in the direction of major showcase kinds of businesses [Channel One and *Special Report*], as opposed to the smaller, less capital-intensive properties [*18 Almanac*, the *Wallpaper Journal,* the *Nutshells*] that had built the business.

"Also he wanted to run the show both internally and externally. He'd always run it externally, but either Phillip Moffitt or myself had always run the show internally. So we agreed to disagree. I said, 'Hey, it's your company. If you want to do it that way, I don't think it's going to work. But take your best shot.' We worked out a very agreeable deal and I went home. But we stayed in touch."

It became a one-man show. Purposely leaving Glover's chair vacant, Chris took total command. The wunderkind from Etowah thought he had enough ambition, talent, and self-confidence to single-handedly lead his troops up to the $1 billion annual revenue pinnacle. Unfortunately, he did not. But Chris would not discover that he had overreached himself until it was too late.

———

It took Chris and his colleagues nearly a year to come up with what they considered a viable scheme for Channel One. They worked in secret and zealously guarded the confidentiality of their research. In such a totally new idea there might be many potential bugs. They wanted time to identify and eliminate unexpected stumbling blocks in advance.

Their first challenge revolved around the question of immediacy. In addition to being youth-oriented, their news report must be as up-to-the-minute as NBC's *Today* show or ABC's *Good Morning America*. Otherwise they couldn't hope to command the attention of the teenage audience. To guarantee such freshness meant discarding the idea of doing it via video tape; obviously Channel One must be broadcast by satellite. That was expensive, but it could be done.

Problem number two was that American high schools were not equipped with satellite dishes to receive such a broadcast. Furthermore, none would have an appropriate system of VCRs, cable connections, and TV sets for showing the news report in homerooms.

"It was quite clear to us," says Chris, "that given the dismal state of finances in most school districts, few educators likely would recommend the expenditure necessary to install what was needed to receive Channel One. Especially since it was something totally new and untested.

"Our estimate was that putting in the satellite dish, VCRs, and TVs, and hooking them up, would run about $30,000 per school."

That did not daunt the Channel One planners. Whittle decided to offer all the needed equipment free to each school that signed up for their broadcast.

They proposed to beam a twelve-minute news broadcast from New York to all Channel One schools, Monday through Friday, patterned on traditional network style, with some of the verve of MTV added. Ten minutes would be devoted to news and features, the other two minutes would be reserved for four thirty-second commercials.

The program would be prepared in New York by Channel One's professional staff, utilizing the same traditional news services available to the networks and newspapers. Channel One would employ its own correspondents and camera crews to produce special features. On leased time the newscast would be beamed from Home Box Office's transmitting dish at five A.M. to GTE Corporation's G Star II satellite, which would relay the signal to receiving dishes at schools anywhere in the United States. There it would be automatically recorded on special Channel One VCRs in time to be reviewed by the school principal before being piped into homerooms.

If as many as eight thousand schools could be signed up for

Channel One, the Whittleites estimated sponsors would fork over $100 million a year for the advertising spots. Sponsors would pay $200,000 for each half-minute commercial on the full network. With that kind of revenue, Channel One could rather quickly recoup the enormous cost of donating satellite dishes, cable hookups, and free TV sets to every school.

At that time nobody in Knoxville headquarters had the least doubt Channel One would be a tremendous success. Chris expected to hear ringing applause from American educators. Surely they would gladly welcome such a snazzy innovation as piping television news for teens into their classrooms.

Chris and his cohorts planned a marketing strategy that included a quiet trial run in six widely separated high schools. They intended to line up a nucleus of Channel One subscriber schools before going public with their new project. But the story somehow leaked to Knoxville newspapers, forcing premature announcement of Channel One. When the news spread coast to coast, a furious response erupted all over the educational landscape. Chris was stunned.

The explosion was set off by the fact that Channel One would carry commercials. Chris and his colleagues, whose entire careers were predicated on thinking up new vehicles for big advertisers and thus were inured to the acceptability of commercials in any venue, had failed to recognize things would look different in the school room.

The *Wall Street Journal* credited Chris with a business stratagem that "seemed brilliant, cornering a captive audience of young, impressionable consumers" that would generate millions in advertising revenue, but asserted "virtually the entire American educational establishment is up in arms over the plan."

State authorities in New York and California, among others, barred Channel One from their schools, angered by the prospect of commercials in the classroom. Bill Honig, California's superintendent of instruction, was irate. "The problem is they want us to sell access to our kids' minds. And we have no right, morally or ethically, to do that."

Another spearhead of the attack on Channel One came from Peggy Charren, founder of Action for Children's Television, based in Cambridge, Massachusetts. Opposed to the use of television to sway children, she never let up. "We'll have advertising in text-books next," she warned.

The National Association of Secondary School Principals was also an early and fierce critic. "I'd be surprised if Whittle could get more than five hundred or six hundred schools to participate," said its executive director, Scott Thomson. "Not only are commercials inappropriate, but it's easy to overpromise what TV will do. Kids don't retain as much from TV as they do with an ordinary teacher."

From the outset, however, Chris had widespread, quiet support from educators who thought he was on to something. But even in his own circles there were doubters. For instance, friend and banker Richard Holbrooke, listening to him describe Channel One, observed: "It's a great idea—but have you read any George Orwell?" Holbrooke suggested playing down the advertising and playing up the educational benefits. Other friends suggested he launch the network on a smaller scale, but he seemed too cocksure of success to do so.

A fighter, Chris struck back at his critics, using his favorite sounding board, the *New York Times.* He ran nine full-page ads trumpeting the dire state of American schools. The first was a page vacant except for a giant headline DINNER'S READY! followed by one line: "For too many students, this is the 6:00 news." His second ad consisted of fifty-seven blank spaces above a line which read, "Here's a list of everyone willing to donate $250,000 to schools" (The amount refered to the cost of the equipment he invested in the Channel One test run).

In a series of newspaper and television interviews, Chris defended his endeavor and emphasized the need for current events education in high schools. "These days," he quipped, "many students think Chernobyl is Cher's full name."

For a time even Ed Winter grew doubtful of the scheme he had largely originated. "I thought we would have to call on fifty schools to get six to test this," he says. "But the first six we approached accepted. That's what changed my mind."

The pilot schools, selected to provide a broad geographic and socioeconomic cross section for a five-week test, were Eisenhower Middle School in Kansas City, Kansas; Mumford High School in Detroit; Gahr High School in Cerritos, California (a private school not subject to state control); Billerica Memorial High School in Billerica, Massachusetts; Withrow High School in Cincinnati; and Central High School in Knoxville.

As the opposition grew, Whittle Communications tried an appeasement strategy, dropping the requirement for mandatory viewing by homeroom students and adding two commercial-free channels, one for educational programming for students and another for teachers, with greatly-desired instructional technique updates from around the country. They improved the semantics as well, creating an umbrella organization to cover this called Whittle Educational Network.

When the Channel One pilot run ended in April 1989, the *Knoxville News-Sentinel* reported it received "glowing grades from students and teachers in the test schools." Likewise, said the newspaper, these participants "downplay the advertisements."

However, critics continued to assail the entry into the classroom of television commercials—such as the thirty-second spots showing teens traipsing along in Levi's 501 jeans looking "cool, sexy, and happy." Peggy Charren was appalled. "Here, we're going to tell them they need expensive jeans in order to be popular. We shouldn't do that—one student in five in this nation is at or below the poverty line."

David Elkind, producer of a teenage show airing on three hundred public television stations, told the *News-Sentinel* that the Channel One commercials put "images on the screen that tend to romanticize and idealize life. It sends the message that if they're are not like that, then something is wrong with them. It plays . . . with a kid's self-esteem. Most teenage girls do not look like Brooke Shields."

In the face of new opposition from groups like the National Parent-Teachers Association, the American College for Teacher Education, the Montessori Society, and the state departments of education in Alabama, Wyoming, and Rhode Island, producers and broadcasters familiar with Channel One praised several elements used to attract teens' interest. For instance, high impact graphics, including extensive use of maps to help students pinpoint places on the globe. "Educators have complained," said the Knoxville newspaper, "that today's students, even college students, are woefully ignorant of geography."

The pilot broadcasts used teen anchors, including Ken Rogers, son of singer Kenny Rogers, and guest appearances by other TV

teens such as Malcolm Jamal Warner, who played Theodore Huxta-
ble on *The Cosby Show.*

To give the news from a teenager's perspective, one report featured youngsters living in a homeless shelter. Others examined the
lives of teens in Cuba and the Soviet Union, the daughter of an
American hostage in Lebanon, and a drug dealer gone straight.

Mary Lou Ray, vice-president of a public broadcasting network
based in Denver that supplied some of the Channel One test programming, told the *News-Sentinel,* "I think Channel One is one of
the best productions I have seen in relevance to teenagers and its
ability to attract and hold their attention."

Even while Ed Winter's team still analyzed the data collected in
the pilot run, "a lot of people—inside and outside the company"—
were advising Chris to cut and run. Chris now recalls:

> The really dark days of Channel One were right after we
> announced, and did our early test. We, in quick succession,
> lost both California and New York. And this was before we
> were even out of the starting gate. We didn't have one
> school installed.
>
> A lot of companies would have folded their tent right
> there, saying if you lost the two largest markets in the coun-
> try you were just not going to succeed. The reason we didn't
> is because we had done a tremendous amount of research
> with schools and they said in significant numbers they
> thought it was a great idea.
>
> Our belief was that if we could ever get to those schools
> and get there fast enough we would succeed because they
> would adopt the product, they would like what we did, and
> we could adopt a lasting relationship with them. Which is
> exactly what happened.
>
> I think our opponents thought by knocking us out of
> those two markets they would just end the game. Out strat-
> egy was that we wanted this to be a national system, and we
> just kept at it in the other forty-eight states.
>
> It was a tough period. It was not a stretch of time I want to
> go back through.

In the summer of 1989 Chris Whittle could not be dissuaded
from officially launching Channel One. Feedback from the pilot

program was mainly positive. Opinion in Knoxville headquarters was that in time the educational establishment would have a change of heart. As the positive nature of piping in teen news began to show itself, bitter criticism of the commercials would assuredly diminish.

One indication this might happen came, ironically, from rival broadcasters. Two other groups—Turner Broadcasting and the Public Broadcasting System—revealed they were also considering copying the Whittle invention of news programs for high schools. But taking note of the brouhaha over advertising spots on Channel One, they elected to not include commercials. And not, of course, give away satellite dishes, VCRs, cable hookups, and TV sets.

At the time of roll-out there was yet no let up in opposition to Channel One. A long letter came to Chris from his former partner Phillip Moffitt. They had not communicated for two years, having parted on less than friendly terms. Their friends say Moffitt's letter was a scathing denunciation of Channel One. "Reportedly," said one published account, "the letter made a good case for Chris being the Devil, a man for whom selling was the only goal."

Both were asked to comment on the letter. Each refused. Both gave the appearance of having enough respect for their old partnership to resist washing dirty linen in public, but their conversation left a distinct impression they still harbored grudges.

Moffitt's letter was a mere glitch in the sales campaign launched from Knoxville to recruit eight thousand schools for Channel One. The going was tough—and nowhere any rougher than in the trenches with Whittle sales reps. As they fanned out across the country to make their initial pitch to school officials, often they would encounter an opponent from the National Education Association handing out "I Hate Whittle" literature. Peggy Charren was also sending out slick notebooks full of anti–Channel One articles. "We get those waved in our faces a lot," Dave Southard, vice president of Whittle field sales, reported to his bosses.

Trying to sell Channel One to a school board was decidedly frustrating. Usually the sales rep had to show up and sit through three or four hours of trivial business before getting a chance to speak. It sometimes took three or four such visits to sign up a school.

"I walked into a meeting at a school in West Memphis, Arkansas, and said 'Hi,' " reported sales rep Rick McDaniel. "Not one person responded. They all had their legs stretched out and their arms crossed—I could read the body language. The superintendent started out by saying, 'Mr. McDaniel, you're wasting your time. We're not interested and we're completely against Channel One.'

"They were total skeptics, but I just went on with my presentation. I told them this was a rare opportunity for them and that some of the things they had heard about Channel One just weren't so. I said, 'You owe it to yourselves and your school to listen.' At the end they were all excited about the program and wanted to get it. They talked about what they could do with it, like start an in-house broadcast-journalism program. It was an amazing transformation."

Another sales rep struck out in Springfield, Illinois, because one distraught mother organized seventy-five parents into a boycott, although they had not seen the program. In Idabel, Oklahoma, sales rep Susan Anderson was giving a presentation to the superintendent and two principals when one of her charts snagged her pearl necklace, breaking the string. The four of them got on the floor to pick up the scattered pearls. "All the superintendent's secretary could see was the four of us underneath the table laughing our heads off," said Susan Anderson. "It really broke the ice, and they did go for Channel One."

In Santa Rosa County, near Pensacola, Florida, a parent group fought sales rep Janet Dearden viciously. "They spread rumors I was sleeping with the superintendent, and that's why he was for the show. At the school board meeting, they said Time Warner was trying to take over the world and this was how they were going to get the young people. It was ridiculous. They did everything but burn me at the stake. That ruined the whole Panhandle; none of the counties wanted anything to do with Channel One after that."

At the beginning of August 1989, the Whittle team had contacted 155 schools and signed up only 14. Chris was undaunted. "Our critics have totally underestimated us," he told the *Wall Street Journal*, predicting that when Channel One officially aired on March 5, 1990, 1,114 schools would be receiving the program with another 5,000 signed up and committed.

He knew he was taking a big risk. Failure of Channel One could easily leave him $150 million in the hole.

"We'd be digging out of that mess for twenty years," he admitted, ruefully.

The Channel One war was a long way from over.

═══

Tom Ingram, continuing in his role as Chris's political consultant, watched his client become deeply absorbed in the Channel One controversy. "That kind of took over his schedule, including his political exploration," says Ingram. "Channel One just kind of knocked everything else off the scope for a while.

"And not only did it dominate his time, it illustrated to him, I think, the way things were frequently approached by the public sector and the way he was approaching them from the private sector.

"And it graphically illustrated to him points that Lewis Lavine [Ingram's partner] and I had been making—that that was the kind of thinking, the kind of criticism, the kind of process and debate that he would have to deal with on a regular basis if he were in government.

"And that, in fact, what he was doing by creating Channel One and implementing it was very important. And he was doing that from a private business position. He didn't have to be in a public elected or appointed position to do that. In fact if he were, he probably couldn't do it."

According to Ingram, Chris Whittle could resolve his political dilemma because "he realized he had more options as a private person. It wasn't a decision he made on one certain day. It was more like, I just don't have time to do it anymore. So it was moved to a side burner and put on hold—as opposed to thoughtfully cancelled."

As the Whittle political dream took a back seat, the ax fell on *Tennessee Illustrated*. There just wasn't enough advertising revenue to support it. The second year brought another $1 million deficit. On May 4, 1990, Chris suspended publication.

═══

To continue innovation and growth meant maintaining a high-powered cadre of executives. It was no easy task; the chairman was choosy. Chris was only interested in big-time thinkers who were totally devoid of "corporate cholesterol." At the beginning of the 1990s Whittle Communications was loosely organized into five divisions, each run as a separate business by its president and named for him.

"That personalizes performance," Chris explained. "Besides, there is no other way to define them since a division may be working in books, magazines, wall media, or something else at the same time."

Each division president had to be able to deliver. Ordinarily they were executives plucked from big business because they had displayed independence and creativity. They were charged with creating new properties and marketing and running them. Whittle gave them high standards to meet.

"We raise the bar very high around here," Chris explained. "To give you an example of how we grade the internal report card: Ten percent growth [in a division] is a complete failure, 20 percent is embarrassing, 30 percent is not bad. Forty percent you can begin to strut a bit."

A few disasters, however, would not get an executive fired. "We encourage people to fail," Nick Glover once said. "The people who are feared at Whittle are those not brave enough to try things." In fact, about one out of every five new ideas fizzled before it ever got out of the starting gate.

Each potential project was expected to aim for a 20 percent profit margin, meaning that as the company grew so did the pressure to generate ideas that create ever bigger revenue. As Chris Whittle often said, "It takes almost the same talent to pursue a $100 million idea as it does a $5 million idea."

Steady growth required strong leaders. Besides, the direction of the organization was undergoing a lot of change in goals and methods, which also needed careful thought and action.

Whether in his battery-charging sojourns to the Swiss Alps, shooting the rapids in the Grand Canyon, working out in his home gymnasium, on an early-morning walk, or at one of the frequent executive retreats, Chris was constantly studying the future. Deliberately he tried to peer five years ahead for his company and himself. Once he decided on a project or a schedule, it was immediately jotted on the yellow pad he kept in reach.

In his search for talent to augment his entrepreneurial cadre, Chris proved to be a vigorous suitor. He relied heavily on a New York headhunter, Don Ross. The persistence with which they pursued a quarry was demonstrated when they targeted the number-two man at Turner Broadcasting System, chief operating officer Gerry Hogan.

They knew Hogan had already turned down an offer from Rupert Murdoch to develop Fox Broadcasting. But they were impressed that Hogan started with Ted Turner in a one-station operation with barely $1 million revenue and in twenty years had helped develop it into a $1.5 billion Goliath, four or five times larger than Whittle. That they were trying to lure a frog to leap from a big pond to a small puddle deterred neither.

Ross could not get past Hogan's secretary but scrounged his unlisted home number and called him one night to ask if he'd consider a job change. Hogan said no. Ross persisted, urging Hogan to at least talk to Chris. After thirty minutes, Hogan gave in that much. Chris flew to Atlanta and they talked over lunch.

"I found Chris interesting," Hogan says. "But, I still said no."

Chris wouldn't give up. For the next three months he and Ross badgered the Turner executive by phone to meet once more and explore possibilities. "They were enormously persistent and tenacious," Hogan recalls. They raised what he calls "valid points" that made him ponder his career status, but again he said he wasn't interested in moving to Whittle.

Two weeks later Chris was again on the phone. "Would you mind," he asked, "making a list of the reasons you wouldn't join us and giving it to me so I can at least understand the problem?"

By now Hogan was irritated. They were imposing on his time. But he was intrigued enough to agree to do it. "There were only four or five items on my list," he says. Hogan was mainly concerned about his chances of breaking out of the role of number-two man. Chris flew to Atlanta, picked up Hogan's list, and said thanks.

A week later Chris phoned again. "I'd like to go over this list with you," Chris said. "Because I've got an answer to all these and I have reasons why this is the right thing for you to do."

When they met again, Chris answered all objections and presented what Hogan called "compelling reasons" for joining Whittle Communications as a vice-chairman. Hogan then talked to Ted Turner to ask what timetable existed for Ted to retire and Hogan to become CEO. Becoming number one was a big concern to Hogan; he had observed CEOs like William S. Paley of CBS, who kept day-to-day control into his eighties. Ted Turner, not much older than his COO, discussed his plans for eventually turning control of Turner Broadcasting System to Hogan. It was a friendly talk, but the timetable left Hogan disappointed.

At that juncture Turner's right-hand man decided to get serious with Chris. He introduced Mrs. Hogan to Chris and went to Knoxville to look over the company and see what it would be like to live there.

"Chris made me a very attractive offer in terms of the financial package," Hogan says, but he declines to spell out details. "During all these sessions Chris had painted a picture of his dream of what this company might be and what role I might play. My first fifteen or seventeen years at Turner were spent building the company. For the last two to four I basically did day-to-day operating. Chris is a wonderful salesman. He opened my eyes to the reality that what I enjoyed was the building, not the operating. He held out a new opportunity."

Hogan was bombarded with memos, charts, and letters from Chris. They had more face-to-face meetings, and talked frequently by phone. "Don Ross, Chris's headhunter, was involved, too," says Hogan. "They kind of double-teamed me. Don would act as sort of my confidant."

They tried to convince Hogan, who had turned forty, that he would enjoy a new challenge, escape his current management headache of dealing with four thousand employees, and focus instead on building a business. "I was sold into this. There is no doubt about it."

Chris almost stumbled by failing to recognize the glamor element accompanying the number-two job at Turner Broadcasting. "We were making movies and dealing with the entertainment community in Hollywood and so forth." says Hogan. "That was a component I think Chris undervalued perhaps because he didn't have any experience with it. But over time they learned a lot about me and what my hot buttons were and what kinds of things interested me. That's what they focused on. If they couldn't address a problem like the glamor side of Turner, the Hollywood side, they tended to move me off that issue, put it deep in the background as nothing significant rather than trying to confront it. That slowed down the process."

In early September 1990, Hogan agreed to take the Knoxville job and went in to tell Ted Turner he was leaving. "Ted was very angry. Very hurt and disappointed. Ted felt I was disloyal. I felt it was like a divorce, tearing apart a deep, personal relationship.Ted asked me to draw up a plan for shifting my responsibilities. The second day he implemented that. The third day he reopened all issues and asked what he had done wrong, and were there things he could do to fix it. I told him it was too late. He again became angry, and our communication was essentially over. In April 1992, through mutual friends, we had lunch and to some degree buried the hatchet, but our relationship obviously can never be the same."

The Knoxville job didn't turn out to be quite what Hogan had expected. "I was surprised both positively and negatively," he says. "I was surprised positively by the number of bright people who were in the company. I was very surprised at the depth of talent Chris had assembled for the size of the company. I was surprised on the negative side by the small amount of financial resources we had at that time to search for new opportunities."

Hogan had calculated Whittle Communications was perhaps five years behind Turner Broadcasting in development. "The reality was it was about ten years behind."

The new vice-chairman was assigned to oversee the drifting core business—the single-sponsored publications that the company had been founded on—and to lead Whittle Communications into the retail environment and event marketing. But being short of capital hurt him. Hogan had to scale back on his ideas. "But Chris did an enormous amount of work to try to mobilize what resources we had for me, so that we could do some things."

Hogan quickly tackled a promising ongoing project called Highway One, which was an attempt to market new automobiles to people visiting shopping malls.

Whittle had discovered something Detroit was also finding out—that many people were reluctant to visit dealers' showrooms because they were subjected to hard sell. The Whittle concept was to create a "large automobile and entertainment center" in a mall where people could walk in and find cars from as many as ten different manufacturers displayed along with high-tech, computerized information devices. The computer screens would show comparisons on cars' cost of operation and maintenance, and simulate various features. In the back would be something like a superstore travel agency offering free maps and trip ideas.

"The idea was to draw people, give them exposure to these cars, answer their questions in a friendly way without trying to sell them anything," says Chris. "If a visitor was interested there were phones available to make arrangements for an immediate test drive. It was a nonthreatening vehicle for introducing consumers to new automobiles."

The Highway One concept was planned for malls throughout the United States. Each month would have a different theme—such as sports utility vehicles, convertibles, medium family sedans.

The Chrysler Corporation immediately signed up—at a cost of between $10 million and $20 million. General Motors made a tentative agreement. If Ford had also come in it would have been difficult for Toyota and other manufacturers not to sign.

But from 1991 to 1992 the auto industry was in too much turmoil, and Highway One, unable to get enough sponsors to break even, was shelved. Hogan felt frustrated but moved ahead on other new Whittle ventures.

The next big-name hire was Hamilton Jordan, coming off distinguished careers in the public and private sectors. Manager of Jimmy Carter's campaigns for governor of Georgia and president, Jordan (pronounced JER-dan) was Carter's White House chief of staff. Later he wrote a book, *Crisis: The Last Year of the Carter Presidency*, and from 1987 through 1990 was chief executive officer of ATP/ATP Tour, the governing body for men's international professional tennis. During that time the organization's marketing revenues rose by over 400 percent. Chris named him chairman of corporate communications.

About this time, however, the game of musical chairs got into high gear in the executive suite. Several projects were being altered or abandoned; important new ones, such as Channel One, were taking center stage. As needs developed, Chris had no compunction about switching his men from one post to another. At times such changes were forced by outside events, as when "Ham" Jordan took a leave of absence to go to Dallas and codirect the Ross Perot campaign for president. Jordan was back in Knoxville in a matter of weeks.

Jordan's next assignment was to create something patriotic, similar to America's celebration of the bicentennial, that would get the jump on the advent of the twenty-first century. It was tough going, and by the time Jordan left Whittle Communications he was complaining that he had wasted several years—"the most frustrating" of his career.

Countered a fellow executive in Knoxville, "He was disappointed that he wasn't treated as a chief of staff. The fact of the matter is, he wasn't the chief of staff."

At one point there was much gossip among Knoxville businessmen about Whittle Communications. "Chris has got a lot of new million-dollar men over there," said one observer. "They look to me like 'trophies.' I don't know how he can use all of them."

Chris conceded he heard that talk. "I didn't agree with it. The most important thing in business are the people within it. That's particularly true of a business that's in a development stage. And my belief, particularly if you have an agenda like ours, is that you need a number of very talented people. By definition, you are going to make some mistakes. Some of those people aren't going to work out. But that shouldn't be a reason not to bring them in. And in our case most worked out. We try to be patient, and if you really run through the list, we've done pretty well."

In this period of development Chris recruited a series of top-notch executives, including his political guru Tom Ingram, whom he shoved into a leadership role for the flagging *Special Report* operation. Others freshly hired or promoted to key positions included Mike McAllister, who had been vice-president for marketing at Wrangler jeans and Luchese boots; Douglas J. Greenlaw from MTV Networks, where he was executive vice president; Tim Nichols, who had created media research at Chiat/Day/Mojo in New York; and Ray Gaulke from Gannett's *USA Today*, where he was president of the *Weekend* supplement.

———

Even before any one project fully took form, Chris Whittle's imagination usually had already galloped ahead conjuring up something else. That was certainly true with the advent of the 1990s; he was on a creative rampage. Half a dozen singular and fresh ideas were jostling inside his brain to stormily emerge and produce headlines in the media and educational worlds.

Corporate executives rarely had time to glean the information they needed from books and magazines. Why couldn't those thick "doorstopper" books be thinner, quicker to read? Instead of seven hundred pages, perhaps only one hundred?

Enlisting editor in chief Bill Rukeyser, Chris set out to solve that problem. "What a lot of executives did," says Rukeyser, "was not to read books anymore but to read reviews, and feel guilty. We began to consider whether we could create serious nonfiction books on topics that business people would know they ought to know about, and get authors already known to them."

What Chris and Rukeyser first had in mind was offering serious business-oriented topics in small sponsored booklets of about eight pages. Initially Chris rejected the scheme but later reconsidered and commissioned a closer look. Research and focus-group interviews convinced them that experienced authors could boil a serious book down to one hundred pages and that executives wouldn't give up before finishing one that length.

But the kicker was they saw their short books as a perfect medium for carrying advertising from a single sponsor. Once again, Chris Whittle was ready to jump the traces of convention.

Moreover, Whittle books would not be peddled through bookstores among the fifty thousand published annually but sent free to 150,000 "opinion makers" across the country—all paid for by the sponsor. Of the one hundred pages, twenty would be reserved for the sponsor's message. It would be expensive, the advertiser paying about $13 per book.

Offering a $60,000 advance for each manuscript, they quickly signed up such authors as David Halberstam, John Kenneth Galbraith, William Greider, George Gilder, Edward J. Epstein, James Atlas, and Robert Waterman.

Chris pitched the first of these Whittle Direct Books, known as the "Larger Agenda" series, to his fellow Tennessean Frederick Smith, chairman of Federal Express. It was a quick sale.

Established book publishers were critical. None said they would follow suit. Said one publisher: "I'm not sure I want to read a book and find an ad for baby powder, or worse." Paperbacks had tried ads in the 1960s but dropped them after postal authorities and authors protested.

Once again a Chris Whittle brainstorm had become an important money-making concept. The *Knoxville News-Sentinel* gave him an editorial pat on the back: "Leave it to Chris Whittle to find a different way to do something. Whittle's latest innovation . . . likely will carve another notch in the belt of his publishing empire. . . . 'It will not be the biggest part of our business,' Whittle said, 'but it will be a very prestigious part.' . . . While we are waiting on the books, we are impressed with Whittle's creativity that gives a big boost to Knoxville."

Quickly a second series was launched: the "Grand Rounds Press," which explored issues in medicine aimed at physicians and health care policy makers, and sponsored by various pharmaceutical and health care–related companies.

A third series, "The Chief Executive Press," announced in June 1992, was an eight-book deal sponsored by Cessna Aircraft and sent to CEOs and senior executives in about eleven thousand companies. The second Chief Executive Press book was the much talked about *What Are You Worth?—The New World of Executive Pay,* by Graef S. Crystal, a well known compensation consultant.

In less than three years, nineteen Whittle Direct Books had been published. Though generally well received, the "giveaway" tag that stuck to them, as it did to their targeted publications, secretly rankled the Knoxville entrepreneurs. Yearning for acceptance and legitimacy in the publishing world, Rukeyser and Chris worked to effect some hookup with established book publishers.

They did so by entering a licensing agreement with W. W. Norton and Company for the six titles from its first "Larger Agenda" series to be published—minus, of course, the advertising pages. The first, *The Disuniting of America,* by Arthur M. Schlesinger Jr., was on the *New York Times* bestseller list for nine weeks.

Whittle Communications actually got into the mainstream of book marketing and distribution in the fall of 1992 by entering a three-year agreement with Penguin USA. In that arrangement, Penguin USA agreed to publish, each year a minimum of four titles previously issued or commissioned by Whittle, with the two parties sharing the revenue fifty-fifty.

With that contract the Knoxville company had finally achieved the status it yearned for. With considerable satisfaction, Bill Rukeyser told the *Knoxville News-Sentinel* the deal "is a validation from the conventional publishing world of the appeal of what we're publishing."

16

A MANHATTAN
LOVE STORY

Chris Whittle discovered the girl of his dreams—in the best love song tradition—across a crowded room. But there was a major complication. It was not the standard boy-meets-girl romantic scenario. The woman was already married and even had a child at home.

The fateful episode began when his decorator Liza Lerner invited him to a surprise fiftieth birthday party for her husband Porter Bibb, an investment banker, a writer and producer for television, and author of a biography of Ted Turner.

The party was held April 4, 1987, at a dance studio called Steps on New York's Upper West Side. Chris knew some of the fifty guests, but not all. The one who stunned him was a striking stranger, tall, slender, with a confident air and dark hair streaming halfway down her back. Liza Lerner introduced them. "Priscilla Rattazzi," said Liza Lerner, pronouncing her first name with an Italian accent—Pre-SHEE-la.

Taking her hand, Chris turned on his charm. Priscilla smiled back, warmly. It was a magic moment for both of them.

Chris also met her husband, Claus Moehlmann, a German national who was an investment banker with First Boston Corporation in New York. And before the evening was over he learned that at their Upper East Side townhouse they had a one-year-old son, Maximilian.

It was instantly clear to Chris that here was the woman who met all his carefully engineered criteria for a perfect wife. That she already had a husband was merely an unexpected complication.

"When Chris sees something he wants," says a woman who knows him well, "even if it's something he's not supposed to have, he lets nothing stand in his way."

But, he did not see or speak to Priscilla again for at least eight months. Their next encounter took place in December 1987 at a Christmas party in Manhattan.

In his passion for new art treasures Chris searched many places—on foot, on the phone, and through catalogs. With further plans to build and refine his collection, in the fall of 1987 he hired Lori Ciancaglini, a private adviser and art dealer in New York.

"He was really bitten by the art bug," says Lori Ciancaglini. "Collectors fall into three interest categories: mild, moderate, intense. Chris was intense. Art collecting was a pleasure for Chris, not a business. More like a sport. It was a civilized hunt, and fun."

Lori first met Chris at the Dakota in January 1985, introduced by Peter Marino. Marino had her helping search for several paintings needed to complete the living room in the Dakota apartment. She recommended an Oriental work, *In a Rug Bazaar,* by George Henry Hall and *Lady on a Gold Couch,* by American Impressionist Frederick Carl Frieseke. Frieseke had painted a richly patterned portrait of his wife reclining on a French settee in 1906 at Giverny. It was grand scale, five by six feet.

Chris bought both paintings and was impressed by her art knowledge and expertise. A few weeks later Peter Marino asked Lori to prepare a catalog of the 120 art works already hanging in the Dakota apartment.

"I spent about a year and a half doing the catalog," she says. "It was almost like detective work. I spent a lot of time over at the Dakota alone with the art collection and at the Fricke Art Reference Library. The apartment was very quiet, serene, and stately. Almost like a private museum. After the catalog was finished, I had a meeting with Chris, and a serious new acquisition program was launched in November 1987. We tried to develop an effective strategy for collecting."

Manhattan galleries and auction houses were visited by collector and adviser. They received identical magazines, gallery bulletins, and art auction catalogs. That led to some amusing incidents.

In *Antiques* magazine, she saw a painting offered by a Boston gallery "that would be great." She phoned. The gallery owner said, "Oh, a man from Kentucky called yesterday about that painting!"

"Are you sure it wasn't a man from Tennessee?"

"Yes, it was a man from Tennessee."

"Chris Whittle?"

"Yes."

In the end, Chris and his adviser decided to pass on it.

Then a similar coincidence happened. "I received a brochure from a Cincinnati gallery," says Lori Ciancaglini. "In the brochure I saw a beautiful portrait of a young girl by an American artist named Elizabeth Nourse. When I phoned to inquire, the owners of the gallery who knew I was Chris's adviser said, 'Well, Chris was in town yesterday and came in and bought that work.' Our being on the same art path was kind of magic. I found it a lot of fun."

On every trip to Europe, Chris was on the lookout for art. In London he saw two men remove a huge marine painting from a truck in front of a gallery. He followed the painting into the gallery and bought the work, by William Wyllie.

Lori Ciancaglini explained what inspired his love of art. "I understand the motivation. I love art, and when I meet another person who loves art in this strong way it makes complete sense to me. Chris is such a discriminating person. He enjoyed the cerebral, intellectual selection process and the intuitive emotional response to a painting. Chris was very focused on collecting, but I realized it was just a small aspect of the very dynamic and complex life he was leading."

Chris credits his mother's influence in his formative Etowah years for giving him a latent artistic bent. This passion to collect paintings was ignited by his need to decorate his Dakota apartment. In one of our interviews, he explained:

> Let me start by saying that my collecting is not very educated. Meaning it is much more an intuitive pursuit. Maybe a better way is to say it is not very studied. I've done it because I enjoy it. I've kind of taken to it very naturally. It's

been more hobby and fun. I don't think of it in any way as labor.

In the beginning I was working on the apartment, and the art flowed out of that. My tastes are pretty specific. They run from about 1870 to 1915, mainly American and British and Scottish and Scandinavian.

A painter friend of mine described my paintings as the most singular collection he had ever seen in that most of the art had a very particular sensibility. I'd never thought of that—that the pieces were very connected, and that each had a certain atmosphere, a certain mood.

I think there is some truth in that. And as you say, poetic and romantic is a pretty good description of it.

Art collectors, of course, need deep pockets. Chris's were fairly deep but not bottomless. He sent his adviser to a New York gallery to examine a small Thomas Dewing portrait of a standing woman. "It was very lovely and poetic," says Lori Ciancaglini. "We agreed it was of good quality, but it was too expensive. However, the Dewing reminded me of a work I had seen a year earlier by John White Alexander entitled *Onteora*. It depicted a woman in a gown standing in a doorway holding a bowl of flowers. Oddly, Chris's apartment had a similar curtained doorway between hall and living room."

They located *Onteora,* and bought it. When asked why he seems partial to paintings of women, Chris merely smiles. He decided to acquire more of Alexander's work. Another of the artist's portraits, *Alethea (The Blue Dress)*, went on the auction block at Sotheby's in New York. Chris sent Lori to bid—and gave her a limit. Very discreet, she refuses to mention the figure, but art auction sources indicate it was close to $500,000.

"There was ferocious bidding between me and another gallery," she says. "I didn't get the painting and I wanted Chris to know right away." The auction house phones were all busy. She rushed by cab to her West 76th Street apartment.

"I was unlocking the door when I heard the phone ringing. It was Chris calling to find out what happened. I still had my coat on. *Alethea (The Blue Dress)* was magnificent, and he was very anxious to get it. He just couldn't resist it. A few weeks later the gallery that had won the painting at auction put the work on exhibition. Chris went in on a Saturday and bought it."

At all hours, from his home, airports, the office, his car, Chris would phone to discuss paintings. "I received early morning telephone calls from London dealers and packages of art information constantly," Lori Ciancaglini says. That was fine with her. "We were both aware of the competitive art market at the time and did not want to miss anything." Frequently she would leave a folder of art photos with her recommendations on his desk at the Dakota.

"You would get a sense of order and decorum in the apartment until you walked into Chris's study. A million proposals and contracts on his desk—it was overflowing with art catalogs. Stacks of books. There was wall-to-wall information in that room. It was always interesting to see what he was reading. History books. A biography of Thomas Jefferson. *Brideshead Revisited. The Road Less Traveled.* A well balanced selection. Not just art books.

"Leaving my blue folder was interesting. I'd put it on top of the stack on Friday because he would usually come in on weekends and go through his papers. When I went back, my blue folder was usually buried, but I would always find his notes to me in it.

"Chris relies on a lot of specialists to do things for him, and you feel a great deal of trust. I started to feel so terribly comfortable in that apartment. I was spending so much time there. The majority of the art was there. He had other works at his offices in Tennessee and New York. At one point there was so much he had to store paintings in a warehouse. There was no room to hang anything else. Paintings were leaning against the walls in the hallways. The apartment looked like an artist's studio at the turn of the century."

For several years, Chris and his adviser devoted themselves to the search for important acquisitions for his collection. But as his personal and business lives became more complicated and intense, his interest in collecting dropped back to mild. He told Lori Ciancaglini, "I believe I'll put collecting on hold for a while."

In January 1988 the Claus Moehlmanns separated, and Chris started to pursue Priscilla. She didn't seem to mind. "Priscilla was totally enamored of Chris," says a mutual friend. "What woman wouldn't be? He is quiet and charming. Very considerate of a woman's feelings. And, oh, so self-effacing."

When they first met, Chris did not know he had fallen in love with a scion of Italy's perhaps wealthiest and most powerful family. Her mother, Susanna Agnelli, is the granddaughter of the founder of the Fiat conglomerate, headquartered in Turin. Not only a maker of cars, the multibillion-dollar corporation is involved in shipping, oil refining, banks, newspaper and book publishing, department stores, professional athletic teams, insurance, plastics, and scores of other enterprises. Susanna's brother, Gianni Agnelli—known in New York as Johnny—has headed Fiat since 1966. Gianni once had a grand affair with Pamela Harriman.

Priscilla's father was Count Urbano Rattazzi, born in 1918 in Genoa, Italy. He married Susanna—known by the nickname Suni—on August 18, 1945, in Forte dei Marmi, Italy. Between 1946 and 1956 they had six children, two daughters born in Rome, a son and a daughter born in Buenos Aires, and a son in Lausanne, Switzerland. The last was Priscilla, born on July 20, 1956, in Rome. Not much later her parents divorced.

A pampered life awaited Priscilla. She was educated in boarding schools in England. At eighteen she came to New York, where years before the Angelli clan had established a strong American presence. (Priscilla's great-grandmother was a Virginia belle who married into Italian nobility. Moreover, her uncle "Johnny" Agnelli was a frequent visitor to New York and Detroit on financial and industrial business.)

In 1974 Priscilla enrolled at Sarah Lawrence College in Bronxville, New York, graduating in 1978 in liberal arts. She concentrated on photography, taking classes for seven semesters in that subject. Priscilla is remembered for her "endless curiosity and modesty" by Dr. Joseph Papaleo, director of the college's writing seminars and author of three novels and forty-five short stories published in the *New Yorker, Penthouse,* and other magazines. As her don, or counselor, he conferred with her twice a month.

"I think she was aware of what she didn't know," says Papaleo, "and that meant she was more intelligent. She had a wisdom beyond her young years. She was easygoing. To use the language of the sixties, there was an aspect of her that was really laid-back."

Louis Sgroi, a New York painter who taught photography at Sarah Lawrence College from 1970 to 1980, says his class—limited to fifteen—was already full when she applied, carrying a handful of her pictures. "After I talked to her awhile," Sgroi says, "I was impressed. I don't know how the hell you are supposed to react to people. I felt a sincerity there. She was shy, but that didn't bother me at all. I managed to sneak her into my class."

Sgroi suggested Priscilla buy a simple, reliable camera; she got a Nikon. "The camera is just a tool. Don't get crazy with gadgets," he told her. Sgroi did not know Priscilla was wealthy until she came in one day "almost crying."

"I said, 'What the hell is the matter?' She said, 'I can't go home!' Well, there was a scare in Italy over some kidnappings, and she was afraid for her own safety because of—what do they call that?— ransom. I said, 'What do you mean?' And she said, 'My family is connected with Fiat.' "

Sgroi also got a glimpse of her connections when she casually remarked she was going to photograph movie actress Sophia Loren. "I said, 'Sophia doesn't want anybody to take her picture!' Priscilla said, 'Oh, I know her. She's a friend of mine.' "

On another occasion she told Sgori that her mother had gone into politics, becoming mayor of the Italian seaside town of Porto Ercole, later joining Italy's Parliament as a senator. Suni Rattazzi would also serve in Rome as vice secretary of state for foreign affairs before finally abandoning political life in the late 1980s.

From the Sarah Lawrence campus Priscilla set out on a career as a freelance photographer in New York—using her keen eye for available-light shots and family connections to open doors. She served an apprenticeship with famous society and fashion photographer Hiro in Manhattan. Then she was taken on as a protégée by the late Diane Vreeland, the influential editor of *Vogue* magazine. She became a busy photographer, shooting pictures for the *New York Times,* and other publications. She began thinking about doing a book of photographs of celebrities with their pet dogs.

By the time she was in her twenties, Priscilla was dating the *Vogue* editor's grandson, Nicky Vreeland. Then she met Alex Ponti, son of movie producer Carlo Ponti and stepson of her friend Sophia Loren. Priscilla married Alex, but it proved a mistake. Their marriage lasted only a few weeks.

The March 1990 issue of *Vanity Fair* quoted a friend from those days: "She was always very sweet. Priscilla was never flashy, and she had a very sympathetic personality. Men loved her, and you could understand why—she was Italian royalty, but she didn't have an attitude." After her divorce she married Claus Moehlmann, and their blond son Maxi was born in 1986.

Details of Chris Whittle's vigorous courtship of Claus Moehlmann's wife are not widely known. Chris, when questioned, is not very forthcoming. Priscilla is adamant about keeping their romance private. A few of her friends talked about her personality, such as agent Ed Victor's comment, "Priscilla is one of those diaphanous women made of steel." But most friends stonewalled interview requests. Priscilla urgently telephoned Liza Lerner and Porter Bibb, begging them to not talk about her romance with Chris.

Not long after separating from Claus, Priscilla began moving toward divorce. Moehlmann was reported to have gone to London or perhaps Germany. Quietly, Chris and Priscilla began dating. The forbidden element of their romance seemed to invigorate her suitor, according to *Vanity Fair*. The magazine said:

> "She and Chris had to keep their relationship secret quite awhile," says a friend of Whittle's. "But I think Chris loved that. He loves intrigue, and there he was, having an affair with an Italian princess. . . . He appears to be quite smitten— at a recent dinner party he kept one eye on Rattazzi at all times. ... Whittle's work schedule has not slackened. He usually sees Rattazzi only on the weekends. . . ."

In Knoxville Chris talked about his dream girl only to relatives and a few close friends. Almost immediately she triggered profound changes in his life-style, most particularly in his places of abode.

"There were reasons," Chris says, "for these changes in my life. My decision to sell my farm in Vermont, my moving out of my log cabin in Knoxville, and ultimately my selling the Dakota—and this is particularly true of Vermont and the cabin. She likes those a great deal. The reason we left Vermont is because the farm at Waitsfield is very difficult to get to with a family. You basically can't do it. It was one thing for me as a bachelor to go up there anytime I wanted to, but to take children and nannies, it just didn't work. Even though she loved the place and I loved the place."

He could not expect her to appreciate being quartered in Knoxville in the tumbling-down log cabin he adored. So to have a decent and traditional place he spent about $700,000 for a two-story, four-place apartment building, known locally as the Van Dyke "Mansion" on Kingston Pike, with a view of Fort Loudon Lake. He converted one of the apartments into his own deluxe residence and turned one into guest quarters. Another was made into his personal gymnasium, with the fourth used for storage. To decorate his new place Chris flew in Liza Lerner from New York.

Reportedly for $8 million, Chris bought a large rambling beach house at East Hampton, on Long Island, that a physician had built in 1933 on what is called Georgica Pond, a hurricane-formed lake that measures about one-third by one and one-half miles. The pond is separated from the Atlantic Ocean by a sandspit fifty yards wide. Chris commissioned Peter Marino to remodel the residence and make it deluxe.

According to the December 1994 issue of *Vanity Fair*, the two-story, fifteen-room mansion "is done to perfection inside, from the grand balconied living room to the last bit of wainscoting on the back stair. The dock where several sailboats are moored is private, the tennis court is hidden behind a thick wall of evergreens, and off to one side there is a guesthouse so beautifully decorated that it rivals many of the area's main residences."

At the time Chris bought the property, Priscilla Rattazzi was spending summers at the Agnelli family beach place, which was conveniently located just across Georgica Pond. The Agnelli family has since sold that residence.

When their dating became serious, Priscilla made clear that she did not like his Dakota apartment. "It is incredibly dark and gloomy, too masculine," she told a friend—and obviously Chris as well. He put the "bachelor" apartment on the market at $2.7 million. Even though he had invested years in creating this "crown jewel," he realized it would be too small and otherwise unsuitable for a married man. He loved the Dakota, so he purchased a twelve-room apartment on a lower floor that the owner had created by combining two side-by-side, six-room apartments, and commissioned Peter Marino to decorate it for a family.

"We knew we were going to get married," Chris says, "but there were legal complications"—meaning it took three years for the Italian heiress to divorce her husband.

Though Chris kept their romance quiet for about a year, he couldn't resist finally showing her off in New York City in 1989 to a few select Knoxville colleagues and their wives. Priscilla's Mona Lisa–like beauty, obvious intelligence, and engaging personality won them over instantly. They were impressed that she spoke five languages.

Chris had to share Priscilla with her continuing career as a photographer. She was shooting celebrities and their canine companions for a book, *Best Friends,* which was published by Rizzoli in April 1989.

Actress Glenn Close posed with her Coton de Tulear "Gabby" nestled on her bare feet; socialite Brooke Astor, who had four rowdy dogs, managed to quiet her Schnauzer "Maize" for a woodland portrait. Priscilla Rattazzi told *Time* magazine that snapping director Franco Zeffirelli and his Maremma sheepdog "Boboli" gave her the jitters. Henry Kissinger and Ivan Lendl gave no trouble; they refused to pose. With all the hassles, asked the *Time* reporter, why do a book featuring dogs? Her answer: "I hate cats."

To keep her eye sharp, Priscilla was committed to a daily ritual of unlimbering the Nikon and shooting at least one roll of film. Often her subject was little Maxi. Looking at the photos she took of her son gave her the idea for a second book—celebrities and their children. Rizzoli, pleased with the reception accorded *Best Friends,* promptly gave her a contract to produce it.

The stir created by the dog book publicly lifted the cloak hiding the Whittle-Rattazzi love affair. One New York gossip columnist reported they were engaged. Chris assured the *Knoxville Journal's* "Whispers" column that the New York item was "premature." He said they had been dating for a year and were "just very good friends."

Yet Chris had already begun to build his life around Priscilla. They were often apart, both traveling, he the most, either on business or mountain treks. Her photo appointments frequently took her abroad. In winter she customarily joined the Agnelli clan—along with Roman princesses, descendants of doges, or dashing *sportivi*—on the snowy slopes of Italy's Cortina d'Ampezzo, site of the 1956 Winter Olympics. The December 1988 *Town and Country* magazine showed her there with Maxi, both ready to ski.

In New York, Chris and Priscilla kept close watch on progress of

Case Number 65267–90 in New York County's state supreme court—Moehlmann, Claus *vs.* Moehlmann, Priscilla R., for divorce. Until the decree in that lawsuit was granted the lovers could not marry.

The Moehlmann marriage was finally dissolved without contest, and on July 16, 1990, the decree was recorded in the Manhattan court clerk's office. (It was just about then that Chris and Priscilla attended the Long Island dinner at the Ed Victors' Two Barns beach house where Chris first met Benno Schmidt and debated with him about reinventing education.)

Now that Priscilla was free they plunged into wedding plans. They picked a date—August 12, 1990—eleven days before his forty-third birthday. She had just turned thirty-four on July 20th. The ceremony would take place at Chris's East Hampton beach house, but that posed a problem because carpenters were still sawing lumber and hammering nails to complete the remodeling. Their solution was to order a tent and have the ceremony staged on the lawn.

About one hundred guests were invited. Priscilla's mother, Suni Agnelli, and her sister Ilaria, a child psychologist, flew over from Italy. Chris brought his immediate family by plane from Knoxville: his parents, his sisters Camille Hanggi and Karen Ellington with their husbands, and the two Hanggi children, Matt and Sarah.

"I like Priscilla a lot," says sister Karen. "She's super. I told Chris he really picked a jewel. She's really sweet. She's very well educated and on top of things."

During the civil ceremony, says Bob Hanggi, "Chris got a little choked up. Why? Because when he makes a commitment—you'd better believe it!"

Longtime friend, journalist, and author Richard Stengel was best man. Maxi, four and a half, was ring bearer, joined by two four- or five-year-old flower girls, Zoe Bibb, daughter of the Porter Bibbs, and Anna Kennedy, daughter of Michael, a well-known Manhattan attorney, and Eleonora Kennedy. Photos taken at the wedding appeared in the November 1990 issue of *Vanity Fair*. Shown along with close-ups of the bride and groom were artists Keith Sonnier and Nessia Pope playing with their daughter Olympia, architect Peter Marino and his Westie "Nella" amusing the guests, and Richard Stengel posing with Susan Calhoun. The *Vanity Fair* picture page carried a succinct caption:

WEDDED CHRIS

What made media mogul Chris Whittle, forty-three and seemingly a confirmed bachelor, finally take the plunge and marry Agnelli scion Priscilla Rattazzi? "I love her," he says. "It's as simple as that."

The wedding was page-one news in the Knoxville newspapers. It was soon followed by the public announcement that they were expecting. This item appeared September 18, 1990, in the *News-Sentinel*:

ANOTHER WHITTLE IS ON THE WAY

Chris Whittle, who recently became a husband, is going to be a father.

His wife, Priscilla Rattazzi, is expecting in January, Whittle confirmed Monday.

Whittle, 43, and Rattazzi, 33, a photographer, were married in August in a ceremony attended only by family members. It was his first marriage; her third.

She has a 4 1/2 year old son from a previous marriage.

Ten days later Chris gave further news about his impending fatherhood to the newspaper—"It's going to be a girl."

Barbara Aston-Wash, the *News-Sentinel* society columnist, interviewed him September 28, 1990, when he and Priscilla came to Knoxville for a $125-per-person black-tie dinner that premiered an exhibit at the Knoxville Art Museum of one hundred paintings from his Dakota collection. Priscilla, whose physician presumably had made an ultrasound examination, was on her first visit to Tennessee as Mrs. Whittle.

Chris had not only loaned his paintings for hometown showing but had also provided his art curator Lori Ciancaglini to hang the show, which lasted a week. He had never before exhibited his collection.

"The first and probably the last time," Chris told the society writer. "Already I miss it. Walls at my apartment, the offices, and all our houses are bare with hanger nails sticking out. It is not a pretty sight."

That fall and winter the Chris Whittles occasionally returned to Knoxville for brief visits but primarily remained in the bachelor apartment in the Dakota while work continued on the larger one, which would have three bedrooms, in the same building.

On January 4, 1991, in their New York City apartment, Priscilla woke Chris up at 2:30 A.M. Her time had come.

They rushed to Lenox Hill Hospital. Chris went with her into the delivery room. At 4:30 A.M. the six-pound, fourteen-ounce girl was born. "It was pretty exciting," Chris said, relaying the news back to Tom Ingram at headquarters in Knoxville.

Three days later, "tired and happy," Priscilla took the baby home to the Dakota. They considered several names and finally settled on Andrea Leigh. "We call her Andie," said the new father.

=17=

FROM A TO Z, AND BACK TO R

In twenty years of managing R. J. Reynolds marketing in the United States, Europe, and the Far East, Nick Glover never found executives who ran a business quite the same way Chris Whittle and Phillip Moffitt ran the 13–30 Corporation in 1982.

"When I got on the scene to try to fix some of their problems, I found a lot of surprises," Glover recalls. "The company was still operating as a kind of college project–type thing. It had no real structure. Chris told me that's not something they knew anything about."

Glover considered himself a keen student of entrepreneurism. Once RJR's director of all marketing in the United States and one of its youngest vice-presidents, he gained his expertise by hands-on work.

"I had managed RJR subsidiaries and others in many parts of the world, and seen different dynamics. And it was a real shock to see all of these things going on in this little company in Knoxville, Tennessee. Completely by instinct!

"One aspect of Chris's genius is an incredible instinct for doing the right thing. Without having studied it. Neither one of these guys, as far as I know, had ever taken a business course. They were doing it by instinct. But their instincts were right."

Glover, who spent a year as a consultant before joining the little company as COO, adds, "I'll tell you why Chris was able to do this. Chris is the only person that I've ever known personally who is capable of doing what I'll describe to you, though I'm sure there are others. But most people—and I can't use the right terminology because I'm not a psychiatrist, but I'll give it to you in layman's terms.

"Most people tend to think down one of two paths. You have the sort of rational, logical, linear thinkers that go A, B, C, D, and on to Z. And those tend to be your marketing guys and your lawyers and people like that.

"And then you've got the more creative people who think, what I usually characterize as spirally. Their thinking progresses up a chain but it's not linear. It kind of bounces from one side of the spiral to the other. They will wind up at, say R, just like the linear guy, but it is not through some sort of logical path that they can track back. All they know is that they are at point R and instinctively they think that's the right place to be."

Nick Glover thinks the linear person has less chance of error, explaining, "Because he has kind of covered all bases as he's gone A, B, C, D, E. But there's little creativity in that process, so he's only going to get the same answer that anybody else would get going down that path.

"The strength of the spiral thinker is that he may break through and come up with a completely different answer that no one else would have thought of, but he can't prove it's the right answer. And he's likely to make more mistakes that way.

"Chris is the only person I have ever seen who can think down either path or both paths at the same time."

As his colleague for a decade, Glover observed thousands of episodes of Chris Whittle's creative thinking and problem solving firsthand.

"You know Chris got there by just instinct, and he went through that spiral path and went—bam! bam! bam! and saw here's what we ought to do. But then he can turn around and track it right back down through its logic why it makes sense to do it.

"So as a result of that he made very, very few decisional mistakes. And he can bring people along with him, where a lot of creative thinkers—and we saw this in our editorial and television production departments—that a lot of really good creative thinkers can't bring other people along with them because they can't explain why they're doing what they are doing.

"But Chris is such a master at explaining what he does that he can bring people along with him. And to me that has always been the kind of fundamental, at least half the fundamental, aspect of his genius."

In discussing elements of ambition, Glover suggests that Chris Whittle's personal drive is fueled by his almost insatiable thirst for knowledge. "He has more than anybody I've ever seen. And he's just constantly absorbing new data, and he has always been driven to kind of understand who he is, and how he operates, to better capitalize on what it is that he does."

Another longtime colleague impressed by Chris's so-called linear-spiral mental process is Ed Winter, who came to 13–30 from a vice presidency at Dallas's Tracy-Locke advertising agency in 1984 and later became head of Channel One. To the advertising man from Texas, Chris represented a free spirit enjoying the best of both the business and creative worlds.

"I was clearly drawn to him," Ed Winter says. "He was very hip, very loose. When he's on the case to convince you, he's really convincing. I think part of it is that Chris never wastes a single word. He is the most focused man I have ever seen in business anywhere. He doesn't waste a minute of time, not a single word. He draws you into that directness. And you want to be kind of on his side, on his wavelength. There is something that takes over that is sort of mesmerizing.

"It's the boyishness, the smart things he says, and the way he says them. You never lose track, and go, 'This guy's bullshitting me,' or, 'He doesn't know what he's talking about!' He's just so focused, he tends to get you right between the eyes."

One great advantage Chris has in business relationships, Winter believes, is being able to present his "own reality." Winter explains, "He sees the world the way he sees it, and he brings you around to his reality. That's why he has been such a great salesman. And why he is so effective at what he does. He creates and dimensionalizes a vision, so you believe it."

Most people, Winter believes, think in terms that are one-dimensional, "seeing only what is in front of them." Not so with Chris. Winter explains, "It is amazing the way the man's mind works. Chris always describes his way to me as looking at things through two or three prisms. And one prism may just see the facts. The second prism may see an alternative. And the other prism may come at the subject from the back side. And his mind is more like a kind of X-ray. He can extrapolate and put so many different things together, and keep them focused, and always approach things originally."

Winter cites as an example his discussion with Chris about a potential movie theater project. "I thought I was a pretty adept thinker, entrepreneurial, open-minded, smarter than the average. All the facts on this scheme were laid out. And the facts basically said we couldn't afford to do that business because the cost of doing a film every week and sending it to enough theaters to get a large enough audience wouldn't work.

"So we were going through this idea and I said, 'Chris, look at the facts. It just doesn't make sense. We might go in and install a satellite dish on a movie theater and do it that way.' He said, 'Isn't the big hang-up here the cost of printing and getting copies of the film? What exactly does that cost?'

"I gave him the figures. He said, 'Well, over a three-year period we could do X number of films. I don't think there's a problem here.' And I said, 'Well, look at the facts. It just costs too much money.' And he said, 'You haven't thought of one thing. If you were going to order that many prints from a film production facility you would be their primary business. Have you ever thought about buying the film production company, owning it, and making it a profit center, and using it?'

"My mouth just dropped open. I went, 'Hell, I never thought that was an option.' Chris said, 'Yeah, if you take away their profit margin and economies of scale, we'd be better off owning the facility. I'd bet that if we owned it and used it other times, not only would we cut our cost in half, we'd make money. Why should we be all of the volume for an outside supplier?'

"And that's a perfect example. Some people just don't go to the third or fourth prism and think around an issue—one of his big strengths!"

In making his own assessment of his skills, Chris Whittle does not rank himself "in classical terms of great intellect." In one of our interviews he said, "I didn't think of myself that way. I thought I worked hard. I thought I had more discipline than most, but probably until thirty I didn't think I was very smart.

"In terms of am I aware of how things get created? Yes! And I don't think it's very magical. I think, for example, one way you create things is to take things apart. And you take them and put them in all different pieces and say, Now how can you put this back differently? Or, What if we added this to it? . . . And that's like building blocks. . . . And organize it differently. And I think creativity is relatively logical. I think there are flashes, and I get mine after a hard workout in the steambath."

For fifteen years Chris regularly worked out at Knoxville's downtown YMCA at 605 Clinch Avenue. Then he installed exercise equipment, or gym rooms, in each of his residences.

Chris adds, "Generally I will get flashes and I will go, Oh! There's something interesting! Why? Well, I think it is relaxation. I do notice it again and again."

Brient Mayfield relates to some of these steam-bath inspirations. In the 1970s when he was a *Nutshell* partner, he and Chris habitually went to the Knoxville downtown YMCA around six-thirty P.M. to battle each other in two or three furious games of racquetball. Glistening with sweat from the strenuous exercise, they would spend ten or fifteen minutes in the steamroom.

"I remember that Chris got some of his ideas relaxing in the steambath," Mayfield says. "Directly from the Y we'd go about eight o'clock out to dinner, usually to the Copper Cellar on Cumberland Avenue near the University of Tennessee. We did a lot of brainstorming there. Usually we'd get together there with Phillip Moffitt and David White, sometimes others. We were regulars and had our own booth."

The Copper Cellar, a hangout for collegians, was a Moffitt favorite for business discussions. "The food was good," he recalls, "and it was close to the office. You had some privacy in the booths. It was downstairs, and you could spread out papers because it had a big, long table. Besides—I liked the waitresses.

"It had an energetic atmosphere in those days. It has changed now. But in those days it had a sense of energy about it. And the thing about creating something out of nothing—which we've done so many times—is that you've got to have a lot of belief. So you want to be in an *up* atmosphere.

"We brainstormed all the time, going back to when David

White was still there and active. Sometimes it would be David, Chris, and I. Sometimes Chris and I. Just all sorts of people. Editorial, mainly. Laura Eshbaugh would be involved. For a number of years Chris and I did more of that than anybody."

Chris Whittle never tried to steal credit from his fellow innovators, but frequently he put his own spin on their proposals. And usually for the better.

Keith Bellows, who catapulted from magazine group editor in 1982 to the inner circle of *Special Report*, says characterizing Philip Moffitt as the editorial guru and Chris only as the brilliant marketing expert is a mistake.

"No question on the surface that's true, but Chris is very gifted," Bellows says. "He could have been a good editor. He understands what people want. Has very good instincts. A very clever man. That always struck me in the probably hundreds of development meetings I've been in with him. He's as likely to come up with an interesting editorial twist on things as he is to come up with a marketing twist. And he has the ability to make you play on a higher plane. You can't just go in there and give him the same refried beans. So when you are in a development project you are constantly pushed."

If Chris is offered "refried beans," how does he react?

"Well, he won't tell you it's a lousy idea. He'll just go, 'Hmmmmmmm . . . I don't know about that.' And then he'll throw in a counter idea or a spinner on your idea, and generally that will elicit a counter. . . . You almost compete with him in a sense. He pushes you in a way, but it's not demeaning or derogatory.

"This has always been a creative sandbox. The real allure is that you're constantly pushed to do things in a different way. You could go to a big publisher and put out magazines, and they'd be good magazines. They'd be magazines like all other magazines. But here there is a constant push to stretch the envelope. To do things differently. To think of new forms.

"We were probably the first company to really look at the idea that information can be packaged in a lot of different ways. It doesn't need to be just a magazine. It could be a magalog, which is a cross between a catalog and a magazine. It could be a poster. It's fairly liberating to say, 'Here's the mission. You figure out how to solve it!'

"And in many cases we came up with ideas that were far ahead of the time. One example, I think was in 1985, I worked on a project that was for Seagrams, and it was going to be taking old rock songs and cutting them to new videos and packaging them as Seagrams ads for distribution in music clubs. This was just as MTV was emerging as a force and just as music clubs were reviving, and we, as we sometimes do, charged too much. Seagrams said no.

"And then all of a sudden four or five other companies jumped into the market with exactly the same idea. A lot of times that has happened to us, where we've had very good ideas. Our hit rate is probably forty percent, or was when we were really in the generation stage of coming up with ten or fifteen different properties a year."

Bellows adds, "And a lot of our ideas that didn't make it in the marketplace have since come into the marketplace. Ideas that we had like *Moviegoer* magazine, which was a wonderful magazine. When R. J. Reynolds pulled out of that, we made a sort of half-hearted effort to remarket it.

"We couldn't get our numbers to work because we insisted on outrageous profit margins. And what happened was that *Premier* magazine came into the marketplace, and that was six years ago [1986] and it has done quite well.

"I recall going to Chris pained that we were going to walk away from this franchise. 'Chris, this is crazy. This is a great idea. Movies are going to be hot!' He said, 'Keith, I know that we can do this magazine, but it will never make money.' I said, 'Chris, you are wrong!' He was right. When *Premiere* was six years old [in 1992] it still had not turned a profit.

"So Chris is pretty prescient on these things. Just eight years ago [1984] he said the networks were in trouble. Well, eight years ago the networks were nowhere near in trouble. But I was reading a *New York Times* article yesterday asking, 'Where are all the audiences going?' We've known for two or three years there is an erosion in the network audience, but it seems now that the level of panic in their ranks has reached fever pitch, and they just can't seem to figure out what to do to stem the tide. Chris was right.

"I think Chris also realized pretty early on that the future of marketing was going to have to lie in much more precise targeting. Our system of delivering media to market is pretty effective though there are some Achilles' heels—one being we have incredible lead time, which means a lot of our material isn't as fresh as it might be. And engaging in an environment has its down side as well, and there are a lot of competing factors for your attention. But he was pretty prescient in knowing that we're at an age where the public is just overburdened with information.

"There are very few places—the home especially—where people really have the time and inclination to sit down and concentrate, especially on print, and TV to an even greater degree. So we've got to get people where they have some down time. Doctor's offices, for instance.

"Chris has a real ability to see things, to put things together in novel ways, and to see things before other people tend to see things. That's probably the hallmark of a great entrepreneur."

Explaining why he considered the company "grown-up," Bellows explained, "To a large degree the arc of this company has been very similar to that of a human being. Like a kid, as a young company it was brash and nobody knew who we were. We were dismissed largely as just youngsters, and that allowed us to forge our way relatively unseen. Nobody picked us up on their radarscope. And we were free and happy and having a lot of fun and doing a lot of things.

"Then we suddenly emerged into adolescent years. And I would characterize those adolescent years as probably starting about 1982 when there was a certain amount of *chutzpah*. We had *Esquire*, and suddenly we started strutting our stuff, and we thumbed our noses at people. We started being much brasher, and we were probably insufferable little brats. Then for about three or four years it was like we were in college—we knew everything. Nobody was right; we were the only ones who were right. You know how that is when you are that age. Our parents are stupid and we are feeling our oats. And we overreached a little bit.

"Then about 1991 we suddenly grew up. We realized that we were adults now and it was time to make our way in the world, to forge alliances, to be more responsible. To have a little clearer strategy about who we were, and what we wanted to accomplish.

"I think Chris has sort of gone through similar arcs. He continued to want to stir the pot. As he often said, 'I want to leave a warm campfire, and we should be over the next hill before anybody gets here.' And he still wants to be a thorn in the side of society to some degree. He likes to do that."

Keith Bellows was making his assessment only months before the roof started to cave in at Knoxville. Gerry Hogan, when lured away from being Ted Turner's number-two man, discovered a night-and-day difference between his old boss and his new one.

First of all, Hogan surprisingly found it difficult to assimilate into the Knoxville company. "There was a very different culture at Whittle than there had been at Turner. Probably the most obvious was that Whittle was a very collaborative company. Decisions are made with a management team, and there is an enormous amount of compromise, and enormous time spent trying to make sure everybody is happy.

"Turner is a very autocratic place. Ted would say, 'This is what we are going to do.' And the whole company did it. And a lot of his style was transferred to me. I could do the same thing. I didn't have to sit down and convince everybody it was absolutely the best thing to do. Here it became a little frustrating. Chris looks for consensus and compromise, and often things didn't get done very quickly. Sometimes didn't get done at all because we couldn't satisfy everybody's needs or wants."

Hogan saw Chris regularly, the reverse of his relations with Ted Turner. "I only saw Ted a couple of days a month—maybe three—because he essentially lived in Montana and didn't come in to the office very much. Ted's strength was more in vision and leadership as opposed to day-to-day operating. I'd speak to him on the phone a couple of times a week. I see Chris far more.

"Chris is very hands-on, particularly on the marketing side. He's directly involved in creating the selling strategies, working out individual strategies for clients. His weaknesses? Perhaps not being able to pull back and focus on bigger issues and vision and leadership. The team he assembled relied heavily on him for the day-to-day, hands-on things.

"Chris is obviously very bright. He works very, very hard, enormously hard. Ted Turner is gifted. Things occur to him without an enormous amount of physical work. Chris has to work harder for it. I think both get to the same place but Chris puts in an enormous amount of time exploring options and working on strategy."

Hogan never had any discussion with Chris about brainstorming but closely observed his tactics and methods. He says, "He takes an enormous amount of input from a variety of people. I mentioned earlier that he's very collaborative; he welcomes input. There is an old joke they tell about Turner that I reminded Chris again of yesterday. Conversation with Ted Turner is like having a conversation with a radio. You just turn it on and you listen; that was the conversation.

"Chris is true conversation. There's give and take. There's exploring of points, and he challenges thinking, and all of that goes into his subconscious, and from that over time he comes forward with these visions or dreams of what might be."

Chris Whittle was not handicapped by failure to take college business courses. Hogan says, "I didn't take any. Neither did Ted Turner. He was a classics major. He did not know a thing about business. As a business executive, Chris's strength is on the creative side."

As an example, Hogan cited a session where Chris was working on refinancing the company's debt. "A typical CEO, classically trained, would have, if not hands-on experience with that, would certainly have an education, either formal or informal, as to how that is done. Chris didn't have a clue. Not the first idea of how things are done, and in fact had a list of goals he wanted to accomplish with the refinancing that were well beyond what would have been done in a typical financial transaction.

"And what he did is he created a new reality in which these goals of his made enormous sense. And what he did then, or we all did, is to convince people to buy into this reality. In broad terms, I guess it is salesmanship. And perhaps the best thing Chris does is sell his ideas to people."

Does Hogan believe Chris is guilty of overselling?

Hogan responds, "I think there's no doubt that a good salesman does tend to oversell and promise too much. One of the challenges Chris faces is reconciling this new reality with what's possible, and perhaps instead of overreaching on every project that a little more time is spent on thinking about what's possible, and what's the fallback position, and what happens if we don't achieve what we say we are going to achieve."

At the time Gerry Hogan was being interviewed, Chris Whittle was unfortunately already snared in the supersalesman's trap of overreaching.

18

THE BIRTH OF
EDISON SCHOOLS

Speaking to a teachers' convention in Knoxville on October 27, 1989, Chris Whittle boldly called for the president of the United States to give $1 billion to the "one hundred best people you know" with orders to reinvent American education and open fifty model schools within four years.

His pie-in-the-sky chatter got only small headlines and no national attention. At the time it didn't impress even him a great deal, although it espoused certain of his underlying idealistic beliefs. Education obviously had been brought to the forefront of his mind because of the hours he had spent answering criticism of Channel One.

Even so, his remarks before the East Tennessee Teachers Association led directly, albeit slowly, to the boldest, brashest, and most risky venture he ever undertook—the Edison Project.

"It was just a speech," he said later. "I didn't have any plan to do anything."

Not only did he impetuously call for a total remake of the public schools, he suggested how to do it. Not by requiring more pilot programs, experiments, Band-Aids, nor even powering up "with a new four-barrel carburetor."

"We need to disassemble the old structure and then, using old and new parts, put it all back together in some fundamentally different way. What does that mean? What does the New American School look like? And how do we ever get there from here?

"The moon was easier to get to. We could see the moon. We knew it was there. It is difficult to see the New American School. It's like trying to explain a car to an ancient chariot driver. 'Instead of your horse, we're going to have this thing made of the same stuff as your sword that drinks yellow-green liquid and that growls. It will go ten times faster than your horses. And everyone will have one— not just the pharaoh.'

"So when I describe what I think the New American School will look like, don't think: farfetched nonsense, as would have the chariot driver."

Chris said the new schools should spend a lot more time teaching students *why* they should learn. Schools would be open year-round and offer day care. Each student would have a computer, and teachers would have private offices and phones.

"The day of the typical classroom is over. Instead you may see work stations arranged in circles with the teacher coming to the students. Tests will be a thing of the past. There will be a disk updated annually—and if students want to take something home, they will just print it out. But they probably will not take it home. I think there will be no more homework. If they are going to school year-round, why do we need our children to work nightly, too?

"To keep costs down, I think the big breakthrough will be that we will triple the number of people involved in education and decrease the student-teacher ratio perhaps to five to one. How could that be possible? We need millions of assistant teachers; young people can teach other young people. Many have called for a new kind of national service for young people. Why not bring them into education to help teach their peers? And then what of retired people? Many would gladly volunteer services to help train the new generation.

"Just as it took the federal government to guide us through the depression, to rally us to war, to fund the Manhattan Project, to inspire our interstate highways, it will require the federal government to create the blueprint for the New American School.

"I did not say build it or run it. The idea of the federal government running our schools is about as appealing as a federally-run fast-food chain. I said redesign it."

His audience stirred when Chris slapped the podium and barked that almost anything is possible. "I believe that, at the risk of sounding fantastic, humans can fly without the aid of technology or ancient wings that they strap on and flap. We just haven't figured it out yet. And probably will not any time soon. But we could!"

Polite applause rewarded him; several teachers later shook his hand and agreed he had voiced "very interesting and progressive" goals. But for the moment, that was that. Just a speech.

Somehow, now that he had espoused it, the Edison Project seemed real. The embryonic idea began to haunt Chris. He had broached the subject carelessly; now he could visualize actual Edison Schools. He was struck by their potential and business prospects.

Several days later Chris addressed corporate executives at the Tennessee Business Roundtable. He gave the identical speech. He actually drafted the speech for the Roundtable and had tried it out on the teachers. Lamar Alexander, then president of the University of Tennessee, phoned and said, "That was a phenomenal speech." Alexander's attitude about the idea would later become significant when he was appointed secretary of education in President Bush's cabinet in 1991.

Meanwhile, for his column in the Winter 1990 edition of his ill-fated *Tennessee Illustrated* magazine, Chris unlimbered his laptop and took another whack at "An Education Edison."

His opening sentence was: "America's schools need massive restructuring." And he went on from there, harping on the fact that only the federal government, not local school boards, can finance the "New American School."

> . . . And merely fine-tuning current methods will not work. We need a complete redesign of the way we teach our children, founded on one premise: the education of those children must be conducted in the context of today's world. That means we cannot begin with the system we now have. Great new innovations require visionary leaps of human consciousness. When Edison invented electric illumination, he didn't tinker with candles to make them burn better. Instead he created something entirely new: the light

bulb. In the same fashion, American education needs a fundamental breakthrough, a new dynamic that will light the way to a transformed educational system.

By now what he was dubbing the Edison Project began to emerge in Chris's imagination. "What happened," Chris says, "was when I first proposed this, I didn't have any intention of us [the company] doing it. I just thought it was a good idea. Right? I just went, The creation of a new school system from the ground up by significant new research and development was something that the country needed to do. It was really just an idea I was floating. Then a couple of things happened. One is I began to go, This really is what should be done. I believed it when I said it, but began to go, We really should do this and maybe we should do it as a company. And the second thing was the appointment of Lamar Alexander as secretary of education. He phoned and wanted to know if some of these ideas could be incorporated in President Bush's educational program. I said yes. I thought we ought to just kind of give them the idea. And we'll do it privately, and they can do it publicly. That way we'll be attacking on two fronts."

Eventually, Chris's brainstorm became a key ingredient in President Bush's educational initiative, which even incorporated the banner "The New American School."

To his dismay but not to his surprise, Chris found the federal government unwilling to put up a billion dollars to reinvent American education.

Even while occupied deeply with business problems, Chris was still haunted by Edison. The tiny seed he had planted at the East Tennessee Teachers Association convention sprouted and began to grow wildly. In his imagination Chris visualized it turning into a Jack's Beanstalk—towering higher than anything he had ever dreamed of before. All at once it hit him—he had a rare business opportunity that could yield billions. Wasting no time, he gathered his top lieutenants, and everybody got cracking.

―――

It was a secret project. In Knoxville work went on for nineteen months behind closed doors. Finally Chris and his Edison team created the framework for a new American school system that could be launched as a money-making business.

On May 16, 1991, the daring scheme was unveiled at a news conference in Washington, D.C. and got immediate page-one attention across the country. The Edison Project was huge—and expensive. It called for building one thousand model schools at a cost of $2.5 billion raised from corporate investors. The first two hundred would open in 1996, the others by 2010, serving two million students. Chris, of course, intended to head up the corporation that would operate the new schools—for profit.

Chris's yellow pads were studded with key lists, cost figures, educators to check out, ideas to explore, places to visit. Nothing was in complete or final form. It wasn't up to him to reinvent the schoolhouse; that was a job for real experts. It was not known that Chris was doggedly pursuing Benno Schmidt, often talking with him on weekends in Manhattan, pressing him to leave Yale and become leader of the Edison Project.

In his own extensive research and study, Chris mainly wanted to survey possibilities, gathering ammunition to show the limitless possibilities of revamping the educational system. Under his plan, the first step would be to recruit one hundred "innovators" from education, business, science, and other fields to come to Knoxville and work as a team to totally revamp the American educational model. At a cost of $60 million they would be given three years to develop a new curriculum, textbooks, and new architectural layouts, as well as schedules that would probably mean year-round classes and longer hours, plus new video and computer resources for twenty-first-century schools.

Not only was Chris's aim to create schools that would rank as the best the world, he decreed that tuition be held to the 1991 cost per pupil in public schools—about $5,500 a year. The Whittle schools would also avoid the attitude of private academies: Chris asserted pupils would be randomly selected from applicants and there would be no entry requirements. An average of one-fifth of the students would be on full scholarship. "We think," Chris said, "the answers exist as to how to run an educational system better. . . . There are pieces of the answer all over the globe." He cited the Boy Scouts, business schools, and military training—but vowed his attitudes about discipline were not militaristic. "I'm not going to be on the law-and-order side. One of the biggest problems with education may be that it's compulsory. Edison Schools will actually be parent-friendly; we intend to regard both children and parents as clients. Had the old model been parent-sensitive, we wouldn't have latchkey kids."

To tackle the "motivation" of kids, Chris considered an idea obviously spawned by his summer in Czechoslovakia as a University of Tennessee student. On his yellow pad he noted that rather than teach geography and foreign language in a void, it might be possible to offer twelve-year-olds the chance to live in another country for year-long stints. They would learn geography and language as preparation.

As one means of holding down expense, Edison Schools would use parents, senior citizens, and even other older children as teachers and day-care operators. Part of his scheme was to offer a form of kindergarten or day care for three-month-olds.

As a diligent student, Chris had learned one of the most valuable lessons of history—avoid repeating past mistakes. Though ready to spring forth with his audacious Edison Project, he was on guard. He had foolishly startled and angered the educational establishment in 1989 by bringing out his controversial Channel One with no advance warning or consultation. In unveiling Edison, he had no intention of suddenly and brazenly striding out into the middle of the highway and letting his critics roar down at him.

Hence public announcement of the Edison Project was carefully orchestrated in advance. Days before his news conference in Washington, D.C., at the National Press Club, Chris and his colleagues began a round of private briefings with a dozen influential government and education officials. This time he wanted to be sure the establishment, at least, would not suddenly be hit with his intention to create the new American school—as a business, for profit. On his agenda for briefings were the American Federation of Teachers, the National Association of State Boards of Education, the National Education Association, and top officials in the Department of Education.

The *Knoxville News-Sentinel* managed to get a one-day scoop on details of the Edison Project, and the headlines dominated the top half of page one. Through leaks from friendly sources, the *Wall Street Journal* and a few other national publications were able to jump the gun with May 15th stories on what would be revealed next day.

There Chris revealed that the first two hundred schools would enroll children one to six years old, and each succeeding year would expand by one year. Explaining how it would be possible for Edison schools to turn a profit of 12 to 15 percent, he pointed out that he hoped to spread his brand of education to the public sector, either by contracting with public school systems to run their schools or by selling Whittle Schools software and other technology to public schools.

Reaction from the national educational community was mixed but cautiously supportive. Bill Honig, California superintendent of schools, a confirmed Whittle-basher, appeared with Chris on *Larry King Live*. Surprisingly, Honig said, "There may be some promise in this idea. As you know I have been a sharp critic of the Channel One idea of selling goods to kids, but . . . if [Whittle] figures out something we can use, more power to him."

Later, however, Honig told the *New York Times:* "I'm somewhat skeptical. . . . because the dangers are if you have a profit-making institution, who's to say that cutting costs and cutting corners won't be undertaken to increase profit margins."

June Million, a spokeswoman for the National Association of Elementary School Principals, which had received one of Chris's advance briefings, told reporters: "We wish him well. But it will be very interesting to see if he can operate schools that can be replicated without any of the ties that bind us."

Albert Shanker, president of the American Federation of Teachers, said, "Chris Whittle has a right to do this. He might come up with something that is damn good. But [the schools] could also be crassly commercial."

Announcement of the Edison Project came close on the heels of a strikingly similar "America 2000" plan launched by the Bush Administration as its new strategy to overhaul the nation's schools. At President George Bush's behest, two dozen top business executives organized the New American Schools Development Corporation as a catalyst for educational reform, undertaking to raise $200 million from concerns such as Exxon, Boeing, AT & T, and Xerox. From this fund Education Secretary Lamar Alexander intended to issue research and development grants to the private sector for projects to invent 535 new public schools that would serve as models of excellence and could be replicated nationwide.

Washington reporters, noting Chris's longtime business and social friendship with Alexander, asked if Whittle Schools and Laboratories, as he named his Edison venture, would apply for one of the government-sponsored grants.

"No," said Chris. "We, of course, support President Bush's strategy. But we will not request one of those grants."

In part, Chris was avoiding any possible conflict of interest stemming from his ties with Secretary Alexander, as was pointed out by the *Knoxville News-Sentinel*.

"For that reason," said the *News-Sentinel*, "the company will apply for no federal grants to help fund the concept. A recent *Wall Street Journal* story revealed that Alexander received $125,000 in fees as a consultant for the now-folded *Tennessee Illustrated* magazine published by Whittle. In addition, Alexander in 1987 was given an opportunity to buy shares in Whittle for $10,000, which were issued in [his wife] Honey Alexander's name. A year later, when Time Warner bought half the company for $185 million, Whittle bought back the four shares for $330,000."

Indeed, Lamar Alexander's shadow continued to hang over the Edison Project through Tom Ingram, who not only had been his campaign manager and chief of staff as Tennessee governor but had also helped Alexander in assembling his Washington staff when he left the presidency of the University of Tennessee to join the Bush cabinet.

Within days after the formal announcement, Chris summoned a small team of his executives to a retreat at his East Hampton home to figure out just how to organize and staff the project. The primary need was for someone with a sufficient grasp of education to take day-to-day charge of coordinating Whittle Schools until the core team of innovators, whom Chris termed education's Mercury Astronauts, could be chosen and in place with their own staff—by January 1992.

The job went to Tom Ingram.

======

In November 1991, six months after the Edison Project was announced, Chris phoned Lee Eisenberg in London. The former editor in chief of *Esquire* during the Phillip Moffitt–Whittle reign had just launched a British edition of *Esquire* for Hearst Magazines and was packing to return to New York.

"Chris proceeded to give me a sales pitch that was absolutely intriguing," Eisenberg says. "I knew zilch about his school scheme, but he equated Edison's challenges to the kind of creative challenges I enjoyed in journalism—creating material that was effective and informative, as original and dynamic as the best journalism, albeit for children."

Three weeks later Eisenberg found himself at Blackberry Farm in the Smokies, sitting around a table with a handful of other candidates for the Edison core team. In all, a dozen men and women from business, science, and education were summoned to weekend retreats at Blackberry Farm. They were finalists culled from a list of five thousand assembled by Tom Ingram and his staff.

Eisenberg got an offer. He pondered whether to change professions and move to Knoxville. Finally he reacted affirmatively, concluding Edison had an 80 percent chance of success.

Three women and two other men joined Eisenberg as "founding partners" of the Edison Project under three-year contracts. They were John E. Chubb, an expert on public policy in education and energy and a senior fellow with the governmental studies program at the Brookings Institution, a Washington think tank; Chester E. Finn Jr., professor of education and public policy at Vanderbilt University in Nashville, a former federal assistant secretary of education and adviser to presidents Reagan and Bush; Sylvia A. Peters, the black principal of an inner-city elementary school in Chicago who became a national "heroine" by leading parents and activists to build a safe haven for her pupils in a crime-infested neighborhood; Dominique Browning, assistant managing editor of *Newsweek* magazine and once an editor at *Esquire*; and Nancy Hechinger, a writer and producer, who founded the independent multimedia "Hands On Media."

Hired as consultant for one year was Daniel Beiderman, president of the Grand Central and 34th Street Partnerships in New York and a pioneer in funding and management of public services by the private sector.

By January 1992, the core team had gathered; four moved to Knoxville (Eisenberg, Hechinger, Peters, and Chubb). Chris took the role of leader. About once a month he would convene the team for three or four days in a convenient location. Sessions were held in Knoxville, New York, Washington, D.C., and once at Chris's East Hampton home.

"Chris led us in pretty wide-ranging discussions about the task that lay ahead and how we could best organize ourselves to begin it," says Eisenberg. "They were fascinating and provocative sessions. In the *Esquire* days, most of my work has been with Phillip Moffitt. This was the first time I got to be in a room with Chris when there was conceptualizing being done. And I think I can speak for everybody in saying it was a very exciting time. He brought to each meeting a real sense of creative excitement and would not let us fall into the trap of setting our sights too low in what the Edison schools could be. Chris would never let us settle for that. He kept reminding us in an encouraging, not reprimanding, way to try to effect a paradigm shift in how schools are thought of in this country."

Chris's sense of excitement and challenge motivated his Edison team, Eisenberg adds. "This was a particularly interesting and gratifying time for the core team. Here we were, seven very disparate people from different fields. The creative opportunity and challenge that Chris insisted hovered over our heads kept us from disuniting. He really kept the dynamic of the room working right."

The founding partners examined the many facets of what they recognized as a gargantuan undertaking: "curriculum, management, personnel, bricks, and mortar." Eisenberg says one "haunting, pedestrian question" dominated early meetings. "We kept asking ourselves, 'How do we *begin*?' There were two broad ways we could go. One was to set ourselves up as a sort of commission, which is to say, bring in experts and interrogate them, assess what they told us, write up a report with our recommendations. Or, we could do some of that, but basically hold our noses and dive right in, try to design in a state of relative innocence before too much conventional wisdom could blunt our creative instincts."

They opted for the second course, dividing themselves by ones and twos into a series of design teams. Each had the identical—and competing—assignment: creating in elaborate detail the full design of a new American school system.

"That's how we spent the next six to eight months," says Eisenberg, "working maybe forty percent of the time on these individual designs and meeting the rest of the time as a group, putting on seminars for one another, educating ourselves."

At one in-house seminar atop a gleaming long conference table at Whittle headquarters lay a goodly heap of colored construction paper, pastepots, string, packets of glitter, crayons, and kindergarten scissors. Eight grown men and women including Chris Whittle, eagerly sorted through this child's pile. Each was picking out items to use in creating his or her own visual "autobiography."

This assignment was sprung on them by Sylvia Peters. Using scissors and paste in this childish fashion, she promised, would perhaps "emancipate" their individual cerebral initiatives. The challenge triggered many dark or puzzled frowns. Chris, cocking his eyebrows and sometimes giggling, scrutinized the tabletop assortment for a couple of minutes. He discovered a pile of popsicle sticks and grabbed a handful.

Somehow his subconscious must have reverted to memories of his carefree days as a child in Etowah; with the little sticks he created two objects: the figure of a little boy about five or six and a crude stockade or fort.

"I don't know why I made those particular things," he says. "But we all had fun."

Incongruous or not, this exercise was but one of many paths the Edison principals followed in their search for the mystical design of the new American school. To force their brains to attack the project from every angle, they took turns at the head of the table. Some ran the seminar more traditionally—detailing the New York City school budget, a "creativity seminar" led by Chester Finn, long conversations about pedagogy, day care, the architectural history of schools, and so on.

Mrs. Peters's session was described as "diverting, distinctive, dramatic, and a little weird." Said Lee Eisenberg: "We sat around furiously cutting and pasting. I don't think we created any lasting works of art. Don't make any more of it than it was—something only done for an hour or two. A lark, more or less—one of many different kinds of 'searching' exercises."

As they worked on into the late spring of 1992, none of the core team had the least notion Chris was in pursuit of Benno Schmidt.

"We knew from the beginning," says Eisenberg, "there would be a CEO. But we were not kept informed as to who Chris was talking to. The betting among us was that he would select some captain of industry with an interest in education, as many of them have. Or possibly a university president, maybe one who was proficient at raising money and who also had academic and intellectual credentials."

Thus at that stage of the game, when summoned to Chris's rambling beach house on Long Island, the Edison core team believed they merely faced another working session. But their leader had news for them—sensational news. Chris gathered them in a room, asked their attention, surveyed them with a warm and mischievous smile, and said he had finally secured a leader, a CEO.

"The president of Yale University—Benno Schmidt!"

That took every founding partner by surprise. There had been no leak; that Chris had been wooing Benno Schmidt was a deep, dark secret not only to the press and virtually all of his Knoxville colleagues, but to the trustees of Yale as well.

Says Lee Eisenberg: "I don't believe that Benno had yet told his trustees at Yale. This was, in fact, the Memorial Day weekend at Yale, which is the traditional commencement weekend. At such a time a college president talks to trustees and important alumni. Benno was within a day or two of telling them he was resigning to join the Edison Project. For this reason we were asked to keep this totally confidential. So we had a few days to keep this under our collective hat.

"Shortly after Chris told us, we assembled on his porch overlooking Georgica Pond to await Benno's arrival. We all had a pleasant chat on the porch for an hour or two, and then Benno went off to New Haven where he presided over his final commencement."

At Yale the president's final days were less than pleasant. His New Haven critics became vocal, accusing him of departing with unseemly haste. Students brandished page one of the *New York Times*, which carried an interview and photo of Schmidt and Chris obviously prepared prior to public announcement of his resignation.

Metropolitan newspapers took note of the catcalls that followed Schmidt to the Edison Project. Typical was this report on July 21, 1992, in the *Washington Post:*

What Schmidt leaves behind at Yale is perhaps another story—bruised feelings and anger that he cut his deal (and talked to the *New York Times*) without telling his board of trustees, a malaise about the mess he left behind in the university's leadership, a renascent sense that he never cared about Yale in the first place (he commuted from New York where his wife works), and, of course, the sometimes envious scorn directed at anyone who moves from the scholarly priesthood to the capitalist mud-wrestle (for as much as a million dollars a year).

Benno Schmidt's response was blunt: "I think that is a lot of crap, frankly."

In our interviews he said that as soon as he decided to join Edison, in mid-April, he flew to Chicago to tell Vernon R. Loucks Jr., the senior Yale trustee. Loucks was chairman of Baxter International, the world's largest hospital supplier.

Schmidt explains, "Vern was extremely good about my decision. He said, 'I really hate to see you leave. You've done a good job for Yale. I basically agree with you that if you can create a new model for schooling that can help turn around education, that's our country's biggest problem.' "

Schmidt says they decided to not phone other trustees but wait and break the news face-to-face when all trustees met in May in New Haven for graduation weekend. He adds, "And there I told the trustees I was anxious none of this be revealed before the actual graduation ceremonies. I didn't want to interfere with that day for the seniors."

The resignation was announced on Monday, May 25. It was to take effect promptly. Benno Schmidt said he didn't want to continue at Yale as a lame duck. Besides, he was eager to start developing the Edison model.

19

ELECTRONICS ON DOCTORS' DESKS

Crucial business problems suddenly began to descend on Chris Whittle in 1990, disrupting his new and blissful family life, and they steadily grew worse in 1991. He prized dining by candlelight with Priscilla in the Dakota apartment, on Italian dishes she whipped up in her own kitchen, or rocking Andie in her antique cradle. Out in Central Park, Chris would swing Maxi by his heels and promise to show him how to build an Etowah-style fort.

These pleasures were interrupted more and more as crises started exploding at Knoxville headquarters and elsewhere, with unexpected twists and turns posing considerable danger. Since Whittle Communications L.P. had always been primarily a one-man show, few significant decisions could be made until Chris put his spin on a problem.

The business was slipping into a stressful evolutionary upheaval that threatened its entrepreneurial climate and cultural harmony as well as its growth and profits. The dilemma confronting Whittle was how to adroitly shift its core business from magazines and print to video and television. Chris watched in dismay and frustration as the *Special Report* venture that had held such rare promise started turning sour in the startlingly short span of about two years.

The advertising business was in a general downturn. Several of the *Special Report* sponsors dropped out, forcing a frantic effort to sign up new accounts. Chris decided to cut back, issuing the magazines only three times a year. The wall media *Physicians Weekly*, posted forty-eight times a year in staff lounges in three thousand hospitals and medical centers, was going strong. However, not so robust was *Southern Style*, sponsored by Procter and Gamble for distribution in beauty parlors. Broadening its circulation and renaming it *American Style* was not enough to keep the magazine alive.

Still showing a profit were a variety of properties, such as *Pet Care Report*, featuring how-to booklets and wall media for veterinary offices, *Go!*, subtitled *Girls Only*, a magazine for girls eleven to fourteen, along with *The Best of Business Quarterly*, a compilation of business articles published elsewhere that was sent to executives. The attempt to launch a male companion to *Go!* proved a howling fiasco. It was named *BANG!*, subtitled *Boys and Not Girls*. When editors unveiled the test mock-up at a Muscatine, Iowa, school the eleven- and twelve-year-old pupils giggled. One boy read the logo and subtitle as a sentence. "Bang boys and not girls?" he smirked. "I don't think the principal would okay that!"

At the outset Chris had a board of directors that considered him a wunderkind and gave him almost carte blanche on launching new ideas, regardless of how off-the-wall or eccentric they might appear. Largely this was because the original Whittle system called for finding and selling a single advertiser on sponsoring a new property, usually with a three-year contract. That, in effect, provided the up-front capital—as well as the prepaid profit—for new ventures. Whittle was not really risking much more than the expense of brainstorming and engineering the concept.

The situation changed with the launch of Channel One, which required an investment of around $180 million, largely borrowed from banks. Chris was more intrigued than ever by the challenge, and asked Time Warner to forego its option to buy more of Whittle Communications. "I went to Time," he says, "and said can we tear up the back half of our agreement. Why? Because the original plan was that I was going to leave and sell the business, and now I didn't want to do that. Time granted my request."

Reg Brack, a Time Inc. member of the Whittle board, professed in a November 1990 *Wall Street Journal* interview to be "happy" with the partnership and "delighted" that Chris had abandoned his political ambitions and wanted to devote full time to the business and continue as chairman.

"We've always made it plain that he was the key to the business," Brack told the newspaper.

Even so, other Time Warner executives privately acknowledged that Whittle Communications had not "performed as well as originally expected, in part because of the tough advertising climate."

As the chief visionary, Chris was handed the laurels for most successes but had to accept major blame for failures. Sir David English, one of Lord Rothermere's executives on the Whittle board, was critical of the waiting-room magazine venture. "We were the first to spot that the *Special Report* magazines were not going to work," he says. "We were terribly impressed with their look but disappointed in their content." Lord Rothermere, in an interview for this book, was asked what was wrong with the articles in the magazines. "They just weren't good enough," he said.

To their credit, Chris and his colleagues came up with a new property to replace the waiting-room magazines—WRTV, waiting-room television, eventually named Special Report TV. Instead of magazines in racks, doctors were given a twenty-seven-inch screen television set, supplied by Whittle, on which would be played an hour-long news and feature video, dotted, of course, with commercials. To emcee the program, Chris signed Joan Lunden, cohost of ABC's *Good Morning America*, to a moonlighting contract. The new project went well but was another expensive start-up.

In his public persona, Chris, now in his early forties, still appeared the boyish eccentric with his mopish hair, trademark bow tie, striped shirt, and usually baggy suit. He maintained his shy smile, wrinkling his eyes but seldom showing his teeth. Behind the scenes—inside the company—he was different: usually calm and reasoned, always determined, frequently stubborn, and once in a while irate. "One of my weaknesses is I'm not very tough," he said. "I wish I were—because I think it's a problem of mine."

Chris wanted to keep his private life and business career entirely separate. "Not physically possible," he admitted ruefully. Executives saw him as the consummate loner. Said vice-chairman Laura Eshbaugh: "Chris thrives on risk. The hotter the fire, the tougher the metal." Editor Keith Bellows observed that Chris "wants to control reality" and does not know how to be intimate—"though he does have a relationship with his houses."

In defense of his self-confidence, Chris says he chooses not to see potential risks and pitfalls. "Is that being naive? I call it robust naïveté, or conscious innocence." Chris does not deny he is driven—success is not possible without it in some measure. And he concedes bad moments. "The more drive you have," he says, "the more fear you have, that is a rule of emotional physics. You have to get fear in perspective. You must push away irrational fears and not deny real fears." Says Laura Eshbaugh: "Chris will always pick a way to win."

Chris Whittle, a hands-on person, is a stickler for details. In 1990, while the $50 million Historic Whittlesburg office complex was rising as a four-story skeleton of steel girders in the heart of downtown Knoxville, Chris kept fretting whether it would have precisely the Ivy League look he envisioned. Insisting on wood-framed windows, he directed architect Peter Marino to create a mock-up so he could personally decide whether the bricks were red enough.

While it has the look of one large structure, the headquarters is three buildings connected by large corridors. To give the courtyard the aura Chris and Marino wanted, thirteen forty-foot-tall pin-oaks were hauled in from New Jersey and planted along with six magnolias from South Carolina and scores of maple trees. The landscaping included 6,500 square yards of sod, with a pop-up sprinkler system.

Chris Whittle's office, on the fourth floor at the head of the grand staircase, measured twenty-four by twenty feet, with hardwood floors, pale oak paneling, and a fireplace with marble surrounds and a dark oak mantlepiece. The connecting library served as a private sanctuary and meeting room. Chris's private bath, the only one in the complex, included a shower.

Chris considered that another prime requisite for Whittle executives, especially himself, was convenient air travel. Saving time was essential, since editorial and business offices were located in Knoxville and New York, with television studios on the West Coast. Sales pitches were being made to corporate advertisers all over the country. The company leased two seven-passenger jets, a Cessna Citation III and Mitsubishi Diamond, with a staff of eight pilots, mechanic, and scheduler. Virtually every day found Chris in the air. He could swoosh from Knoxville to New York in eighty minutes. Chris, the most frequent flier in the company, estimated that in twenty years he spent 1.7 years on airplanes. Said chief pilot Tom

Barber: "In our jets he can accomplish in one month what it would take eight to do by airline. Recently flew out for ten A.M. meeting in New York, then to Sacramento, California, and back to New York same day. He was exhausted but he got an awful lot done that day." Barber estimated the private jets were as cost-effective as flying first class by airline if each carried five company passengers.

Internal change and turmoil plagued Knoxville operations. The abrupt shift from print to video displaced scores of writers, editors, and production people, leaving them dangling in uncertainty about their jobs and the company's future. They were frightened by rumors that the company might shift to a major new direction—retail marketing. Hinted at was point-of-sale advertising in malls that might culminate in ventures to peddle by telephone such diverse products as lawnmowers or automobiles. Details never were spelled out to the rank and file, who found the scuttlebutt alarmingly weird.

———

Abolishing Nick Glover's role as "Mr. Inside" had been a serious mistake. Chris began to realize that while "Mr. Outside" was off hustling business someone had to run the show back in Tennessee. Chris reached out to Bill Connell, the ex–Procter and Gamble beauty-care chieftain and Cincinnati friend whom he initially consulted on entering politics.

While they lunched in New York, Chris abruptly asked Connell to become president of Whittle Communications L.P. and chief operating officer. Connell recalls, "Chris said, 'I'll handle the outside of the business, which is generating revenue and whatever financial support we need, and you manage the inside—the internal culture and the cost structure and those kinds of things. We'll work together in taking this company into its second and third stages of medium- and large-company development.' "

The pledge of working together was a myth; it is not in Chris Whittle to share power or control. Connell joined the company, which was now twenty years old, on September 8, 1990, but the "Mr. Outside–Mr. Inside" partnership was doomed from the start.

Connell thought their mission was to consolidate the company, manage it for medium-term profit, and whip it into shape to turn over to Time Warner in a few years. "But early I learned that Chris was not planning to consolidate and turn the company over to Time Warner but instead wanted to remain a partner and personally build into a huge company."

Chris was "absolutely driven" in his quest for growth. "He was hiring people and spending money at a prodigious rate. He was bringing in some outstanding talent. His rationale for that was that if we were going to build a billion-dollar company, we had to have genuine outstanding talent in place and give them resources to exercise their talents and fuel tremendous growth. That was a totally different strategy than I had envisioned. I disagreed with it. The company was in dire need of consolidation. It had been growing too fast. It had not built in anything like the cost and operating discipline that are essential to putting money on the bottom line. And programs like Channel One were still very, very tenuous."

When Connell warned the chairman they needed to consolidate and manage the bottom line before expanding, he got nowhere. Chris listened, but took no advice. "Chris is very nonconfrontational. He will sit and listen and will acknowledge many of the things you say. Then he will say, 'Yeah, but I've thought about this, and I'm going to approach it this way and this way and this way . . . and I know it's going to be tough and a struggle. But I've been through this many times before and, Bill, believe me—we'll pull it off!' "

For the 1990–91 fiscal year, Chris projected a profit of $26 million. Connell was astonished. His own analysis of the books indicated about $15 million. He confronted Chris. "There's no way in bloody hell we're ever going to deliver $26 million this year," Connell said. "We ought to cut the forecast."

Chris wagged his head. "Bill, you just don't understand how this business works. Sure, we gotta go out and make some sales, but this is like an airline, once you hit your load factor it all falls to the bottom line."

Curiously, Connell went away not sure that Chris wasn't right after all. "If you went back over the company history," Connell says, "Chris had a twenty-one-year track record in which the company grew at a compound rate of 27.6 percent. He had never had a down year in sales and had, I think, only two down years in profit, when he was investing in things. The guy started twenty-one years ago doing something that people told him was impossible to do. And every year he went out and did something else that was new and which all convention and traditional business wisdom told him wouldn't work and couldn't be done. He did it on the edge. In every one of those situations they were very dicey. They were often in jeopardy, but he always pulled them out at the last minute."

Connell reflected that he had emerged from Procter and Gamble, "a staid structure . . . that is the epitome of tradition and conventional wisdom. So why should he have accepted my judgment? Particularly when he was getting a lot of reinforcement from very smart people like Reg Brack [a director and Time executive] and the rest of the folks at Time Warner, from Charles Sinclair [a director and Associated Newspapers executive], who is a very smart, sophisticated player. So I looked at this and said, Hey, the guy may be right.

"People will tell you that Chris Whittle is a snake oil salesman and he bullshits you . . . on his plans and projections. Chris does not bullshit. If Chris says something, Chris absolutely believes it. I've been through a number of very painful situations with Chris where he would not shade the truth one iota. So when Chris tells you that a property is going to deliver two hundred million dollars three years from now, in his mind he absolutely believes it will, and he can make it happen."

Connell argued that bringing in "hotshots" with an emphasis on spending was a very dangerous game.

"You're like running ahead of a steamroller, Chris. If you stumble, you are dead meat."

"Bill, I can't stumble. I can't afford to stumble. Stumbling is not an option."

Chris believed that, Connell says. "Chris will tell you—I'm sure he has—that the way he drives himself is that if he wants to learn to swim he goes down to the twelve-foot end of the pool and jumps in. So that he has no option but to succeed."

And Connell, though basically impotent as COO, saw an effective exercise in Chris's dogged will to achieve the $26 million profit projection.

"We got down to the last two or three months of the year, and Chris and I and others went out and made sales—and the net of it is we made $28.6 million profit. We over-delivered! Boy, it was really a bitch. But I look back and say they've done this every year forever."

═══

Employee morale became a definite problem. In the yeasty days of 13–30 staffers were willing to give 110 to 120 percent; they felt the company was "family." Now the atmosphere—on the eve of moving into their new faux Ivy League headquarters building— lacked the vivid and warm sense of collegiality that for two decades had kept staffers working long hours as free spirits. Now they grumbled among themselves—the company didn't care about them. Furthermore, Chris was going back on his promise that print would always be the premier part of the company.

Chris was torn two ways. Despite setbacks, the company was definitely growing. Annual revenue was about to hit a record $207 million. At an employees' yearly luncheon the chairman could confidently predict that the future looked enormously bright, with annual revenue zooming into "the multi-billions" by the year 2001. But despite his outward optimism, he was feeling panicky because of runaway expenses.

Drastic action was needed, and Chris took it. Ushering in a new era of cost-consciousness, he called a special meeting in November 1990 with full partners and senior management. Citing concerns about the downturn in the national economy, he asked the assembled group to figure out ways to reduce expenditures in all divisions—chiefly on travel, supplier services, and material purchases.

And then to emphasize the seriousness of cost-cutting, Chris asked his limited partners to take a voluntary, one-time pay cut of 15 percent. "As the people responsible for leading our efficiency initiatives," he explained, "it's important for us to set the example."

Chris's unprecedented request was aimed at saving millions to offset some of the heavy spending on the launch of Special Report Television and the expansion of Channel One. The goal was to cut out about $30 million from the annual expense budget of around $250 million.

Chris's lieutenants pitched right in. Connell bragged that by booking two weeks early he got a $750 coach ticket from Knoxville to New York for $499. "We spend about $12 million a year on air travel. If everybody called ahead and got discounts, we could cut that by 20 percent. That's $2.4 million on savings, more than we make on some single-sponsor publications."

By using Time Warner clout, Whittle executives obtained substantial hotel discounts and under Time Warner's MCI contract were able to reduce long distance rates in Knoxville from sixteen cents a minute to eleven cents, saving $10,000 a month.

The cost of distributing each issue of *American Style* magazine was cut $100,000 by unearthing the cheapest UPS and postal zones and distributing copies from those points. Clay Shwab, vice-president of field services, initiated $800,000 in annual savings by cutting back on hiring and "encouraging my people to take on more stops on their routes." That meant buying fewer replacement vans, resulting in less expense for gasoline.

Shwab's cleverest thrift wrinkle came when *Special Report* introduced SRTV, rendering the oak bookcases in which the magazines had been displayed obsolete. "Instead of spending company money to haul them off," says Shwab, "I had my zone managers give them away to doctors, patients, or anyone else who happened to be in the waiting room. That saved forty thousand dollars. We got rid of about 95 percent of the cases that way. I'm sure a lot of them are going to gather dust in people's garages, but that's their problem."

There is more than a little irony in the fact that Chris Whittle's quest for a business fortune gradually shifted gears and more and more began to ride piggy-back on the American physician. Chris is, of course, the son of a country doctor and as a child often went along on house calls in his dad's battered VW.

At first Whittle Communications looked at the doctor's offices as merely a consumer "trap" where patients—mainly housewives and mothers—had to sit for about thirty minutes in the waiting room. Into that idle half hour were injected the place-based *Special Report* magazines, carrying ads for soap, coffee, butter, and other household products.

Later, after making a number of amateurish mistakes that dangerously crippled this promising publishing enterprise, Chris and his colleagues veered away from print and plunged into video. Instead of glossy magazines, they tried to capture the eyes and ears of the patients by equipping waiting rooms with a twenty-seven-inch TV screen that showed the soap opera-flavored *Special Report* features, interlarded with commercials.

The big corporate advertisers who were footing the bill—and it was pretty steep—did not maintain their initial enthusiasm for either venture. At renewal time their Madison Avenue agencies, ignominiously bypassed by the brash Whittleites who made their initial sales pitch directly to corporate executives, now got a chance to exact revenge by pooh-poohing the impact Whittle claimed on consumers. The ad men said there was no valid yardstick to prove results; the sponsors just weren't getting their money's worth.

That developing scenario triggered panic back at Knoxville headquarters. A financial setback was in the making. Ideas began percolating to resolve the *Special Report* fiasco. Chris says the solution just bubbled up out of the collective entrepreneurial culture that had been energizing the company since the 13–30 days.

"What I recall was that we had seen how our print vehicles in schools evolved into our video system. We began to say to ourselves, I wonder if the same thing can happen with our medical print vehicles? Can they evolve into video productions? And I'm sure someone, three or four years ago, said, If we can do a Channel One for schools, can we do a Channel One for medicine?"

The idea was sparked by Charles Vogel, who understood problems in the medical profession from handling advertising for *Physician's Weekly*. By his estimate, each of the 600,000 physicians in the United States received sixty or more medical journals monthly and couldn't begin to read them all. Pharmaceutical companies were spending $400 million a year advertising in these journals—wasting their money. Why not cash in on the market with a telecast that winnowed the most important news for the busy doctor?

It also dawned on the marketing experts in Knoxville that they had been foolish to devote all their attention to the patients instead of the most important people in doctors' offices—the physicians themselves. They leaped to the task of creating the model for a medical Channel One—a daily straight newscast for physicians that would be supported by drug company advertising. They named it Medical News Network. Alan Greenberg was designated chairman of MNN and put in charge with a small development staff. But the scheme, the planners soon discovered, presented numerous problems. For one thing it would be difficult, if not impossible, to convince the advertisers that physicians paid attention to the broadcast. The drug companies needed some gauge of whether they were making worthwhile use of their promotion dollars.

"We can talk to physicians," Greenberg said. "Wouldn't it be wonderful if they could talk back to us? Channel One is one-way; what if we could make MNN two-way?"

Greenberg knew of no current technology that would make such an interactive system possible, but he challenged Philips Electronics in Knoxville, a branch of the Dutch conglomerate, to design and build a desktop unit containing a television set, a microprocessor, a VCR, a telephone, and a keyboard compact enough to sit on a doctor's desk.

To achieve two-way communication, Medical News Network would utilize half a dozen direct link-ups and three or four side connections. The principal element was the twelve- to fifteen-minute broadcast, *NewsPulse*. Originating in New York, the newscast was to be beamed by satellite five nights a week throughout the country to dishes atop professional buildings occupied by subscribing doctors. Hooked to each dish was a central computer and VCR to record the broadcast and store it for two days. Doctors' desktop units were wired into the computer so that at their convenience they could hit the PLAY button, watch *NewsPulse,* and even rewind to take a second look at its most interesting parts.

The unique elements of MNN were that doctors, by using their keypads, could respond to polls, request in-depth news reports to be faxed or mailed to them, take continuing-education courses needed for certification, and get additional information on the drugs advertised in the programming.

Each daily *NewsPulse* broadcast would carry a two-minute commercial in the middle plus another two-minute ad at the end. By buying this time for informational pitches, drug companies could reach doctors directly. Through MNN's interactive function, the physician could request more information on the product (receiving it instantly by fax or later by mail), ask for a rep visit, and order samples (which physicians are always anxious to get), signing for them with a digitized signature pad on the keyboard.

One aspect of Medical News Network struck the Whittle executives as almost magical. By means of electronic switches, as many as nine versions of *NewsPulse* could be beamed out of the New York studio at once. The advantage was that all would be recorded by each receiving computer, which would automatically deliver the broadcast edited for that doctor's specalty to each desktop unit by means of implanted codes. The initial MNN was directed only at family physicians, general practitioners, internists, cardiologists, gastroenterologists, and people influential in medicine. Each got a tailored newscast.

Greenberg found "extraordinary interest" in MNN in the drug industry. Within three months seven companies—Abbott, Ciba-Geigy, Glaxo, Johnson/Ortho, Marion Merrell Dow, Merck, and Pfizer/Roerig—had signed up to sponsor a one-year trial run at a total cost of $80 million. The target date for launching the trial broadcast was March 1993—to a test group of five thousand physicians. If successful, it would go into phase two and expand to fifty thousand offices. Chris and Greenberg also talked of possibly taking the concept to Europe and then on to the Pacific Rim.

Working toward a nerve-wracking deadline, MNN faced several critical tasks: establishing a worldwide news-gathering organization, building the desktop units, outfitting a production facility, refining the programming to a must-watch level, and building Whittle's third television production team.

The first step was hiring Geoffrey Darby, former director of Canadian TV network news and top Nickelodeon executive, as president of MNN programming. "We have to create a package of brilliant TV," Greenberg said. "Darby can bring us that." As managing editor, MNN tapped physician Bruce Dan, former senior editor of the *Journal of the American Medical Association*. Of course, the producers of MNN would not expect their viewers to put faith in news from medical newcomers, so the staff—working out of Washington, D.C., and Rockefeller Center in New York City—consisted of several physicians as well as veterans in medical journalism recruited from organizations like *Science*, the *Washington Post*, and the Associated Press. The latest graphics software was installed on the network to permit "incredible" illustrations in 3-D animation.

Dan predicted viewers would applaud how quickly MNN responded to developments in the medical field. "Doctors are in the forefront of technology—lasers, MRI, CT scans," Dan said. "But the ways they get information are most primitive. Once a month a doctor gets a journal that was published a month before, with articles that were submitted *nine* months before that. In contrast, MNN will provide immediate, daily, interactive stuff."

Pilot newscasts were shown by MNN executive vice-president Tom Lombardo to focus groups of physicians across the country to gauge reaction. "Nine out of ten docs loved it," Lombardo reported. Physicians also welcomed MNN offering continuing education courses in medicine. Those are advanced studies that state laws and professional organizations require doctors to take periodically, which can mean having to spend days at a time at local hospitals or traveling to distant conferences.

Lombardo said, "Doctors don't like to shut their offices for days. They lose five thousand to ten thousand dollars a week when they're not in practice. Now they'll get a chance to gain hours of credit sitting right at the desktop unit in their office."

Medical News Network produced continuing medical education (CME) programming in conjunction with a consortium of medical education centers—the University of Wisconsin at Madison, the University of Alabama at Birmingham, the University of Michigan, the University of South Dakota, and the University of Southern California. Each hour-long course was written by an expert from one of the schools. At the end of each of the four, fifteen-minute segments, the doctors would take a multiple choice test through their keypads.

Their answers would go back to the central computers in Knoxville, which would forward them to the university that worked on that course and which eventually awarded the credit. Doctors got two weeks to study each segment and could work on three courses at once. For example, "Part I of Managing the Difficult Patient," "Migraines," and "Hyperlipidemia" would be telecast to the doctors' MNN units at the same time. "This gives the doc enough time to work their CME into an already busy schedule," Lombardo observed. The doctors' desktops would show how much they were being used. Each time the physician logged on at his desktop keyboard, the central computers would record when, how, and how long he used the system. For the first time, Whittle Communications could eliminate guesswork in evaluating the true impact of an advertising device.

In the glow of what they considered "an impending, stunning

success," Alan Greenberg and his MNN team woke up to the broader possibilities that this interactive technique posed far beyond the medical field.

"Just think," Greenberg told Chris, "we could target professionals such as lawyers. All kinds of trade applications are possible. The system perhaps eventually could be adapted for home news. What about a business-news network that could compete with business magazines for audience and advertisers?"

Chris Whittle nodded agreement. "You're right. MNN is wonderful. And it barely scratches the surface."

That was true. But Chris Whittle and Alan Greenberg were heading into a fatal trap they did not foresee. The start of Medical News Network was unfortunately out of sync with the fast-developing upheaval in America's health care industry.

———

In the spring of 1991 Chris Whittle came to the painful realization that his war chest was not large enough to exploit his current ventures much less finance new start-ups taking shape on the drawing board. Millions of dollars, actually tens of millions, would have to be invested. The answer was to bring in an additional partner— one with deep pockets. He broached that strategy to current partners Time Warner and Lord Rothermere's newspaper group. They agreed.

"We made a list," Chris says, "and started talking to a lot of people."

Within months Chris had winnowed prospective new investors down to two, and negotiated with them. One was the Wall Street investment firm of Forstmann Little and Company. The other was one of the world's largest electronics manufacturers, Philips Electronics N.V. of Eindhoven, the Netherlands, which had $30 billion in annual sales, a consumer subsidiary in Knoxville, and 250,000 employees worldwide.

Philips agreed to pay $175 million for 25 percent of Whittle Communications L.P. At that price Chris's company was now valued at $700 million, almost double where it had stood not quite two years earlier when Time Warner bought a one-half interest for $185 million.

But when Chris notified Forstmann Little, the New York investment firm, of his intention of dealing with Philips, chairman Theodore Forstmann said, "Wait! You haven't heard our best offer."

They soon came up with a decidedly better proposition: $350 million for a one-third interest, meaning—by their calculations—the Whittle company had jumped in value to more than $1 billion. Elated, Chris and his board of directors signed a letter of intent on September 4, 1991, to close the deal with Forstmann Little and Company.

With civic pride and considerable amazement, Knoxville got this news while watching the culmination of a storied, seven-league leap by the successful remnants of the little band of entrepreneurial collegians who had started so unpretentiously two decades earlier. From their ramshackle pillow factory they had been forced, by steady growth, to gradually migrate into the Arnstein building and spill over into two or three others in the business district. But now, on the 1991 Labor Day weekend, the Whittleites were leaving a scattering of motley offices and moving into the stunning, just-completed $55 million Georgian headquarters in the heart of downtown Knoxville. Chris felt passionate about the beauty and style of Historic Whittlesburg, with its copper-domed clock tower and grassy Ivy League courtyard behind one-ton wrought-iron gates, and scheduled a public open house for October.

But while he was still enjoying his architectural triumph, Chris was staggered by two jolts that came in abrupt and dramatic succession.

The first explosion was a near revolt in the ranks. His troops were unhappy. For months resentment festered over deep and caustic feelings that loyal staffers had been slighted while top executives enjoyed lavish perks and high pay. The rank and file were really distressed when word filtered down from president Bill Connell's office that the expected customary annual bonuses had been eliminated. Four days later, on September 25, 1991, Connell proudly announced the appointment of twenty new vice-presidents. That only added to the disgruntled workers' outrage.

On lunch break the next day ninety employees cornered Connell in the courtyard. Connell spotted a *Knoxville News-Sentinel* reporter looking on, apparently tipped off that trouble was brewing. The wary Connell quickly led the angry-eyed employees into the privacy of the fourth-floor boardroom.

The president tried to smooth things over. He conceded that the timing of the veep announcements was "lousy" but argued that the new men were necessary. The company, he said, had been hard hit by the heavy expense of getting Channel One and Special Report Television up and running. Therefore profit margins were not sufficient to pay bonuses for fiscal year 1991, except to a small group of "special contributors."

Alerted that the confrontation was in progress, Chris went to the boardroom, stood in the back looking stricken, but did not get involved. He heard a litany of complaints shouted at Connell: "We want you to know how we feel—dismayed." "We've seen properties die, and we are terrified we won't have a job." "We depend on bonuses to make up for the salary we get." "It's not just that our feelings are hurt. We're the commodity in this company: talent. And we're going to be leaving if things don't change."

After several minutes Chris left. Connell continued to defend the company's actions, explaining at one point, "Chris said the money is just not there" for bonuses, and pointing out that the partners had taken a 15 percent pay cut the previous January. An associate picture editor shot back: "It rings hollow for the soldiers in the field to hear that someone making two hundred thousand dollars took a fifteen percent pay cut . . . and for you to lease new cars for the twenty new vice-presidents!" One of the writers jumped in: "Don't shed tears about the poor partners taking a pay cut! We hear they'll divvy up about one hundred thirty million of that Forstmann Little buy-in."

Chris recognized that some complaints had validity. The healthy, intimate "family" atmosphere from the 13–30 days seemed in imminent danger of disintegrating into a "screw the company" mentality. More importantly, his top lieutenants were restless and nervous, increasingly badgering him to change the company strategy.

To cope with this turmoil, Chris reserved rooms at Blackberry Farm, a small, expensive Smoky Mountain resort fifty miles southeast of Knoxville. He remained there in November 1991 with twenty top management executives for two days, in a quiet guesthouse that had featherbeds and mountain vistas but no telephones or television. In the opinion of many there, it was the most crucial two days in the company's history. Chris was given a chance to slow his expansion strategy down and stave off disaster for Whittle Communications L.P. But he did not.

Writing later about the Blackberry Farm sessions, Chris would comment: "For two decades we had grown by more than twenty percent per year, so typically these meetings were upbeat, filled with discussions of our future. This one was not. A certain unease permeated the two days of talks. We wondered aloud if we were attempting too much but concluded after some minor adjustments that we would stick with our game plan. In my mind, that discussion marked the beginning of a difficult, three-year stretch in Whittle history, one filled with pressure, occasional victories, and serious defeats."

At the Blackberry Farm sessions Chris received candid and straightforward dissent from his lieutenants. The executives—including such battle-tested leaders as Bill Connell, Tom Ingram, Hamilton Jordan, Ed Winter, Gerry Hogan, Mike McAllister, and Nick Glover—argued that the company had excessive staffing, needed to cut back on spending, and focus on very few new projects.

As usual, Chris was nonconfrontational. "He listened," says one of those present, "and we did cut back. He did all those things just enough to appease everybody, but not enough to make a difference. Chris really thinks he is an infallible genius, and he doesn't think he can do anything wrong. He wanted to do what he wanted to do, and didn't care whether it worked for the marketplace or not. But you can't ignore the dynamics of the marketplace. You've got to be responsive to them. Chris just consistently made bad decisions, and you can't do that in business. It catches up with you."

Meanwhile, efforts were under way to finalize the Forstmann Little buy-in. Before signing, their top executives wanted to visit Knoxville, inspect Historic Whittlesburg, and check the books—a process known as "due diligence." Their coming made Whittle brass nervous. Headquarters supervisors were directed to make an overnight inspection of carrels and offices in the newly-occupied building. They pounced on and immediately whisked away about thirty ungainly items—personal coffee pots, desk lamps, heaters, and so forth—which editors and artists had brought along from old offices. That produced another howl of rage against "deplorable confiscations" by "Big Brother."

Whether the desks were tidy enough apparently would not have cut much ice, if any, with the visitors from Wall Street. Feisty Ted Forstmann and his colleagues were little concerned about trifles;

they started having second thoughts about the big picture. Chris stood to boost his personal fortune substantially in the deal, because $130 million was to be shared by existing partners. A sum of $120 million was allocated for paying down bank debt, $100 million was reserved for an acquisition that did not come off, and only about $20 million to $30 million would have been plowed into developments.

To Chris's surprise—and shock—Forstmann Little reneged. First, the New Yorkers attempted to substantially lower the price they were willing to pay for the one-third interest. When that ploy did not succeed, they entirely backed out. As reported by Whittle's employee newsletter, *Fred*:

> Forstmann Little gave us the kind of examination that makes a draft-board physical seem polite. Through it all we had to try to explain Whittle. The potential investors wanted, understandably, a clear personality profile. We explained that we couldn't put a tidy label on ourselves because we never know what we'll think of—or do—next. That was a bit too ethereal for them, and they were a bit too stodgily substantive for us. When the culture clash showed up in the numbers, both parties decided to reject the buy-in plan.

Stunned, Chris hurried back to Philips Electronics. He was on good terms with the top officials and believed he could rekindle their interest. Whittle and Philips already had major business ties: Most of the Channel One equipment had been purchased from Philips Consumer Electronics Company, which had a large operation in Knoxville. In business in the United States since 1933, the Netherlands concern marketed products under a number of brand names, including Philips, Magnavox, and Norelco. Chris was impressed by what he considered their preeminent position as a leader in technology development—a lead they shared with Sony—and figured that would give Whittle Communications an advantage in creating video networks for the Edison Project and its medical satellite broadcast operations.

"We knew them well," says Chris. "I believe we were their largest customer in the United States."

Chris negotiated by transatlantic telephone with Jan Timmer, Philips Electronics chairman. In New York and Knoxville he dealt with Stephen C. Tumminello, president and CEO of North American Philips Corporation; Donald F. Johnstone, president and CEO, Philips Consumer Electronics Company of Knoxville; and L. P. H. (Rens) Das, senior director of corporate mergers and acquisitions of Philips Electronics, N.V.

Jan Timmer was still interested in acquiring an equity position of 25 percent for $175 million. Furthermore, on the basis of Chris's optimistic sales pitch, Philips would take a two-year option to increase its stake to 33 percent if forecasts of increased earnings held up.

Electronic equipment obviously would play a critical role in reinventing the American school, and the Philips officials were also willing to invest separately in the developmental stage of the Edison Project.

To make this one-quarter interest available in Whittle, Time Warner would reduce its holdings from 50 to 37 percent, Associated Newspapers from 33 to 24.6 percent, Chris from 11 to 8.5 percent, and the other limited partners from 6 to 4.9 percent.

Because of Philips-dictated conditions, the $175 million was not to flow immediately into Whittle coffers but be paid in increments that depended on meeting business goals. (Because of these restraints, the investment did not effectively materialize for two years.) The negotiations were complex and laborious. The deal was not announced until February 5, 1992.

The Whittle Communications board was enlarged to thirteen to add four Philips Electronics members: Timmer, Tumminello, Johnstone, and Das. Time Warner's members were Gerald M. Levin, president and CEO of Time Warner Inc.; Donald L. Elliman Jr., president and publisher of *Sports Illustrated*; Joseph A. Ripp, vice-president and CFO of Time Inc.; and Reg Brack, chairman and CEO of Time Inc. On the board to represent Associated Newspaper Holdings were Lord Rothermere, the *Daily Mail* and General Trust plc; Sir David English, chairman of Associated Newspapers Limited; Peter Williams, finance director of the *Daily Mail* and General Trust plc; and Charles J. F. Sinclair, managing director of Associated Newspapers Holdings Ltd.

Over the months Chris kept his right hand pulling levers to

complete the Philips deal. With his left he struggled to correct insidious problems at Whittle—the most troubling, after revenue shortfall and heavy expense, was worker morale.

In a two-day period in late October 1991, Chris and Bill Connell conducted face-to-face Q and A sessions with all employees. Many questions concerned pay. Chris said 3 percent of Whittle employees earned less than $13,500 annually, which the government defines as the poverty level for a family of four, 75 percent exceeded $20,000, and 50 percent $25,000.

When asked about the gap between rich and poor, Chris said: "It's like the story of a Russian farmer. If an American farmer has one horse and his neighbor has three, he wants two more. The Russian farmer just wants his neighbor's three horses to die."

One copy editor disagreed with his analogy, saying, "There's a striking scarcity of covetousness or nasty feelings here about the top people."

Chris had a candid message for anyone who thought himself being taking advantage of by the company. "Test it. You don't have to leave. Just go find out. We don't set out to be exploiters. I think we'll never solve the money issue. People have talked about it since before Christ, and they ain't got it right yet."

Months later Tom Ingram would candidly concede that the workers' discontent "told us that our company's culture was all messed up and that we needed to fix it. Most entrepreneurial enterprises go through a creative period and then have to take the steps necessary to build themselves as long-term businesses. These steps are all about our culture—they protect it by redefining it and helping us get on with business."

About this time Chris Whittle came to the conclusion he needed a new deal on his "Mr. Inside–Mr. Outside" combination. He summoned back Nick Glover.

20

THE 21ST CENTURY SCHOOL

Designing a brilliant model for the Edison Schools was fairly easy; getting money to launch them was hard.

National attention on the project intensified when Chris announced in May 1992 that Benno Schmidt would be his partner, and it remained high for at least six months. Both of them made speeches around the country, explaining Edison Schools. They appeared on television shows, including *Larry King Live* on July 1, 1992, answering phone-in questions. Together they stood at the lectern at the National Press Club in Washington, D.C., on September 17, 1992, and held their own with skeptical reporters.

Edison began to get good publicity for a change; it was a venture still on the come, but one beginning to look like it had a chance to work. Schmidt, a legal scholar versed in educational management who had raised millions for Yale, had proved a catch for Chris, giving the Edison Project an enormous and sorely needed cachet of credibility.

Schmidt immediately tried to defuse criticism of Edison's "profit" motive. In a *Wall Street Journal* op-ed article on June 5, 1992, he asserted an unorthodox approach was now necessary because education reform efforts for twenty years had bogged down. It was time to try again—and harder.

He wrote, "The evidence that U.S. schools are not working well is depressingly familiar. One in five young American boys drops out of high school. Nearly half of all high school graduates have not mastered seventh-grade arithmetic. American thirteen-year-olds place near the bottom in science and math achievement in international comparisons. One-third of seventeen-year-olds cannot place France on a map of the world. Only about one in ten high school graduates can write a reasonably coherent paragraph or handle pre-college mathematics."

America had doubled per-pupil spending since 1965, Schmidt wrote, but the primary problem was not lack of financial resources available to schools or good people who teach. "The problem, I think, is the system itself," he opined, adding, "If our young people were doing well, we might accept this inherited system as the best we can do. But they are not. The system virtually cries out for radical change."

Schmidt added, "Critics of the Edison Project have charged that there is an inherent conflict between educational quality and profits. There is no more reason that this should be so with respect to schools than with respect to newspapers, books, or computers. Competition, choices, diversity will be a spur to innovation and progress in education as in other areas. This project can provide public schools who wish to adopt changes with tested innovations, new models and structural reforms that they simply cannot develop and test themselves."

To be able to go out and convince corporate that America their project was a wise investment, Chris and Benno needed something to show, an actual model of the Edison Schools. They were held in check through the final months of 1992 while behind the scenes those specific elements were created in Knoxville. Finally, in the first days of 1993, the design team proudly wrapped up its work on the for-profit private school for the twenty-first century.

Now came time to raise the first part of the $2.5 billion Chris estimated was needed for bricks and mortar, equipment, personnel, and start-up expenses. Benno Schmidt scowled with concern at this enormous financial obstacle. Chris was unruffled and undaunted. He airily dismissed all expressions of doubt: Don't worry, we'll get all the money we need!

Chris's most recognizable Achilles heel was trusting his own vision as infallible. Huffed one colleague: "It's okay for Chris to dream, but does he have to dream out loud!" Lamented another: "Chris is a visionary and when he looks into the future, he doesn't see possibility or probability, he sees facts!" And another: "Why in the world did he ever mention $2.5 billion? He doesn't have any figures for that! Sounds like something just scribbled on the back of an envelope."

Chris's price tag was much too high. And within a few months the astounding start-up cost would emerge as a stumbling block that threatened to leave the venture stillborn. On the other hand, educational circles generally applauded the freshly conceived Edison Schools model, although its designers readily admitted, "We are shooting for the stars."

Benno Schmidt set forth the "philosophy and values" of Edison Schools on the premise that education was the nation's "missed opportunity" because most schools were mired in a basic nineteenth century model that "virtually guarantees waste, inefficiency, and mediocrity." He added, "As a result, our nation itself is seriously at risk. . . . The Edison Project exists to bring together the vision, the people, the resources, and the will to effect a revolution in America's schools. We will create schools that achieve quantum gains in the academic performance of American students, in the quality of their lives, and in the well-being of our nation. . . . Edison schools will be technologically sophisticated as only a system based on careful research and development can be—in contrast to schools so untouched by modern technology that the majority of classrooms do not even have a phone line."

Waxing poetic, Benno Schmidt promised new teaching methods would be exciting and cause Edison schools to "hour after hour . . . ring out with surprise, delight, and discovery." Students would be immersed beyond the academic domain "to four other essential realms: the physical, the creative, the practical, and the ethical and moral."

For all this lofty preamble, the Edison design did not totally abandon the outmoded meat-and-potato concept, but significantly broke the mold by piling more work on students, teachers, and parents, while supplying twenty-first century tools.

The striking changes included keeping Edison schools open year-round, with only six weeks vacation, from July 1st to August 15th, and extending the school day by as much as four hours. Starting with day care at 7 A.M., the school day would run to 6 P.M., closing with sports. The extra time adds nineteen weeks to the current school year. Schmidt pointed out that with accelerated curricula this would add "the equivalent of more than six years—that's right, *six years*—to what is now a typical kindergarten-through-twelfth grade academic career."

Not unexpectedly, the Edison design leans heavily on electronic technology. Each student and teacher has a personal computer linked via a video satellite network to distant libraries, world-class lecturers, interactive town halls, newscasts, as well as all other Edison Schools. The student's computer is installed at home, which permits parents to send teachers E-mail and also get early warnings before their child falls hopelessly behind. Even children four to eight carry a small-screen "Rad Pad" on which to doodle with a stylus and record their ideas. School records and textbooks are on-line, and students can carry a two-page printout of the day's lesson instead of a backpack of books weighing eight pounds.

Edison teachers forge a close partnership to support the children, meeting frequently to share materials and ideas. Families have a wealth of print and electronic material, so they can reinforce at home what their children are learning in school. They may also use their home computer, logging on to pursue their own educational objectives, such as learning a new language or math.

Another distinctive break with tradition was to organize each Edison campus of 1,320 students into six small schools-within-a-school called academies, because students tend to learn faster in small settings. The academies are determined by grade level: preschool, which accepts three- and four-year-olds; kindergarten through second grade; third through fifth grade; sixth through eighth grade; ninth and tenth grades; and eleventh and twelfth grades. In each academy students will spend two to three years, giving teachers a chance to know them. They are not promoted grade to grade but by completing the requirements to move up to the next academy.

The Edison model made its "most profound change" in creating "a new breed" of "master teacher." Each campus would have thirteen of these, under a school director aided by four executive managers and two principals. They would be supported by nineteen senior teachers, thirteen teachers, and twenty resident teachers, the latter in training like hospital interns. All instructors would be paid about 25 percent above the prevailing wage and share in profits. Their work would extend beyond the classroom, advising clubs and problem students, and coaching sports. The teacher-student ratio would be about sixteen to one, but this is not considered critical because in Japanese schools, which are superior, this ratio is often forty or fifty to one.

Critical in twenty-first century teaching, however, is which subjects are taught and at what age. Edison designers concluded a curriculum "does not need to be routine, watered down, or tedious," but instead should be delivered in "dynamic and original ways" to emphasize creativity "in such fields as art, music, design, character and values, physical fitness, and practical skills."

Math and foreign languages were singled out for emphasis, along with science, development of character and ethics, and physical fitness. The Edison design book said, "To be blunt, math may be the worst taught, least understood, and most feared and loathed of all subjects offered in schools." During Edison elementary years math and reading are on equal footing.

With more hours in class, students are required to learn the *meaning* of fractions and by graduation know calculus as well as probability and statistics. Science classes, too often an afterthought in most schools, begin in kindergarten, directing children's curiosity toward wildlife, plants, and natural systems. In the ninth grade, students learn college-level biology, chemistry, and physics.

Students are taught to read, write, speak—and understand the words of others. "Words are basic . . . the ability to speak and listen well is closely related to the ability to read and write," said Schmidt. Even in the second grade students keep daily journals. By the fifth grade they will read plays, poetry, biographies, and speeches, memorizing outstanding passages. Students will climb by the eleventh and twelfth grades to literature like *Canterbury Tales, Don Quixote, The Federalist Papers,* and *Crime and Punishment.*

The formerly dry pursuit of social studies—history, civics, and geography—would "spring to life, replete with heroes, tyrants, and exotic journeys."

Schmidt said, "Each Edison student learns at least two foreign languages, studying Spanish in preschool, and achieving fluency by the fifth grade. Courses will be offered in Italian, Hebrew, Chinese,

Russian, and Arabic." Latin is required. The core team felt a working knowledge of Latin helps students better understand the mechanics of mastering other subjects.

Schmidt added, "Students spend an hour a day in art or music classes. They will get into architecture and design. The curriculum is so rich, an Edison student could graduate with the "equivalent of *two* years of college."

"Edison graduates will be ready for life," said the core team's design book. There are no classes in "shop" or home economics, but students must learn practical skills equal to those of Eagle Scouts—to cook, take a bicycle apart and put it back together, to garden, speak in public, excel in photography, understand bank accounts, mortgages, tax returns, and stock exchanges.

Student behavior was to be strictly monitored. An "honor code" begins in the fifth grade. Violations of the straightforward discipline policy results in punishment, usually by "restitution—the righting of wrongs." Students could be suspended or expelled for "intolerable actions" that endanger or harm others, threaten the schools' core values, involve the use of drugs or alcohol, possession of weapons, criminal activity, or physical or emotional abuse.

A "simple, versatile dress code" was put in effect. It calls for: solid-colored shirts or blouses, with collars; blue or khaki skirts or slacks—no jeans or sweatpants; sweaters or blazers, if desired; socks and plain shoes—no sandals, high heels, or cowboy boots; good personal hygiene; no excessive makeup, bizarre haircuts, elaborate jewelry, gang jackets, or other efforts to draw excessive attention to one's appearance.

The original intent was to build new Edison school buildings from the ground up, and designers proposed to further break the conventional mold in the way they were constructed. The core team employed three outstanding architectural firms to create a new design, but before that effort could begin the Edison Project shifted gears and decided to use existing public school buildings.

The architectural parameters that were drawn up, but not used, would have produced highly unusual structures. The design team wanted portions of the foundation, walls, and beams to be visible so students could see and understand the relationship of one section of the school building to another.

In the words of the design team, the new school building should "encourage a child's natural desire to explore and discover. We want to create 'intelligent' buildings that will be greater participants in the teaching and learning process." Ideally the building might include a sky-viewing station (with telescopes and weather-analysis instruments), broadcasting equipment, and outdoor gardens that would be planted and tended by children. "Lessons in architecture, biology, engineering, the natural sciences, and anthropology would spring from our buildings. Imagine a school basement that had been finished to look unfinished, with windows on the soil beds and with the pipes, wires, beams and footing labeled and colored for teaching."

In every respect the Edison school model was truly twenty-first century stuff, many education experts agreed.

To counteract concerns that Edison Schools would be elitist, thus robbing inner-city youngsters of the chance for quality education, Chris Whittle had initially planned giving scholarships to 20 percent of the students. When the decision was later made to operate in public schools instead of charging individual tuition, that point became moot.

———

With the scheme now fully spelled out, the search for financial and governmental support for Edison schools began in early 1993. Benno Schmidt responded to inquiries that began coming in from all across the country. He went on the road giving his sales pitch to leaders in education, industry, and politics, including at least twenty governors.

Some, such as governors Roy Romer of Colorado and William Weld of Massachusetts, were impatient with Chris's priorities and timetable. Chris's initial idea was to design the private Edison school, build, open, and operate a few, thus demonstrating their effectiveness. With that proof, Whittle Schools would bring the Edison inventions and techniques into managed public schools.

"Don't wait to get the Edison schools running," Schmidt was told. "If you have worked out the answers, let us have them right now."

Chris was dismayed by the bad vibes stirred up by Edison's announced $2.5 billion price tag. He said, "We projected that as roughly what it would cost to build one hundred of these original campuses and also fund start-up. We didn't have to have two and a half billion dollars at one time. We started seeking one hundred seventy million, which would cover us for a stretch of time."

Then, acting on suggestions from governors Romer and Weld, among others, Chris and Schmidt significantly altered the Edison strategy.

Chris said, "When we began we had a concept of building what we call O and O's, which are owned-and-operated schools. And we would build the campuses, charge tuition, and that was basically the plan.

"After Benno joined us we started getting a lot of inquiries from governors, superintendents, and school boards basically saying, 'Would you be interested in running a public school of ours, using the Edison system? You wouldn't have to put up buildings because we already have them. We would contract with you to in effect run a magnet school for the public system.'

"As we got into that we began to like it more and more and the reason is, it radically reduced our capital needs. We would be able to get out of the brick-and-mortar business. And the other thing is that we would achieve what we really set out to do in the first place, which is to bring quality education to ordinary kids because our hope from the beginning was the public schools would copy what we were doing. So what we have gone through is a large shift to what we call a PSP strategy—public school partnerships."

═══

Even though the "big picture" looked bright on the outside, at Knoxville headquarters Chris was hounded by problems. Most, unfortunately, arose because of his iron grip on the company.

At odds with the boss for a full year, Bill Connell finally gave up. Chris readily let Connell step aside and persuaded Nick Glover to come back and take over his old post of "Mr. Inside." Connell, retaining the title of president, was given special assignments. Glover was designated a vice-chairman.

Nobody genuinely functioned as chief operating officer. Chris let division heads shoulder the day-to-day routine but was not about to relinquish calling the critical and strategic shots himself. As any insider could see, the problem confronting the company was simple and straightforward: Expenses were too high and income was too low.

Chris, still the artful dodger, could not stomach the dirty work of firing executives, cutting pay, and laying off editors, writers, and artists, or withdrawing perks. But Glover argued for six months that costs had to be reduced by $30 million a year—quickly. Finally Chris gave in and swung the long-overdue economic ax. Glover said, "We've kept delaying all the little pieces of pain until we had to cut our damned foot off."

There was plenty of pain in Glover's restructuring. Ten of the eighty limited partners were discharged; executive salaries were cut 25 percent. (Chris volunteered to take a 30 percent reduction.) Auto and travel perks were curtailed. One hundred and eleven staffers were laid off, most of them in print—8 percent of the work force.

Summoning all employees on May 13, 1992, to Knoxville's Tennessee Theatre, the closest auditorium that would hold all eight hundred, Chris walked out on the stage and personally delivered the bad news. Despite rumors, his audience was stunned by the depth of the retrenchment. Chris, too, was overcome by emotion. He choked up at the microphone, tears misted his eyes, and he asked for a five-minute break. He retreated to the wings, then returned to announce that a program was being set up to retrain terminated staffers, provide them with psychological stress counseling, and help them find new jobs.

Looking back on that experience, Chris said the shocking reaction to the layoffs caught him by surprise, but he agreed it had been a serious "mistake" to postpone the decision to restructure.

"One of our central themes," he said, "is that we went through a transition that has caused a lot of stress in this business—going from a print company to an electronic company. One particularly difficult aspect is that as we introduced electronic they often cannibalized our print business.

"We had a print business called *Connections* [a wall poster] in high schools, and we introduced Channel One in high schools, and all our clients went, 'Channel One is a much superior product than *Connections!*' We devastated our *Connections* business, which ran about ten million dollars in revenue. But we built Channel One, which was about a hundred-million-dollar business."

From a business standpoint, Chris regarded that as proper. "The folks at *Connections* obviously didn't like it. One of the ultimate results was that we were unable to continue to employ all of our print staff. And I did drag my feet on it. I didn't want to cut loose people from the print operation, and yet what was happening was we were hiring rapidly in the electronic businesses. And so at some point we had to start letting people go in the print business, and it caused a lot of tension in the company."

The firings triggered a strong wave of resentment. But when a delegation of one hundred employees later confronted Nick Glover for explanations, he took a hard stance. "It is true that our growth has been created by people and will always be. The reason people are here is they like doing new things, love excitement, and like entrepreneurial challenge. If I were a person who wasn't comfortable with new things, this is not where I'd hang out. But we are totally dependent on people. People create new things, and there will always be tremendous opportunities here for people, but it won't always be the same people."

═══

In his private life, too, Chris was encountering major turmoil and complexities—especially because it required three years to convert his new large apartment in the Dakota into his new "family" home.

"I was going nuts," Priscilla lamented. "I have no patience for the process. I want to move right in and put my roots down, and never move again."

Chris was more patient. "I understand you have to take time. You don't really get a place that you are going to love in six months."

Nor did Chris and Priscilla get an entirely free hand in rearranging their rooms. The masonry-bearing walls that separated the two units in their Dakota apartment could not be touched, which resulted in a long central hallway. Priscilla turned to architect Peter Marino and threw up her hands. "It was intimidating," she says. "Then I realized a hall is a wonderful place to hang your pictures. Now we call it the train."

Moreover, the once-distressing hall proved the unexpected key to taming the enormous space to make the apartment satisfy multiple needs. The hall had entrances at each end, making it convenient to locate the new formal rooms, the couple's two studies, children's rooms, and an eat-in kitchen off the hall. Says Priscilla: "It's like two apartments tied together by the kitchen, the heart of the house."

The hand of a woman was obvious in the design of the new apartment. Whereas Chris's bachelor place had been "incredibly masculine, incredibly dark," this apartment was magnificent, lighter, and cheerier. "I like this far better," Chris said, "and that's attributable to Priscilla." Marino had stuck with dark, hand-rubbed mahogany woodwork, but made the walls lighter and "more welcoming," adding "comfy" chairs, some of which were "squishy." Priscilla had demanded the place be "grand and formal for entertaining, but cozy for me and child-friendly for the kids."

Obviously Chris didn't walk away and leave too many favorite things back in his old apartment. He found plenty of wall space for his scores of paintings, giving prominent display to his large John White Alexander's *The Blue Dress* and the artist's equally sizeable and impressive *Onteora*.

This time Marino skipped a decade and made the mood of the apartment Edwardian, "about 1905." Everything was elegant—and expensive. No two sections of wallpaper were exactly the same; each was hand-printed from wood blocks. It took artisans in Italy a year to make the delicately lined curtains for the bedroom. Cupboards and closets were covered inside with hand-fashioned textiles and wallpaper.

In the kitchen, Priscilla hung nearly two dozen photographs from her own collection, including many she took with her Nikon. In her study she had three fabric-lined corkboards on which she tacked photos and page proofs from her new book, *Children*. (The Italian edition was titled *Bambini*.) On the desk in Chris's study she placed another of her favorite photos, *The Torso*, a nude by Alfred Stieglitz and Clarence White.

The editors of *House and Garden* magazine obviously considered the collaboration of Marino, Chris, and Priscilla a distinctive success. In the March 1990 issue, the magazine had featured Marino's work in designing the bachelor apartment. Now the editors sent a writer and photographer to explore the new apartment and scheduled a laudatory eleven-page spread for the October 1992 issue, with a close-up of the Whittles' candlelit kitchen table on the magazine cover.

Both Whittles—husband and wife—received a lot of newspaper attention in Knoxville in 1992, only a month prior to his Tennessee Theatre downsizing announcement. Chris was honored as Knoxville's "Man of the Year," Priscilla came to town for that ceremony.

Because her second picture book, *Children,* had just been published and Knoxville's curiosity about her was not yet fully satisfied, she actually got bigger write-ups than did her husband.

The Man of the Year award was presented in April by the greater Knoxville chapter of the Juvenile Diabetes Foundation International (JDFI) at the Cherokee Country Club, for Chris's "contributions to the community and his interest in the education of the youth of America." Most men among the 350 dinner guests wore bowties, copying Chris's trademark. J. Richard Munro, chairman of Time Warner board's executive committee and international chairman of JDFI, flew down from New York to present the award. "Chris won't settle for the world as it is," Munro told the guests. "He's a dreamer, a planner, a doer."

News-Sentinel society columnist Barbara Aston-Wash interviewed Priscilla in the paneled library at Whittle headquarters and found her relaxed, friendly, and willing to share "some of her thoughts about family, politics, education and her art book, just published by Rizzoli, New York."

Under the blaring banner "Priscilla's Picture Book," the interview and pictures filled two full pages in the newspaper and stands as the most candid interview the usually shy photographer had given. She considers *Children* in some ways her "visual autobiography." The book contains many shots of her son Maxi. (In one he merges nude from the surf.) Chris is also in the book, photographed swinging a laughing Maxi by the heels in New York's Central Park. Daughter Andrea Leigh arrived too late for the photos inside, but is shown on the back jacket cover with her mother and half-brother.

Priscilla's dedication on the flyleaf reads: "To Chris, who has given me the courage to grow."

"Chris is wonderful," she told Barbara Aston-Wash. "He's bright and kind, thoughtful. Very supportive. He encourages me to do and be more. While I tend to moroseness, he has a wonderful sense of humor and tease. He lightens me up when I need it. He also has the best manners of any man I know. He's just a unique person—a wonderful father to our daughter Andrea and a good role model for Maxi. They are the best of friends."

The text of the book was written by Priscilla's sister, Ilaria Rattazzi, a renowned child therapist in Italy who helped her "explore the essence of childhood." The book contains ninety-eight photos, many in color. Some of the moments captured are a kindergarten pasta-making session, toasting marshmallows on the beach at East Hampton, a Christmas pageant, trick-or-treating, running in the park, and playing "Ring Around the Rosie."

Priscilla was considering doing a book of landscapes. She said, "I love the beach, the sand, the dunes and other scenery around our East Hampton house. I want to photograph that. But I don't plan a new book anytime soon. Barbara Walters was quoted as saying you do two out of three things well when it comes to marriage, family, and career. That may be true. The career is now the least important thing to me."

The Whittles were spending most weekends at East Hampton, where they sail and play tennis. "I love to ski, but I gave up wind surfing when it hurt my back. I guess I am sportive, but you can have more fun together with your children when you like sports, I think. Certainly Chris and I have lots of fun."

She finds it more convenient to live in New York because Chris travels so much. "I really couldn't stand living in the city were it not for Central Park. Despite the press to the contrary, it is a wonderful place. We spend lots of time there. When we are out early enough in the morning, I walk Maxi across the park to school fifteen minutes away. If we are late, we take the crosstown bus and walk through the park after school."

In their Dakota apartment the children were under strict discipline. "Andrea is already learning to pick up her toys. The children take their plates to the sink after they eat . . . I don't want them to grow up as I did—having everything done for them. I want them to know how to do things for themselves, to have summer jobs, to develop self-confidence by doing things. Often an 'advantaged' childhood ends up being a personal disadvantage, as I felt was my case. Chris is a perfect role model to make the point."

The Whittles had a housekeeper and a nanny, but Priscilla spent much of her time with the children and cooked some of the meals. "At least three times a week I do the cooking, and since New York City has wonderful ethnic restaurants, we sometimes have takeout Chinese or Mexican. We eat out at little restaurants [located] around the apartment. I don't like the chic, famous restaurants where you have to make reservations six months in advance."

The newspaper columnist asked how she would feel if Chris

revived his previous political ambition? "I'd support him, of course, in whatever he wants to do, but I have often told him that I feel he can do more for the country as a private person. I would certainly prefer that." She said she knew the wife of a candidate would have to be good at public speaking. "I simply cannot do that. But if Chris ever gets involved in politics, I am sure I will learn." Education is more to her liking, and she had some definite thoughts on the subject.

"Having been brought up in Europe where passing final exams is necessary before one can graduate from high school, I think they are powerful incentives to achieve. I know exams are not popular, but students who know they are not going to graduate unless they give time and attention to learning are likely to do so.

"Also, I feel vacations are too long in this country. In Europe, educators say six weeks is as long as students can be away from the classroom and remain focused, retaining information they learned the semester before. Three-month vacations let children become bored unless they are learning new skills or having a summer job. Perhaps if vacations were broken up differently, it would help."

She believes more life-style courses would be beneficial. "Students need to know practical things like how to unstop a sink, fix the hinges on a door, something about electrical appliances. They need courses in child care and parenting. Courses in marriage— how to stay married, to grow together. Something of how to fight and not to fight, conflict resolution. The family is the most important asset we have, and we are doing little to preserve it."

=====

The Public School Partnership (PSP)—idea triggered Chris's imagination. He got out his yellow pad, jotted down notes, and was hit by a thunderclap. The enthusiastic reception PSP got was contagious. Suddenly Chris thought he caught a clearer view of the big picture. They were sitting on something very potent; here was a climate that definitely offered much more than merely a chance to finance the Edison start-up. The opportunity was enormous, big enough, he told his people, to serve as the vehicle for attracting a very large and immediate infusion of capital. And new partners bringing big bucks couldn't come any too soon. The company was drowning in red ink, chiefly because of the enormous expense of research and project start-ups. Furthermore, revenue for the fiscal year ending June 30, 1993, dropped 5.5 percent, down from $213 million to $201 million.

And there was another critical problem—the partnership with Time Warner. They were anxious to sell their 37.5 percent stake—or a large chunk of it. Time Warner, heavily in debt in the wake of its own mammoth merger, had decided to "monetize" non–income-producing assets such as its Whittle stake, as well as its interest in Turner Broadcasting Corporation. Their relationship with Chris and his other partners had proved tricky. Time Warner had not yet lost faith and their men on the board usually supported Chris. One significant aspect of the partnership was that all partners were locked in; not one, not even Chris, could sell his interest without the unanimous agreement of the others.

That was not a sticking point, however. Price was the element that might hold up Time Warner's exit. They wanted around $300 million for the share that had cost them $185 million.

In his enthusiasm over the good reception Edison was getting so early, Chris decided to be more ambitious than limit his efforts to finding partners interested in investing solely in Edison Schools. Why not just bundle together all the elements of Whittle Communications and offer corporate America a chance to buy into his whole company? That made an attractive package, he reasoned. On that premise he would solicit investors to buy out Time Warner as well as supply funds to move along the remaining magazine operations, expand Channel One, and roll out the next phase of Medical News Network. He turned to the New York investment bank of Salomon Brothers Inc. to manage the search for new investors willing to back his dreams with $1 billion.

Chris's proposal definitely attracted attention in corporate boardrooms, and soon the limousines began pulling up at Historic Whittlesburg. John Sculley, then Apple's chief, came to look and listen. So did Michael Eisner, chairman of the Walt Disney Company, bringing eagle-eyed accountants to go over Whittle Communications' books. Chris and Benno Schmidt did not hole up exclusively in Knoxville; they hit the road to make their high-decibel pitch to other corporations. In Seattle they made a ninety-minute presentation to Microsoft's Bill Gates, but struck out.

According to the press, Chris made his pitch to such marketing and consumer giants as Paramount Communications Corporation, Viacom International Inc., McDonalds, PepsiCo Inc., Tele-Communications Inc., the Tribune Company, publisher of the *Chicago Tribune* and producer of TV programs, and also to a leading cable-TV and newspaper conglomerate, Cox Enterprises Inc.

Cox took a long look and was intrigued—but backed off. "The education component is fascinating," David Easterly, president of Cox Newspapers, told the *Wall Street Journal*. "And we want to see it given a try. But the risk was just a little beyond our comfort level. It's unlikely we will go back and look at it again."

Chris carried on his most serious and lengthiest negotiations with Disney chairman Eisner, who was given an initial hour-and-a-half sales pitch in Los Angeles.

"This is just an overview," Chris told the Disney chief. "We can't do it justice in such a short time. To really understand this you need to come to Knoxville and spend a full day."

Eisner did.

For six hours Eisner and four top lieutenants sat around a Knoxville headquarters conference table and heard a stirring presentation by Chris, Benno Schmidt, and other Whittle executives. "And those guys weren't bored for a second," says Nick Glover, who took part in the sales pitch. "It was spell binding."

Business Week reported that Disney was interested in acquiring 80 percent of Channel One and Edison. Investment bankers told the magazine that Chris's asking price was $1.3 billion. Disney considered that too steep. "Whittle lowered his price to around $700 million," the magazine reported. Even so, Disney, with its new Paris theme park a money-eating quagmire of its own, did not buy the deal.

Recalling the negotiation with Eisner, Chris says, "We presented a combination of vision and detail. Vision that is not rooted in detail is not worth much. Blue sky doesn't get you anywhere. What you've got to do is go, *Here's a vision, but now let's go through how this can actually be executed. And what the details of that are, and how it will function, and why it will work.*

"And what we did in that day was to try to take him through two businesses—Edison and Channel One, in particular what the future ramifications were. They were intrigued. Disney ultimately declined, but like most people they found Edison fascinating. In those early days it was hard to know whether it was going to work. Today that's becoming much more evident. But there was a lot of skepticism about the scale I was trying to do in the early days."

Eisner was critical of Chris's intention of launching the Edison Project with twenty schools in the first round. Chris says, "He told me, 'You don't have to start with twenty. That's too many! Do a few.' That was a general reaction at the time. And, by the way, they were right."

Asked about the Eisner rejection, Chris said, smiling, "I have a rule in business. I don't discuss clients on a detailed basis. I'm happy to talk about my wife, but not my ex-girlfriends."

The investor search ultimately fizzled out. The year 1993 turned into one of Chris Whittle's worst business nightmares. "I have had five tough stretches in my career," Chris said. "The launch of the 13–30 was extremely difficult. The takeover of *Esquire,* meaning the first couple of years of that—that stretch was very hard. The parting with Phillip was very difficult. Didn't have much to do with operations of the business, but it was a very complex and tense stretch. And then this period was really the fifth. They all had their dangers and their fears."

Beyond doubt, however, the 1993 investor hunt became the most public and demeaning of the Whittle nightmares. His struggle to bring in big investors and his obvious failure in this mission was harshly derided in the business news journals, even lampooned in some.

At that juncture, Whittle Communications had difficulty presenting the pretty face of a successful business belle to attract stalwart suitors from big business. The Knoxville company was no giant; only a $200 million-plus annual revenue producer. Besides, it was now losing money, still snarled in the awkward switch from print to video. But Chris pursued his strategy with desperate intensity, saying, "I worked on this twenty hours a day."

A wave of bad publicity developed, built around reports that Whittle was "scaling back" and "scrambling for money." Clearly the news reports led the public to conclude that the Edison project, announced at $2.5 billion, had somehow been cut to $1.2 billion— and finally a mere $750 million.

Chris conceded that he got carried away with feeling there was wildfire optimism about Edison and made a grievous mistake by deciding to bundle up everything in the company into one package and offer that to investors.

"I should have done these one at a time," Chris said. "I should have gone out and raised the Edison money separately and the Time Warner money separately. By bundling them, I made it more complex than it needed to be. And then, finally, if that weren't enough, my timing was not smart, in two respects. I never intended to go out at this time and raise funds for Edison. Frankly it was a little early, since Edison is still kind of forming. Then the other reason is that we did have one significant problem area in our business—*Special Report.* So my timing was not very good. Add all that together—it was a failed strategy."

Was his board of directors opposed to that strategy?

"No, they weren't. I had myself convinced and I think I had everybody else convinced. Well, we actually had offers. And so the strategy wasn't that flawed, but the offers that we got weren't either at the price levels that we would prefer, or on the terms that we would prefer. So we decided to pass."

Reporting on the failure to raise $750 million, the *Wall Street Journal* said: "People familiar with the talks said one problem was the high valuations that Whittle placed on its own properties and the Edison project. While they said some companies were interested in Whittle properties, such as the advertiser-supported Channel One news program for schools, Whittle was said to be asking too high a price."

Chris put the best face possible on the licking he took. He announced that although Time Warner would not put any more money into the Edison Project, his other two partners—the Dutch giant Philips Electronics and the British Associated Newspapers—would invest more. In addition, Chris would put in more personal funds. Altogether, Edison would have an additional $40 million to finance the next eighteen months of operation, carrying the project into the spring of 1995.

At a time Chris Whittle's abilities as a successful educational entrepreneur were yet to be demonstrated, his reputation as a media wunderkind suddenly began to tarnish. *Advertising Age*, the bible of Madison Avenue, reported that although "smart, aggressive, and pioneering," Chris appeared to be running out of gas because investors rejected his Edison project. The magazine asserted

Chris had good ideas and was more willing than others in media to push the envelope. But in doing so, the Whittleites "tend to run when they can walk, and that's what gets them into trouble."

Even good ideas can self-destruct if pushed too fast, the magazine said, and entrepreneurs who are too aggressive get labeled hucksters filled with hype and promises but little capacity to deliver. It added:

> To some degree, that is happening to Chris Whittle. If he would only slow down a little, take it a day at a time and finish what he starts before leaping into the next Big Idea, perhaps his fortunes and those of his worthy ideas would improve.

21

STARTING THE
DOWNHILL SLIDE

In early August 1993 Chris Whittle flew to Los Angeles to face severe interrogation by his angry board of directors. The board had
become alarmed about over-ambitious schemes that threatened to
sink Whittle Communications, L.P., despite Channel One's presence in 12,000 schools. The financial plight was close to desperate.
Now they wanted straight answers. In the prior year revenue had
sunk while costs escalated. *Special Report* television was losing serious money. Medical News Network was ninety days into its test run
and looked good. It was everyone's hope. Channel One revenues
had flattened out, despite the fact that Chris had just invested another $20 million. The Edison Project, still in the embryonic stage
despite millions spent, was not programmed to earn its first dime
until at least 1996. Chris had been trying to soothe the directors'
anxieties: *Don't worry. My dream is intact. We are going to be a $3
billion company*.

But Donald F. Johnstone, one of three Philips Electronics men
on the board, feared Chris had lost his magic touch. So did other
directors, especially *Time*'s Reg Brack. For three days in a suite at
L.A.'s Hotel Bel-Air, the board questioned Chris and his chief lieutenants.

Johnstone felt he had a big personal stake in clearing up the
mess. Head of the Philips consumer products division in Knoxville,
he had met Chris while selling 300,000 television sets to Channel

One. Highly impressed, he had persuaded his Dutch superiors to buy their one-quarter share in Whittle Communications.

Like other directors, Johnstone had been mesmerized by Chris's ability to pull rabbits out of his hat. Time after time he had raced to the brink and waltzed back with a contract worth millions.

"Chris is so bright and so talented," says Johnstone. "He could talk the board into anything. He got a whole good intelligent group of pros on the board to go along when it was as clear as the noses on their faces we were in deep trouble. But he commanded the board meetings with such skill; he spent all his time on these damn presentations. He never left us any time to discuss anything. It was always presentations, presentations, presentations . . . and we'd go home."

Busy in their own careers as executives at Time Warner, Associated Newspapers of London, and Philips Electronics of the Netherlands, the twelve directors had willingly ceded a throat-hold on company control to Chris, who was also a director as well as chairman. A single partner's vote could have vetoed any of Chris's schemes. The directors believed in his dreams. Now it was difficult to second-guess themselves.

"We all invested in him," Johnstone says, "and we believed in him. We, Philips, put all our money on Chris Whittle so the last thing in the world you want to do is say he isn't the greatest thing since the nickel cigar. When people disagree with him, he's so nice. Somebody challenge us, we'd say, 'Oh, you're full of crap!' He doesn't. He just sits there and says, 'Oh, yeah?' And smiles. It goes in one ear and out the other. It never took. He's sitting there saying, 'Anybody who disagrees with me is halfway loony.' He has such a nice personality he never comes across as confrontational or critical of your input. He never criticizes. He never loses his temper."

Chris had time after time been able to blindside the board. He cornered his divisional chiefs just before board meetings for personal, challenging pep talks. "He would put them through their paces," Johnstone says. "It was, 'You mean you can't do this?' Nobody wants to displease Chris. So of course these guys said, 'Yeah, I guess I can.' But their hearts weren't in the numbers they presented to the board. They would forecast revenue that did not materialize. First Chris convinces himself that something is possible. Then he can sell his reality to anyone."

Directors were also slow to grasp the severity of the mounting costs. Johnstone adds, "Chris just had a lot of waste, redundancy, and people on the payroll he didn't need. We had an organization to run a billion-dollar company and we were running around $200 million. So all these things were starting to be perceived. But Chris is very optimistic and stubborn about not taking the kinds of actions that a seasoned, prudent generalist would take. It was the ego thing. He wanted to control the entire business as he had in the past."

Now clearly aware of danger, the board woke up in Los Angeles and took corrective action. No longer would they tolerate one-man control. The directors repudiated Chris's laid-back leadership by ordering two important changes. First, a competent chief financial officer would have to be brought in immediately to fill a critical position Chris had left vacant for two years. Second, a task force would be appointed and empowered to examine the company from top to bottom and recommend fixes.

Chris did not resist, urging a close look at expenses. He conceded the need to hire a CFO.

This crisis came on top of considerable executive suite dissention that had already existed under the Knoxville clock tower. Nick Glover, although brought back to direct headquarters operations, had been emasculated by Chris's iron hand. His suggestions got the same cold shoulder that had stymied Bill Connell in his short reign as "Mr. Inside."

"Both Nick and Bill tried to tell Chris he was making mistakes," says Johnstone. "He listened, but ignored them. They both finally just gave up."

Other key men jumped ship. Gerry Hogan, the prize catch from Turner Broadcasting, felt frustrated and disgusted. He scouted around for a new job and landed the presidency of Home Shopping Network and moved to St. Petersburg, Florida. Hamilton Jordan, also disenchanted, headed back to Atlanta.

The company quickly hired a new chief financial officer, Randy Greaves. He had served as the number-two executive of Insilco Corporation of Midland, Texas, a $600-million-a-year producer of goods ranging from automobile transmissions to school yearbooks. He seemed perfect to be Whittle CFO. He had just worked out a $1 billion refinancing for Insilco, and fascinated and intrigued by the media schemes, was eager to come to Knoxville.

Greaves was quickly disillusioned. "I thought Chris and Nick Glover were tremendous people at the time I was being recruited," says Greaves. "I was shown financial information that was very solid. However, as soon as I really examined the books, I discovered I had been misled one hundred and eighty degrees." That statement surprises Chris. "I had one short interview with Randy Greaves," he says. "Nick and the partners brought Randy in because he was a turnaround expert."

Confronting Chris and Glover, Greaves threatened to quit. Instead they worked out a new contract. Greaves, sharp-eyed, young, and tough, wrote it himself—a thirty-page agreement that required a vote to discharge him by at least three partners and guaranteed $1 million in severance pay if the company failed or was sold.

"The partners winced," he recalls. "But they all signed, including Chris. Then I had to jump right in and start fighting alligators."

First, the new CFO undertook to soothe bankers who had lent the company over $100 million. "They were incredibly angry. The company was thumbing its nose at them. Promises were not being kept. The bankers wouldn't even sit in the same room with Chris. They thought their money was being thrown down a rathole. They just wanted to get their principal back and wash their hands of Whittle."

Chris says, however, the company never defaulted on any payments of interest or principal, and that he maintained cordial relations with Gerald Hassell, executive vice president of the Bank of New York and head of its credit department.

Greaves struck a deal that kept the bank consortium, headed by the Bank of New York, at bay. He agreed to truncate, or cancel, the unused part of the existing $150 million line of credit, easing the banks' scrutiny by regulatory agencies. To augment that, he proposed the Whittle general partners ante up more of their own money to cover revenue shortfall and keep the company going.

Time Warner refused. Says Greaves: "So Philips and Associated took a disproportionate share of funding the operating losses after the banks shut us off."

To weather the storm, Philips and Associated Newspapers agreed to jointly put in a total of $60 million. "But no more. When that was spent, that was it."

Don Johnstone organized the task force in November 1993 and

began summoning every department head to the ornate executive conference room on the fourth floor of the headquarters building. Assisted by Greaves, Glover, and financial expert Andy Rounds, sent over from London by Lord Rothermere, Johnstone mercilessly dug for hard information on every phase of the company.

"It was an unbelievable situation, how bad it was," says Johnstone. "So I put together a task force report for the general partners. It said we ought to close down *Special Report* immediately, and we ought to get forty million dollars in costs out of here overnight—or the place is not going to make it.

"You really didn't have to be a pro, which I am, to see how much waste there was. Forty or fifty million dollars could come out of here. [Chris disputes the term "waste," contending the only way expenses could be cut $40 or $50 million was by closing down entire departments such as *Special Report.*] Our people understood what they needed to do. They were all scared to death, but still saying with a lot of bravado how we are going to pull a rabbit out of the hat."

That, precisely, is what Chris was attempting once more. "I was devoting all my time trying to raise money to launch Medical News Network," Chris says. "Working twenty hours a day."

Chris told the board that abolishing such a large component of the business as *Special Report,* the TV and print system for thirty thousand physicians, would damage his client search to get MNN going. He argued that he deserved an unhampered opportunity to complete this mission.

The bankers, too, were stunned by the heavy losses in the *Special Report* operation. They felt they had a written pledge—a loan covenant—that Chris would close down *Special Report* in September 1993 unless it started at least breaking even. That deadline passed with no action taken.

The board was fearful and confused. Chris persuasively asserted he had an 80 percent chance of signing up two or three more big pharmaceutical companies—just give him another month or six weeks. He already had pledges of $147 million for the MNN rollout; a total of $200 million would do it.

Once again Chris won the board over. The task force report was shelved. He was again given free rein to try to pull his rabbit-hat trick. Whittle Communications continued to skid downhill.

However, to Knoxville and the business world in general, the Whittle company presented a confident posture. Every press release was upbeat. No hint of the turmoil in the executive suites leaked to the outside world. The crisis continued into 1994 and deepened by the day.

Now with a hard-nosed chief financial officer on the scene, present at all board and executive committee meetings, for the first time Chris's hand was being called on the revenue forecasts he presented to his directors. In the January 1994 meeting Chris predicted the fiscal year ending June 30th would show a loss of $25 million.

The CFO broke in to challenge that estimate. Says Greaves: "I stopped him and said, 'No, it would be more like seventy to a hundred million.' And that marked the beginning of the end of the whole thing in the eyes of the owners. We had already booked thirty million dollars in losses at the time Chris told them he'd come in at twenty-five million. [This comparison was inaccurate, Chris says, because Greaves included anticipated costs of shutdowns and ignored the profits that traditionally materialized in the last half of the year.] There was an inability to come to grips with reality. Part of my job was trying to get people to embrace reality. If people could be real about what you've got, you might be able to save something. But they let it go way too far."

Chris Whittle kept shaking off his critics. He felt certain that Medical News Network would pull the company out of the hole. In June 1992 it had looked like a sure winner when he and Alan Greenberg first took it into the marketplace. "It met with phenomenal success," Chris says. "In one hundred and twenty days almost one hundred million dollars was pledged to the MNN test by seven pharmaceutical companies, and four others signed contracts to be on the waiting list. We had never experienced anything like that. The test itself, between February 1993 and February 1994, went far better than we expected in every respect. And those two things made us extremely bullish on MNN."

Results of the $100 million MNN one-year test, which beamed the satellite program from New York to five thousand physicians' offices across the country, were just in. They looked good, in a fashion that should be convincing to sponsors. Forty-two percent of the doctors turned on their desk computers daily to access the news, education, and informational broadcasts. By comparison, 40 percent of television viewers watch the Super Bowl.

But while the test was underway MNN got blindsided like an innocent bystander by the surprise earthquake that rocked the drug industry—President Clinton's health care reform crusade.

"The 1992 election threw the entire health care industry into a state of shock," Chris says. "Every pharmaceutical company became concerned about where it was going. That's the first thing. Then, in the context of the Clinton health reform act, the drug companies began to question whether individual physicians were going to be important decision makers in the future. And finally, in response to those first two things, the pharmaceutical industry went into an acquisition frenzy in which large pharmaceuticals began buying up pieces of the managed care industry."

As examples, Chris cites Eli Lilly's $4 billion acquisition of PSC Health Systems, Merck merging with Medco Containment Services, and SmithKline Beecham buying Diversified Pharmaceutical Services.

"All these were multi-million dollar mergers that occurred literally in the stretch of seven to nine months in which we were trying to secure the roll-out contracts for MNN."

Chris defied these new heavy odds facing him. Brashly, he called a news conference February 23, 1994, in New York to announce the national roll-out of MNN in the fall. The goal was to hook fifty thousand physicians and four thousand managed care and corporate benefit executives into the satellite system within two and a half years.

Chris admitted the launch would cost $200 million. Only $147 million had been pledged by three pharmaceutical company sponsors, but negotiations were "going very well" with five others to raise the remainder. Meanwhile, he told the New York reporters, the shortfall would be made up from other Whittle Communications revenues.

Even though the Knoxville headquarters staff knew the media derided the company as a "spin machine," Chris's New York statement sounded weird to anyone who knew the company's true dire financial straits. Managers wondered how in the world could properties that were heavily losing money be milked for anything like $50 million? Now that would take real magic!

All of his partners knew Chris was working one hundred hours a week, sparing nothing in his frantic pursuit of his dream. But the rainbow still eluded him. The Tennessee wunderkind was going down the tubes—and taking them with him. Something had to change. The directors had to make a reluctant and hard decision. It was time to take some aspects of control away from Chris—and install a new chief executive officer to serve as the key operational executive while Chris did what he did best. The board recognized his strengths in certain areas—vision, capital raising, and marketing—but were aware of his weaknesses—lack of toughness in cost control and operational issues—and had to do something about those weaknesses.

For a replacement they didn't even have to go outside their board room. Don Johnstone was the logical man. He had joined Philips at a time the company was hemorrhaging red ink and its Magnavox sales were lagging. During Johnstone's eleven years at Philips—a company ten times Whittle's size—it had doubled its sales, reaching more than $2 billion in 1993. That same year its Magnavox brand bumped Zenith for the second-largest color TV brand share in the United States market. RCA was first.

Sixty-four years old, Johnstone was slender, sandy-haired, wore big silver-rimmed glasses, lacked humor, and was all business. He had a master's degree from Harvard Business School and previously was a senior manager at Litton Industries and General Electric.

Johnstone had settled permanently in Knoxville, building a mansion in 1992 for about $2 million on an eighty-foot bluff overlooking the Tennessee River. "It is a dynamite house with all the electronics befitting the president of an electronics company, built for the year 2000." Johnstone, however, built "Cliffview" for the view. He adds, "It's a religious experience looking out. All you can see is the river and the forest."

His superiors asked if he was willing to resign and rush over to Whittle headquarters to try to rescue the sinking ship. The Philips company proposed to replace him by transferring their lighting division head from the East Coast to Knoxville, "robbing Peter to pay Paul."

"I had another year to go before retirement," says Johnstone. "But I knew the right thing to do for Philips was to try to save their investment. My God, from the time they came in, they were losing a million bucks a week damn near! So I agreed to make the change."

With the ax over his head, Chris resisted. Ironically, being un-seated had been one of his greatest fears for years. He had studied the careers of other pioneer entrepreneurs—Fred Smith of Federal Express, Steve Jobs of Apple Computer, and Bill Gates of Microsoft among them. John Sculley's ouster of Steve Jobs in 1985 at Apple had shocked and alarmed Chris.

"I'm a fan of Steve Jobs," Chris recalls, "and I think he did great. Basically Jobs founded the business and Sculley came in later, and Jobs wound up out of the company. And that's something that hap-pens from time to time where the founder and entrepreneur in the business is replaced by the, if you will, professional manager. And it's really not a fate that I would wish upon myself."

"It was not personal," Johnstone says. "He just didn't want any-body to take his place. For this company to survive, Chris would have had to come to grips with the fact that he is an outstanding, marvelous, visionary marketeer, salesperson, product developer, great guy, good people skills, damn near could be a cult leader—has all these wonderful skills, all those things helped him get where he was. But it's just like all of us, when you take your skills, and he controls everything, then he wants all the power. This is where he came to problems with Moffitt and Glover before. Who's going to run the place? 'I'm going to run it!' So Moffitt left. Glover left. I wasn't there then, but that's the story. And Bill Connell, a good man from Procter and Gamble—Bill learned you can't stand up to Chris. My point is that Chris would have to have had the kind of insight that's tough to come by—and part of it is ego—to say, 'I need to step aside and let professionals run this business.'"

There was no way for Chris to escape that he was going to have to significantly share power with Johnstone. True, he had what he considered an iron-clad management contract; it required unani-mous consent of all four general partners to cancel it. However, having traded in his majority interest for a multi-million dollar per-sonal bank account, Chris was in a vulnerable minority position. It was not that he held only 7 percent of the stock, but because his partners' cash was essential to continue in business.

Gracefully, he accepted the board's decision. It was all handled in a polite and gentlemanly fashion. The new game plan was that Chris would remain as chairman so that he could manage the reve-nue and product development of the company. Johnstone and

Chris were supposed to work together, with Johnstone holding the purse strings and Chris driving the revenue.

Chris put his best public face forward. In Knoxville, where the February 28, 1994, announcement of the change—just four days after his MNN roll-out news conference in New York—dominated page one of the *News-Sentinel,* he told reporters, "We needed to bring very strong executive management into the business because we have a very challenging plate over the next two or three years. Don's career is running complicated businesses, and his experience in the whole world of technology will be very important to us. Don's appointment will free me to devote time to product development and conceiving businesses. My strength is not putting in place very intricate and complex management systems. Don has thirty more years experience in that area than I do."

Changing chief executives was merely the first step. Drastic and immediate action was needed to pull Whittle Communications back from the brink. If revenues could not be raised, certainly costs could be cut. And interim funding had to be obtained. The banks, with about $125 million so far at risk, had completely cut Whittle off. The two general partners, Philips and Associated, who were shouldering the mounting deficit, had set not a date but a dollar-certain cutoff. When the additional $60 million they invested was gone, the game would be over!

In Johnstone's first day on the job, the Special Report Network was shut down. Doing so was long overdue, even though this TV and print system that reached thirty thousand physicians' waiting rooms was at one time the company's most promising media property. Surprisingly Chris Whittle agreed, telling reporters, "From a financial perspective, this takes a tremendous burden off the company." One hundred fifty staffers were let go; Tom Ingram, who had vainly struggled with *Special Report* for a year and a half, joined the exodus of top-flight executives from the company.

The new CEO kept his ax swinging. A few days later he closed Whittle Books, leaving in limbo William Rukeyser, the editor in chief Chris had purposely hired in 1988 from Time Inc. to give his Knoxville company big-time cachet. In a single month—by April 1, 1994—Johnstone cut expenses by $40 million, about $30 million of that coming from closing *Special Report.*

"It was simple," says Johnstone. "It was easy to see what to elim-

inate. All the frou-frou—flowers, all kinds of personal things. Closing down *Special Report,* changing the traveling habits of people,
cancelling the jet-plane leases."

Johnstone summarily suspended the feisty and irreverent employee publication *Fred,* closed the company cafeteria, the library,
and community relations department, and kept looking for additional "waste," and ways to trim the payroll.

The situation remained dangerous. The banks had not yet been
repaid. Losses continued. Survival was not certain without a new
infusion of capital. Randy Greaves, under deadline pressure, feared
that when the Philips-Associated $60 million guarantee ran out
creditors might try to force Whittle into Chapter Eleven bankruptcy.

He urged the board to "disaggregate" the assets and let Channel
One stand alone. "It was our only plow horse," he says. Greaves
proposed to go into the high-yield debt market and borrow about
$150 million secured by Channel One, which he considered
"credit-worthy," and pay off the creditors.

"The wolves were about to come in and take everything away,"
says Greaves. "There was not a single agreement at Whittle that
involved the extension of credit that the company was not violat-
ing. Not a single one. Whether it was aircraft leasing, keeping up
mortgage guarantees on the headquarters building . . . There was
nothing that wasn't screwed up. And everybody in the company
wanted to keep their head in the sand about it."

The owners accepted Greaves's bail-out scheme and recruited
prominent New York investment bank Goldman, Sachs and Company to handle the bond offering, assisted by Dillon, Reed. The
investment bankers, exercising due diligence, checked the Whittle
financial records. They discovered what they called a sticky problem in the possibility of a "fraudulent conveyance."

As Greaves explains, "Channel One as an entity was credit worthy. Everything else was a total abyss. There's a little thing here and
there worth a couple of millions. But basically there was nothing
left but huge liabilities. People had extended credit to Whittle on
the whole thing, including Channel One. You can't pull out the
best assets and leave all the bad for the old credits. That's called a
fraudulent conveyance. To sell bonds against only Channel One,
the partners, being Phillips and Associated, had to agree to come in

and stand behind the old obligations. That number was huge—hundreds of millions of dollars. They refused to do it. And when you refuse to do that the only thing left is to sell the company."

Nor was that to be a simple matter. The board retained the prominent New York investment bank Goldman, Sachs and Company to find a buyer. Of course the investment bankers, exercising due diligence, checked the Whittle financial records.

"Goldman, Sachs knew we weren't able to pay our own bills," says Greaves. "And that we were about to spend the last of the sixty million. They could see that Whittle Communications had a gun to its head. So they tried to cut a very, very tough deal."

Greaves describes the offer from Goldman, Sachs as "very strange," not a straight-out purchase of the company. "They were going to agree to handle the bond offering to raise $150 to $175 million," he says. "Then they would loan us the rest of the capital we needed, about $50 million. In return for that they wanted 55 percent of the equity on top of the loan."

Those severe terms so riled the owners that Philips considered buying Whittle Communications outright. The Dutch electronics magnates privately mulled over the pros and cons for several days and finally dropped that idea as too risky.

Greaves had another option up his sleeve. "I told them to run an auction. There's no telling what the price for the owners would be. But if you don't run an auction and you're dealing with only one guy and he has a monopoly and he knows that the clock is running, he's going to take advantage and drive a very hard bargain. Goldman changed the terms, and they were taking more and more as time went by."

But Philips and Associated were too frightened to challenge the Goldman offer. Says Greaves: "The reason we didn't run an auction and go out and find the right buyer at the right price was because it took too much time. An auction generally takes nine to twelve weeks to get information out to everybody, to do due diligence and run the beauty contest. The owners were unwilling to keep funding the losses long enough to run an auction. They simply weren't going to do it. Times Warner basically said, 'Screw it. It can go into bankruptcy for all we care. We're not giving this guy another penny!' The owners themselves were the ones that made it a one-horse race. They put the gun to their own heads."

The Goldman agreement moved forward. In July 1994 the board was summoned to New York to start crossing t's and dotting i's. The night before the meeting, Greaves went to dinner with two top Philips executives who were Whittle directors, Stephen C. Tumminello and Rens Das.

Greaves hit them with another last-ditch maneuver that might escape Goldman's "terrible" deal. Says Greaves: "I had a friend at Dillon, Reed who suggested I contact K-III Communications Corporation about buying Channel One." K-III is controlled by the leveraged buyout firm of Kohlberg, Kravis, Roberts and Company. It owns several magazines, including *New York, Seventeen,* and *New Woman,* as well as the *Daily Racing Form.*

Greaves continued, "I showed them a very impressive profile of K-III and said I could talk to them next day about buying Channel One. They said no. They said if we started talking to K-III Goldman would pull its offer. Then who knows what K-III would do. 'We're out of money. We're not going to put any more money in this, so don't run Goldman off.' "

The K-III possibility was discussed at the board meeting next day. Greaves was instructed to stay away from K-III.

"It was shortly thereafter," he says, "that the letter of intent that would have locked this thing up with Goldman, Sachs was circulated among the owners. Time Warner signed it. Associated signed it, and Philips signed it. And the only signature that was left was guess who? Chris. It was sent to Chris and Chris wouldn't sign it. The reason Chris wouldn't sign it was because he was trying to get Goldman to cut a deal to pay him a bunch of money on the side."

This was no secret. To get the partners to keep funding operations during the Goldman negotiations, Chris had voluntarily torn up his management contract, surrendering all his benefits, salary, severance. "If you keep the company going through this crisis," he told the partners, "you don't owe me anything." He thus felt he had a right, with the most valuable part of the company on the block, to try to arrange his own compensation.

While this furor raged in New York, the crisis at Knoxville headquarters took two new tragic turns.

The national launch of Medical News Network was cancelled. Chris made the announcement on August 1, 1994. He just couldn't raise the necessary additional $50 million. Chris said, correctly, the blame fell on drug industry turmoil. "We thought this uncertainty about health care reform would diminish this year. It has not. We were wrong. We continue to believe there will be an electronic highway for the health care industry. Much of the work in MNN is relevant to that, but our timing simply isn't right."

Two hundred more employees were laid off, leaving only about six hundred in the Ivy League headquarters designed to house one thousand. The shutdown also cut loose one of Chris Whittle's closest colleagues, Alan Greenberg, MNN's chairman. From the 13–30 days Greenberg had been the founder's chief rival as a "star" salesman and a frequent architect of business strategy. Greenberg promptly sold his $2.2 million Knoxville mansion that once belonged to author Alex Haley. With his wife and two children he moved to Atlanta to take a one-year sabbatical before starting a new career.

Knoxville was also totally surprised to learn that the stately Ivy League headquarters building was up for sale. Barely three years old, it cost more than $50 million, contained 225,000 square feet, and was one of the largest office buildings in Knoxville. Furthermore, the United States government was interested in buying it.

That came about in a backhand way. One morning Randy Greaves and Don Johnstone were conferring in the latter's fourth floor office. From across the street they heard the rattle of bulldozers and looked out the window.

"They're really clearing that block," Greaves observed. "New federal courthouse, isn't it?"

Johnstone started, and suddenly a light came on. "Hey! Wouldn't it be a crime if they build a new courthouse there, next door, and meanwhile we have to sell this building!"

They got busy—and lucky. The bid for erecting the new U.S. courthouse came in way over budget, and work stopped. The courthouse was redesigned, made smaller. "They came up with some absolutely horrible looking architecture," says Johnstone. "And still over budget. So we put in an unsolicited bid for the government to buy our building and remodel it into a courthouse. They were interested, and we started talking."

Johnstone was anxious to deal—even on fire sale terms. He was reported willing to sell the Whittle headquarters for about half its cost. The big question for the government was to determine how expensive and feasible it would be to convert the Ivy League building into courtrooms. One remodeling estimate was $14 million. It soon looked like a deal was in the making.

At that time in New York, the Channel One–Goldman, Sachs deal still hung fire. More than unhappy, Chris was angry. "They're squeezing and squeezing and squeezing," he told a Wall Street friend. "We should not just let somebody steal our company."

Making personal demands, Chris abruptly crashed into the deal-making because he could not afford to come out empty-handed; he was in severe personal financial straits and Goldman, Sachs knew it. Not only were they permitted to examine company books, they got access to Chris's personal net worth statement. Gossip on Wall Street said it showed Chris had hard assets of $35 million, chiefly real estate, art, and antiques, but owed the same amount in personal bank loans, mostly to Morgan Guaranty Trust.

The Goldman offer, says Randy Greaves, would have given Chris nothing for his equity. "That's the reason he wouldn't sign the letter of intent. He was trying to get Goldman to cut a deal to pay him a bunch of money on the side. I've heard he wanted thirty million dollars, over time. Personal money for his services to continue to operate Channel One as chairman. An article in the *New Yorker* said Goldman offered him five hundred thousand dollars a year for two years, plus a piece of the upside he kept insisting is there. That wasn't good enough. Even though Chris was sitting with me when the board flat-out prohibited contacting K-III, he did anyway."

Chris concedes he went ahead strictly on his own. Instead of a direct approach, Chris used a Dillon, Reed friend to contact William F. Reilly, K-III chairman and CEO. Reilly, former Macmillan Publishing executive, quickly saw Channel One as a good fit for his media company, especially at a bargain price. On Sunday, July 31, 1994, Reilly phoned Chris at his Dakota apartment and began negotiations.

"Chris brought back a letter of intent from K-III that did two things," Greaves says. "First, it offered a higher price. But the key was Chris got K-III to agree to fund the interim losses while they did their due diligence. That meant the owners didn't have to come out of pocket any more. And, gee, they offered three hundred million and even if they dropped the price way down, it's better than the Goldman deal. [The actual offer was $260 million, although the higher figure was deliberately leaked to Wall Street reporters to discourage rival bidders, and the true purchase price eventually dropped to $240 million.] So they cut Goldman loose, and told them to stick it. And K-III, being a reputable and good organization, with real business reasons for owning Channel One, ultimately consummated the deal."

By becoming a lone wolf negotiator with K-III, Chris says he saved his partners $60 million. "If we hadn't made the K-III deal," he says, "the bridge loans would not have been repaid and the company would have been bankrupt. Everybody told me not to do it. And I was afraid to do it. If it had failed, I would have been beaten to a pulp by my partners. But it worked, and saved them an enormous amount of money."

Chris believes it was one of the most courageous moves of his career. He got his hoped-for personal deal—about $10 million. He signed an ironclad agreement giving K-III 50 percent of his business time as a consultant, which included a clause prohibiting him for five years from competing in the industry he created—sending TV news into schools. Chris received $7.5 million up front plus $1.25 million annually for three years.

Greaves says, "All the other money that K-III paid went to pay liabilities. There was no equity distribution, to my knowledge."

The purchase price didn't stay at $260 million. When K-III auditors scrutinized the Whittle Communication books, they found that Channel One had not paid property taxes in any state where they installed TVs and VCRs in schools, which was unbeknownst to Chris, as well. That negligence might flare back on K-III, so the purchaser withheld a reserve of $10 million. K-III, holding the whip hand in a distress sale, also insisted on other price reductions to establish funds for several possible liquidation contingencies. When the transaction was finalized on October 1, 1994, the purchase price was not disclosed but reportedly had dropped to $240 million.

Though the K-III saved Whittle Communications from bankruptcy, it caused the selling off of all the company's main operations and effectively wiped it out as a business concern. By mid-January 1995 the liquidation was essentially complete. Robert E. Hope had bought the Whittle Ventures division, which he had headed, and moved it to Atlanta. Johnstone also sold off the few remaining viable "properties" like *Physician's Weekly,* the oversized wall poster for doctors' lounges in hospitals, and the sampling business that served college campuses and health clubs. For less than six figures, the Time-Mirror Company bought what Johnstone described as "intellectual properties," meaning technical apparatus, from the defunct Medical News Network, and hired some MNN staffers.

And finally, the federal government made the courthouse deal. For the headquarters building the Whittle liquidators received $22 million in cash plus the previous courthouse site across the street, a city block valued at $3.6 million. But that land, plus $7.1 million in cash, was forthwith handed over to the city to satisfy Whittle obligations for municipal financial assistance that had made Historic Whittlesburg possible. Later the federal government paid an additional half-million dollars for the Whittle building's furniture and fixtures.

The liquidation let the company just break even. Don Johnstone told the *Knoxville News-Sentinel:* "All creditors will be paid, and the only losses will be to investors." Everybody lost "on paper" in terms of what their stock would have been worth if the company had continued to grow as it had for twenty-plus years. But only two investors lost heavily in cash.

Time Warner saw about $120 million of its $185 million buy-in price disappear, and Philips lost its $175 million investment. (Philips did not come up completely empty-handed, Johnstone points out. It profited handsomely from the sale of more than 300,000 TVs and VCRs for Channel One and on terminals designed and built for use in the MNN test run. And it still owns 10 or 15 percent of Edison Schools.)

Chris had taken in one hundred limited partners who chipped in a total of $2 million. Over time these investors took out about $20 million. But many complained that the collapse of the company deprived them of much more. And it did, but just on prospective value of their shares, not cash.

Lord Rothermere and his Associated Newspaper concern gained big by gambling on Chris Whittle in the early days. Over time they took out profits of at least $100 million. Fortunately for Associated and Philips, the $60 million they put up to meet the dying company's last-gasp payroll was scheduled to be repaid in the final liquidation.

Just what the end of the dream did to Chris financially is not clear. "I don't know exactly what I made," Chris says. "But I made profits over the years. One way to look at it is, if you were in the first twenty years you did fine. It was the last three or four that hurt." For many years Whittle's top executives shared another benefit—a princely life-style with first-class or private jet travel, $500–hotel suites, leased Porches, and salaries thought to range from $400,000 to $800,000.

As everything else collapsed, Chris clung desperately to his partial ownership of what he considered his brightest of all dreams, the Edison Project. He firmly believed America's educators would eventually embrace his concepts for the twenty-first-century school—and pay for the privelege. His partners, Time Warner, Philips, and Associated Newspapers, definitely were not so sanguine. Time Warner had become disillusioned much earlier with the supposed magic of Whittle innovation. They had better places to invest their money, so they had totally withdrawn from the Edison Schools scheme. That left Chris sharing the partnership with Philips Electronics and Associated Newspapers. The latter two had already invested so many millions they felt they had to continue to gamble, even though the plan to reinvent American education still looked difficult.

When Don Johnstone began dismantling the Whittle empire in the latter months of 1994, the Edison project virtually stalled. It badly needed a new infusion of capital. None was forthcoming, or in sight. The design was available, and Benno Schmidt and his aides were getting nibbles of interest from many school districts. But Edison would need between $25 million and $75 million in its kitty to guarantee the Edison Schools launch. The cost of wiring one school for a video-computer network was estimated at $800,000.

Strapped for funds, Edison started downsizing. As their contracts ran out, most core team members were dropped. Benno Schmidt and about ten other key executives, totally convinced they had a sound and promising model to sell, kept up the search for investors and school contracts.

Chris and Benno had high mutual respect for the other's talents, but the frustation and financial worries that beset them and dragged on for months ate steadily into this close bond. They began bickering. When Chris attracted a lot of bad publicity in the wake of the Whittle empire collapse, Benno Schmidt openly suggested Chris's business reputation probably raised a red flag in the face of any investor Edison went after. The two practically quit speaking. Their colleagues, seeing them pursuing different possible sources of funds, considered they had actually begun a contest to see which could take over the school venture.

"There was a fight to see who would get credit, if the thing lived," said one Edison colleague.

By July 1994 Chris was trying to stave off disaster on two separate fronts. He was about to get squeezed out of Channel One. And the Edison Project also had a noose around its neck. Chris didn't have enough personal funds to keep it going. Neither did Benno Schmidt. The two corporate partners, Philips and Associated Newspapers, were sick of the fruitless struggle to get it going.

Bluntly, both informed Chris that if new financing could not be raised by the end of 1994 they would close Edison Schools and just write off their losses.

That news jolted Chris. He saw no hope of swaying Philips or Lord Rothermere. The New York investment bank of Dillon, Reed and Company was managing the search for new Edison investors but having no success. With all his other problems, Chris had to somehow yank a hare out of a hat again, or stand by and see the plug pulled on Edison Schools. His deadline was a little less than six months away.

———

His rainbow collapse left Chris, who had always lived with the flair of a Gatsby, personally hard up for cash. In mid-1994 he was obligated for $600,000 as his annual payment to fund Whittle Scholars. Instead of writing a check he deeded the University of Tennessee a tract of land valued at 10 percent higher than the due amount, as permitted under terms of his $5.2 million endowment. At the same time U.T. eased his burden by agreeing to reduce the number of incoming scholars for the next few years from twenty to ten.

From the day it was apparent that survival of the Whittle empire was hopeless, a steady stream of key executives—most of whom took a bath in paper value as limited partners—left the company, many remaining in Knoxville to launch business ventures. Among those who became local entrepreneurs were Tom Ingram, Nick Glover, Bill Connell, Keith Bellows, William Rukeyser, and Laura Eshbaugh. Chris's hard-working and affable brother-in-law Bob Hanggi retired to a horse farm he had been running with his wife Camille twenty miles from the city limits. Even Randy Greaves, who walked out of headquarters carrying a check for $1 million the day after the K-III deal closed, liked Knoxville well enough to keep his home there and go into business leasing wide-angle movie theatres to science centers. Among the lucky few, Ed Winter and Jim Ritts were retained as senior managers by the new owners of Channel One.

The day the headquarters building was sold only ten of a peak of nine hundred employees were still inside—Don Johnstone and a small liquidation staff needing "six months or a year" for the windup.

The collapse left Knoxville more sad than mad, in Johnstone's opinion. "This was a home-grown company that went national, with a charismatic leader, a big building, flashiness, that brought in all the top-level executives and gave millions to local charities. The people here do not think Whittle is a charlatan. They just think it's sad this had to happen. The community hasn't given up on Chris Whittle. It thinks he will come back. When you add it all up there are a whole lot more pluses than minuses, what they've done for this town. The only losers are Philips and Time Warner, and a lot of people's careers. They went up in smoke, too. That left some angry people. They bought into the dream and it didn't come true. So they want to take out their anger on the head of the dream factory."

Tom Ingram agrees that there was a lot of local sympathy for Chris. "Studies show that per capita Knoxville is one of the most entrepreneurial cities in America. A lot of risk taking. People start businesses that fail and then come back and start again. One of the richest men in Knoxville right now is Jim Clayton [a builder] who bankrupted and started over, and is now on the *Forbes* richest list. Chris is thought of in that light, somebody who took a lot of risk and moved the city forward. Everybody just feels he moved too fast with too little horsepower behind him. Generally people are disappointed but feel Chris was good for the community, and now say, 'Let's pick up where we are and keep going.' "

Ironically, at the height of her husband's meltdown, Priscilla Rattazzi was asked by Knoxville's Museum of Art to exhibit her best work as a professional photographer. The show, in November 1994, was warmly praised by the *News-Sentinel* for presenting "images, mostly in black and white, of serene landscapes and moments of life—children at play, dogs in harmony with their owners—captured and infused with warmth by someone who makes art of the things and people she loves."

The reporter found her nervous and shy. "I feel very insecure," she told him. "Every time I do something public—a book, a gallery show—I feel totally vulnerable. I'd like to hide ten feet underground and just observe people visiting the show."

Priscilla, just turned thirty-eight, confided to friends she was again pregnant and expecting her second little Whittle, another girl, in mid-1995. Chris said, "On the personal front, that was the best news of the year."

Shaken, incredibly saddened by his business reverses, battered by caustic magazine articles and business press jabs that castigated him as a "huckster and failed visionary," Chris Whittle spent hours searching his own soul. He thought he owed some explanation to the people of Knoxville. He hunched over his laptop computer and put together a lengthy *mea culpa* statement that the *News-Sentinel* published on page one, October 2, 1994.

Though he shouldered personal blame, Chris largely attributed the collapse to the hurried leap from running a group of thirty small, successful print properties to interactive electronic ventures that cost $150 million to start—and bad timing. *Special Report* died of "self-inflicted wounds" because, he wrote, "we were arrogant" because of earlier successes. MNN was caught in a tidal change in the drug industry. "It was like building a dam during a monsoon."

He hailed Channel One as a total victory and said the story was yet to be told on the Edison Project. In his 1,500-word article, he also wrote:

> It has been said that success has a thousand fathers, but
> that failure is an orphan. In our case, the company's suc-

cesses should be attributed to a great team. Our mistakes, largely, have a single parent, me, and stem from a single source: I didn't discipline and control the company to the extent that I should have. When we were a collection of 30 small businesses, this problem was less obvious and less consequential. But with the scale of enterprises we undertook over the past six years, discipline became an increasingly important and missing ingredient.

Why did I make this error? By nature, I am an "in-the-field-with-my-troops-commander," and my relationship with those that I work with is collegial and inspirational, versus hierarchical. It's a trait that does not lend itself to discipline and control.

This deficiency has three manifestations, the largest being that we tried too much, too fast, not distinguishing large products from the many small ones we created in years past. Everyone wanted to launch something. I didn't say "no" often enough.

The second most significant symptom was that I wasn't tough enough. When folks didn't perform, I gave them not two chances, but three. Sometimes that paid out, but most times it did not. And without question we were too lenient about expenditures (a trait easy to fall into when revenues had risen every year for two decades).

Finally, we did not put in place quickly enough the management infrastructure required to run the size enterprise we were building. There were other mistakes. . . . Some observers think we hired too many star players from other companies. Perhaps. But when you undertake not one, but four major start-ups in as many years, you need lots of great talent. In fact, as not everyone works out, you need some redundancy.

Some think our leniency about costs was in the extreme. I would quarrel with that. Invention, in particular the high-speed variety that we have practiced, is not efficient. Efficiency comes after you invent something, not before. And the benefits of invention far outweigh the wastes inherent in the process.

As 1994 wound down, Chris Whittle was furiously fighting to salvage his entrepreneurial life. He still saw an outside chance to save the Edison Project and recapture his elusive rainbow. But the odds were heavily against him.

22

RESCUE AT THE 11TH HOUR

As chipper and optimistic Benno Schmidt flew around the country putting on his dog-and-pony show seeking Edison school contracts, he gradually underwent a dangerous change of mood. He slipped from upbeat to depressed, irritated, and finally angry and rebellious. For example, Benno had to stall when school officials, as in Charleston, South Carolina, in August 1994, wanted to see proof that Edison had enough money to finish what it started.

Looking very Ivy League in his conservative gray suit and breast-pocket handkerchief, he kept his poise and finally muttered a syrupy but vague assurance. His round face, described as "chipmunk" by one journalist, remained solemn and the "eagerness" the board president observed in the ex–Yale president's eyes, behind large silver-rimmed spectacles, did not dim. Though short and chunky, Benno bounced around as he showed his slides and charts with more athletic agility than might be expected of a fifty-two-year-old. But he was sweating.

What upset him most in making his Charleston pitch was getting sandbagged by the board president with an even more critical question: Tell me, if Chris Whittle can't even keep his own business going, how can we trust him to experiment with our school kids?

Pointedly, Benno had not even mentioned Chris's name or troubles in his ninety-minute presentation, much less identified

Edison as Chris's brainchild. He didn't have to. The Charleston school officials read newspapers and magazines. The dramatic debacle in Knoxville was receiving a lot of ink nationally.

So Benno, who had been invited down because Charleston was seriously interested in giving Edison a tryout, went back to Manhattan empty-handed. Charleston superintendent Rodney LeBeouf set a follow-up meeting for October.

"We kept asking for financial statements," the superintendent says. "They always made excuses. They never sent anything." So LeBeouf canceled negotiations. However, Charleston remained intrigued by the Edison idea; LeBeouf said in early 1995 he might be willing to take another look if the program succeeded elsewhere.

By no means was the Charleston concern a singular event. Nearly everywhere Benno and his team went they were challenged about their finances. The taint of the Whittle empire's collapse was spilling over and dangerously undermining the Edison sales campaign. Chris had become an embarrassment and a scandalous detriment to the school venture and ought to step aside.

Benno told Chris that to his face. Though some thought otherwise, Benno said it was not personal animosity—just business. Schmidt still strongly admired Chris's nimble brain. But his reputation had become a roadblock—turning off not only skeptical school officials but prospective investors as well.

Their conflict began in gentlemanly fashion. They tried to settle it in private. Not even their core team colleagues were initially aware that Benno wanted to dump Chris. Chris, of course, would have none of it; he would not step aside. Benno said Chris was being selfish; Chris said Benno was being opportunistic, and made no effort to help him through the crisis.

Then Benno played hard ball. In an Edison board meeting in September 1994 he vigorously demanded Chris distance himself from the project, not be in control of the business, not be its chairman, and have little or no role in it. Chris, who was present, wouldn't budge. Benno became actively "evangelical" and tried hard to convince partners and other investors of his point of view.

Chris had strong and definite reasons for refusing to be ejected. First, he was willing to concede Whittle Communications's dangerous problems but argued strongly that Edison could survive. He told a friend, "To say that I had to distance myself from my best idea was an odd contest. It was like saying Whittle was your idea, but Edison wasn't. Edison was my most important idea!"

Second, Chris was convinced he was "important" to Edison and that the team he and Benno put together was a combination of entrepreneurs and educators. In this marriage of capitalism and education, Chris was the only person with significant business and entrepreneurial experience. Without him aboard, the ship might sink.

On top of that, now that the Knoxville empire had collapsed Chris was free to devote all his skills and talent to Edison. He told a colleague, "I look at my life now as being a major force for change in schooling." Nothing else—such as building hotels or running an airline—"excited" him.

In late 1994 Chris and Benno battled for control of Edison. "There were periods," Chris conceded, "where I did not think I was going to come out on the other side in good shape."

They were smart enough to keep their feud reasonably out of sight, but overcoming Edison's visible shortcomings proved difficult without exposing an internecine impediment. Gradually, a few schools signed up. Edison was getting poised to actually go into business in the fall of 1995, operating four elementary schools. Letters of intent which eventually became contracts were signed with Wichita, Kansas, and Mount Clemens, Michigan, near Detroit. Massachusetts granted a "charter" for an Edison school in Boston. Negotiations that later proved successful were underway to operate one grade school in Sherman, Texas.

By estimates Chris made publicly, to install equipment and actually start up twenty Edison schools would require at least $40 million on top of the $40 million already spent in research and development. That money was nowhere in sight. Chris's two remaining partners, Philips and Associated Newspapers, adamantly refused to invest another dime, preparing to let Edison Schools close.

Of its three owners, only one was willing to continue gambling money on Edison—Chris. Of course, Time Warner had dropped out early, at the time it was spun out of Whittle Communications as a separate venture. Philips and Associated Newspapers stayed in, each owning 40 percent. Chris had the other 20 percent.

When Philips and Associated first balked at putting up any more money, Chris stepped into the breach. Rather than see his "dearest business child" go to the grave, Chris boldly decided to invest more personal funds. Calling a press conference on August 2, 1993, he had personally guaranteed to come up with $24 million of his own to assure Edison could go ahead to end of 1994. On the plus side for Chris, his guarantee of cash actually diluted the stakes of Philips and Associated, leaving the three of them equal partners, each with one-third of the stock.

However, there was no escaping the most critical fact: that he had to come up with more funds.

By an oblique twist of fate, an aggressive young Wall Street "deal maker" who was a stranger to Chris Whittle was belatedly thrust into a pivitol role in deciding whether the Edison Project lived or died.

He was Patrick Boroian, recently hired by the Sprout Group, the $750 million venture capital affiliate of Donaldson, Lufkin and Jenrette Securities Corporation, to scout prospective investments for Janet Hickey, a Sprout senior partner.

In the beginning neither was impressed with Edison. Pat Boroian stumbled into Chris's dilemma while sniffing around the proposed sale of Channel One to get an idea, for a different deal—how much school satellite televisions tie-ins were worth.

While with New York investors Odyssey Partners three years earlier, Boroian had investigated Educational Alternatives Inc. (EAI), a for-profit school venture similar to Edison, started in 1986 with little notice by Minneapolis businessman John T. Golle. Educational Alternatives, already a public company in 1991, asked Odyssey for a $15 million investment. Boroian recalls, "Odyssey said no. EAI within two years went from two and a half dollars a share to forty dollars. Odyssey would have made a bloody fortune. The stock [on the Nasdaq market] went back down to seventeen or eighteen dollars, but it would have been a terrific investment."

After stumbling with early ventures in Minneapolis, Arizona, and Florida, Golle made his first real breakthrough in June 1992 by landing a five-year, $133 million contract to operate nine inner-city public schools in Baltimore. EAI meanwhile acquired as partners KPMG Peat Marwick, a major accounting firm, and Johnson

Controls World Services Inc., a national facilities management company.

In its Baltimore contract, EAI says it can save money, streamline school bureaucracies, clean up buildings, enliven classroom teaching, and raise student achievement. In addition to updating computer systems, bringing in intern teachers from universities, and policing other expenses, EAI relies heavily on an individual plan for each student, which is closely tracked. A major element is its trademarked curriculum, Tesseract, designed to turn bored children into active learners. Golle, who had been designing education and training programs for big corporations since 1970, decided to take on public schools largely out of personal frustration that developed when his learning-disabled son failed to improve in Minneapolis's special-ed classes.

Results of the Baltimore experiment were mixed in 1994. Some students gained, others lost. Though profitable in Baltimore, overall EAI was losing money but expected to show profit later. Nearly twenty school districts across the country subsequently rejected EAI, but it appeared to score big again in October 1994 by landing a five-year, $1 billion contract to manage all thirty-two public schools in Hartford, Connecticut.

But within eight months, EAI discovered it had undertaken too big a task in Hartford. John Golle announced that only five schools would get the full Tesseract curriculum, but the other twenty-seven would be cleaned and financially managed. In June 1995 EAI began seeking approval for its modified plan, with teachers, parents, and politicians raising a ruckus about staff reductions and increased class size. Such confusion could be expected, Dr. Henry M. Levin, a professor of education and economics at Stanford University, told the *New York Times,* because neither EAI or Edison as yet had a track record. He said, "They're learning reality, basically. But they are learning it at taxpayer expense."

Golle insisted EAI was not a "get-rich-quick idea" and expected only small profits from helping improve schools. Answering critics, he told a reporter, "Sometimes I feel that I'm between the hydrant and the dog. If you make too much money, they say, 'How dare you make too much money off these children?' If you don't make any money, they say, 'You're a bad businessperson.' "

Chris Whittle shrugged at the notion Educational Alternatives represented serious competition that might knock out Edison Schools before he could launch them. First, he said, the Edison model and curriculum were much more comprehensive than EAI's Tesseract and certain to guarantee superior student improvement. The universe of schools was so great, and there were so few contenders, Chris said, "we won't be running into each other."

Though not a lot of companies were in EAI's and Edison's business, fifteen or twenty entrepreneurs around the country leaped into the business of serving public schools, some offering management, others an advanced curriculum. One of the latter was Educational Management Group (EMG) of Scottsdale, Arizona. EMG provided information on subjects such as math and science, written on demand by two hundred college professors, to television sets, faxes, and printers via telephone wires and satellite for one million students in 3,500 schools.

It was hearing about EMG and checking it out that obliquely sparked Pat Boroian's interest in the Edison Project. In early 1994, he alerted Janet Hickey, his boss at Sprout, a venture capital firm, that EMG had huge potential, recommending that Sprout offer $20 million for the company. He worried that Channel One with a similar satellite "pipe" into twelve thousand schools, might harm EMG. Just when he decided to do a little spying on Channel One, he learned that investment bankers Dillon, Reed had offered to sell Channel One as part of the package to raise money for Edison. Thus Boronian didn't have to snoop. He had a contact with Dillon, Reed senior partner Mack Rossoff, who was handling the Edison deal for Chris and Benno. A major player in mergers and acquisitions, Rossoff, forty-two, had played key roles in the RJR Nabisco and Time Warner mergers. He readily provided facts about Channel One.

"I just needed to know about the pipe," Boroian says. "Sprout wasn't at all interested in Channel One. Too many people take a dim view of advertising in schools."

Mack Rossoff suggested Sprout buy into Edison. Boroian says, "Mack said if EAI was worth one hundred and forty million, Edison ought to be valued at a hundred million. Edison intended to open twenty schools in 1995 and needed to raise fifty to seventy-five million. I have never seen Sprout fund a start-up over twenty million. The Edison deal was so ridiculous I wouldn't take it to Janet."

Still pursuing EMG, Boroian kept talking to Rossoff to learn more about Channel One. For that reason he agreed in June 1994 to confer personally with Benno Schmidt and John Chubb at Edison's New York office.

"Chris wasn't present," Boroian says. "I listened, but their price was ridiculous. I became impressed with Benno and learned about their technology and curriculum. I was struck by how well thought out it was, how comprehensive. I was generally more impressed than I thought I would be."

In the course of discussing what effect Channel One might have on EMG's future, Boroian finally outlined the Edison proposal to Janet Hickey. She concurred that Edison was not a venture for Sprout, and they concentrated on trying to acquire EMG. Eventually they were outbid by Simon and Schuster, the nation's largest textbook publisher, who reportedly paid between $65 million and $75 million for EMG.

Thus, in the summer of 1994, while Chris Whittle was fighting for his professional life on two fronts, the Sprout Group dropped all interest in the Edison Project.

"Their one-hundred-million-dollar valuation is ridiculous," Janet Hickey repeated to Pat Boroian. "Just forget it!"

Pat Boroian intended to do that, but fate decreed otherwise. By autumn he would be back playing a pivitol role in the Edison crisis, bringing along Janet Hickey.

———

Executives who joined Chris and Benno at the outset caught on quickly that their large egos would propel their leaders into a shoving match for credit if Edison became a success. The two differed significantly in points of view.

"Their sensibilities are in conflict," said one colleague. "It was clear that the world Benno was coming from and the one Chris represented professionally were totally divergent. If Benno were to tell you he was never comfortable that Edison could sit close to the Whittle marketing culture, that wouldn't surprise me. He would be wary of that. It's probably not the best thing for Edison to be close to [Whittle Communications] because of all the conflicting messages it gives to prospective customers, the education community."

The relationship between the two men was described as "an uneasy peace," but in late 1994 another top executive said privately:

"My guess is Edison, by hook or crook, will continue. Whether Chris will still be part of it is an open question. Of course, Benno feels the Whittle company demise is an embarrassment to Edison. But I think it is more a matter of Benno sees an opportunity to edge Chris out."

During the 1994 financial crisis, Chris kept a low profile in the sales campaign. For instance, he did not go to Charleston, nor contact school officials there. In fact, tied down by his frantic pursuit of financial saviors, he couldn't spare the time. "Chris never intruded on Benno's operational turf," said a colleague. "They were very clear about that from the beginning."

In the end, he said, each knew they had no hope of going forward without the other. "Chris had a huge investment in Edison. He put a lot of his own money on the line and any kind of open warfare between them would absolutely doom chances of Edison finding any money at all. By the same token, Chris understood that the education credibility of Edison was totally tied to Benno, and it would be very hard for him to go out and find somebody else without creating a huge amount of discordance, and the project would fail as a result of that. So for better or worse, they were married and they'd better do what they could and allow the marriage in some form or other to survive for the good of the children."

To Chris, Edison had always been "the dearest of my business children," as he told a confidant. "When it was conceived, I viewed it as the most important thing I was doing. Then, unfortunately, all the issues at Whittle began to completely absorb me. So I was in a strange kind of period where I did not get to spend much time on what was most important to me.

"One way I think of Edison is that in 1990 and 1991 I spent a good bit of time conceiving it and recruiting folks into it and getting it ready to go. But from 1992 into 1994 I spent less and less time because of Whittle problems. And frankly, were Edison not as good an idea as I think it is, it could have been impossible to save it."

As to Chris's regard for the Edison Project, Bill Connell recalls, "I remember something he said back about 1989 when his interest in pure politics was waning a bit and his interest was shifting to education. He said that one hundred years from now nobody will remember who was the president of the United States, much less who was governor of Tennessee, but they certainly will remember the person who revolutionized education in America. And I think he began to take on a real dream at that point."

Fearful that lack of funds would slowly doom Edison, Benno Schmidt, despite his continuing tense feud with Chris, rushed around the country trying to tap sources of his own venture capital. It was tough going. Meanwhile, the core team disbanded. With the Edison model already sculpted, their work was essentially complete. The next phase would be the roll-out. Six of the seven principals in the research and design phase—Lee Eisenberg, Sylvia Peters, Chester Finn, Daniel Biederman, Nancy Hechinger, and Dominique Browning—were leaving as their contracts expired at the end of 1994 to resume old careers or start new ones. Ms. Browning went to *Mirabella* magazine as editor and three months later to *House and Garden,* also as editor.

The lone design executive remaining was John E. Chubb, who worked in New York with Mike Finnerty, a former Yale financial officer and Edison's CFO. Chris and Benno also had an expensive marketing department in New York.

===

In September 1994, Sprout's Pat Boroian launched his regular round of calls and letters to eight hundred personal contacts on Wall Street. He phoned Mack Rossoff at Dillon, Reed. "What's new?" he asked. "And, by the way, how are you doing with Edison?"

Not at all well, Rossoff admitted. Nobody was willing to invest. Chris and Benno had dropped their valuation to $60 million or $80 million and now hoped to raise only $25 million to $50 million.

Boroian recalls, "I said, 'That's more interesting. But too tough. Sprout wouldn't go for that. You plan to open twenty schools?' Mack said, 'Yes.' 'They've never opened a single school. How do they know these things will work? You'll be spending sixteen million to open twenty. Why don't you just open five, or three, or one?' Mack said, 'Oh well, they've got the demand. They have people ready to sign up, ready to write checks.' I told him Sprout wouldn't be interested, and hung up."

In early November Pat Boroian again called Mack Rossoff and found him desperate. "Mack said, 'Pat we're down to the end game on Edison. Basically, no one's come to the party. This horrible article about Chris came out in *The New Yorker*. He's getting hammered in the press, the *Wall Street Journal*, the *New York Times, Business Week*. They're just hammering this guy. Nobody wants anything to do with this project. Nobody wants anything to do with Chris. It's incredible. It's a crime because it's a great business, it's a great opportunity. But this is going to hit the wall, and it's going to blow up!' "

Then Mack Rossoff switched gears and asked Boroian to propose the kind of financing Sprout would accept. That was what the deal maker wanted to hear. He saw possibilities in Edison, knew the market was huge, their model was superb, and made sense. Their conversation quickly got serious.

Rossoff said Edison had a $16 million annual overhead. Boroian said to cut it back to $3 million or $4 million. But Edison couldn't, and support twenty schools. Boroian said, "Mack, forget twenty schools. Forget raising fifty million. Try a handful of schools first and see that they work. Mack said, 'Oh, Jesus.' I thought that was the end of it."

Instead it was the beginning of desperate negotiation.

One week later Rossoff summoned Boroian to Dillon, Reed offices at 535 Madison Avenue to meet Mike Finnerty, Edison's CFO. They showed him a budget that cut overhead to $12 million.

"Mack, you're not listening to me," Boroian said. "This isn't going to fly. It's got to be one-third of that."

On Tuesday, November 22, 1994, Rossoff phoned, saying Chris and Benno were trying to make deeper cuts in overhead, and got Boroian's home phone number in New Jersey so he could reach him over the Thanksgiving weekend. Boroian recalls, "Mack said, 'I'll call you at home. This is really coming down to the end game. Phillips and Associated—the partners with money are all saying if they don't get a commitment in hand, a letter of intent to invest by the board meeting on Wednesday, December 7, they are going to pull the plug on the whole thing and go out of business.' "

On Friday, November 25th, Rossoff sent the Sprout man a fax showing a breakdown of all Edison salaries. "I nearly passed out," Boroian says. "There were a lot of million-dollar salaries. [Boroian was exercising a little hyperbole; Edison was paying only one executive, Benno Schmidt, $1 million a year. The next highest salary, for five others, was $400,000.] Sprout had never funded a start-up where the CEO made more than $200,000. Never. So I said to Mack, there is no way! I'm not going to ask Sprout to even look at this. The boss would have my head examined. He'd throw me out."

Rossoff asked what it would take.

"You've got to get those salaries below two hundred thousand dollars," Boroian said.

Edison executives had employment contracts, Rossoff protested. It was not possible to slash paychecks by 80 percent.

"That's your problem," Boroian responded. "You figure it out. For Christ's sake, give them stock in the company. Key executives ought to own 10 to 20 percent of the company, and all reduce their cash income. They'll think the same way we do, reduce the cash flow, grow equity, and make money as opposed to milking it for a high salary whether the thing makes money or not."

On Sunday, ten days before the board's deadline, Mike Finnerty got back to Boroian with a budget cut to $5.5 million and a question: Would Sprout be comfortable with management owning 20 percent of Edison stock? "I said, absolutely yes."

Sprout then speeded up negotiations. On Wednesday, November 30th, they brought Benno Schmidt, Mike Finnerty, and John Chubb to their offices on the forty-second floor of the Marine Midland Bank building at 140 Broadway. The Edison emissaries spent the entire day making their sales pitch to a group headed by Richard Kroon, Sprout's managing partner. Boroian recalls, "The deadline was seven days away. The impression we all had was very favorable. We liked Benno. We liked the story. And we liked the fact there was a real financial need or the thing was going to blow up."

Kroon wanted senior partner Janet Hickey—who was out of town—to decide on the deal. Kroon had doubts about it. Ms. Hickey, fifty years old, had long experience in managing pension fund investments and handling new business start-ups. She was sufficiently battle-tested to be in the venture-capital industry's Hall of Fame, based largely on her eighteen-year career at the General Electric Company.

It was not until Monday, December 5th, that Janet Hickey returned. She had only one free day, Tuesday, before the Wednesday noon deadline because she was flying to California for a partners' meeting.

Janet Hickey spent all of Tuesday, December 6th at the Edison Schools offices at 529 Fifth Avenue. Boroian recalls, "Janet called me on her way to the airport. She said, 'I was impressed more than I thought I would be. I think we should submit a letter of intent.' I was emotional, stunned, thrilled, fearful for Sprout but excited about the potential. I said, 'But, Janet, you are going on an airplane. This letter has to be in their hands by noon tomorrow!' She said, 'I know, Pat. I'm taking my laptop. I can write it on the plane.' "

She wrote the letter on the red-eye flight to San Francisco, and at dawn on Wednesday, December 7th, faxed it back to Sprout head-quarters, where it arrived at eight-thirty A.M. It was carefully checked, retyped on Janet Hickey's letterhead, and faxed over to Benno Schmidt at Edison's office.

"They got it at eleven o'clock, just an hour before the board meeting," Boroian says. "That's how close this came to blowing up."

The people at Sprout sat back smugly awaiting a good-news phone call from the Edison board, confident that Janet Hickey's last-minute deal would be accepted.

They were in for a surprise—and a big disappointment.

===

The last act of this life-or-death drama was played out that December 7th afternoon at the New York headquarters of North American Philips Corporation at 100 East 42nd Street. Chris Whittle knew he was up against thousand-to-one odds, maybe million-to-one. The Sprout deal wasn't good enough to save Edison. Chris was certain it would be rejected. But he refused to give up and just let his great idea perish.

In a twenty-third-floor conference room, Chris joined the North American Philips president and CEO Stephen C. Tumminello. This was actually a meeting of the general partners rather than the board. Only four people participated, two by transatlantic speakerphone: Rens Das, Philips's chief of mergers, from the Netherlands, and from London, Charles Sinclair, managing director of Associated Newspaper Holdings. Time Warner was no longer a partner, although it had—despite vowing to never invest another dime with Chris—given Whittle Communications a $3 million short-term loan to keep the Knoxville company afloat long enough to conclude the K-III purchase of Channel One.

Though none of the Edison owners had been directly involved in the Sprout negotiations, they already had a pretty good idea of the proposed deal from information passed on by Benno Schmidt. Via their phone hook-ups, Das and Sinclair asked questions and made brief comments. There was not much to discuss. The owners stood ready to reject the offer—Associated, Philips, and Chris, as well.

In the letter from Sprout, all found three major flaws. First, it was not a commitment to put up immediate money but to "consider" investing after further weeks of due diligence and negotiation. Sprout, secondly, mentioned investing only $6 million and seeking another $4 million from outside sources, although by Chris's calculations to launch Edison would require at least $30 million. Sprout also made a serious strategic error by dealing only with Edison's management; at that point Chris and executives at Associated and Philips had not yet met Janet Hickey or Pat Boroian.

If Chris Whittle had sat silent at that Philips conference table and thrown up his hands, by sundown the Edison Project would have been history. Philips and Associated were adamant; they were out of patience and would not give Edison another dollar.

Fearing this precise death knell, Chris had been in nightmarish torment for weeks, struggling to concoct an alternative scheme by which he could personally keep Edison Schools alive. And to this meeting he came prepared.

Later Chris told a confidant: "So I had a decision to make there, and as I look back on my life this was one of the most important and, I think, boldest things I ever did."

To be able to make his move, Chris had begun by marshalling all his financial resources, chiefly by disposing of several of his homes. In New York, he put his Dakota apartment on the market, and it was snapped up in a week by Connie Chung and Maury Povich for a reported $5.8 million. The husband-and-wife television journalists already lived in the Dakota in a smaller unit. Cutting his last residential ties with Knoxville, Chris sold for $1 million his Van Dyke Mansion on Kingston Pike, and for $72,000 the log cabin that in pillow factory days two decades earlier had harbored him and his ambition.

Chris had purchased in 1993 an $11 million Manhattan townhouse on East 79th Street, proposing to commission Peter Marino to spend $10 million more renovating the five-story residence into the new Whittle family domicile. That was another dream knocked awry in the financial collapse. Chris sold that building, at a slight loss, and acquired a less expensive location, the $3 million townhouse on East 91st Street being vacated by Gloria Vanderbilt. It is near the private school his stepson Maxi attends and where daughter Andrea will go. "Unless," Chris adds, "we have an Edison school in New York." The Whittles retained their sixteen-acre Georgia Pond estate at East Hampton, Long Island.

On the auction block also went the impressive art collection Chris had painstakingly acquired at a cost of $10 million. The Whittles retained a few deeply loved paintings, but sold the bulk of the collection through a series of sales at Christie's.

After satisfying his creditors, Chris emerged from this fire sale of holdings with liquid assets of around $15 million. Every dollar of that he was willing to risk in an 11th-hour gamble to avoid closing Edison. "I'm not a good poker player," he told a friend, "so I just plunged in head-first."

Philips and Associated were not totally surprised because Chris had started dropping hints in November that he wanted another last-ditch chance to pull a rabbit out of his hat.

The deal Chris offered was to buy out his two partners and take over total control of Edison, personally shouldering all operational expenses, which ran about $2 million a month. "Starting tomorrow," he told Tumminello, Das, and Sinclair, "you will no longer have any funding obligations. None. Zero." Chris proposed to buy 70 percent of the Edison stock, provided the partners gave him an option valid through January 1995, allowing him time to arrange financing. Associated and Philips would together retain a 30 percent interest. In addition, Chris pledged, if successful, to repay out of his share the $40 million they had spent over two years to keep the company going.

By sundown the deal had been struck. Philips and Associated ceded total control to Chris Whittle. All he had to do was come up with $30 million within the next seven weeks!

The Edison crisis was not over. Chris, now obligated to dole out about a half-million a week from his rapidly dwindling cash pile, needed to move fast. So he went back to Sprout. When Janet Hickey heard what he had done, she called him a lunatic. "Every one of my advisers were against the buy-out," Chris admitted. "But I could not see my dearest child perish."

Chris looked on Sprout as his last hope for financial support. He and Janet Hickey immediately began toe-to-toe negotiations. Chris's chief demand was to retain control and own the biggest share of stock. Hickey resisted, posing the threat of stalemate. Each held a whip hand. Chris could queer the deal, since he held all the Edison votes; Sprout could kill it by pulling out.

Hickey and Whittle talked daily by phone, often on weekends. They began to draw closer on terms. She would not hear of launching twenty untested Edison schools. Chris agreed to limit the first wave to four. To slow the up-front "burn-rate" of capital, Edison's overhead was slashed; the ten-person marketing staff was cut in half.

Hickey later recalled: "Chris had gone out and hired stars at *Fortune* 50, not *Fortune* 500, salary rates. By that I mean the salaries were typical of companies that took in billions as opposed to a company that had no revenue." Benno Schmidt agreed to reduce his pay to $200,000 a year, and take equity options. Chris, who received no salary, relinquished his consultant fees.

The dangerous feud between Benno and Chris had been resolved, Sprout thought. Chris told Hickey that immediately after the December 7 buy-out he and Benno had met pleasantly and pledged to work together to create the new financing. They also agreed to let Sprout, as the new partner, make the decision whether Chris should continue as chairman. Benno wrote a memo to that effect, Chris told Hickey.

Before making up her mind, Chris urged Hickey to investigate his business career closely, promising she would find his reputation good among educators dealing with Channel One and Edison. "I think it's important I remain chairman," he told her. "That's what my role is about. I am the founder. I am the largest shareholder, and I think I can contribute."

After checking out Edison clients, Sprout agreed in early January 1995 that Chris was not a detriment and should remain chairman. When Benno Schmidt was told, he blew up. Says an Edison source: "He never thought Sprout would agree to that. He went crazy. He said he'd pull out if Chris remained chairman."

Benno's abrupt reversal reopened the old feud—and put it right in Janet Hickey's lap. Unless she could patch up the quarrel, and keep Schmidt aboard, there was no hope that even with sufficient money Edison would ever get off the ground. She was realistic enough to understand Schmidt's opinion that Chris was still tainted by the "failed in business" stigma. She bluntly recalls, "I didn't want to invest in a situation where Chris had control of the checkbook." On the other hand, she did not consider Schmidt acceptable as the "nitty-gritty day-to-day operator." Chris proposed, and she agreed, to employ a high-caliber chief operating officer, experienced in managing a large multi-site organization, "a chain of hospitals, for example."

To resolve the dilemma, she suggested Chris step aside as chairman, leaving the office temporarily vacant. Schmidt would continue as president and chief executive officer. Chris would be designed founder and "principal proprietor."

That did not appeal to Chris. But he realized that if he did not go along, his high-risk 11th-hour rescue package would fall apart. He confided to a friend: "It was a terribly bitter pill for me. I was upset for weeks. Deeply upset. I had two choices. I could play poker with my dearest child, or I could just bite the bullet and go, 'I'll live with it.' And that's what I did. I don't know whether it was the right decision or not. I'm not a great poker player. I did realize I had a satisfactory governance agreement with Sprout, and we all understood what my role was going to be, regardless of title. I decided this is—bitter as it is—largely cosmetic. And I went, 'Live with it, Chris, and get it over with.' And that's what I did. It is not necessarily permanent, and obviously that was conveyed to me. But that didn't make it any sweeter, frankly."

With this conflict again relegated to the back burner, if not totally buried, agreement was reached in February 1995 setting up $30 million in financing for the Edison schools. Chris invested $15 million through his holding company, and Sprout pledged $12 million. The remaining $3 million was invested by Benno Schmidt and two friends, Joel E. Smilow, chairman of Playtex Products, Inc., and John W. Childs, formerly in a Boston investment form.

Without a chairman, Chris and Sprout shared control, holding equal positions on the board of directors. At the outset, since most of Chris's funds went in first, he owned or controlled 75 percent of the stock. That was scheduled to decline to approximately 50 percent by the middle of 1996 when Sprout began infusing its cash into the operation.

The refinancing was announced on March 16, 1995. Just one month later Edison formally signed the Sherman, Texas, school as number four in its first wave of start-ups.

Hickey was both optimistic and cautious. She said, "It is essential that these first four schools open on time, be well staffed, deliver the curriculum we think we are going to deliver to the students. They have to operate on budget. And they have to be excellent. There is no margin for error. Every national media is going to be standing outside these schools. There's going to be intense interest by educators, parents, the local community, and the national community. To think you could open twenty schools in one fell swoop was, I think, very naive. Opening four, we've got a shot. Edison must deliver on its promises. We have a credible plan. But it's risky, not a sure shot."

Chris praised Hickey as "a very experienced investor" and applauded her vision. "Basically I think she sees what we see, and that is a crying need for improvement in schooling in the United States," he said. "Also Sprout believes the whole world is going to explode in new companies in many ways and she sees the parallels between the managed health care industry, where Sprout has invested, and the whole area of managing schools. I think they believe in what I call the category, and, secondly, they are very impressed with Benno, with the team, and with all the work we've done."

At the end of his struggle to rescue Edison, Whittle waxed philosophical. He said, "Now there are some interesting plusses in all this that I would never have imagined. There was a stretch in July 1994 where I was about to be eaten alive on Wall Street. If you had said then come next March 16th that I'm going to be the largest shareholder in Edison, I would have laughed—I don't see how that's going to work out from where I am.

"One of the reasons it worked out is that in an odd twist of fate the kind of collateral damage that Whittle caused Edison in effect made the share prices much cheaper by shaking the confidence of some of the shareholders, thereby creating an opportunity for people who had faith and courage that it was going to work. So that has been a distinct plus for me.

"It has been very hard and painful to do because the only way I could do it was sell homes, and I didn't like that. But at the end of the day the most important thing to me has happened. And that is, one, the Edison launch, and, two, that I remain in an important and influential role in it. And that's what I wanted to happen."

Chris Whittle believes one measure of a man is his ability to survive difficulties and keep his work and goals intact. "Something I don't believe people understand about me," he says, "is that I always viewed myself as passing through business toward something else. If you go back to the days when I left the University of Tennessee kind of asking myself, What am I going to do? I consciously dealt with, Am I going into politics right now? And I went, No, I don't think that's a good idea because I really don't know much. So why don't I go into business for a while? Then after that my career was a series of decisions as to whether I was going to continue in business or go into politics. And a point I would make is that a sense of mission was always present, that what is called simply financial success was not what I was about from the beginning. I grant some people think that. But over two and a half decades I've been searching for what *was* that mission. And a few years ago I think I found it."

He means Edison schools. It will be his first priority for at least fifteen years, until 2010. Chris adds, "I can make a case that the birth of Edison killed its mother, which was Whittle Communications, but the child survived." The lessons learned in Whittle Communications—"good and bad"—will be reflected in the school project. "And I think my career is pretty linear, though on the surface it looks anything but. And that goes from unsophisticated publishing of a local guide through pretty sophisticated news programming all the way to the running of an entire school."

In Chris Whittle's view, the educational reform market is enormous. America has 100,000 K–12 schools spending $6,000 each on forty-five million students, or $260 billion a year. Within twenty years he expects that 20 to 30 percent of public schools will be under private management. "You are seeing the birth of a new industry. With luck, we will be in the forefront. Think of it, thirty percent of 260 billion rounds out to a new 75 billion category. You see the pond we are fishing in. Edison should have a big piece of that market. I'm very bullish on it."

Edison will receive between $3 million and $3.5 million per

school under its first start-up contracts, totalling $12 million or $14 million. "That won't pay our R and D and our headquarters cost," Chris says. "But in three years we'll be making money."

Even Pat Boroian, the deal maker, calls that a good bet. He says, "I have been exposed to thousands of entrepreneurs. Chris is very unique. He takes big risks. He's had big rewards, and he's had big failures. That doesn't scare me. Remember Babe Ruth—the year he led the league in home runs, he led the league in strikeouts. And Ray Kroc went bankrupt twice before he hit on McDonalds in 1954. Chris Whittle is cut from the same cloth. His greatest business triumph may be yet to come."

===

On the 1995 Memorial Day weekend Chris Whittle sailed across Georgica Pond in his catboat *Andrea* enjoying the Long Island sunshine, recalling a photo snapped outside his log cabin when he was twenty-six. He saw it a few weeks earlier while cleaning out his old desk in Knoxville. The 1973 picture showed him surrounded by twenty-six other free-spirited hippies, the 13–30 staff celebrating the debut of their *Vega* magazine. The scene made him misty-eyed.

"When I get reflective," Chris confides, "ninety percent of the time it's about the future. Edison's all I think about. I don't often dwell on the past. But that picture brought back a lot of good memories."

In the thirty years since graduating high school in Etowah, Tennessee, a country doctor's son with no clear career goal, he had been on a wild ride. Despite ups and downs, he had managed to fairly well stay on top. Ringing "the pond" he had such celebrity neighbors as movie producer Steven Spielberg, fashion designer Calvin Klein, Revlon chief Ron Perleman, home decorator guru Martha Stewart, Atlanta's Cox publishing family, and his intimate friend, Manhattan attorney Michael Kennedy.

Though battered, Chris Whittle was still in pursuit of his dream. He had pulled another rabbit out of the hat. He had snatched the Edison Project from the brink at the eleventh hour. Now the first Edison school was scheduled to open in Sherman, Texas, on August 7, 1995—just twenty-two days before his forty-eighth birthday. The other three, in Kansas, Michigan, and Massachussets, would be running by the end of September. In all, 2,100 youngsters would be pioneers in privately-managed public education for the twenty-first century.

Furthermore, Chris and Benno Schmidt were already lining up their fall 1996 second wave. That included adding middle schools—four of them—in their launch cities. Also, Edison would open seven elementary schools in additional cities being selected. The first new school for 1996 would be in Colorado Springs, Colorado. Chris was sure Edison Schools would start turning a profit, on schedule, in the third year.

Getting clobbered financially by the Whittle Communications collapse had hurt, but Chris adroitly salvaged assets sufficient to keep Priscilla's kitchen from running out of pasta anytime in this century. His best news of the year was the arrival of a second daughter, born June 26, 1995, at 7:25 P.M. in Lenox Hill Hospital in New York. She was healthy, weighed seven pounds and fourteen ounces, and was named Sasha Marie.

Though Chris had to sell three of his four homes and most of his art collection to save Edison, the way he spends his time didn't change much; but his lifestyle was pretty well uprooted. Chris said, "We lead a pretty simple social life, with a fairly tight-knit group of friends. Go to dinner and to movies. Give little dinner parties. Just six or eight friends. Casual. Mostly at East Hampton."

His business life was exclusively devoted to Edison Schools. In the New York office his yellow legal pads already had notations for some possible spin-offs, including educational software. He has Edison inked in on his calendar for the next fifteen years.

As expected, Chris still works out on a regular basis, trying to keep fit. At East Hampton he converted the attic of his rambling old mansion into a gym. His health is good. He is not broke. He is happy. If Chris Whittle heard the deal maker's prediction that his greatest business triumph is yet to come, he just might agree.

NOTES AND ACKNOWLEDGEMENTS

Not surprisingly, Chris Whittle was edgy when he discovered I had a publishing contract to write his biography. He phoned me in Kentucky and debated thirty minutes whether to cooperate. After grilling me again by phone, he agreed to see me in Knoxville and tell me his decision. When we met, Chris announced that his friends at *Time* magazine had given him a look at their morgue file of my life as a journalist and author, and that he had also tracked down former *Nashville Tennessean* publisher John Seigenthaler to ask about me. "He was in Czechoslovakia," Chris said. "I phoned him in Prague."

My credentials apparently passed scrutiny. Chris agreed to make himself available for interviews, to authorize access to company information and officials, and to encourage his family to delineate his background. In return I agreed to let Chris review—but in no way censor—my manuscript.

Biographers usually do a better job when their subject cooperates. That is not always possible. The late Happy Chandler, the former Kentucky governor, senator, and commissioner of major league baseball, discoursed over a span of months at his cheery fireplace. Charmingly but candidly, he gave his recollections of eight decades—because I, of course, was writing *his* autobiography. Initially Sam Walton couldn't talk to me; he was under exclusive contract to ghostwrite his own book. He hired one writer, then another, and finally a third. All disappointed him. He fired them, threw up his hands, and canceled his contract. Then, knowing he had terminal cancer, he called and invited me to Bentonville, Arkansas, volunteering to help with my book. We spent a couple of days together; he gave me a lot of fresh material. Later he struggled again with his autobiography, using his fourth coauthor, and that book was published shortly after his death. (Sam had obviously liked my book; his Wal-Mart stores bought and sold 340,000 copies.)

Fred Smith, on the other hand, relentlessly shut me out when I wrote his Federal Express story. However, his mother and sister cooperated, giving me long and valuable interviews on family history. Scores of Fred Smith's friends and colleagues also willingly provided important data.

It was not possible for me to talk to E. W. Scripps. His corpse, wrapped in a shroud of double canvas and weighted with two hundred pounds of lead, was buried in the Atlantic Ocean off the west coast of Africa from his yacht *Ohio* nearly sixty years before I started *The Astonishing Mr. Scripps.* But the "damned old crank"—as he called himself—gave me enormous posthumous assistance by leaving behind 350,000 pages of personal correspondence and diaries. From them, and interviews with people who knew him, I fashioned a 490,000-word biography. Alas, I had to cut it in half to get it published, but even so the book was awarded the University of Missouri's Kappa Tau Alpha/Frank Luther Mott award as the best book on journalism published in 1992.

I believe my agreement with Chris Whittle proved beneficial to all parties. I am indebted to his parents, Dr. Herbert and Rita Whittle, who have a beautiful retirement home on the southern shore of Lake Loudoun, Tennessee, and his sisters, Karen (Mrs. Patrick) Ellington, whose husband is a physician in Maryville, Tennessee, and Camille (Mrs. Bob) Hanggi, who raises show horses on a farm just outside Knoxville in Clinton, Tennessee, and whose husband was a longtime executive in Whittle Communications L.P.

Dr. Whittle is a charming raconteur, delightfully candid and entertaining, with wry humor. It is easy to see why he is so highly admired and respected as an "old-time family doctor" in Etowah and neighboring Athens. Chris's mother, after some reluctance, also warmed up to the book project and gave much insightful help.

As in earlier books, my wife, Elzene Miller Trimble, a researcher of infinite talents, was my collaborator. In trips to Etowah to mine Chris's boyhood our work was facilitated by many residents of the quaint, friendly little town, including close family friends Judge William and Nancy Cantrell Dender, Jim and Kathleen Frost, retired druggist David Murphy, Mrs. Evelyn Alsip, Mrs. Billie Ruth Elrod, and Mrs. Harley Wear.

School days were recalled by Chris's pals Jim Alsip, Dr. Charles Bivens, Sandi Brewer, Kay Derrick Keller, and two of the junior high girls he dated, Karen Wear (now Mrs. Marvin Taylor of Rex, Georgia) and Janet Elrod (now Mrs. Charles Pickens of Tallahassee, Florida).

Other assistance in Etowah came from Janet L. Constant, local editor of the *Post-Athenian;* Mary Lou Harris, who for years was the Whittle housekeeper; Robert Cobb, who was Dr. Whittle's handyman; former Scoutmaster Eugene Witt; Willard Yarbrough, Etowah native and retiree from the *Knoxville News-Sentinel;* former mayor Mike Cantrell; librarian Mary Holsclaw; piano teachers Louey B. Dickson Palmer, now of Athens, and Grayce Reynolds; and the late R. Frank McKinney, retired editor and publisher of the *Enterprise,* who gave me an interview in his Etowah nursing home a few months before his death.

To reconstruct the momentous years at the University of Tennessee at Knoxville, I am primarily indebted to Chris's fellow 13–30 founders, David

White, Phillip Moffitt, and Brient Mayfield. Professors Tony Spiva, Anand Malik, and Richard Marius, now at Harvard, contributed valuable recollections, as did Dr. Milton Klein, the university historian, and Dean Charles Burchett. Others who filled out the university days were Dr. Jack Reese, Jimmie Baxter, Ann Alexander, Katherine Pearson, Becky Nanny Batson Brown, Ron Leadbetter, and Wayne Carpenter. University president Joseph Johnson facilitated research assistance in school archives.

The most prodigious genealogist of the Whittles proved to be Idele Whittle Robinson of Maryville, Tennessee, who spent years meticulously tracing family ties back to the 1700s. On a tip from Dr. Whittle, I tracked her down in a retirement home, and she generously shared her records with me. In tracing Chris's forebears on the maternal side I obtained efficient assistance from Mary D. Cockrell Gambill of Little Rock, Arkansas. Among Gatlinburg residents who were helpful on lore from that area were Beulah and Lucinda Ogle, Mary Bolt, and Nancy Lee Saltonstall.

Much valuable insight on the nearly three decades of company history from deep-in-debt *Nutshell* publisher to the days of Edison, Channel One, and MNN came from a host of past and present colleagues and associates, including: Frank Finn, David Sharp, Laura Eshbaugh, Pat Westfall, Mike Collins and his wife Christy, Ed Winter, William Rukeyser and his wife Elizabeth, Nick Glover, Ron King, Keith Bellows, Gary Hogan, Alan Greenberg, Bob Hanggi, Ellen Barrentine Shwab, Shelly Williams, Hope Dlugomisa, Tom Ingram, Jim Omastiak, Bill Longley, Kathy Hall, Hamilton Jordan, Charles Vogel, Warren Guy, Michele MacDonald, Donald Johnstone, and Randy Greaves.

Joe Opre of Los Angeles provided details on the critical Datsun travel guide, and Jim Kobak of Darien, Connecticut, recounted how he guided the merger with the Bonniers, leading to the eventual acquisition of *Esquire*. Interviews with Benno Schmidt and Lee Eisenberg supplied much material about the Edison Project. Lord Rothermere discussed his long partnership with Chris at some length.

To learn firsthand of Chris's political efforts in Connecticut and his purchase of a retreat in Vermont, I went to Wally Barnes, Louis Friedman, Fletcher Joslin, Donald Joslyn, Peggy Macdonald Smith, Bruce Wade, Terrence J. Boyle, Ann Marie Simko DeFreest, Bob Lang, and Liza Lerner.

My sources about *Esquire* magazine and New York events include: Daniel O'Shea, Betsy Carter, Cindy Still, Tricia Brock and her mother Patty, Lori Ciancaglini, who was Chris's art adviser, Clay Felker, as well as Byron Dobell and Lee Eisenberg, who were good enough to vet portions of the manuscript dealing with the takeover of *Esquire*, advertising executive Dick Jackson, Columbia University's Catherine Davidson, literary agents Mort Janklow, Ed Victor, and Marianne Strong, authors Jesse Kornbluth, Donald Katz, Porter Bibb, and Gay Talese.

Others who helped the research in one way or another are Joseph Papaleo and Lou Sgroi from Sarah Lawrence College, Mark Landler of *Busi-*

ness Week, Patrick Reilly of the *Wall Street Journal,* Jolie Solomon of *Newsweek,* Dan Thomasson and Jay Gourley of Washington, D.C.; Judy Trott, women's dean at University of Mississippi, Francesca Paolozzi of New York, and Tom Toch of *U.S. News and World Report.*

I am especially indebted to fellow author Cheryl MacLachlan for convincing her husband Phillip Moffitt to break his silence on Chris; to Dr. Joel Markowitz for his willingness to discuss his role as Chris's psychiatrist—fully respecting the bonds of doctor-patient relationship—which adds a certain dimension to the Whittle persona; and to journalist and author Richard Stengel for crafting an intimate portrait of his friend Chris. The priceless drama of the eleventh-hour rescue of Edison Schools was recounted chiefly by Janet Hickey, Patrick Boroian, and Mack Rossoff, to whom I tip my hat.

I feel much indebted to my esteemed friend Harry Moskos, editor of the *Knoxville News-Sentinel,* who not only made the resources of his newspaper available for my research but went further and vetted the manuscript to check for possible gaffes in a Tennessee-based story he knows perhaps better than anyone. My appreciation to his society columnist Barbara Aston-Wash, business editor Lois Reagan Thomas, former art critic Gail Gudge, Washington correspondent Richard Powelson, and chief librarian Shirley Carter.

And finally I gratefully acknowledge the friendship and encouragement of publishing celeb Richard Marek and the extremely helpful hands-on editing of this text by Carol Publishing's forthright Hillel Black.

INDEX

INDEX